Lone Star Tarnished

Texas pride, like everything else in the state, is larger than life. So, too, perhaps, are the state's challenges. *Lone Star Tarnished*, Second Edition approaches public policy in the nation's most populous "red state" from historical, comparative, and critical perspectives. The historical perspective provides the scope for asking how various policy domains have developed in Texas history, regularly reaching back to the state's founding and with substantial data for the period 1950 to the present. In each chapter, Cal Jillson compares Texas public policy choices and results with those of other states and the United States in general. Finally, the critical perspective allows us to question the balance of benefits and costs attendant to what is often referred to as "the Texas way" or "the Texas model."

Jillson delves deeply into seven substantive policy chapters, covering the most important policy areas in which state governments are active. The second edition includes completely rewritten first and second chapters, as well as updates throughout the book and revised figures and tables. Through Jillson's lively and lucid prose, students are well equipped to analyze how Texas has done and is doing compared to selected states and the national average over time and today. Readers will also come away with the necessary tools to assess the many claims of Texas's exceptionalism.

Cal Jillson is Professor of Political Science at Southern Methodist University and a former Chair of the Political Science Departments at CU, Boulder, and SMU. He is a former member of the Council on Foreign Relations and a frequent commentator on domestic and international politics for local, national, and international media. He is the author of *Pursuing the American Dream: Opportunity and Exclusion Over Four Centuries*, *American Government*, *Texas Politics: Governing the Lone Star State*, and *Congressional Dynamics*, and editor of *The Dynamics of American Politics*, *Perspectives on American Politics*, and *Pathways to Democracy: The Political Economy of Democratic Transitions*. He has also served as Associate Dean for Academic Affairs of Dedman College at SMU.

Lone Star Tarnished

A Critical Look at Texas Politics and Public Policy

Second Edition

Cal Jillson

Southern Methodist University

Routledge
Taylor & Francis Group
NEW YORK AND LONDON

First published 2015
by Routledge
711 Third Avenue, New York, NY 10017

and by Routledge
2 Park Square, Milton Park, Abingdon, Oxon OX14 4RN

Routledge is an imprint of the Taylor & Francis Group, an informa business

First edition published 2012 by Routledge

Library of Congress Cataloging in Publication Data
A catalog record has been requested for this book

ISBN13: 978-1-138-78360-7 (hbk)
ISBN13: 978-1-138-78361-4 (pbk)
ISBN13: 978-1-315-76860-1 (ebk)

Typeset in Garamond 3
by Swales & Willis Ltd, Exeter, Devon, UK

Remembering
Old Sam Jacinto & Mr. Sam

Contents

Illustrations

Figures

Tables

Map

Preface

Lone Star Tarnished describes how the Texas political culture, the Texas way of thinking about and practicing politics, shapes the state's politics and public policy. This book is intended for use in Texas Politics courses in the state's colleges and universities, but it is not a standard textbook. *Lone Star Tarnished* is designed to be used in conjunction with a basic text, which will cover political processes and institutions, in courses that want more coverage of Texas political culture, history, and public policy. Though the book was written for a college audience, Texas politics junkies of any age are, of course, welcome.

Most of *Lone Star Tarnished* is dedicated to describing the meaning of "the Texas way" and tracing out its impact on Texas public policy in separate chapters on jobs, income, and poverty, education, health care and social services, crime and punishment, transportation, energy and the environment, and tax policy. The thesis of this book is that Texas is in thrall to a myth that blinds it to social and economic changes that threaten its future. We begin with the irrefutable point that there is a romantic reading of Texas history in which most Anglo Texans revel. The myth is that Texas has always been and remains big, bold, open, and vibrant and that these attributes assure dynamism, growth, and prosperity. In Texas history, the defenders of freedom at the Alamo and San Jacinto and the planters, ranchers, wildcatters, and high-tech entrepreneurs who followed in their wake are the exemplars.

The Texas way, as Governor Greg Abbott and former Governor Rick Perry continue to call this distinctive outlook on life, rests on the pillars of individualism, personal responsibility, low taxes, and limited government. The Texas way presumes that individuals build families and businesses and create wealth. Sometimes individuals join together to seize opportunities or solve problems, but they do so on their own terms and usually in their own neighborhoods and communities. There is a place for government where individual and community effort is insufficient to solve pressing problems. But government should limit itself to the essentials, defending persons and property, promoting an economic infrastructure of

ansportation and utilities, and establishing courts to enforce the rule of
w. In this environment of freedom, some will succeed and some will fail,
ut all will deserve and should own the results that they achieve. In many
ays, this is an attractive view of life and politics.

But virtually no one still denies that for most of Texas history the state's
ommitment to individualism, personal responsibility, and limited gov-
rnment encompassed only white men and served particularly well the
eeds and interests of wealthy white men. Far fewer recognize that today
he Texas way, rather than marking the path forward, obscures growing
hreats to our future security and prosperity. Touting the Texas way as if it
pplied to all Texans, when, in fact, it is the heritage of an ever shrinking
nglo portion of the population is an excuse for political and policy inac-
on. Anglo Texans have not yet fully realized that the days in which they
ould succeed even as Texas blacks and Hispanics lagged are fading fast.

The challenges facing Texas are no secret; they involve the interaction
f demographic change, educational attainment, and income distribution.
emographic change is an old story in Texas. But once the Anglo majority
n Texas was established by the 1830s, it ranged from two-thirds to three-
uarters of the total population into the last quarter of the 20th century.
s late as 1980, Anglos accounted for 66 percent of the Texas popula-
on, blacks for 12 percent, and Hispanics for a little over 20 percent. By
050, Anglos are expected to be just 28 percent of the population, blacks
ill be 10 percent, and Hispanics will account for more than 50 percent.
hese are massive changes, but massive changes do not have to be worri-
ome. If Anglos, blacks, and Hispanics in Texas enjoyed equal educations
nd incomes, there would be no reason to worry, because demographic
hange would not affect the state's overall competitiveness and productiv-
y. Unfortunately, this happy possibility does not pertain in Texas.

The problems posed by demographic change in Texas emerge most clearly
hen we look at educational attainment and income by race and ethnicity. In
010, Texas ranked 50th, dead last among the 50 states, in the proportion of
esidents 25 and older who held a high school diploma, at 82.6 percent com-
ared to 87.2 percent nationally. High school graduates in Texas by race and
thnicity break down this way – Anglos 91 percent, blacks 83 percent, and
Hispanics 57 percent. Because Hispanic educational attainment lags that of
nglos and blacks, so do Hispanic incomes. Median family income in Texas
n 2012 for Anglos was $78,388, for blacks $44,282, and for Hispanics
41,151. Unless Hispanic educational attainment and income improve as
he Hispanic share of the population grows, Texas will become a poorer, less
ynamic, less effective wealth producing state.

For many Anglo Texans, bred in the Texas way of individualism, personal
esponsibility, and small government, this seems like a boot strap issue. If
ck of education limits income potential for many Texas Hispanics, then
he answer is to study harder in school, go further in school, and work

harder in the private economy once you leave school. Alternatively, to view Hispanic educational attainment as a major public policy problem, requiring significant investments in the state's poorer schools, would be expensive and the money would have to come at least partially from the pocket of wealthier Anglo school districts. The political dilemma is in two part and is quite simple; (1) nothing in Texas history suggests that Anglos will provide the revenues necessary to support high quality public schools for minority children, (2) but, if they do not, the state's economic growth and prosperity will decline.

We seek to unravel this dilemma by approaching Texas politics and public policy from historical, comparative, and analytical/critical perspectives. The historical perspective provides the scope for asking how Texas politics and public policy have evolved and developed, often with a qualitative discussion reaching back to the state's founding and with substantial data for the period 1950 to the present. In each chapter we compare Texas public policy choices and results with those of other states, usually including California and Florida as they are similarly situated, and the United States in general. Finally, the analytical/critical perspective allows us to question the balance of benefits and costs attendant to "the Texas way" or "the Texas model" and to think about how we might do better.

All of the tables and graphs in this book have been crafted with teacher and students in mind. Data is usually presented in straightforward numbers, with statistics rarely more complicated than percentages. Student can easily grasp their meaning and teachers can easily introduce them for class discussion. Most importantly, these clear graphic presentations allow class discussions to begin from a foundation of fact. All political discussions end in argument and debate, but they should not and do not have to begin there.

Lone Star Tarnished is comprised of ten chapters divided into three sections. Part I is entitled "The Great State of Texas?" The goal of Chapter 1, "The Texas Way," is to show that a distinctive view of the role and purpose of government has long, indeed always, characterized Texas. In this new edition, we highlight the work of the prominent cultural geographer Wilbur Zelinsky to better understand the stability so clear in Texas political development. Zelinsky's "Doctrine of First Settlement" helps explain the lasting impact of the early Anglo settlement of Texas out of the American South. The foundation of Anglo dominance laid then helps explain the racial and ethnic tensions that persist in Texas today.

In Chapter 2, entitled "Texas: The Myth vs. the Reality," we highlight and attempt to get control of the boosterism and braggadocio that pervade Texas life in general and Texas politics in particular. In this new edition, we confront one of the broader myths of Texas history – that the state is culturally western or southwestern, rather than southern – with compelling new evidence. While Texas elites have sought for decades to foster a western image over a southern one, we show that the bulk of the state's population, economic activity, and political weight have always been in the state's most unambiguously southern cultural regions. We also show that while Texas has done very well on population and job growth, its ranking among the states on income, education, social services, criminal justice, and the environment have been stagnant or falling for decades.

Chapter 3 highlights the rapidly changing demographics of Texas. Demographic change is nothing new to Texas, but from the Austin colony of the 1820s through the current decade Anglos (whites to the wider world) were the dominant ethnicity. They still are, but in 2005 Anglos fell below 50 percent of the Texas population, compared to Hispanics at 36 percent, blacks at a little less than 12 percent, and Asians at about three percent. By the early 2030s Hispanics will be the majority in Texas, though Anglos will still control the wealth and likely the politics of the state. We ask what these demographic changes mean for Texas politics and public life in the coming decades. The recent release of the 2010 census provides rich new demographic data for our consideration.

Part II, entitled "The Reality Thus Far," is composed of six substantive policy chapters. These chapters cover most of the major policy areas in which state governments are active; including the economy, education, health and human services, crime and punishment, transportation, and, especially in Texas, energy and the environment. We ask what Texas says it is trying to do, how hard it seems to be trying to do it, with what results, and for whom. In chapters dealing with economic and social policy issues like income, education, and health care, we have added substantial new detail that highlight troubling differences in opportunity and achievement by race and ethnicity. In each chapter we compare Texas to a relevant selection of states and usually to the national average of all fifty states. We want to know how Texas has done and is doing compared to selected states and the national average over time and today. Is Texas above or below the national average, say in education expenditures or access to health care, and is it falling behind or moving up? What we find is that Texas's firm commitment to low taxes has starved state government funding of programs in most of these policy areas and comparisons with other states have worsened.

Part III, entitled "The Coming Reality," is composed of one concluding chapter. Chapter 10, entitled "The Way Forward," explores the history of Texas tax policies and asks how Texas might change its revenue system to better confront the problems that loom clearly on the horizon. In recent years, Texas has consistently ranked among the lowest of the low tax states, ranking 45th in 2010. We ask what tax reforms and new tax sources would provide the additional revenues needed to bring Texas to the southern average for tax effort, and then to the national average, and to what uses those funds might be put.

Books take time and their authors – at least the lucky ones – draw on many kinds of support. I am deeply grateful to Southern Methodist

University for its ongoing support of my work. This book originated in conversations with Harold Stanley and matured in daily conversations with Brad Carter, Dennis Ippolito, Joe Kobylka, Dennis Simon, and Matt Wilson. I am also grateful to the students in my Texas Politics classes, the journalists with whom I frequently talk Texas politics, and the reviewers who took the time to offer advice and suggestions when the manuscript was in draft. Many of the improvements found in this new edition can be attributed teachers and students of Texas politics who have used the book and suggested how it might be strengthened. My wife Jane continues to expand the calm in my life. Finally, this is the fourth of my books that Michael Kerns has seen through the production process at Routledge. He is ever faithful. These are the relationships that define and sustain me and upon which I place great value.

Part I

The Great State of Texas?

The Texas Way

I happen to think America would be a whole lot better off if Washington did things the Texas way.[1]

(Texas Governor Rick Perry, 2010)

n January 1822, Jared Ellison Groce rumbled into Stephen F. Austin's ew colony at the head of fifty covered wagons containing his family, ousehold goods, and agricultural equipment. Behind the wagons some of .is ninety slaves drove herds of horses, mules, oxen, cattle, sheep, and hogs. Groce immediately became and long remained the colony's richest citizen. He received the largest land grant in the colony, eventually totaling eleven :agues or 44,000 acres of prime Brazos River bottom land. With ready noney and an experienced labor force, he soon had the best of his land in :otton and his famed Bernardo Plantation rose on a bluff overlooking the iver.[2]

Jared Groce, like most of the early Austin colonists, called the "the)ld Three Hundred" in Texas history, came out of the American South. iroce was born into a prominent Virginia family in October 1782. Eager o make his own mark, Groce acquired a South Carolina plantation in 1802 t the age of 20. In 1804 he moved to Georgia and in 1814 to Alabama vhere he established a plantation called Fort Groce. Just a little more han six months after Stephen F. Austin arrived in Texas to take over his leceased father's colonization venture and one month after Austin himself rrived on the Brazos, Groce's party arrived. Austin, the *empresario* or real state developer and leader of the colony, needed wealthy immigrants like iroce to bring people, agricultural expertise, and development capital to he colony. Groce generally cooperated with Austin, but always on his •wn terms. A fellow colonist described Groce as "a warm friend or bitter :nemy Just as his Immidiate Interest is Effected. . . . his Excentricities and :xalted notions of himself is his worst foibles."[3]

Groce's reputation for self-interested aristocratic eccentricity became legend- ry. In 1828 a proud Mexican official named Jose Maria Sanchez fumed to his diary that Groce had treated him with studied contempt. Sanchez wrote, "The did not deign to offer us shelter in the house, even though they saw us campin, under the trees. Later, they asked us into the house for the sole purpose of show ing us the wealth of Mr. Groce and to introduce us to three dogs called Ferdinan VII [then King of Spain], Napoleon [former Emperor of the French], an Bolivar [the hero of Latin American independence movements]." But Groce self-interested hauteur was not reserved for Mexican officials. William Fairfa Gray, a Virginia lawyer, military officer, and land agent, commonly referred t as Colonel Gray, was allowed to stay in the house while visiting Bernardo, but h also used his diary to criticize Groce. Gray attended the convention c March 1 to 17, 1836, that declared independence and wrote the Texa Constitution, spent March 18 to 21 at Groce's, and prepared to join th "Runaway Scrape" of Texas civilians fleeing East before Santa Anna's advanc ing armies. As Gray and his party prepared to depart, some were concerne that they had imposed on Groce's hospitality. Colonel Gray reports that, "Thi delicacy was cured when . . . he presented each with a bill for $3 per day, ma and horse."[4]

Another of "the Old Three Hundred," the sugar plantation owne Sterling McNeal, also arrived in Texas in 1822 and took up a land grant i what became Brazoria County. Like Groce, he prospered and his plantatio became a common stop for travelers. In 1848–49, future U.S. Presiden Rutherford B. Hayes of Ohio visited the region. He described McNeal a "A shrewd, intelligent, cynical, old bachelor. . . . Very fond of telling hi own experience and talking of his own affairs." Hayes went on to observ that "The haughty and imperious part of a man develops rapidly on on of these lonely sugar plantations, where the owner rarely meets with an accept his slaves and menials."[5] While comparatively few men arrived a did Groce and McNeal with their fortunes in hand, many assumed that th lush new country would soon yield them a fortune, so they practiced th haughty planter manner in confident anticipation.

A prickly defense of individual interests, a fulsome self-regard, an intolerance of outside authority, whether emanating from near or far, soo came to characterize the white male population of Texas. Several leadin, mid-twentieth-century scholars have described in very similar terms th mind-set or world view of early Anglo Texans. T.R. Fehrenbach, forme head of the Texas Historical Commission and author of the iconic *Lon Star: A History of Texas and the Texans* (1968), argued that, "the poore whites and larger cotton growers . . . held very similar world views. Botl were atomistic, . . . ferociously self-motivated and self-reliant, pridefu and intolerant, hard-working and ambitious . . . both were impatient witl government (which inevitably followed them) except as it served thei wishes and interests."[6] D.W. Meinig, the prominent cultural geographe and author of *Imperial Texas: An Interpretive Essay in Cultural Geograph* (1969), made a similar point at greater length, saying:

The Texan . . . is strongly individualistic and egalitarian, optimistic and utilitarian, volatile and chauvinistic, ethnocentric and provincial. . . . Such a person regards government as no more than a necessary evil, distrusts even informal social action as a threat to his independence, and accepts violence as an appropriate solution to certain kinds of social and group problems. . . . There is an easy acceptance of equality among one's own kind but a rigid sense of superiority over other local peoples, and a deep suspicion of outsiders as threats to the social order.[7]

W.W. Newcomb, the respected mid-twentieth-century anthropologist and Director of the Texas Memorial Museum, wrote that "Texans . . . came to regard themselves as a breed apart, perhaps, too, a chosen people in a chosen land."[8]

In thinking about the three quotes above and many that will follow, the reader is always well advised to keep this question in mind—who are they talking about, who are the Texans that are being described? With a little thought, it will usually become clear that they are not talking about "all" Texans. In fact, they are not talking even about "most" Texans. They are talking about the "iconic" Texan: the "mythic" Texans of John Wayne's *Alamo*, Larry McMurtry's *Lonesome Dove*, and Edna Ferber's *Giant*. Leigh Clemons, a scholar of contemporary media and culture and author of *Branding Texas: Performing Culture in the Lone Star State*, argued that a "white male, brazenly independent, and typically larger-than-life stereotype has defined the common perceptions of what it means to be a Texan, who does and does not have access to that identity, and what impact . . . that identity has on the state's relationship with the rest of the country and among Texas residents."[9] Texan iconography does not have a place, certainly not an equal place, for blacks, Hispanics, Native-Americans, or women.

Until well into the twentieth century, the reminder that the appellation "Texan" meant whites was unnecessary. Everyone knew that "Texan" referred to white people, though it was occasionally necessary to explain that to Yankees and Europeans. For example, N. Doran Maillard, an Englishman and editor of the Richmond, Virginia, *Telescope*, toured Texas from January through July 1840. In 1842, Maillard published *The History of the Republic of Texas*, explaining to his readers that, "The white population of Texas are called 'Texans' . . . The Texans are generally styled the first offsprings of America, and the grand-children of England."[10] Even in recent decades, scholars have felt the need to remind readers that history changes the meaning even of familiar words. Texas historian Billy D. Ledbetter opened his classic 1973 paper, "White Over Black in Texas: Racial Attitudes in the Antebellum Period," by writing, "In this paper, the word 'Texan' refers only to white Texans—the accepted ante-bellum definition of the word."[11] Our initial inclination might be to think that the word "Texan" is no longer used so narrowly, but would we be right? Let's leave that question open, but front of mind, for now.

In this opening chapter, we trace the origins, development, and political impact of "the Texas way." No one will be surprised to find that the "empresarios" of early Texas and the leaders of the Texas Republic worked hard to attract wealthy white men, their families, property, and capital. From the perspective of white men, women were valued family members, but by no means equals, slaves were useful, even economically essential, while Hispanics, and even more evidently, Indians, were in the way. Yet, many will be surprised to find that the cultural assumptions of early Texas survived so robustly into our own time. We trace the southern cultural heritage of early Texas and its evolution through Texas history—always supporting the primacy of male social and economic elites, personal autonomy and individual responsibility, small government and low taxes, and a deep suspicion of foreign, meaning federal as well as international, influence and authority.

The Southern Cultural Matrix of Early Texas

Cultural geographers have long understood that early settlers establish social, cultural, economic, and political matrices into which those who come later must fit. Pennsylvania State University's famous cultural geographer Wilbur Zelinsky initially offered "The Doctrine of First Settlement" in 1973, the year he served as president of the American Association of Geographers. Zelinsky explained that:

> Whenever an empty territory undergoes settlement, or an earlier population is dislodged by invaders, the specific characteristics of the first group able to effect a viable, self-perpetuating society are of crucial significance for the later social and cultural geography of the area, no matter how tiny the initial band of settlers may have been. . . . Thus, in terms of lasting impact, the activities of a few hundred, or even a few score, initial colonizers can mean much more for the cultural geography of a place than the contributions of tens of thousands of new immigrants a few generations later.[12]

Texas was not unoccupied before the Anglo-American influx, but it was very thinly occupied. As late as 1820, Mexican Texas numbered only three or four thousand non-Indian inhabitants, mostly in the San Antonio and Goliad areas, with a smaller mixed Anglo-American and Mexican population at Nacogdoches. But the opening of Texas to Anglo immigration, and especially the founding of the Austin colony in 1821, brought uncontrollable change. By 1835, there were about 25,000 non-Indians in Texas; 80 percent of them Anglo-American and after independence the Anglo tide rose rapidly. The weight of the population and wealth were in the Austin colony's rich Brazos and Colorado River bottoms.[13] Texas historians report that the bulk of Anglo immigrants were southerners and brought with them southern habits and expectations. Randolph B. Campbell, author of *Gone to Texas: A History of the Lone Star State* (2003), wrote that, "Most of the planters and plain folk who settled in antebellum Texas were southerners, and they built an overwhelmingly agricultural economy highly similar to that found in the older southern states."[14]

D.W. Meinig's well-known description of the cultural geography of antebellum Texas, reported that:

> East Texas . . . was entirely Anglo-American and very largely from Alabama and other Gulf states. East Texas was thus the western extension of the older Deep South. . . . It had an economy based upon cotton, corn, cattle, and hogs, a wholly rural society . . . in which slaves, who made up a third or more of the total population, were an integral part of the economic and social structure.[15]

When Meinig and others refer to East Texas, they do not mean just the piney woods of far East Texas adjacent to Louisiana. Rather, they also, even principally, mean the green, well-watered, humid, low lands North of Galveston and Houston, East of Austin, and between the Trinity and Colorado Rivers, centered on the rich Brazos River valley. Michael Lind, like Meinig, described East Texas as "the westernmost extension of the Deep South. The society of East Texas . . . was biracial and hierarchical. . . . It was a clone of the society of Alabama, Mississippi, Georgia, and northern Florida."[16] East Texas was the center of plantation wealth and so set the social and cultural tone for early Texas.[17]

But the plantation aristocracy of early Texas faced a more threatening reality and faced it far longer than did their cousins back home. The courtly plantation life of Virginia and South Carolina, even of Alabama and Mississippi, never really came to Texas. All of Texas, including the Austin colony, was a contested and often bloody frontier in the 1820s and 1830s. Civil institutions remained to be built so order was maintained by voluntary, including vigilante, effort. In 1825 Jared Groce provided 30 armed slaves to Stephen F. Austin to assist in putting down Karankawa raids. In 1833 when Groce divided parts of his original estate among his children and moved several miles north to establish a new plantation at Groce's Retreat, he took twenty armed slaves to deal with Cherokee raids. Even after the brief but bloody fight for independence in 1836, two invasions by Mexican forces, both of which occupied San Antonio briefly, occurred in the early 1840s. Statehood in 1845 was expected to bring peace, but Comanche raids plagued the state's western frontier for three more decades.

The leading early settlers of Texas had the social expectations of plantation aristocrats sharpened by the demands and dangers of frontier life. Many fought Indians across the southern frontier, carried slaves with them to Texas, and fumed at Mexican rule once they arrived.[18] These early settlers "brought with them a long history of dealing with Indians and blacks, while the experience of the Alamo and the Mexican War served to crystallize and affirm anti-Mexican prejudice."[19] The Anglo elite had an unshakeable expectation of social deference and political and economic primacy that they were prepared to enforce. They did not equivocate or compromise with enemies; they pushed most Mexicans, including Tejanos, south of the Rio Grande and exterminated those Indians that refused to leave the state.

The plantation culture of deep racial distinctions and Anglo dominance was entrenched in East Texas before meaningful settlement took place in North Texas and in the broad expanses of West Texas. When settlement did come to North Texas in the 1840s and 1850s, it had a different cultural source and feel than East Texas. Meinig describes the Blackland Prairie of North Texas as "distinctly Border South country, drawing most heavily from Missouri, strongly from Arkansas and Tennessee, and significantly from Illinois." There was little cotton, at least initially, and few slaves: "agriculture was more diversified . . . ; settlement was more compact; towns a more vital part of social organization; and contrasts between rich and poor rather less prominent. In short, there existed here between North and East Texas the same difference as between Kentucky and Alabama."[20] Nonetheless, the Brazos plantation elite assumed the right to lead and the farmers and small town folk of North Texas did not contest it.[21]

As the Civil War approached, Texas elites were unequivocal about their southern roots and cultural assumptions—slavery was a positive good for whites and blacks and they would fight to defend it. In 1856 Lorenzo Sherwood, a Galveston lawyer recently immigrated from New York and even more recently elected to the Texas legislature, opined that slavery, while perhaps necessary now, sat uncomfortably with democracy and would probably fade away in the next century. The state erupted in outrage. The Dallas *Herald* declared that, "A man, a Texan, a southerner who could get up in the legislature of a southern State, *of the most southern State*, and deliberately outrage the feelings of the whole people without distinction of party, on a question so directly affecting their most vital interests, by uttering sentiments that strike at the foundation of their social and political rights," was not fit to serve.[22] Sherwood resigned his seat. In 1857, the *Galveston Weekly* declared, "Those who are not for us, must be against us. There can be no middle ground. Those who denounce slavery as an evil, in any sense, are enemies of the South, whatever may be their pretended conservatism."[23] Moreover, the Texas Secession Convention, meeting on January 28, 1861, voted 166 to 8 to secede from the union. The Convention defended its recommendation for secession in its famous "Declaration of

Causes." Secession was necessary to protect the "'beneficent and patriarchal system of African slavery' against 'the debasing doctrine of the equality of all men, irrespective of race or color.'" The declaration went on to say that the U.S. and certainly Texas were founded "exclusively by the white race, for themselves and their posterity; that the African race had no agency in their establishment; that they were rightly held and regarded as an inferior and dependent race, and in that condition only could their existence in this country be rendered beneficial or tolerable." The "Declaration of Causes" barely mentioned issues other than slavery; fully 95 percent of the document was dedicated to a defense of slavery. The remaining 5 percent dealt with border and frontier security. States' rights was mentioned, but barely, and then only as a defense of slavery.[24] Texas approved secession by a vote of 46,154 to 14,747 on February 23, 1861.

Though the Civil War and Reconstruction temporarily loosened the grip of established elites, they restored their dominance by the early 1870s and fastened it down in the Constitution of 1876. James McEnteer writes that, "the Texas Constitution of 1876 reflects the Alamo values of 1836, affirming states' rights, decentralized government and the supremacy of the white race. Frequently amended, that document has never been rewritten and remains in force."[25] White supremacy remained the dominant Anglo Texan attitude toward others well into the mid-twentieth century.

The last great migration into Texas in the nineteenth century was the post-Civil War exodus of busted whites out of the Old South. Robert Calvert and his colleagues write that,

> Residents of states that had been devastated by the Civil War and post-1865 economic stagnation sought out a fellow ex-Confederate state with cotton lands and similar racial attitudes in which to resettle. . . . Thus (in descending order) Arkansas, Alabama, Mississippi, Tennessee, Missouri, Louisiana, and Georgia sent the majority of the in-migrants to Texas. . . . The influx of new people did little to alter the previously formed cultural regions that had determined the course of prewar politics.[26]

New Texans and old, these defeated southerners had decades of rebuilding to do. They had to regain control of their state and then slowly rebuild it on the old white supremacy model. Slavery was gone, but white supremacy could be restored behind a strict segregation of the races.

The post-Civil War battles for social and political control of the South were fought with all of the weapons that could be brought to hand. The great historian of the South, C. Vann Woodward, wrote that, "Southern whites . . . . used craft and guile, force and violence, economic pressure and physical terror, and all the subtle psychological devices of race prejudice and propaganda at their command."[27] By the first decade of the new century, restrictive voter registration, the white primary, and the poll tax were in place, assuring elite Anglo control. T.R. Fehrenbach correctly asserted that, "Texas entered the 20th century" with white supremacy restored but "with its basic society a full two generations, or about sixty years, behind the development of the American mainstream. Industry was in its infancy; among the people themselves the norms and patterns of the industrial society had no root. . . . The early 19th century American values were in no way eroded in Texas."[28] Texas elites wanted to attract northern capital, but not at the expense of southern social and cultural traditions.

West Texas was not cleared of Indians and hence ready for settlement until after the Civil War and Reconstruction. Even then West Texas was an unforgiving land that broke the first generation of farmers before being fenced for ranching in the late 1880s. Critically, as we will see in detail in Chapter 2, there was never anything remotely like a balance between the cultures of southern traditionalism and western individualism, because the vast majority of the population always lived in the region dominated by southern traditionalism.[29] The southern traditionalism of East, Northeast, and South Texas was the dominant cultural matrix of early Texas. Yet, during the twentieth century, Texas elites seized on the West Texas cattle culture of the two or three decades immediately surrounding the Civil War to argue that Texas was a mix of the Old South and the Old West, perhaps even distinctly southwestern, but certainly not simply southern. Anglo Texans wanted a restored southern order, but they also wanted a national reputation partly, even mostly, western or southwestern as that reputation would be less sullied by slavery, rebellion, and defeat.

In fact, the fundamental social assumptions and commitments of Anglo Texans have been remarkably stable from first settlement to today. Anglo Texans have demanded independence, personal and collective, small government, low taxes, light regulation, and personal responsibility. These ideas were not unusual in nineteenth-century America, though Anglo Texans were keenly aware of differences in emphasis and implementation between North and South. In Texas, as in the South more generally, the idea of freedom, to be unrestrained, was so important to whites because its opposite, black slavery, was so immediately before their eyes. What is unusual, however, is that Anglo Texans have held to these ideas more tenaciously and for longer than others, without seeing, one hopes, that historically they were the underpinnings of the doctrine of white supremacy.

More Freedom Requires Less Government

Many have wrestled with the singularity of Texas and how both Texans and others react to it. Two famous statements by Sam Houston, the dominant figure in Texas from independence to secession, show that the broad confidence that many have seen as hyperbole has surrounded Texas from its earliest days. Sam Houston's first appearance in Texas was widely thought to be as a scout for his close friend and political associate, President Andrew Jackson. In 1833, Houston wrote to Jackson, saying "I have travelled near five hundred miles across Texas, and am now enabled to judge pretty near correctly of the soil, and the resources of the Country, and I have no hesitancy in pronouncing it the finest country of its extent upon the globe."[30] This might be discounted as early Texas bluster, but his declaration that, 'Texas could exist without the United States, but the United States cannot, except at very great hazard, exist without Texas," is uninterpretable outside of Texas.[31] What Houston meant—and Texas leaders from that day to this have shared variations on this vision—was that an independent Texas might expand westward to the Pacific faster than the U.S., perhaps, even in some sense, displacing it.

Houston's vision was of two Anglo republics sharing, uncomfortably, the continent, with the Texan republic more dynamic, more energetic and aggressive, than its elder cousin. Anglo Texans knew the United States; it had been home for most of them. They viewed their new home as freer, more open, more entrepreneurially dynamic, and less burdened by government and regulation than the United States. U.S. President James K. Polk understood, if he did not fully share, this vision and acted to preempt it by welcoming Texas into the American union. Anglo Texans entered the union gratefully, aware that their decade of independence had been a struggle, but worried that being embedded in the United States might limit their ability to act at discretion—limit their freedom.

The first settlers into Texas understood as clearly as any developer does today that land values and commercial opportunities hinged on population growth so they told tales of free land, rich soil, and unlimited opportunity. In the early decades of the Austin colony, the Republic, and statehood, these "tales shone the shimmering image of a fabulous empire, of broad vistas and plateaus where a man could see for miles, of barbaric Indians and millions of buffalo and cattle hardly less wild. This was a country where a man could be a man, and a good man could make himself a king. In these years a lasting legend was born."[32]

The early legends of a rich and expansive land open to domination by strong men was deepened into a founding myth by the events of the Texas Revolution. "Crockett at the Alamo" seems to "set the state's tone, capture its essence . . . , as an expression of the culture's fundamental values, or at least those that it wants to cultivate."[33] Don Graham, a Texana scholar at the University of Texas, reminds us that "the most frequent formulation of the Alamo's great theme is freedom."[34] The power of the "Alamo myth" is both in what it highlights and in what it leaves in shadow. It highlights Anglo sacrifice, courage, and determination. Free men, choosing death over escape, stand against tyranny until overwhelmed. Similarly, Houston's army, civilian recruits collected along the line of retreat, trained only haphazardly as the enemy closes in, astoundingly victorious in less than half an hour over a well-drilled but cowardly Mexican enemy at San Jacinto. Government is in the shadows, squabbling and ineffectual, in fact, barely present, as free men, almost spontaneously, carry the day.

Texas historian T.R. Fehrenbach sharpened this point by writing that, "Until this time," meaning 1835, "self-government in Texas had really meant the absence of government. In a province where everyone had land . . . no government was needed to clear the wilderness and plant cotton."[35] Anglo Texans might come together to confront danger, but when it passed, they adhered to a highly personal view of freedom. As the Englishman William Boellert wrote in 1842, "Their land costs them but little, . . . It is their own and their children's, no proud lord to look up to, no tythes or taxes, no game laws, and to use an American expression, 'One feels freed and one is free.'"[36] This sense of freedom, understandably, still appeals to many in Texas. When Governor Rick Perry was questioned in early 2013 about the possibility that Texas Democrats might become competitive as the Hispanic population increased, he rejected the possibility out of hand, saying, "It's because of freedom. People in Texas truly aspire to freedom. They don't want government coming in and telling them how much of this or how much of that. . . . Texans have never been for that, and Texans never will."[37]

For the first Anglo Texans, the fact that there were dangers about did not mean that strong government was needed for protection, it meant that men needed to be assertive, even ruthless, in defense of their interests. Historians Patrick Cox and Michael Phillips of the Dolph Briscoe Center for American History at the University of Texas contend that, "During the early statehood years (1845–1860), the framers of the Texas Constitution intentionally created a weak central government in order to hamper dissent and ensure the rule of economic elites."[38] Minimizing government maximizes individual freedom and choice, especially for elites.

"We Pay No Taxes"

Like the American Revolution, the Texas Revolution began as a tax revolt.[39] By the early 1820s the Mexican government had concluded that populating its northern frontier would require opening it to Anglo-American settlers on attractive terms. Anglo *empresarios*, led by Stephen F. Austin, negotiated contracts permitting them to bring settlers in, distribute free or cheap land, and suspend taxes, usually for six to ten years, to get the settlement or colony started. Not surprisingly, Texans that paid no taxes in the early years were reluctant to begin paying taxes once the exemption period ended. The most heated anti-tax protests and, eventually, battles took place at Anahuac in the early 1830s. Anahuac was a Mexican town and fort responsible for collecting taxes on goods entering the Austin colony from the gulf. Jim Bowie and William B. Travis entered the Texas resistance to Mexican authority through the anti-tax protests at Anahuac.[40]

Famously, even as tensions built between Texas and Mexican authorities, an Anglo East Texas land commissioner from Nacogdoches wrote in 1834: "Come what may I am convinced that Texas must prosper. We pay no taxes, work no public roads, get our land at cost, and perform no public duties of any kind."[41] Central to the Texas way, both in the early years and thereafter, has been a fierce individualism, free from taxes and public service, allowing men to concentrate on their own interests.

While Texas's decade of independent nationhood was financially troubled, with bankruptcy threatening particularly during President Mirabeau B. Lamar's term, the republic depended on import fees, business fees, and a few luxury taxes. The terms of Texas's admission to the union in December 1845 were highly favorable and brought badly needed financial relief. Five million dollars in Republic of Texas debts were assumed by the federal government and Texas retained title to all of its unsettled lands to offset its remaining debts. After admission to the union, disputes over the boundaries between Texas, New Mexico, and Colorado, provided another opportunity for Texas to benefit. In the Boundary Act of 1850, Senator Sam Houston and the Texas congressional delegation agreed to limit Texas's claims in the Upper Rio Grande in exchange for a payment to the state of $10 million. Debts quickly devoured this $10 million, but a second payment of $7.5 million in 1855 as a final debt payment and reimbursement of state expenditures for frontier defense, left Texas not only debt free for the first time, but with a bankable surplus of $4 million.

Texas historians agree that this federal largesse allowed the state to limit its own tax efforts. George Garrison explained in *Texas: A Clash of Civilizations* (1903) that, "For the six years from 1852 to 1858 nearly all of the taxes collected in the State were given to the counties for local use, the expenses of the state government being paid meanwhile out of the indemnity received from the United States."[42] Fehrenbach concluded that the net result of the federal payments "was that Texas during the 1850s was financed publicly almost entirely by federal money, . . . Schools were endowed, public structures built, and the transportation system enhanced, all without a dollar being raised in domestic taxes."[43] Carl Moneyhon, the noted historian of the Civil War and reconstruction in Texas, weighed both the good and the bad of federal monies flowing to Texas. He wrote that, "prewar state government attempted to provide for the interests of local businessmen and farmers with minimal claims on their individual financial resources. The result was a tradition of limited public services in areas such as education or charity."[44]

When war came Texas was plunged back into debt. More shocking to Texans was the unprecedented taxing and spending of Governor Edmund J. Davis's Republican reconstruction government. During reconstruction, with many whites excluded from the electorate because they had served in

the southern armies and governments, Davis and Republican majoritie
in the Texas House and Senate, elected on the votes of newly enfranchise
blacks, increased spending for police and militia, expanded local govern
ments, and provided free public education for all Texas children, blac
and white. Whites were outraged by armed black police and state militi
and by paying taxes to educate black children. When white Democrat
returned to power in the mid-1870s, after nearly a decade of U.S. Arm
and Republican Party rule, they slashed taxes and government, defunde
the public schools, and returned control of most government activities t
local elites. By 1900, Texas blacks had been moved to the periphery o
society where the Civil War promises of equality and opportunity had lit
tle meaning.

The conservative "Establishment in Texas Politics," which Georg
Norris Green described as "a loosely knit plutocracy comprised mostl
of Anglo businessmen, oilmen, bankers, and lawyers. . . . dedicated to
regressive tax structure, low corporate taxes, antilabor laws, political, social
and economic oppression of blacks and Mexican-Americans, alleged states
rights, and extreme reluctance to expand state services," governed Texas
with brief interludes, throughout the twentieth century.[45] Generation
of elected political leaders, conservative Democrats and, more recently
Republicans, have eagerly done the establishment's bidding.[46]

The traditional establishment view still holds undisputed sway i
Texas. In the 2010 governor's race Rick Perry constantly cast Texas a
an example to other states and to the federal government. At the Value
Voters Conference in Washington in September 2009, Perry declared, "A
a Texan, I'm understandably biased, but I think our whole country coul
use a dose of Texas-style fiscal discipline." In the weeks leading up to th
March 2010 Republican primary, Perry bragged that "We govern with
simple set of principles. Don't spend all the money."[47] Anglo Texans hav
always evinced an unwillingness to tax some to provide benefits to others
Independence, autonomy, and personal responsibility remain central to th
Anglo Texan sense of self. These values also warned them to be alert t
threats from beyond their own borders.

An Intrusive and Overbearing National Government

Texans have always believed that distant authority, whether in Mexico City
Washington, D.C., or even Austin, wished them ill out of greed, enmity
and a lust for power. In 1835, as tax protests built inexorably toward revo
lution, William B. Travis, soon to be fatally in command at the Alamo
wrote to David C. Burnet, soon to be Interim President of the Republi
of Texas, about the political and financial demands of the Mexican federa
government. Travis said, "I wish to know, for whom do I labor—whethe
for myself or a *plundering* robbing, autocratical, aristocratical jumbled u

govt."[48] As soon as Mexican authority was thrown off, Texans looked to the U.S., but warily, for protection. Republic of Texas President Sam Houston and most Texans favored annexation, but his successor, President Mirabeau B. Lamar and others, thought the Republic of Texas might find glory on its own. One of the very first histories of the Texas Revolution, Chester Newell's 1838 *History of the Revolution in Texas* warned of northern animus, saying "There is existing in the minds of the people in many places, if not generally, at the North, a strong and bitter prejudice against Texas."[49]

Southerners arrived in Texas well aware that Americans held conflicting views of federalism. Northerners generally thought in terms of union and southerners in terms of states' rights. Yet, even by southern standards, Texas has been prickly on issues of state sovereignty. While most states entered the union after a period of territorial tutelage under rules established by Congress, Texas did not. A free-standing republic, Texas entered the union almost as an equal after negotiations that produced favorable terms. T.R. Fehrenbach reports that as early as 1849, "Texans tended to resent all national interference."[50] From the beginning, Texas governors felt free to address U.S. presidents peremptorily. "When Texans began to realize that statehood would not provide security, Acting Governor Horton informed President James Polk of the consequences: 'The citizens of the frontier will protect themselves, and retaliate whenever occasion offers, and in a very short time a state of things will thus be brought about which will greatly retard, if not entirely defeat, the wish of the general government, to settle a boundary line between us and the Indians, or make any treaty with them.'"[51]

When the Civil War came, Texas unhesitatingly joined the Confederacy. The Confederacy was structured around state sovereignty and limited national power. Nonetheless, Texas Governor Pendleton Murrah complained regularly about "federal encroachment" by the Confederate government in Richmond on Texas prerogatives. The Texas aversion to national intrusion was deepened greatly by the Civil War and Reconstruction. Texans saw Reconstruction as harshly punitive treatment of the defeated South and they resisted the national government's dictates as stoutly and as long as any southern state. Abraham Lincoln's moderate program of Presidential Reconstruction was taken up by President Andrew Johnson after Lincoln's assassination in April 1865. Johnson, a former states' rights Democratic senator from Tennessee, followed Lincoln's inclination to "let the South up easy." Johnson issued a general amnesty to all southerners except high ranking political and military officials who were required to seek personal pardons. To regain admission to the union and representation in Congress, southern state legislatures were required to ratify the Thirteenth Amendment abolishing slavery, repeal their secession acts, and repudiate debts incurred during the war. Texas was rankled even by these modest requirements and responded only grudgingly.

Though the war was lost and slavery was ended, Texans and southerners could not imagine simply treating the recently freed slaves as social, legal and political equals, nor could they imagine investing in the educational and social services that would be required to close the gap between whites and blacks.[52] Instead, southern legislatures passed laws barring blacks from suffrage and, through debtor and vagrancy laws, tying them to the land, often the land of their former owners. The plantation elite believed that they could not plant, tend, and pick the valuable cotton crop without black labor and blacks would not work without compulsion, which they meant to apply. The Republican U.S. Congress responded by seizing control of Reconstruction from President Johnson and instituting what came to be known in the South as Radical Reconstruction. Five military districts including a district headquartered in Houston, were commanded by U.S. Army generals charged to oversee the construction and operation of loyal Republican state governments. Each state was required to grant suffrage to all adult men, black and white, except for legally excluded former rebels. Each state was also required to ratify the Fourteenth Amendment, granting citizenship and equality to blacks, prior to being readmitted to the union. Only President Johnson's state of Tennessee ratified the Fourteenth Amendment. Every other southern state, including Texas, declined initially to do so.

By June 1868, six southern states—Alabama, Arkansas, Florida, Louisiana, North Carolina, and South Carolina—had reconsidered, ratified the Fourteenth Amendment, and regained admission to Congress. Not until 1870 did the final three states—Mississippi, Texas, and Virginia—ratify and regain their former status as fully enfranchised states. By this time, the Fifteenth Amendment, guaranteeing suffrage to black men, had to be ratified as well, which Texas did on February 18, 1870. President Ulysses S. Grant signed the Texas readmission bill in March 1870 and a newly elected civilian government took power in Texas on April 16, 1870.[53]

The Civil War and Reconstruction deepened the Texan sense that the national government short-changed it out of malice and perhaps hatred. Texans pushing the settlement line into Comanche territory in the 1870s believed the federal government provided an inadequate defense "out of anti-Texas prejudice, or hatred against the South."[54] To this day, Texas politicians argue that national policies are designed to harm Texas with impunity and, perhaps, with secret glee. Former Republican U.S. Representative Henry Bonilla recently said that the Obama administration "just cannot stand that we're a successful red state." Republican Congressman Joe Barton, writing about Obama administration environmental programs, said "I think it offends the administration's sensibilities when ornery Texans go their own way and prosper by welcoming economic activity instead of chasing it away with federal style taxes and regulations."[55] Governor Rick Perry told a Republican women's groups in Midland that, "This administration is interested in punishing Texas."[56]

Restoring the Traditional Order

Texans and other southerners knew that the federal government expended only modest and intermittent effort in restoring their security and economic vitality after the Civil War. Wrecks obstructed southern harbors and rivers for years and in some cases decades while an industrial boom, fostered by Republican Party policy, drove population growth and wealth creation in the North. While the North grew wealthy, the energy of the southern elites was dedicated in the 1870 and 1880s to a ruthless campaign to restore the traditional order of white supremacy.

The Anglo elites of the thickly populated areas of East and Central Texas struggled to turn back the social, political, and economic changes forced upon them by Reconstruction. Confederate Colonel William Stewart Simkins, a Ku Klux Klan leader in Florida after the war and later a prominent professor in the University of Texas Law School, spoke for many white Texans when he wrote that the Freedman's Bureau and Reconstruction more generally "were intended to humiliate the South, enforce the anticipated Civil Rights laws, the germ of which was social equality." Soldiers of the United States, he complained, obeyed the orders of the Bureau in order to "assist in crushing the pride of the South by the elevation of the Negro to political control."[57]

Anglo Texans treated the very idea of black equality as deeply humiliating. They could not conceive how blacks could rise if whites did not fall. How could the bottom rail be on top, in the phrase of the day, unless the top rail went to the bottom? In response, "arose the 'Invisible Empire'. . . composed of the best young men of the land, soldiers of the Southern army, . . . now as fearless in their duty as they had been in the war."[58] Klan violence fell off during the late 1870s, once public authority could be used, or misused, directly to limit black social, political, and economic activity. Cox and Phillips report that, "In 1896, forty Democrats in Robertson County held rifles while surrounding the courthouse to block entrance by black voters. The county judge later wrote, 'I went down to the polls and took my six-shooter. I stayed there until the polls closed. Not a negro voted.'"[59]

As the new century dawned, conservative Democrats moved to legally limit the electorate to its most dependable Anglo elements. In 1902 Texas voters instituted a poll tax aimed principally at blacks but impacting many Hispanics and poor whites as well. The Terrill election law required the poll tax to be paid six months before the primary and nine months before the general election, well before campaigns heated up and potential voters began to pay attention. The law also encouraged all-white primaries at the county level and put additional hurdles in the way of third parties seeking access to the ballot. Voter turnout fell by half to two-thirds from its high-point in the mid-1890s.[60] Amy Bridges' classic study of municipal reform in the Southwest in the first half of the twentieth century concluded that, "In Texas, racial segregation was an organizing principle of social life and urban planning; disenfranchisement of African-Americans and Mexican-Americans the goal of much legislation limiting access to the ballot; the white primary the foundation of one-party politics."[61]

The poll tax and the white primary reduced black turnout to scattered urban precincts during the early decades of the twentieth century. Voting by what prominent mid-century political scientist V.O. Key called "unsponsored" Hispanics also was actively and effectively discouraged. Key noted "a markedly lower voter participation in the counties with large numbers of Mexican-Americans than in other comparable counties. . . . In many counties, unsponsored individual Mexican-Americans meet a barrier to the ballot similar in character if not in degree to that which discourages Negro voting in most of the South."[62]

The traditional social order was fully restored during the first quarter of the twentieth century. Jim Crow segregation was law, blacks were barred from the Democratic primary, and even progressive political reforms were progressive only for whites. The goal of progressive reform in Texas and the South was governance by educated and propertied elites. But where exactly did Texas stand socially and economically in relation to her sister states as the "Roaring 20s" gave way to the 1930s and what would become the Great Depression? Texas was poor, but again securely under the management of its traditional Anglo elites.

Interestingly, 1930 saw one of the first systematic attempts to compare the states to each other on a wide range of economic, social, cultural, and political dimensions. H.L. Mencken, the leading political commentator and social critic of the day, and his colleague Charles Angoff at the *American Mercury* drew on the 1930 *Statistical Abstract of the United States* and dozens of other sources to compare the 48 states and the District of Columbia. They were assisted and advised by professors S.H. Hobbs of the University of North Carolina, Chapel Hill, and James M. Chalfont of Ohio State University. Mencken and Angoff presented 105 tables, 30 ranking all 48 states and D.C. and the remainder presenting the top ten and bottom ten states. The article, provocatively titled "The Worst American State," appeared in three parts in the September, October, and November 1931 issues of the *American Mercury*. Table 1.1 is the summary table, which appeared as Table 72 in the November issue on page 356, ranking the states on the broad dimensions of wealth, education, health, and public safety, plus an overall rank. Texas and South Dakota did not present sufficient data on public safety to be ranked on that dimension. Texas's overall rank was 39. Texas ranked above most of the other southern states, but

Table 1.1 The Relative Standing of the States in 1930

Rank	Wealth	Education	Health	Public Order	Aver. Rank
1	California	Massachusetts	Minnesota	Maine	Massachusetts
2	Connecticut	D.C.	Massachusetts	Vermont	Connecticut
3	New York	California	New York	New Hampshire	New York
4	D.C.	Connecticut	Connecticut	Massachusetts	New Jersey
5	Massachusetts	Michigan	Iowa	Rhode Island	California
6	Illinois	Colorado	Oregon	Connecticut	D.C.
7	Nevada	Utah	New Jersey	New Jersey	Minnesota
8	New Jersey	Illinois	Illinois	Wisconsin	Iowa
9	Rhode Island	New York	Nebraska	Minnesota	Illinois
10	Pennsylvania	Oregon	Washington	Iowa	Oregon
11	Ohio	Washington	New Hampshire	New York	Rhode Island
12	Michigan	Iowa	Pennsylvania	North Dakota	Michigan
13	Washington	Nevada	Wisconsin	Utah	Maine
14	Minnesota	Ohio	Rhode Island	Oregon	Washington
15	Delaware	Indiana	Wyoming	Michigan	Wisconsin
16	Colorado	Wisconsin	California	Pennsylvania	New Hampshire
17	Oregon	Minnesota	Michigan	D.C.	Ohio
18	Iowa	New Jersey	D.C.	Nebraska	Nebraska
19	Maryland	Rhode Island	Vermont	Ohio	Utah
20	Wisconsin	Missouri	Kansas	California	Kansas
21	Maine	Montana	Utah	Delaware	Pennsylvania
22	Nebraska	Maine	North Dakota	Washington	Vermont
23	Indiana	Nebraska	Ohio	Indiana	Colorado
24	New Hampshire	Kansas	Missouri	Kansas	Indiana
25	Kansas	Maryland	Idaho	Illinois	Nevada
26	Vermont	Pennsylvania	Maine	Idaho	Delaware
27	Missouri	New Hampshire	Indiana	Maryland	Missouri
28	Montana	Vermont	Colorado	Missouri	Maryland
29	Wyoming	Wyoming	Nevada	Colorado	North Dakota
30	Arizona	Delaware	Maryland	West Virginia	Wyoming
31	Utah	South Dakota	Montana	North Carolina	Montana
32	South Dakota	Oklahoma	Delaware	Virginia	Idaho
33	Florida	Idaho	West Virginia	Louisiana	South Dakota
34	North Dakota	Arizona	South Dakota	New Mexico	West Virginia
35	New Mexico	North Dakota	Oklahoma	Oklahoma	Arizona
36	Idaho	Florida	Florida	Montana	Oklahoma
37	West Virginia	**Texas**	Kentucky	Wyoming	Florida
38	Virginia	West Virginia	Arkansas	Arizona	Virginia
39	**Texas**	Virginia	**Texas**	Florida	**Texas**
40	Kentucky	Kentucky	Virginia	Kentucky	New Mexico
41	Oklahoma	Tennessee	Arizona	South Carolina	Kentucky
42	Tennessee	New Mexico	Louisiana	Arkansas	Louisiana
43	North Carolina	North Carolina	Georgia	Tennessee	North Carolina
44	Louisiana	Louisiana	Tennessee	Alabama	Tennessee
45	Georgia	South Carolina	New Mexico	Nevada	Arkansas
46	Alabama	Georgia	North Carolina	Georgia	Georgia
47	South Carolina	Arkansas	Alabama	Mississippi	South Carolina
48	Arkansas	Alabama	Mississippi		Alabama
49	Mississippi	Mississippi	South Carolina		Mississippi

Source: Charles Angoff and H.L. Mencken, "The Worst American State," *American Mercury*, vol. 24, no. 93, September—November, 1931, pp. 1–16, 175–188, 355–371.

below the rest of the states. Keep this ranking in mind, because, as we shall see in subsequent chapters, it has not changed much in the more than eight decades since 1930.

The Great Depression: Liberal Action and Conservative Reaction

The state rankings presented in Table 1.1 should not come as a great shock. Throughout the 1930s, the years of the Great Depression, Texas remained a poor, rural, and agricultural state. No one knew this better than Texans themselves and they were searching for ways to bring change. On June 7, 1935, the *Austin American-Statesman* offered an editorial, entitled "Why Not Development of Manufactures," explaining that "Texas is an agricultural state, . . . but the fact remains that the industrial states of America are the wealthy states, and powerful."[63]

Though the discovery of major new oil fields in East and West Texas softened the depression's blows, regular Texans suffered greatly. Much of rural Texas still lacked basic services like electricity, flood control, and decent roads. As Chandler Davidson has noted, "The great causes of the New Deal in Texas included rural electrification, which brought electricity to farm families; banking regulation; Social Security, . . . unemployment insurance; public works projects, . . . home mortgage guarantees; . . . and welfare measures."[64]

Texans in Washington were deeply involved in moving New Deal legislation through Congress, though some had misgivings. Uvalde's John Nance "Cactus Jack" Garner was the Democratic Minority Leader in the House in 1929 and Majority Leader after the Democrats took control in the 1930 midterm elections. Before Garner left Congress to serve as Roosevelt's Vice President from 1933 to 1941, he groomed other Texans for leadership. Bonham's Sam Rayburn became the Democratic Majority Leader in 1937 and Speaker of the House in 1940. Seven other Texas Democrats chaired House committees during some of all of the 1930s: Hatton Sumners of Dallas chaired the powerful Judiciary Committee from 1931 to 1947; Marvin Jones of Amarillo chaired the Agriculture Committee from 1931 to 1940; Joe Mansfield of Eagle Lake chaired the Rivers and Harbors Committee from 1931 to 1947; James Buchanan of Brenham served as chair of the critical Appropriations Committee from 1933 until his death in 1937; and a young Lyndon Johnson worked closely with Chairman Buchanan on rural electrification issues.

The modest resources of Texas state government were quickly overwhelmed by the depression and state leaders had little choice but to look to Washington for help. As Randolph Campbell explains,

> Wanting relief and recovery for their state, they took federal aid but tended . . . to reject the underlying philosophy of big government and

collective social responsibility. They spoke more and more often of threats to states' rights, disliked the increased spending necessitated by social welfare programs, objected to legislation that favored labor unions, and opposed even the discussion of civil rights and antilynching laws. . . . In the long run, the political and social conservatism of most leading Texans could not fully accommodate the New Deal and its increasingly liberal, big-city leadership.[65]

George Norris Green added that "New Deal legislation fostered liberalism, in fact, but in Texas and the rest of the South, it also generated a tremendous counterreaction among the monied interests."[66] Texas oilmen funded and led this reaction. Bryan Burrough has written that "conservative fury was fueled by a fear of what is known today as 'big government,' . . . Texas oilmen shared a deep loathing of taxes, labor organizers, and anyone who looked to change their ways."[67] Sam Rayburn made exactly this point in a December 4, 1933, letter to William P. Hobby, an old friend, former governor, and leading member of the Houston business community. Rayburn wrote, "Some of our people want everything static and always preach that any movement that goes forward is socialistic and destructive. The movement at this time seems to be led by the U.S. Chamber of Commerce and the large city bankers. . . . [T]heir selfish interests do not quite fit in with the interests of the average man."[68] The New Deal strained the Texas Democratic Party to, and eventually beyond, the breaking point. Though Rayburn and Johnson generally stuck with Roosevelt, the court packing debate of 1937 proved too much for Garner and Sumners. Upon returning from one White House meeting with Roosevelt on the court packing bill, Sumners famously said to his congressional colleagues, "Boys, this is where I cash in."

At home in Texas, conservatives worked hard to maintain the old social and economic orders. That traditional order required cheap and willing labor. As late as 1943, amid race riots in the Galveston shipyards and a threat by the Mexican government to suspend the "Bracero program" over pervasive discrimination in South Texas, Governor Coke Stevenson was asked by the U.S. State Department to join in a Good Neighbor Commission designed to ease tensions. Stevenson agreed, observing that "Meskins is pretty good folks. If it was niggers, it'd be different."[69] To insure that white labor remained cheap too, Texas passed the Manford Act in 1943, the first state law to use the phrase "right to work." Several other southern and western states followed suit almost immediately and another set of anti-union laws were passed by the legislature and signed by Governor Beauford Jester in 1947. Right to work laws forbid the union closed shop, whereby a worker must join the union if hired into a union shop. Giving the worker a choice of whether to join or not is presented as an element of individual rights, but it weakens unions by giving workers the option of saving the union dues and free-riding on those who do pay dues.[70]

Texas white workers, especially those in the rural areas, were just as tractable and easily managed as the establishment might have wished. In 1946, LBJ was campaigning in Brenham, east of Austin, and was to be introduced to the crowd by a local lumberman and cotton dealer. LBJ's speech was not as memorable as the local leader's description of the needs and expectations of Brenham's citizens. He explained that, "We are a lot of simple people here in Washington County. We don't ask much from our government. We really want to be let alone if we can be. We need a little money. . . not as much as some people, but we don't like a lot of giveaway programs. . . . All we ask is forty-cent cotton and ten-cent beer."[71] One suspects that this local leader may have underestimated the needs of the common people of Washington County, but it is also clear that he and they knew that their needs did not move the state's politics.

Governors Coke Stevenson, Beauford Jester, and Allan Shivers, presided over the heyday of the restored conservative establishment in Texas. Former governor W. Lee "Pappy" O'Daniel, then sitting in the U.S. Senate, led the conservative Texas Regulars to adopt their own platform for the 1944 elections. Their platform promised "a return to states' rights 'which have been destroyed by the Communist-controlled New Deal,' and 'a restoration of the supremacy of the white race.'"[72] Senator O'Daniel warned that wartime rationing was "a Communistic, totalitarian measure designed to beat the people of the US into submitting to the edicts of an autocratic, bureaucratic dictatorship."[73]

World War II brought the U.S. and Texas out of the depression and changed both, but particularly Texas, forever. World War II made Texas an urban and industrial state. The war machine ran on oil and Texas had discovered massive new quantities of it in the 1920s and 1930s. During the war, "Dallas and Houston boomed. The demand for jet fuel and all manner of chemicals led to the building of dozens of new refineries and chemical plants along the coast south and east of Houston."[74] The military and aerospace industries, drawn by the dry climate, clear skies, and cheap land, moved to Texas in a big way, confirming San Antonio's history as a military town. And Texas companies, most notably Houston's Brown & Root, grew wealthy on military contracts. Brown & Root, a modest road building company in 1935, rose with Lyndon Johnson. "That Brown & Root could grow fat on a steady diet of cost-plus [meaning guaranteed profit margins] government contracts and at the same time defy organized labor as Socialistic" would surprise no one familiar with the Texas establishment.[75] Brown & Root later became Halliburton.

By mid-century, the Anglo elite, led by three-term Texas Governor Allan Shivers was determined to battle the "trend to the left that is carrying us swiftly toward socialism in many forms and guises."[76] For many Texas conservatives, "the line between New Deal liberalism and socialism was thin, if it even existed at all, while the line between socialism and communism was only one of gradation."[77] In the middle of this Texas establishment rebellion, Theodore White, a prominent journalist and future author of the *Making of the President* series of campaign accounts that ran from 1960 through 1976, wrote "Texas: Land of Wealth and Fear" for the May 1954 issue of *The Reporter*. White wrote that, "millions of Texans are convinced that their primary enemies are other Americans. . . . Ardent and devout states' righters at home bellowing and snorting that the 'sovereign' privileges of Texas must not be disturbed."[78] But disturbed they were, and soon.

Conclusion

"The Texas way," while by no means unchanging, has evinced a core set of principles since Anglo settlers first arrived in Texas. They remain recognizable today. The slave republic that Jared Groce, Stephen F. Austin, and Sam Houston founded reflected their social ideals. Plantation owners commanded all that they surveyed; they owned broad swaths of prime land and the people who worked it. They provided direction and disciple on their lands and were subject to few external checks. They commanded and were granted respect and deference. They were the leading men of the community and its governing class.

They recognized the need for government, to manage and distribute the public lands, secure order, protect property, facilitate commerce, and provide defense against external threats. Government should be strong enough to protect their interests and serve their needs, but it should not dictate to them. To ensure that government fulfilled its proper role, it should be peopled by the intelligent tax-paying citizens of the community, its acknowledged elite. The clear interest of the elite was that government should protect their social primacy and their property at as little cost to them as possible. If others had needs, for education for their children for example, let them buy as much of it as they desired and could afford. If taxes were to be levied to provide these services, then those who wanted the services should pay the taxes.

The Texas way has always highlighted individualism, small government, low taxes, and a states' rights interpretation of federalism. Individualism has always meant personal autonomy and responsibility for one's self and one's family. Initially, individualism was meant only for white men, but increasingly it has applied to others, especially in the form of individual responsibility. The social and economic elites of Texas have always argued that small government and low taxes allow wealth to be enjoyed by those who created it, rather than taken from them by a too powerful government. While this is attractive to the poor who dream of becoming wealthy, it is really attractive to those who are already wealthy and eager to keep what they have.

Most Texans, especially the elites, have viewed American federalism as based on state sovereignty rather than national supremacy. Texas against federal intrusion has been an enduring theme of the state's politics. Texas independence, state boundaries, frontier defense, social spending during the depression, civil rights, the recent economic stimulus and health care programs, were all cast as foreign or federal intrusions on the rights and prerogatives of the sovereign state of Texas. As we shall see, these attitudes have been remarkably stable over the course of Texas history.

In the next chapter, we ask how well or poorly the founding ideals and assumptions of Texas's first century have fared in recent decades. Texas has a stirring history and a sense of state pride matched by few if any others. How does Texas compare to its sister states? Is Texas wealthier or poorer than most other states, better educated or less well educated, healthier of sicker, safer or more vulnerable? In later chapters, we look in some detail at the evolution of Texas public policy in regard to the economy, job creation, income, and wealth; public education; social services like welfare and health care; crime, punishment, and prisons; as well as transportation and the environment. History, culture, and tradition—most profoundly the Civil War and Reconstruction—continue to shape Texas, its people, and their responses to the political, social, and economic issues of the day.

Notes

1 James C. McKinley, "A Texas Senator: Now a Challenger Lagging in the Polls," *New York Times*, February 21, 2010, Y14.

2 Noah Smithwick, *The Evolution of a State or Recollections of Old Texas Days*, Austin, TX: University of Texas Press, 1985, pp. 8–9, 48.

3 Gregg Cantrell, *Stephen F. Austin: Empresario of Texas*, New Haven, CT: Yale University Press, 1999, p. 178.

4 The Diary of William Fairfax Gray, from Virginia to Texas, 1835–1837, see http://sme.edu/swcenter/FairfaxGray/wg_136.htm. See also p. 137.

5 Rutherford B. Hayes, *Diary and Letters of Rutherford B. Hayes, the Nineteenth President of the United States*, Columbus, OH: The Ohio State Archeological and Historical Society, 1922–1926, 1: 254.

6 T.R. Fehrenbach, *Seven Keys to Texas*, El Paso, TX: Texas Western Press, 1983, p. 6.

7 D. W. Meinig, *Imperial Texas: An Interpretive Essay in Cultural Geography*, Austin, TX: University of Texas Press, 1969, p. 89. More recently, see David G. McComb, *Texas: A Modern History*, revised edition, Austin, TX: University of Texas Press, 2010, p. 149.

8 W.W. Newcomb Jr., *The Indians of Texas*, Austin, TX: University of Texas, 1961, p. 338.

9 Sean P. Cunningham, *Cowboy Conservatism: Texas and the Rise of the Modern Right*, Lexington, KY: University Press of Kentucky, 2010, p. 125; summarizing Leigh Clemons, *Branding Texas: Performing Culture in the Lone Star State*, Austin, TX: University of Texas Press, 2008.

10 N. Doran Maillard, *The History of the Republic of Texas*, London: Smith, Elder and Company, 1842, p. 205.

11 Billy D. Ledbetter, "White Over Black in Texas: Racial Attitudes in the Antebellum Period," *Phylon*, vol. 34, no. 4, 4th quarter, 1973, p. 406.

12 Wilbur Zelinsky, *The Cultural Geography of the United States*, Englewood Cliffs, NJ: Prentice-Hall, 1973, pp. 13–14.

13 Meinig, *Imperial Texas*, pp. 28–37.

14 Randolph B. Campbell, "Statehood, Civil War, and Reconstruction, 1846-1876, pp. 174–175, in Walter L. Buenger and Robert A. Calvert, ed., *Texas Through Time: Evolving Interpretation*, College Station, TX: Texas A&M University Press, 1991.

15 Meinig, *Imperial Texas*, p. 47. Fehrenbach, *Seven Keys*, pp. 4–5. See also, Chad R. Trulson and James R. Marquardt, *First Available Cell: Desegregation of the Texas Prison System*, Austin, TX: University of Texas Press, 2009, p. 15.

16 Michael Lind, *Made in Texas: George W. Bush and the Takeover of American Politics*, New York: Basic Books, 2003, p. 26.

17 Carl H. Moneyhon, *Republicanism in Reconstruction Texas*, College Station, TX: Texas A&M University Press, 1980, p. 12.

18 Fehrenbach, *Seven Keys*, p. 3.

19 David Montejano, *Anglos and Mexicans in the Making of Texas, 1836–1986*, Austin, TX: University of Texas Press, 1987, p. 5. See also, Ledbetter, "White Over Black in Texas," p. 406.

20 Meinig, *Imperial Texas*, pp. 48, 50.

21 Robert A. Calvert, Arnoldo De León, and Gregg Cantrell, *The History of Texas*, 4th ed., Wheeling, IN: Harlan Davidson and Co., 2007, p. 115.

22 Randolph B. Campbell, *An Empire for Slavery: The Peculiar Institution in Texas, 1821–1865*, Baton Rouge, LA: Louisiana State University Press, 1989, pp. 222–223. Italics added by the author.

23 James McEnteer, *Deep in the Heart: The Texas Tendency in American Politics*, Westport, CT: Praeger, 2004, p. 44.

24 Calvert et al., *History of Texas*, 4th ed., p. 137. See also James M. Smallwood, "The Impending Crisis: A Texas Perspective on the Causes of the Civil War," in Kenneth W. Howell, *The Seventh Star of the Confederacy: Texas During the Civil War*, Denton, TX: University of North Texas Press, 2009, p. 34.

25 McEnteer, *Deep in the Heart*, p. 5.

26 Calvert et al., *The History of Texas*, 4th ed., p. 175.

27 C. Vann Woodward, *The Burden of Southern History*, New York: Vintage Books, 1960, p. 105; Fred Arthur Bailey, "Free Speech and the 'Lost Cause' in Texas: A Study of Social Control in the New South," *Southwestern historical Quarterly*, vol. 97, no. 3, January 1994, pp. 452–477, see page 454.

28 T.R. Fehrenbach, *Lone Star: A History of Texas and the Texans*, New York: Macmillan, 1968, p. 633.

29 Campbell, "Statehood, Civil War, and Reconstruction," pp. 174–175.

30 Fehrenbach, *Lone Star*, p. 219.

31 James Conaway, *The Texans*, New York: Alfred A. Knopf, 1976, p. 241.

32 Fehrenbach, *Lone Star*, p. 132.

33 Milton Ezrati, "Just What Is It About Texas?" *Antioch Review*, vol. 62, no. 4, Autumn 2004, pp. 754–773, at 756.

34 Don Graham, "Remembering the Alamo: The Story of the Texas Revolution in Popular Culture," *Southwestern Historical Quarterly*, vol. 89, no. 1, July 1985, p. 48.

35 Fehrenbach, *Lone Star*, p. 198.

36 William Bollaert, *William Bollaert's Texas*, Norman, OK: University of Oklahoma Press, 1956, p. 109.

37 Jonathan Tilove, *Austin American-Statesman* blog, February 25, 2013.

38 Patrick Cox and Michael Phillips, *The House Will Come to Order*, Austin, TX: University of Texas Press, 2010, pp. 10–11.

39 Arica Grieder, *Big, Hot, Cheap, and Right*, New York: Public Affairs, 2013, p. 99.

40 George Pierce Garrison, *Texas: A Contest of Civilizations*, New York: Houghton-Mifflin, 1903, pp. 153–154, 156, 175.

41 Fehrenbach, *Lone Star*, p. 166; Meinig, *Imperial Texas*, p. 34.

42 Garrison, *Texas: A Contest of Civilizations*, p. 270.

43 Ibid., p. 278.

44 Moneyhon, *Republicanism in Reconstruction Texas*, p. 8.

45 George Norris Green, *The Establishment in Texas Politics: The Primitive Years, 1938–1957*, Norman, OK: University of Oklahoma Press, 1979, p. 17.

46 Chandler Davidson, *Race and Class in Texas Politics*, Princeton, NJ: Princeton University Press, 1990, p. 188.

47 Gromer Jeffers, "Hopefuls Visit Dallas, Spar Over State's Future," *Dallas Morning News*, February 3, 2010, A3.

48 William C. Davis, *Lone Star Rising: The Revolutionary Birth of the Republic of Texas*, New York: Free Press, 2004, p. 125.

49 Chester Newell, *History of the Revolution in Texas*, New York: Wiley and Putnam, 1838, quoted in McLemore, *Inventing Texas*, p. 32.

50 Fehrenbach, *Lone Star*, p. 275.

51 James R. Arnold, *Jeff Davis's Own: Cavalry, Comanches, and the Battle for the Texas Frontier*, Edison, NJ: Castle Books, 2007, p. 63.

52 Cunningham, *Cowboy Conservatism*, p. 14.

53 J. David Woodard, *The New Southern Politics*, Boulder, CO: Lynne Rienner Publishers, 2006, pp. 129–132.

54 Fehrenbach, *Lone Star*, p. 529.

55 Joe Barton, "Texas vs. Obama's Overreaching EPA," *Dallas Morning News*, June 21, 2010, p. A11.

56 Christy Hoppe, "Are Feds Punishing Our State," *Dallas Morning News*, May 3, 2010 A1, A5. See also Christy Hoppe, "Texas Ties Up Feds In Court," *Dallas Morning News*, March 24, 2012, pp. A1, A13.

57 Thomas D. Russell, "Keep the Negroes Out of Most Classes Where There Are a Large Number of Girls," www.statesman.com/multimedia/archive/00440/Article_by_Tom_Russ_440071a.pdf.

58 Ibid., pp. 3–4.

59 Cox and Phillips, *The House Will Come to Order*, p. 18.

60 Davidson, *Race and Class in Texas Politics*, pp. 20–21.

61 Amy Bridges, *Morning Glories: Municipal Reform in the Southwest*, Princeton, NJ: Princeton University Press, 1997, p. 20. See also, Calvert, *History of Texas*, pp. 240–241.

62 V.O. Key, *Southern Politics*, New York: Alfred A. Knopf, 1949, pp. 272–273.

63 Anthony M. Orum, *Power, Money, and People: The Making of Modern Austin*, Eugene, OR: Resources Publications, 1987, pp. 44–45.

64 Davidson, *Race and Class in Texas Politics*, p. 28.

65 Randolph B. Campbell, *Gone to Texas: A History of the Lone Star State*, New York: Oxford University Press, 2003, p. 392.

66 Green, *The Establishment in Texas Politics*, p. 15.

67 Bryan Burrough, *The Big Rich: The Rise and Fall of the Greatest Texas Oil Fortunes*, New York: Penguin Press, 2009, pp. 126–127.

68 D.B. Hardeman and Donald C. Bacon, *Rayburn: A Biography*, New York: Madison Books, 1987, p. 161.

69 Green, *The Establishment in Texas Politics*, p. 81.

70 Ibid., pp. 62, 104–105.

71 James Reston Jr., *The Lone Star: The Life of John Connally*, New York: Harper and Row, 1989, p. 120.

72 McEnteer, *Deep in the* Heart, p. 82.

73 Cunningham, *Cowboy Conservatism*, p. 28.

74 Burrough, *The Big Rich*, p. 154.

75 Conaway, *The Texans*, p. 92.

76 Morehead, *50 Years in Texas Politics*, p. 104.

77 Cunningham, *Cowboy Conservatism*, p. 43.

78 Burrough, *The Big Rich*, p. 233.

2   Texas: The Myth vs. the Reality

> Like most passionate nations, Texas has its own private history, based on, but not limited by, facts.
>
> (John Steinbeck, 1962)[1]

In Chapter 1, we drew on the best evidence from history and the social sciences to describe the political culture, the basic or fundamental values, of Texas. The goal was to show the consistency with which Anglo Texans have held to the values of small government, low taxes, light regulation, thin social services, personal responsibility, and elite leadership from first settlement into the mid-twentieth century. Throughout the state's history, Anglo leaders have argued that these commitments—which many have called "the Texas way"—have made Texas a singularly open, vibrant, and dynamic place. Standing by these commitments, while others have flagged, has made Texas the last refuge of freedom, opportunity, and the American Dream. When Texas Anglo leaders, like former governor Rick Perry, argue that Texas is a model for her sister states and the nation, they do not mean that Texas is the richest state, or the state with the best education or health care systems, they mean that Texas is the most "business-friendly" state in the nation because it is the state where independence, freedom, and opportunity still reign.

In June 2013, Governor Perry went on a business recruitment trip to New York and Connecticut, touting Texas as a better climate in which to do business. The whole trip would have been laughable if there were not some sense in which the governor's claims were plausible, if not simply true. Connecticut is the wealthiest state in the nation and New York is fifth, while Texas is well down the list at twenty-fifth. But the point that he was making is that Connecticut is a "high-wage" state; high wages after all is what it means to be wealthy. Texas is a "low-wage" state, which is attractive to business, assuming the quality of the workforce is acceptable.

In this and future chapters, we confront these claims not just with additional historical interpretation, but with the best objective data available. In this chapter, we begin by showing in stark geographical and population density terms that Texas has been a southern state throughout its history. Then we turn to a quick overview of how Texas compares to the nation and to the other 49 states on standard measures of population and job growth income, educational attainment, access to health care and social services. crime and punishment, taxes and public spending, and much more. We confront the Texas myth, the story that Texas Anglo leaders love to tell, with the reality, the results and outcomes, of Texas public policy. Our goal is to assess the costs and benefits, historically and going forward, of "the Texas way." What are the pros and cons—the tradeoffs—of pursuing a small government vision that necessitates lower spending on education and other social services than most other states?

The Cultural Foundations of the Lone Star Nation

Most analysts agree that the traditional political culture of the South is the foundation of the Texas political culture, but many see elements of Western individualism as well. Others see a changing Texas political culture driven by the state's dramatic twentieth-century transition from a poor, rural, agricultural past to a more prosperous, urban, industrial, high-tech, and service economy present. Perhaps, but if the Texas political culture has changed, we would expect to see Texas public policy change as well. In fact, Texas public policy has not responded to the evolution of the state. This suggests that the traditional political culture of Texas's rural past has shaped its urban present much more than most Texans realize or would like to admit.

Texas's southern roots were never in question during the nineteenth century. From the initial settlement of the Austin colony through the post-Civil War exodus of southern whites to Texas, the state's population stock and its political and social instincts were overwhelmingly southern. As we saw in Chapter 1, Wilbur Zelinsky's "Doctrine of First Settlement" contends that first settlers lay down the social, political, economic, and cultural matrices into which later arrivals must fit. Over the course of the nineteenth century, more than nine in ten Texans were born in the South or born in Texas of southern stock. Yet, as the nineteenth century turned into the twentieth, Texas elites grew increasingly concerned that the Civil War left that strong southern connection tainted with treason, defeat, and military occupation. This was, of course, true of all of the confederate states, but, unlike the states of the deep South—South Carolina, Alabama, Mississippi, and others—Texas leaders came to think they had a way to blur if not blot out the state's history.

Beginning in late nineteenth century, some Texas cultural leaders, abetted by generations of Texas historians, sought to expunge the memory of the Civil War, the Old South, and its failed defense of slavery by refocusing attention on the Texas Revolution as an iconic moment in the great westward advance of Anglo civilization and freedom. They believed that Texas could much more comfortably and profitably be defined in relation to Manifest Destiny, the winning of the West, and the fight for liberty and freedom at the Alamo and San Jacinto than with slavery, the Civil War, and memories of the Lost Cause. The desire to recast or redesign Texas history produced a long—even unending—debate over whether Texas was a southern, a western, or distinctively southwestern state.

The broad outlines of this debate were drawn in the new University of Texas Department of History (initially the Department of English and History). The University of Texas opened its doors in the fall of 1883 and the Georgia-born historian George P. Garrison joined the faculty in 1884. Garrison became chairman of the History department when it separated from English in 1888 and he remained chairman until his death in 1910. Garrison's prominent book, *Westward Extension: 1841–1850* (1906), argued that Texas history was a major chapter in the winning of the West. Charles William Ramsdell joined the History Department in 1906 and published his *Reconstruction in Texas* in 1910. Ramsdell "argued that Texas had southern moorings, which made the state socially and culturally part of the South."[2]

Generations of Texas historians lined up behind Garrison and Ramsdell to battle over the best description of the state's cultural roots. Increasingly, the state's social and political leadership came to see Garrison's western view as the most congenial. Though modern historians are increasingly insistent on Ramsdell's view that "Texas had southern moorings," the Texas establishment is unmoved because "the Texas myth" required western roots. Myth has tremendous advantages in any fight between myth and history. For example, the journalist Erica Grieder's recent defense of the Texas way, *Big, Hot, Cheap, and Right: What America Can Learn from the Strange Genius of Texas* (2013), reports that most recent observers agree that "During the first half of the twentieth century, . . . Texas clearly was more affiliated with the South than with any other region." But she also reports that, "A hundred years after annexation . . . Like the rest of the former Confederate states, Texas was still working through the ruination of the Civil War and Reconstruction. The state's alternative regional identities were as yet inchoate."[3] Think about that last line, "The state's alternative regional identities were as yet inchoate," meaning, presumably, that a plausible story about how Texas was not really southern, had not yet come together. The historian Laura Lyons McLemore, author of *Inventing Texas: Early Historians of the Lone Star State,* was more blunt, saying, Ramsdell's view receded before "a desire to dilute, if not completely dissolve, the inglorious memory of the Civil War by reviving the glorious memory of the Texas Revolution."[4]

Despite a concerted effort by scholars across the humanities and social sciences, the myth of Texas's cowboy heritage continues to be quite pervasive. The prominent Texas folklorist and University of Texas English Professor Don Graham has resisted the quiet editing out of the southern roots of Texas history and culture. Graham recently wrote that the North Texas of his boyhood in the 1940s and 1950s "was scarcely distinguishable from the rest of Dixie." But as the mythic civility of the plantation culture morphed into school desegregation and civil rights fights of the 1960s and later, many sought to replace southern roots with western imagery. Graham notes that, "Just as knowledge of the Southern part of Texas history has faded away . . . the part of Texas that keeps being forgotten or erased—East Texas" fades with it.[5] Similarly, in 1989, Randolph B. Campbell, then a young historian at the University of North Texas, wrote a book entitled *An Empire for Slavery: The Peculiar Institution in Texas.* In 2011, Campbell explained his motivation for writing the book, saying "I wrote it because I believed that the historical record ought to be straight. . . . But it wasn't right for the people in Texas to allow themselves the luxury of saying that we didn't have slaves here or that we had only a handful."[6] As the place of East Texas, plantations, and slavery in the state's history has faded, the place of West Texas, cowboys, and cattle has assumed an importance that history simply cannot support. Glen Sample Ely, the state's most prominent historian of West Texas, author of *Where the West Begins: Debating Texas Identity,* wrote that "For far too long, Texas has cloaked itself in a Western identity to escape its southern legacy of racism, segregation, and lynching."[7] Ely presents West Texas as participating, though in distinctive and attenuated ways, in the state's history of racial and ethnic distinctions and exclusions.

Finally, before turning to the data that will resolve this issue, it must be said that in important ways the whole debate over Texas's cultural roots is absurd. Texas was settled mainly out of the South, was a slave state, joined the Confederacy, and mandated Jim Crow segregation into the 1970s. Texas is southern in fundamental respects, though, as Ely said, not uniformly so. Maybe the best that we can do within the historical literature is to listen to the prominent Texas historian Walter L. Buenger. Like Ely, Buenger wrote that, "All of Texas is connected—each region to the other and each region to the South."[8] Fortunately, there is an obvious and powerful way to measure the weight of East Texas, with its unambiguous southern roots, against that of West Texas, with its more western, but still notably southern, roots. When in doubt, recur to the facts.

Three geographical markers have been used to divide East and West Texas. Two are artificial, just intriguing lines on a map, while the third is strikingly physical. The first is the 98th meridian. "In 1905, Vernon Bailey, Chief Field Naturalist of the U.S. Department of Agriculture, conducted a biological survey of Texas. . . . 'the eastern part of Texas, west to approximately the 98th meridian, agrees very closely in climate . . . with the lower Mississippi Valley.' At the 98th meridian, he discerned a 'well-defined division' between East and West."[9] As Map 2.1 shows, a little more than a third of Texas lies east of the 98th meridian. Others, including Glen Ely, point to the 100th meridian as the beginning of arid West Texas. Ely described the transition zone between the 98th and 100th meridian as the "shatterbelt region" where rough geography marks the transition from East to West. Wilbur Zelinsky also noted this transitional region in saying that "the South finally fades away as one approaches the famous 100th meridian and a critical decline in annual precipitation."[10] The 98th meridian runs north and south just west of Fort Worth and the 100th meridian runs 150 miles west of Fort Worth, near Abilene.

A more concrete way to identify the dividing line between East and West Texas is a geographical fault line called the Balcones Escarpment. The Balcones Escarpment was formed when two of the earth's plates came together and the western plate overrode the eastern plate. The faultline runs from Del Rio in the Big Bend area to just west of San Antonio before running north, passing just west of Austin and Fort Worth to the Red River. To the south, the hills associated with the escarpment rise nearly a thousand feet, while further north they rise about three hundred feet. This rough country lies between the 98th and 100th meridians and is what Ely called the "shatterbelt region." The Balcones Escarpment divides well-watered East Texas from the much drier West Texas. As Map 2.1 shows, the Balcones Escarpment divides Texas approximately in half.

Figure 2.1 shows quite clearly that the population of Texas has always been predominantly in East Texas, however defined, and only thinly scattered

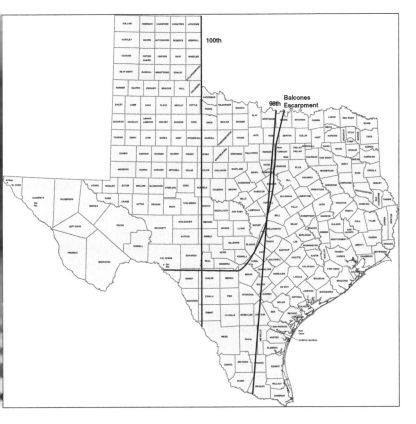

Map 2.1 The Disputed Division between East and West Texas.

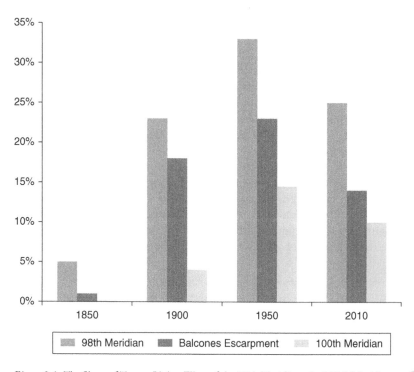

Figure 2.1 The Share of Texans Living West of the 98th Meridian, the 100th Meridian, and the Balcones Escarpment.

through West Texas. Moreover, East Texas was settled first and the weight of social and economic influence has always resided there. The 98th meridian divides Texas about one-third to the east and two-thirds to the west. Still, at no point in Texas history up to and including today, have more than one-third of Texans lived west of the 98th meridian, even though San Antonio, the second largest city in Texas and the nation's seventh largest city, lies west of the 98th meridian. No more than 15 percent of Texans have ever lived west of the 100th meridian. And if one takes the Balcones Escarpment as nature's best definition of the dividing line between east and west Texas, no more than one-quarter of Texans have ever lived in the west. In 2010, just 14 percent of Texans lived west of the Balcones.

So unless we are to believe that the latest settled and most sparsely populated region of the state has driven the state's character and development; or unless we are to believe that reading western novels and watching cowboy movies erased generations worth of southern cultural instincts and assumptions from Texas minds—we must finally treat this debate about whether Texas is southern, western, or southwestern, as absurd. From its origins and to its core, Texas shares in the southern political culture only slightly softened by a West Texas focus on different and marginally less threatening targets of discrimination.

The Stubborn Southernness of Texas in the Twentieth Century

During the first half of the twentieth century, the Texas political culture changed little, but its defenders became more strident as external pressures grew, beginning with the Great Depression and Franklin Roosevelt's New Deal. The unprecedented activism of the Roosevelt administration smacked of socialism to the conservative Texas elite. As the depression waned in the late-1930s, resentment against federal intrusion in state affairs grew louder and angrier. The increasing focus on civil rights in the middle decades of the twentieth century brought a deepening sense on the part of the governing elites that the Texas way was under assault.

John Gunther's political tour of the post-World War II United States, entitled *Inside U.S.A.* (1947), is a generally light-hearted summary of the major figures, party divisions, and issues in each state. In Texas, Gunther was jolted by the intensity of the anti-Roosevelt sentiment, saying, "Nowhere in the United States, not even on Wall Street . . . did I find such a perfervid hatred for Mr. Roosevelt as in Texas. . . . I met men who had been unfalteringly convinced that if FDR won again [in 1944], 'it would mean that the Mexicans and niggers will take us over.' This kind of passion makes for ruthlessness."[11] In fact, this reputation for passion fueling ruthlessness came to characterize the nation's view of Texas from the late 1930s through the Kennedy assassination and beyond.

By 1952, the state's conservative leaders had had enough. When the Democrats chose the liberal governor of Illinois, Adlai Stevenson as their standard-bearer, Texas Governor Allan Shivers led conservative Democrats to Dwight D. Eisenhower, the Republican candidate. General Eisenhower, the former Supreme Commander of allied forces in Europe during World War II, was the first Republican candidate for president to campaign actively in the South. Eisenhower, born in Denison, Texas, but raised in Abilene, Kansas, thrilled southern hearts by standing whenever "Dixie" was played—which was often. Shivers was joined in "Democrats for Eisenhower" by Governor Kennon of Louisiana and Governor Byrnes of South Carolina. Eisenhower carried five southern states in 1952 and did even better when he again faced Stevenson in 1956. Texas went for Eisenhower both times.[12]

In 1960, John Kennedy barely edged Richard Nixon in one of the closest elections in American history. To help in Texas and the South, Kennedy chose LBJ as his running mate. Many Johnson insiders advised that he hold onto his spot as Democratic majority leader in the Senate, arguing that it was more influential and more secure, and Bobby Kennedy famously opposed LBJ on the ticket. John Kennedy knew that he needed LBJ. In fact, even with him, Kennedy carried Texas by just 45,000 votes out of 1.3 million cast. Nationally, Kennedy won 34.2 million votes to Nixon's

34.1 million for 49.72 percent to 49.55 percent. The political climate in Texas grew so fraught as the 1960 election approached that Bruce Alger, one of the first Republicans elected to Congress from Texas after Reconstruction, led a demonstration in Dallas in October in which he carried a sign declaring that "LBJ SOLD OUT TO YANKEE SOCIALISTS." The demonstration spun out of control and national coverage resulted when Lady Bird Johnson was spat upon.

Rising tensions within the Texas Democratic Party prior to the 1964 presidential election led Kennedy, despite the misgivings of Governor Connally and Vice President Johnson, to schedule a fund-raising and fence-mending trip to Texas in November 1963. On November 22, 1963, the day that the president and Jackie Kennedy were to be in Dallas, an ad appeared in the *Dallas Morning News*, outlined in thick black borders, paid for by Texas oilman H.L. Hunt and the local John Birch Society, declaring that "Kennedy was secretly in league with the American Communists." Venom dripped from the scornful greeting, "Welcome, Mr. Kennedy, to Dallas. . . . A CITY that will continue to grow and prosper despite efforts by you and your administration to penalize it for non-conformity to 'New Frontierism.'"[13] The New Frontier was the name given by the Kennedy administration to their mildly liberal domestic policy program and conservative Dallas wanted him to know that they would have none of it. As they prepared in Fort Worth for the brief flight to Dallas, the president is reported to have observed to Jackie Kennedy, "We're headed into nut country today."[14]

Kennedy's assassination in Dallas repulsed most Texans. Texas supported LBJ overwhelmingly in his 1964 run for election to a full term as president, defeated Bruce Alger for re-election, and swept all six Dallas Republicans out of the state legislature. John Connally, elected governor in 1962 and seriously wounded in the Kennedy assassination, had a slow recovery from his wounds but emerged politically invulnerable. A conservative Democrat, Connally increased state spending, especially for higher education, but he made few attempts to change the basic structure of Texas politics. James Reston writes that "John Connally epitomized the big man of Texas. He stood in his elegant boots with the wealthy over the poor, the business executive over the working man, white over black and Hispanic, the glamorous over the commonplace. In short, he symbolized Texas royalty over Texas peasantry."[15] Moreover, the anti-government, especially anti-federal government, sentiment on display the day Kennedy was shot did not abate. George Norris Green noted in the late 1970s that, "Texans believe that there is a difference politically between their state and other states, and that the federal government is almost a foreign menace to Texas rights and privileges."[16]

The electoral system that underpinned white supremacy in Texas and the South came under increasing federal pressure at mid-century. The key exclusionary devices of early registration, the white primary, and the poll tax were all tenaciously defended until Congress and the federal courts struck them down. The Supreme Court declared the white primary unconstitutional in *Smith v. Allwright* (1944); the Twenty-Fourth Amendment outlawed the poll tax in federal elections (1964); and the Supreme Court struck down the poll tax in state election in *U.S. v. Texas* (1966) and early registration in 1971. Texas fought each of these changes to the very end and, in fact, did not ratify the Twenty-Fourth Amendment until 2009. T.R. Fehrenbach stated the matter with characteristic bluntness, saying "Virtually all the political and social reforms of the twentieth century enacted by government have been forced down the Anglo-Texan throat."[17] It often fell to one federal judge, William Wayne Justice of the Eastern District of Texas, to do the forcing.

Judge Justice summed up the Texas record of suppression of minority voting in the case of *Seaman v. Upham* (1982). Judge Justice wrote that this history "stands as a disheartening testament to the perseverance and craft of the dominant political leaders, in their attempt to exclude minorities from participation in the process of self-government." He concluded that, "A century of neglect, sometimes benign, frequently malign, has created a climate of alienation and apathy, mixed with deep-seated resentment in many of the minority communities of Texas."[18] Judge Justice also was involved in a series of cases that challenged segregation in Texas schools, prisons, and asylums. Federal judges still regularly hold that Texas public officials work to suppress minority voter influence. In 2011 and 2012 both the state legislature's redistricting maps and their Voter ID law were found by federal judges to be racially discriminatory. In 2013, after the U.S. Supreme Court struck down the preclearance provisions of the Voting Rights Act, the U.S. Justice Department brought new suits against Texas in both cases.

While the federal assault on segregation overwhelmed the Anglo elites initial strategy of massive resistance, they soon settled on a new and ultimately more effective strategy. Progressive whites, blacks, Hispanics, and other minorities had long argued that discrimination in general and segregation in particular was a violation of the nation's fundamental commitment to equal treatment of citizens. After passage of the Civil Rights Act of 1964 and 1965, the Voting Rights Act of 1965, and the Fair Housing Act of 1968, Anglo conservatives simply said, OK, we agree, America should be a color-blind society. Support for a color-blind society, of course, requires that no group ask for special benefits, even to redress past grievances, because this would entail violation of others' rights to equal protection of the laws. If the Constitution is color-blind, and we believe that it is and must be, Anglo conservatives now said, laws that take account of race, let alone laws that distribute privileges and benefits based on race, even if intended to do some presumed good, are unconstitutional. Liberals sputtered and cursed, but conservatives smiled at having secured an unexpected ideological advantage.

Texas Mythology during the Boom Years

Texas grew rapidly during the 1960s and 1970s. These were the boom years during which oil revenues buoyed individual, corporate, and government bottom lines. Following the institution of a modest sales tax in 1961, burgeoning oil and gas severance taxes allowed Texas to increase expenditures without raising taxes. Citizens and leaders were confident in the future and so politics remained more about personalities than issues. John Connally dominated Texas politics during the 1960s. Connally biographer, James Reston Jr., wrote that,

> The major Texas papers doted upon him: "John Connally personifies confidence. Defeat is not in his make-up," the *Houston Chronicle* purred. "Retreat is not in his vocabulary. Skillfully, he directs this confidence where it belongs: in Texas and her people. In his mind, Texas has everything in her favor—charm, vigor, a reservoir of intelligence, a colorful history, courage for the present, a sense of destiny, abundant natural resources and proud people who are united to make this state the envy of the other 49." In short, John Connally was the personification of Texas, as establishment Texas wanted to see itself.[19]

A new image developed of the indomitable Texan pursuing his own success in a state destined to be the envy of the other 49. This is not the Alamo myth, heroism in the face of overwhelming odds, let alone myth of the Lost Cause masking the bitter taste of defeat, this is the myth of the Lone Star ascendant.

As a business-oriented conservative, Connally "spent a great deal of energy shaping Texas's image as a racially moderate and southwestern, rather than southern, state."[20] He spent far less time on trying to change Texas's standing on key social indicators of education, though he did spend on higher education, health care, and other social services. Reston noted that:

> The social ills of Texas were daunting in 1963. For all its fabulous oil wealth, it was thirty-third in the nation in per capita income . . . thirty-eighth in the country in education and thirty-sixth in public health . . . forty-fourth in adult literacy, and last in per capita expenditure for child welfare services. It had the largest pool of poor in the entire United States.
>
> . . . In its racial attitudes, the state of Texas was only slightly more advanced than Alabama, Mississippi, and South Carolina. Only two percent of blacks actually attended school with whites.[21]

Texas conservatives remained resistant to new spending even when the money was in the till. In 1970, George Mahon, Lubbock's long-time conservative Democratic congressman, declared: "I am a firm believer in the old fashioned virtue of self-reliance, and I hold unwaveringly to the view that individual initiative, drive, and discipline need to be more encouraged in our country."[22]

As T.R. Fehrenbach wrote in 1983, even at the height of the oil boom, rising wealth made little difference to social spending. He observed that,

> Texas, especially in the 1980s, is relatively a rich state, and very rich in terms of resources. It stands at the very bottom of the tier of poorest states, however, in the sums it expends for public health and welfare. Teachers' salaries always hover near the lowest in the nation . . . Petroleum finances a third of all Texas public revenues, but the state gasoline tax in 1982 was the lowest in the nation."[23]

Fehrenbach is widely seen as the classic expositor of mythic Texas, but even he seems somewhat bemused by the fact that the flowing Texas wealth of the early 1980s barely moved the needle on state spending on health and welfare. Others thought that the explanation was quite clear. In 1984, Texas House Speaker Gib Lewis (D-Fort Worth) remarked that, "Most Texans are conservative. They look for a helping hand at the end of their arm."[24]

The Texas myth remained strong into the mid-1980s; largely unquestioned within the state and begrudged if hard to attack from outside the state. In 1987, when political scientist Gerry Riposa and his colleagues wrote *Texas Public Policy*, they reported that individualism was still central to the Anglo Texan self-image:

> Texans like to picture themselves as independent individuals handling their affairs without needing assistance from others. . . . The individualist thread in our culture considers the individual responsible for his or her own success or failure. Social forces, like poverty or racial discrimination, are used by individuals to excuse their own failures, but are not deterrents to those with true ability. Clearly, this theme is inconsistent with extensive government provision of social services.[25]

Similarly, political scientists Anthony Champagne and Edward Harpham noted in *Texas at the Crossroads*, that "Texas is no longer the rustic frontier state of myth and legend. [Nonetheless,] Individualism continues to dominate the Texas psyche. Entrepreneurialism is still valued by a people who crave the opportunity to 'make it big.' But while such values survive, the people holding them and the actual opportunities available to them have changed enormously."[26] Champagne and Harpham also noted the smothering effect of Texas mythology. Harpham wrote that, "The mythos of the frontier, the idealization of the individual entrepreneur, and the idea that the government that governs least is the government that governs best all are well and alive in Texas in the 1980s. All have played a role in constraining a larger policy debate over the responsibility a society has to its poor."[27]

But challenges loomed on the horizon like few times before. Both Riposa's *Texas Public Policy* and Champagne and Harpham's *Texas at the Crossroads* appeared as the collapse in oil prices, followed by devastating collapses in property values and Texas banks, began to bite. Concern battled with confidence in these books and concern was beginning to get the upper hand. Champagne and Harpham tell the sobering story of the collapse in oil prices, though they could not know the depth of the problems that would follow:

> In January [1986], the price of oil had collapsed: it hovered around $12 and $15 per barrel for most of the spring. By July, the price of oil had dropped to a little over $11 per barrel. . . . By mid-summer, unemployment in Texas had topped 10%, among the highest in the nation, and the state that but a few years before had been holding itself up as a land of opportunity for the rest of the nation found itself in the midst of its largest recession since the Great Depression.[28]

Economic Collapse, Diversification, and "Never Again"

The late 1980s and early 1990s were hard on Texas. The old swagger of the boom years did not fully return until the mid-1990s—the Bush years—and then it was muted for a time by the bursting of the tech bubble in 2000 and 2001. While the return of prosperity brought increased state revenues, some went to tax cuts and some went to modest spending increases. Yet, increasingly, economic downturns brought tight budgets and severe budget cuts. Patrick Cox and Michael Phillips write that as the legislature faced deficits in 2003, "Despite the state ranking forty-third in per capita hospital, health, and welfare spending nationally in 2000, and forty-first in state aid per pupil in grades K-12, those budget items faced devastating reductions."[29]

Hard times returned with the global financial collapse of 2008 and 2009. Texas again cut to balance and slipped even further in national rankings on spending for education, health care, and social services. But to listen to state officials, you would never know that Texas had been hit at all. Texas Comptroller Susan Combs, interviewed in Texas Monthly in June 2009, was unrestrained in her boosterism. Combs explained that Texas was far better off than other states because it had learned the lessons of the late 1980s so well:

> The state has enjoyed tremendous growth—incredible sales tax growth of 12 percent three years ago, then 10-plus percent, then 6.6 percent. It has been rockin' and rollin'. In 2008 the state brought in about 71

percent of all new jobs in the country [an over estimate, but more about that in Chapter 4] . . . . We're not sleeping in our cars. We're still largely employed. We're actually fairly lucky. . . . So the state is so much better off than anyplace else. I really attribute that to how badly damaged we were in the mid-eighties. We lost 368 banks and 200,000 to 300,000 jobs, and we said, "Never again; let's diversify. Which we have done."[30]

Very similar themes were articulated by Governor Rick Perry in his 2011 Inaugural Address. In office since late 2000, Perry argued that Texas had survived the financial crisis of 2008–2009 better than most states and the nation because of its open, competitive, entrepreneurial culture. With another four-year term before him, Perry said:

Given our state's economic success compared to that of other states and Washington's ongoing irresponsibility, I believe Texas will lead the way out of this turmoil. . . . Our state is the new, best hope for entrepreneurs and small businesses—the place where Americans can redeem their promise and fulfill their potential. . . . If I've said it once, I've said it a thousand times, and will say it a thousand times more: there is still a place where opportunity looms large in this country, and that place is called Texas.

What Anglo Texas leaders like Perry and Combs miss, of course, is that their triumphalist claims are made at the expense of other Americans. As Laura McLemore described in *Inventing Texas*, "Texans have tended to define themselves as against non-Texans generally."[31] And if Texas is 'a whole other country" and the last refuse of opportunity, what of the American dream and American exceptionalism? American exceptional-ism must have decayed, must have been lost, if it survives in its original vibrancy only in Texas. Naturally, other Americans, proud of American history, the American dream, and American exceptionalism, are, by turns, angry about and dismissive of Texan claims that they have lost faith with the American dream and will only find it again in "that place called Texas." So about those claims—is Texas a model for its 49 sister states or does she have much to learn from them? As we shall see, Texas is a model in some regards, but has much to learn in others.

How Does Texas Compare?

The short answer to the question, "how does Texas compare," is not well. In Chapter 1, we presented a ranking of the states on four dimensions—wealth, education, culture, and public order—that appeared in the *American Mercury* in 1931. *American Mercury* was an ideas and opinion journal and the authors of the article, entitled "The Worst American State," were Charles Angoff and H.L. Mencken. Mencken in particular was a well-known iconoclast and political skeptic, so the ranking attributed to Texas, 39th among the then-48 states and D.C., should be taken with a grain of salt. Even if Texas did rank 39th in 1930, wouldn't rapid economic growth over the last eight decades have moved her up smartly in the rankings. Fortunately, the Federal Reserve Bank of Cleveland, as conservative and staid an organization as you are likely to find (no Menckens working there), attempted to answer just that question. The bank's 2005 Annual Report featured a study entitled, "Altered States: A Perspective on 75 Years of State Income Growth."[32] The study asked of the period from 1930 to 2005, "Why do residents of some states have higher incomes than residents of other states? Why have these income differences persisted for the past 75 years?"[33] Why, indeed!

The Cleveland Fed study points out that the dominant economic model of state income growth, the Solow model, named for the Nobel Prize-winning economist Robert Solow, predicts that if different regions, say the wealthier Northeast and poorer South, start out with different levels of wealth and capital investment, they should converge over time. Businesses stand to gain the most if they invest new capital in states with low wage rates. The study confirms that, "States that had lower incomes in 1930 have tended to grow at a faster pace than those whose incomes were greater at the time."[34] Convergence has occurred, but not enough, even after 80 years, to move the poor states up to the level of the wealthy. Texas lagged the average state income in 1939 by about 13 percent (ranking 31st) and continued to lag in 2004 by about 3 percent (ranking 25th). Two things are happening in this data, the income differences between the states are slowly closing and the states are maintaining their relative rankings. The rich states are generally still rich and the poor states poor, but less so. Finally, the Cleveland Fed study tried to assess the factors that most contributed to state income growth. They assessed education levels, taxes and public infrastructure, patents and technology. They found that higher taxes do not limit growth if the revenues are used wisely for infrastructure development. The factors that did effect income growth were patents, a measure of innovation, education, and industry specialization, measured as the share of the state economy in service and knowledge-intensive activities. Unfortunately, Texas lagged modestly on all three.[35]

To update of the Cleveland Fed analysis, I have taken personal income per capita data by state for 1950 and 2012 (the latest available) to analyze convergence over those six decades. Dividing each state's personal income per capita by national personal income per capita shows how far each state is above or below the national average. Comparing the data for 1950 and 2012 will show how much convergence has occurred overall and which states have moved up (gotten comparatively richer) and down (gotten comparatively poorer) since 1950.

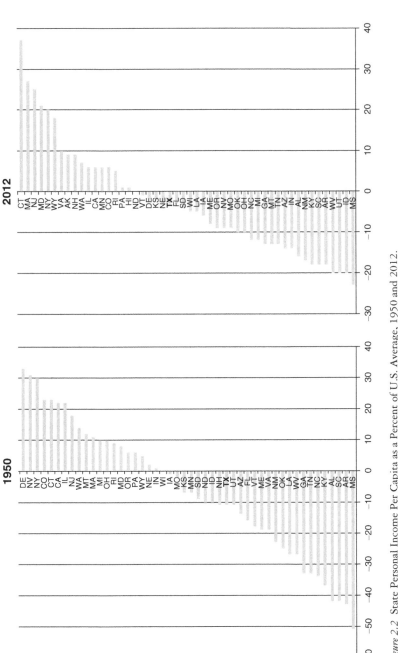

Figure 2.2 State Personal Income Per Capita as a Percent of U.S. Average, 1950 and 2012.

Source: *Statistical Abstract of the United States*, 1952, Table 309, p. 258.

Statistical Abstract of the United States, 2013, Table 693, p. 460. See also http://www.bea.gov/iTable/iTable.cfm?ReqID=70&step=1.

First, in both 1950 and 2012, there were fewer states above the national average for personal income per capita than below it. In 1950, 21 states were above and 27 below, and in 2012, 21 states were above and 29 were below. Second, just as the Solow model predicted, the range between the highest and lowest states closed between 1950 and 2012. In 1950, Delaware was the wealthiest state at 33 percent above the national average and Mississippi was the poorest at 51 percent below, for a range of 84 percent. In 2012, Connecticut was the wealthiest state at 38 percent above the national average while Mississippi remained the poorest state, but at just 26 percent below the national average, for a range of 64 percent. Third, convergence is not as simple as the wealthier states falling toward the national average and poorer states advancing toward it. Poor states like Mississippi, Alabama, Arkansas, and South Carolina made impressive strides. Mississippi moved from −51 percent in 1950 to −23 percent in 2012; South Carolina from −42 to −20; Arkansas from −43 to −19; and Alabama from −42 to −17. However, some wealthy states in 1950 added to their lead. Connecticut moved from 23 percent above the national average in 1950 to 38 percent above in 2012; Massachusetts went from +11 to +28; Maryland from +8 to +22; and New Jersey from +18 to +26. In summary, there is a pattern of convergence overall, with the poorer states coming up nicely, but some of the wealthier states have sprinted away to larger leads.

How has Texas done? The answer is, not bad, but not great. In 1950, Texas personal income per capita, at $1,278, was 11 percent below the national average of $1,436. In 2012, Texas personal income per capita, at $41,471, was 3 percent below the national average of $42,693. In 1950, Texas ranked 29th among the states and in 2012 Texas ranked 24th. Texas has moved up, but just a bit and slowly. Progress is a good thing, but 8 percent over six decades is 1.3 percent per decade. This suggests that a couple more decades will be required to reach the national average for personal income per capita. And what do we make of Connecticut and Massachusetts, two of former Governor Perry's favorite whipping posts, being wealthier than the national average in 1950 and improving by 15 and 17 percent respectively from there.

As the Cleveland Fed study found, high taxes do not preclude growth and low taxes do not assure it. High taxes, well invested in infrastructure and education, can fuel growth. Low taxes, so long as they are not so low as to starve infrastructure and education, can spur growth by encouraging innovation and entrepreneurship. But one must say that it is highly unlikely that a revenue-starved state like Texas is going to overtake the breakaway winners in this century. To understand why, we take two looks at how Texas is doing on a wide range of measures dealing with population and job growth, education, crime, energy and the environment, and more. The first look draws on nonpartisan historical data from the *Statistical Abstract of the United States* and the second draws from recent data prepared by the Texas Legislative Budget Board and Democrats in the Texas Legislature.

Table 2.1 A Troublesome Trajectory: Texas's Rank among the States, 1950–2010

	(1 = best, 51 = worst)						
	1950	1960	1970	1980	1990	2000	2010
Population Growth	14	14	16	10	7	6	5
Job Growth		11	13	8	24	7	8
Median Family Income	30	35	35	27	36	34	30
Inequality (Gini Index)			38	41	41	45	43
Poverty Rate			38	39	39	44	40
Unemployment Recipiency			49	51	49	45	48
Av. Teacher Salaries	18	27	39	32	30	27	29
Av. Spending Per Pupil	31	36	43	38	37	28	43
High School Completion	36	39	39	39	39	44	50
Teen Births as % Total	39	37	37	36	37	42	45
Overall Crime Rate	36	37	38	37	43	39	42
Incarceration Rate	14	35	45	45	35	47	46

Measuring Texas More Broadly, 1950 to Present

Table 2.1 presents a broader comparison of Texas to its peers over the entire post-World War II era. Modern Texas emerged with remarkable speed during the 1930s and 1940s. As the grip of the Great Depression relaxed in the face of preparations for World War II, Texans streamed out of the rural areas and into the new industrial jobs in the cities.[36] For several decades after the war, Texas enjoyed the rapid growth of late-industrialization. Capital, technology, and skilled management flowed into Texas, fueling growth, adding jobs, and creating wealth at rates well beyond those of the more developed parts of the country. While similar growth rates were enjoyed by other late-industrializing states in the South, Southwest, and West, Texas alone stood at the center of the global oil industry. Oil revenues allowed expansion of government services in education, welfare, and transportation to keep up with population and urban growth. Strikingly, however, these were decades in which the national economy was growing strongly too, and while the nation did not grow as rapidly as Texas it spent a greater proportion of its increased wealth on social services, so Texas's ranking among the states barely budged. In fact, on key measures of income, education, and health care, Texas's ranking among the states actually fell and that fall has picked up speed in recent years. The reason that Texas makes little to no progress in national rankings on educational and social services is that every time state budgets tighten the conservative mantra is cut until it is balanced.

Texas pride hinges on the twin facts that population growth and job growth have outstripped national averages and growth in most other states for many decades. The shorthand story is that Texas must be a highly desirable place because people keep coming, voting with their feet, to take up the jobs that they cannot find at home. Aspects of this story are clearly true. Texas has been at the heart of the post-World War II sunbelt expansion. Texas ranked about 15th among the states in population growth from the 1950s through the 1970s and then growth picked up. Texas was 10th in the 1980s and has been between 5th and 7th for the past couple of decades. Only a few states have matched Texas's population growth statistics. During the 1950s and 1960s, the densely populated Middle Atlantic states of Connecticut, New Jersey, Delaware, and Maryland, ran with Texas before falling back. California matched and exceeded Texas's growth rates from the 1950s through the 1980s and Florida kept up through the 1990s. In recent decades, only a few lightly populated states, Idaho, Utah, Nevada, and Arizona, have exceeded Texas population growth rates. In Chapter 3 we explore Texas population growth and, more importantly, demographic change in detail.

With the exception of the 1980s, job growth in Texas has exceeded the national average and those of three-fourths of the states. From the 1950s through the 1970s, a fairly steady group of southern, southwestern, and mountain states, including the Carolinas, Florida, Georgia, Colorado, New Mexico, Utah, and Nevada enjoyed job growth similar to that of Texas. Alaska and Hawaii did so as well once they achieved statehood. The Texas job growth engine sputtered in the 1980s, but roared through the 1990s and 2000s with just a handful of small southwestern and mountain states keeping pace. After 2000, only eight states, Alaska, Montana, New Mexico, Nevada, North Dakota, Utah, and Wyoming exceeded Texas job growth in percentage terms. But Texas alone exceeds these eight states combined in raw numbers for both population and job growth. So Texas does have something to brag about. Nonetheless, there are some stubborn facts.

Texas is not now and has never been a "wealthy" state. During the first several decades of the twentieth century, Texas and the South generally averaged about two-thirds of U.S. median family income. Because oil and agriculture cushioned the depression's impact on Texas, median family income rose to three-quarters of the national average by 1940 and then skyrocketed to 87 percent by 1944. Texas came out of World War II with enough momentum in income growth that it was reasonable to think it would overtake and perhaps surpass national averages in a short time. It was not to be. In 1950, Texas ranked 30th among the 48 states and D.C., at 90 percent of median family income. Texas dropped back into the mid-30s during the 1960s and 1970s, before making an oil-fueled run at the national average, reaching 27th among the 50 states and D.C. in 1980. In fact, as oil prices peaked in the early 1980s, Texas median family income reached the national average, at 101 percent in 1981 and 100 percent in 1982. As the price of oil collapsed, as we shall see more fully in Chapter 4, Texas median family income fell back to the mid-30s. Texas ranked 34th in 2000 and 30th in 2010, just as it had in 1950.

While Texas's rank among the states on median family income has been stagnant for decades, inequality among earners in Texas has increased. The Gini Index is a statistic that measures the degree of income inequality between upper and lower income earners. The index ranges from zero to one, zero being complete equality and one being complete inequality. The higher the Gini Index, the greater the inequality. Over the past four decades, Texas's ranking among the states has ranged from .35 to .50. In 1970, a dozen states had higher Gini Index readings than Texas. In the 1980s and 1990s only an average of ten states had higher Gini Index readings and for the past decade only an average of six states have had higher ratings. In 2002, no state had a higher Gini Index rating than Texas, though D.C., which always ranks 51 (lots of well-paid government workers and poor people) did. In 2010, Texas ranked 43rd on the Gini Index. Compared to other states, Texas has the threatening combination of stagnant family income and high inequality.

Moreover, as inequality in Texas has risen, so has poverty. Poverty has been a national focus since the Great Society era of the 1960s. State comparisons of the proportion of citizens in poverty have been available since 1970. From 1970 to 2000, Texas held steady at 38 or 39, meaning only a dozen states, mostly in the South and Southwest, had a greater share of their citizens in poverty. Texas dropped precipitously into the 40s after 2000 and has remained there in the most recent readings. In 2007, only Mississippi (22.6 percent) and D.C. (18 percent), exceeded Texas's poverty rate of 16.5 percent. In 2008, the Texas poverty rate fell to 16 percent but in 2009, as the financial crisis took hold nationally and in Texas, the Texas poverty rate increased to 17.2 percent. In both years, Texas ranked 43rd among the fifty states and D.C. In 2010, as Texas began to emerge from the recession, it ranked 40th, near its historic norm. Moreover, when Texans lose their jobs they are less likely than workers in virtually any other state to be eligible for unemployment insurance benefits. Texas usually ranks between 45th and 51st in the proportion of unemployed drawing on unemployment insurance benefits. Modest incomes, high poverty, and a thin social safety net make Texas a "business-friendly" state. Notice that no one claims Texas is "worker-friendly," though Anglo leaders do claim that Texas creates lots of jobs and that is good for workers. In the end, though, it is clear that personal responsibility rests lightly on the comfortable and heavily on the vulnerable.

Spending on public schools has consistently limped along below the national average. Two measures are key: average teacher salaries and average spending per pupil. Texas has done somewhat better by teachers (they vote) than by students. Sadly though, compared to the national average and average teacher salaries in other states, Texas teacher salaries peaked in the early 1950s. Texas teachers ranked 18th among the 48 states and D.C. in 1950, before falling back into the high 20s and 30s thereafter. Texas teachers ranked 29th in 2010. Texas spending per student ranked 31st in the nation in 1950 and generally languished in the mid-30s to low 40s thereafter. Texas made a concerted run at the national average in the 1990s, reaching 28th in 2000, before falling back. Texas spending per pupil has ranked 42nd from 2006 to 2008 and 43rd in 2010.

Two sad statistics which track each other closely are high school completion rates and teen births as a percentage of total births. Teen pregnancy is only one of many reasons that students drop out of high school, but most drop outs face a bleak future. Texas ranked 36th among the states and D.C. in high school completion in 1950 and 39th from the 1960s through the 1990s, before dropping to 44th in 2000 and 50th in 2010. Similarly, Texas ranked between 36th and 39th from the 1950 through the 1990s in teen births as a percentage of total births before falling to 42nd in 2000 and 45th in 2010.

Finally, for more than half a century Texas ranked between 36th and 43rd among the states in the overall crime rate. Nonetheless, Texas's response to crime changed dramatically. In 1950, Texas's incarceration rate, the number of persons per 100,000 of population in prison, was modest, ranking just 14th in the nation. But as crime and civil unrest increased in the late 1950s and 1960s, Texas rapidly built one of the most extensive prison systems in the nation. The incarceration rate in Texas has risen dramatically. Texas ranked 35th in 1960, 45th in 1970 and 1980, before federal court decisions forced a slowdown in late 1980s, registered by a rank of 35th in 1990. Once shed of federal court supervision, Texas built more prisons and increased its incarceration rate to 47th in 2000. Texas was still at 46th in 2010.

Ominously, while Texas has led the nation in population and job growth, it has lagged in family incomes and fallen in every other dimension reported in Table 2.1. Can Texas thrive if it is beaten by almost every other state on education, health care, and other public and social services? We will try to answer these questions in detail in subsequent chapters, but before we do, we must highlight the ongoing partisan squabble over Texas public policy and its results.

Partisan Perspectives: The *Texas Fact Book* vs. *Texas on the Brink*

Whether Texas is doing well or poorly has been debated for many decades and is, to some extent, a matter of perspective. Anglo elites tend to believe that Texas is doing wonderfully well and is a model for the rest of the nation, while others tend to see serious problems being left untended. These alternative perspectives on Texas public policy and their results have been clear for many decades, they remain so today, and change is not yet in view. In fact, an exchange in the classic 1952 novel, *Giant*, between the Anglo Texas ranching heiress, Vashti Snythe, and the Virginia-born Lacey Lynnton, Lady Karfrey after her marriage to a minor British nobleman, opposes the upper class Anglo view that Texas leads the nation to the view that Texas has left many economic and social problems to fester. After Vashti posts one more claim to Texas primacy, Lady Karfrey responded, "As you say, of all the states Texas is first in cotton—but last in pellagra [a crippling vitamin deficiency]. First in beef—and forty-fifth in infant mortality. First in wool—and thirty-eighth in its school system. First in mules—and forty-seventh in library service. . . . First in oil—and your hospitals are practically non-exis—."³⁷ Today, as we shall see below, Republicans tend to agree with Vashti and Democrats with Lady Karfrey.

To its credit, establishment Texas is convinced that its low-tax, low-service, business-friendly, model of state government is correct. So convinced are they that state government publishes a number of annual and biannual reports that, at first glance, seem damning, the kind of information that would more likely be suppressed than touted. One of the most remarkable publications of Texas state government is the *Texas Fact Book* (TFB), published biannually on the budget cycle by the Legislative Budget Bureau (LBB). The *TFB* for 2012, along with its predecessors back to 1996, shows where the revenues for state government come from, where they go, and how Texas ranks against the other 49 states and the 50-state average across a wide range of issue areas including taxes, income, education, health, welfare, transportation and the environment. Upon perusing the *TFB*, one wonders why it is published at all since Texas compares embarrassingly on most of the substantive policy dimensions. As we saw in Table 2.1, Texas is occasionally last and often near last. But then one recognizes that Texas is last, dead last, on several measures of state taxing and spending. The *TFB*, while shocking to many, is a fine advertisement for Texas as a low-tax, low-service, business-friendly, state.

On the other hand, since 2003, Democrats in the Texas Legislature have published similar data in a document entitled *Texas on the Brink* (TOB). *TOB* was the brainchild of now former Texas state Senator Eliot Shapleigh (D-El Paso). Each edition of *TOB* has opened with a variation on this claim, "In Texas today, the American dream is distant. Texas has the highest percentage of uninsured children in the nation. Texas is dead last in the percentage of residents with their high school diploma and near last in SAT scores. Texas has America's dirtiest air. If we do not change course, for the first time in our history, the Texas generation of tomorrow will be less prosperous than the generation of today."[38] While Republicans bet that Texas conservatives will appreciate and support the state's lowest of low tax ratings, Democrats bet that middle class, working class, and poorer Texans, especially minorities, will be offended by the evidence of thin, sometimes non-existent, public and social services. Republicans have won this bet over and over again and there is little to suggest that this will change quickly.

First, let's look at Texas as a low-tax state. The 2012 *Texas Fact Book* (reporting 2009 data), reported that Texas ranked 46th among the 50 states in per capita state government tax revenue and 47th on state tax revenue as a percentage of personal income. Texas ranked 50 among the 50 states, dead last, in per capita state government expenditures. Governor Perry frequently says that the simple secret to Texas's formula for fiscal responsibility is "we don't spend all the money." More accurately, Texas takes in less revenue (ranked 46th) than all but four other states and spends less than any other state (ranked 50th).[39] The Democrat's *TOB* leads with the data on Texas's low ranking on taxing and spending. *TOB* (reporting 2010 data) ranks Texas 45th in tax revenue per capita and 48th in tax expenditures per capita.[40]

Few doubt that the most important expenditures that state and local governments make are those for public education. The quality of public education is an important input to the good business climate on which Texas prides itself. The *TFB* reports that Texas has worked hard to keep elementary and secondary school class sizes low (26th at 14.6 to 1) and to pay elementary and secondary school teachers decently (38th at $48,261). Even here the numbers are not stellar, but they are better than the numbers describing per pupil expenditures. In 2011, Texas ranked 43rd in state aid per pupil and 39th in state and local expenditures per pupil. And the educational results are bleak. Texas ranked 44th in public high school graduation rates and 50th in the percent of the population graduated from high school.[41] *TOB* mentions all of these and adds one more: SAT scores, where Texas ranks 47th among the 50 states and D.C.[42]

Texas lags just as badly in health and social services. Both the *TFB* and *TOB* report that Texas ranks 51st in the nation on the percentage of its population without health insurance. It ranks 43rd on the percentage of adults who are obese and 47th on the percent with high cholesterol. Texas ranks 28th on the number of hospital beds and 42nd on number of physicians per 100,000 of population. Texas ranks 43rd in the percentage of its population in poverty and 48th in the percentage of its population who are food insecure. To this litany of neglect the *TOB* adds that Texas is 43rd on percent of the population with employer-based health insurance, 46th on per capita spending on health care expenditures per capita, 48th on percent of the low income population covered by Medicaid, and 50th on per capita state spending on mental health.[43]

TOB focuses intently on what it describes as Women's Issues, while *TFB* presents similar data, though it is scattered throughout the document. *TOB* reports that Texas ranks 48th in overall birth rate and 47th in teenage birth rate, and 50th in the percent of pregnant women who receive prenatal care in the first trimester. Similarly, Texas ranks 47th highest in percent of women living in poverty and 51st in percent of non-elderly women with health insurance. Texas ranks 47th in the percentage of women who have had a dental visit in the past year. And finally, Texas ranks 47th in women's voter registration and 51st in women's voter turn-out. Not a pretty picture, lots of pregnancy but not much health insurance, prenatal care, or dental care. Not surprisingly, given Texas's traditional political culture, not much political participation or voting.

Understanding Texan

How to explain Texas braggadocio when the state has rarely, and never in the last thirty years, reached the national average on median family income and falls well below average on many measures of educational achievement and near the bottom on many measures of health and welfare? One recent attempt was made in an extensive piece in the April 26, 2010, issue of *Newsweek*. Evan Thomas and Arian Campo-Flores, in an article entitled "Don't Mess With Texas," began by quoting Rick Perry saying, "I'm willing to tell anyone that will listen that the land of opportunity still exists in America, and it's in Texas."

Thomas and Campo-Flores then touch upon several key elements of the Texas myth, sometimes without noting how far they have come to diverge from reality. They wrote that,

> not a few Texans wish the past could be their future—if only Rick Perry could show the way. As these people see it, America is turning into a multicultural hodgepodge, sapped of moral strength, run by government bureaucrats. But Texas they believe is different and always has been. 'We don't want to become like them,' says Shuck Donnell, General Manager of Coyote Lake Feedyard in Muleshoe, Texas. (By 'them' he means people living in the big metropolitan areas, especially on the East Coast.)

Forget for a moment that although Texas is one the most diverse and highly urbanized states in the nation, the *Newsweek* authors still managed to find 'Shuck' in Muleshoe—they make a very important point by tying the Anglo Texan's sense of independence to fear of social change, particularly if that change is being abetted by outside—read federal—forces.

Analysts viewing Texas from the outside have frequently pointed to insularity, anger, and suspicion. Thomas and Campo-Flores note that,

The forces of suspicion and anger may be exaggerated in the Lone Star state. They're also compounded by a strong streak of Texas exceptionalism. It dates back to the War of Independence against Mexico and the founding of the Republic of Texas in 1836, says historian David McComb, professor emeritus at Colorado State University. Texans have a "kind of macho, frontier, independent attitude of 'I can do what I damn well please and nobody else can tell me."

Now, to read this description is to immediately recognize that it refers to Anglo Texans, not all Texans. Descriptions of a swaggering individualism, though often attributed to "Texans," does not refer to the 38 percent that are Hispanic, the 12 percent of Texans that are black, or the 3 percent that are Asian. In fact, as Thomas and Campo-Flores note, "The independent strain has a racial dimension. . . . The less dominant whites become in Texas, the more some of them cling to a mythical past of the cowboy and oilman. 'A lot of these conservatives don't want to change. The ground is moving underneath them, and they don't want to recognize that and don't know what to do about it. So they join a tea party group and strap on a six-gun and strut around,' McComb says."⁴⁴

For more than a decade, Anglo Texans looked to Governor Rick Perry to hold the line against undesirable change. Rick Perry was the longest serving governor in Texas history. He held statewide office in Texas from 1991 to 2015, winning twice for agriculture commissioner, once for lieutenant governor, and three times for governor. What made Rick Perry such a formidable Texas politician was that he channeled the Texas myth with confidence and ease. Anglo Texans, because the myths are so flattering to them, respond favorably, but blacks and Hispanic tend to be much more skeptical.

On April 15, 2009, Perry addressed a raucous crowd of nearly one thousand tea party activists and sympathizers from the steps of Austin City Hall. Perry's speech drew national attention and won him some prime time attention on Fox News and other conservative outlets. Less noticed was that Perry was voicing deeply historic Texas themes which, while less resonant in recent decades, were common in the nineteenth century and from the late 1930s through the 1960s. Perry revved up the crowd by saying, "I'm just not sure you're a bunch of right-wing extremists. But if you are, I'm with you! Cause you are a true patriot today in this country. And I might add, you are surrounded by fellow patriots—individuals who embrace concepts like lower taxes and smaller government and freedom for every individual. I'm talking about states' rights! States' rights! States' rights!"

After the speech, in response to a reporters' question about whether he was threatening secession, Perry mused, "There's a lot of different scenarios. We've got a great union. There's absolutely no reason to destroy it. But if Washington continues to thumb their nose at the American people, you know, who knows what might come out of that?" Under additional questioning, Perry observed, "We are very proud of our Texas history; people discuss and debate the issues of 'Can we break ourselves into five states, can we secede'—a lot of interesting things that I'm sure Oklahoma and Pennsylvania would love to be able to say about their states, but the fact is, they can't, because they're not Texas."[45]

Perry rode the "anti-Washington" theme to a decisive primary election victory over Senator Kay Bailey Hutchison in March 2010. His last commercial in that campaign was aimed straight at Washington and, by implication, Senator Hutchison's long service there. It made no mention whatsoever of what Perry would do if he won another term as governor. Clad in baseball cap and signature light brown barn jacket, Perry looked straight into the camera and solemnly warned Texans that, "Washington is broken. As the federal government grows more intrusive with mandates and unprecedented debt, we believe that Texans, not federal bureaucrats, know what's best for our state. That's why I rejected federal dollars with strings attached, and will fight misguided health and energy policies that will raise taxes on our families. As governor, I'll always champion our Tenth Amendment, which is supposed to keep Washington from messing with Texas."

At the June 2010 Texas Republican Party Convention, with Hutchison safely dispatched, Perry continued to aim his ire at Washington and to claim that his general election opponent, Democrat Bill White, former three-term mayor of Houston, was an even greater danger. Perry warned the convention that, "As Washington steadily encroaches on our freedoms, we must not be silenced by their criticisms. The nation is watching Texas to see if our model of state-based solutions will triumph over the Democrats' big-government movement that controls our nation's capital, for now." Perry reminded delegates that, "We're engaged in a struggle for the very heart of our state." While Hutchison had become too comfortable with the ways of Washington, Perry warned that: "Electing my opponent will accelerate the Washington takeover of our state."

Barack Obama's re-election as president in 2012 sparked another round of secession talk in Texas. Just days after Obama's victory, Micah H. of Arlington put a petition on the White House website requesting peaceful separation of Texas from the U.S. Within a matter of days, 116,000 people signed the petition. Peter Morrison, the treasurer of the Hardin County Republican Party in East Texas explained that people were coming "to appreciate that the fundamental cultural differences between Texas and other parts of the United States may be best addressed by an amicable divorce, a peaceful separation."[46]

Conclusion

Anglo Texans are comfortable with, in fact they revel in, the mythology of their state. The myth is flattering to them and has advantaged them in obvious and important ways, both historically and in the present. But like all myths, the Texas myth points to a partial truth while ignoring and even masking much else. As we have seen above and will explore in greater detail in later chapters of this book, Texas is not a wealthy state, though it does have a substantial body of wealthy and privileged people within it. Unfortunately, for many Texans, modest wages, absence of fringe benefits like employer managed health care, underfunded schools, hospitals, and social services, and environmental degradation are the norm. Texas's most prominent contemporary historian, UT's H.W. Brands, has drawn the obvious conclusion, saying "We have prided ourselves on our uniqueness and idiosyncrasies, but you only become a beacon state if people from the outside see something to emulate. And outside of Texas, not many people look at Texas and say, 'we want to be like that.'"[47] Really! Was it the 47th in dental care?

In the mid-twentieth century, the prominent Texas-born political scientist V.O. Key thought that the dramatic economic changes of the 1930s and 1940s would drive political change in the direction of a competitive two-party politics that would allow the poor to better defend their interests against the organized rich. Instead, the fight over civil rights and desegregation drove whites together even as their majority moved from the Democratic to the Republican Party. In the early twenty-first century a business-oriented conservative establishment governs Texas as surely as it did when Key wrote. In fact, in many public policy areas, including the critical areas of education, health, and social services, Texas ranks lower among the 50 states than it did in 1950. Today, analysts frequently argue that demographic change, especially the burgeoning Hispanic population, will drive political change in Texas and nationally over the next half century. It may, but, with Key in mind, we should not expect it to happen quickly. Change is not impossible, even in Texas, though one is always wise to expect it to come grudgingly and only after a fight.

Nonetheless, as we shall see in detail in Chapter 3, demographic change in Texas has been dramatic over the past three decades and will continue through the twenty-first century. Texas was 38 percent Hispanic in 2010 and will be majority Hispanic in the late 2030s. Hispanics have tended, with occasional exceptions, to vote two-to-one Democrat, but have voted at only about two-thirds the rate of Texas blacks and Anglos. As a result, while Hispanic numbers are up, Hispanic political clout is not. In Chapter 3, we look in detail at demographic change in Texas.

Notes

1   John Steinbeck, *Travels with Charley in Search of America*, New York: Viking, 1962, pp. 201–202.

2   Walter L. Buenger and Robert A. Calvert, ed., *Texas Through Time: Evolving Interpretations*, College Station, TX: Texas A&M University Press, 1991, p. xv.

3   Erica Grieder, *Big, Hot, Cheap, and Right*, New York: Public Affairs, 2013, pp. 136–137.

4   Laura Lyons McLemore, *Inventing Texas: Early Historians of the Lone Star State*, College Station, TX: Texas A&M University Press, 2004, p. 73. See also Gregg Cantrell, "The

Bones of Stephen F. Austin: History and Memory of Progressive Era Texas," *Southwestern Historical Quarterly*, vol. 108, no. 2, October 2004, pp. 145–178; and Michael Phillips, "Why Is Big Tex Still a White Cowboy: Race, Gender, and the 'Other Texans,'" in Walter A. Buenger and Arnoldo de León, *Beyond Texas Through Time: Breaking Away From Past Interpretations*, College Station, TX: Texas A&M University Press, 2011, p. 183.

5 Don Graham, *State of Minds: Texas Culture and Its Discontents*, Austin, TX: University of Texas Press, 2011, pp. 19, 32.

6 Brian D. Sweany, "Time Will Tell," *Texas Monthly*, March, 2011, pp. 10–14.

7 Glen Sample Ely, *Debating Texas Identity: Where the West Begins*, Lubbock, TX: Texas Tech University Press, 2011, p. 129.

8 Walter L. Buenger, "Texas and the South," *Southwestern Historical Review*, vol. 103, no. 3, January 2000, pp. 308–324, 310.

9 Ely, *Debating Texas Identity*, p. 8.

10 Wilbur Zelinsky, *The Cultural Geography of the United States*, Englewood Cliffs, NJ: Prentice-Hall, 1973, p. 124.

11 John Gunther, *Inside U.S.A.*, New York: Harper and Brothers, 1947, p. 844.

12 Numan V. Bartley, *The New South, 1945–1980*, Baton Rouge, LA: Louisiana State University Press, 1995, pp. 101–102.

13 James McEnteer, *Deep in the Heart: The Texas Tendency in American Politics*, Westport, CT: Praeger, 2004, p. 112.

14 James Reston Jr., *Lone Star: The Life of John Connally*, New York: Harper and Row, 1989, p. 273; Robert Dallek, *An Unfinished Life: John F. Kennedy, 1917–1963*, Boston: Little, Brown and Company, 2003, p. 693.

15 Reston, *Lone Star*, p. 213.

16 George Norris Green, *The Establishment in Texas Politics: The Primitive Years, 1938–1957*, Norman, OK: University of Oklahoma Press, 1979, p. 3.

17 T. R. Fehrenbach, *Seven Keys to Texas*, El Paso, TX: Texas Western Press, 1983, p. 117.

18 Frank R. Kemerer, *William Wayne Justice: A Judicial Biography*, Austin, TX: University of Texas Press, 1991 and 2008, pp. 230–231.

19 Reston, *Lone Star*, p. 296.

20 Sean P. Cunningham, *Cowboy Conservatism: Texas and the Rise of the Modern Right*, Lexington, KY: University of Kentucky Press, 2010, p. 104.

21 Ibid., pp. 264, 289. See also McEnteer, *Deep in the Heart*, p. 136; and Patrick L. Cox and Michael Phillips, *The House Will Come to Order*, Austin, TX: University of Texas Press, 2010, p. 90.

22 Ibid., p. 121.

23 Fehrenbach, *Seven Keys to Texas*, pp. 112–113.

24 Chandler Davidson, *Race and Class in Texas Politics*, Princeton, NJ: Princeton University Press, 1990, p. 17.

25 Gerry Riposa, ed., *Texas Public Policy*, Dubuque, IA: Kendall Hunt, 1987, pp. 17–18.

26 Anthony Champagne and Edward J. Harpham, *Texas at the Crossroads: People, Politics, and Policy*, College Station, TX: Texas A&M University Press, 1987, p. 3.

27 Ibid., p. 270.

28 Ibid., p. 9.

29 Cox and Phillips, *The House Will Come to Order*, p. 182.

30 Evan Smith, "Rain, Rain, Go Away," *Texas Monthly*, June 2009, pp. 142–147, 189–190.

31 McLemore, *Inventing Texas*, p. 95.

32 http://www.clevelandfed.org/about_us/annual_report/2005/pdf/essay2005.pdf

33 Ibid., p. 7.

34 Ibid., p. 9. See also, G. Andrew Bernat Jr., "Convergence in State Per Capita Personal Income, 1950–1999, *Survey of Current Business*, June 2001, pp. 36–48.

35 Ibid., p. 17. See also, Brian Chappatta, "States Lacking Income Tax Get No Boost in Growth," BGOV Barometer, Bloomberg News, June 24, 2012.

36 David G. McComb, *Texas: A Modern History*, revised edition, Austin, TX: University of Texas Press, 2009, p. 145.

37 Edna Ferber, *Giant*, Garden City, NY: Doubleday & Company, 1952, p. 359.

38 *Texas on the Brink* (TOB), A Report from the Texas Legislative Study Group on the State of Our State, March 2013, p. 4, http://texaslsg.org/texasonthebrink

39 *Texas Fact Book* (TFB), Texas Legislative Budget Board, 2012, p. 24, http://www.lbb. state.tx.us/Fact_Book/Texas_FactBook_2012.pdf

40 TOB, 2013, p. 5.

41 TFB, 2012, pp. 18–19.

42 TOB, 2013, p. 5.

43 TFB, pp. 21–22; TOB, 2013, p. 6.

44 Evan Thomas and Arian Campo-Flores, "Don't Mess With Texas," *Newsweek*, April 26, 2010, pp. 28–32. See also Ezrati, "Just What Is It About Texas," *Antioch Review*, p. 761.

45 Paul Burka, "The Secret of My Secession," *Texas Monthly*, June 2009, p. 8.

46 Manny Fernandez, "With Stickers, a Petition and Even a Middle Name, Secession Fever Hits Texas," *New York Times*, November 24, 2012, A11.

47 William McKenzie, "175 Years of Texas," a Q&A with H.W. Brands, *Dallas Morning News*, February 27, 2011, 5P. See also Public Policy Polling, "State Favorability Poll," February 21, 2012, at http://publicpolicypolling.com/main/2012/02/state-favorability-poll.html. Texas ranked 37th among the 50 states.

3 Demographic Change and Its Implications

One of the basic rules of politics is that demographic change produces political change.

(Paul Burka, 2011)[1]

More than a century ago, Associate Justice John Marshall Harlan stood alone on behalf of racial equality in the infamous case of *Plessy v. Ferguson* (1896). Justice Harlan reminded his colleagues that "in view of the Constitution, in the eye of the law, there is in this county no superior, dominant, ruling class of citizens. There is no cast here. Our Constitution is color-blind, and neither knows nor tolerates classes among citizens." Tragically, Justice Harlan was on the wrong end of an 8 to 1 majority that found in favor of Louisiana's right, and that of other states (i.e., states' rights), to separate blacks and whites in public places. Justice Harlan's claim that the Constitution was meant to be color-blind was rejected by his colleagues.

In *Parents Involved in Community Schools v. Seattle School District #1* (2007), United States Supreme Court Chief Justice John Roberts wrote that "The way to stop discrimination on the basis of race is to stop discriminating on the basis of race." American law, the Chief Justice declared, should be color-blind. This view strikes a positive cord with most Americans; every school-child knows that the most famous phrase in the Declaration of Independence is that "all men are created equal." Yet, as Paul Burka suggests in the quotation above, race and ethnicity have been touchstones of American life throughout our history. White majority status has always commanded privilege, even if only in the absence of road blocks, while minority status has often meant limited opportunity. Is Chief Justice Roberts right today to argue that America could become a color-blind society if government simply stopped recognizing race, or, is he as wrong today, just in a different way, as Justice Harlan was more than a century ago?

Race and ethnicity have been profoundly important in American and Texas history. Distinctions of race and ethnicity were written into every U.S. immigration statute from the 1790s through the 1950s and remain central to our discussions of immigration today. Similarly, Texas used its constitutions and laws to define who was welcomed, who was excluded, and with what degree of force. As the Anglo majority that has governed Texas since its independence fades into history, what kinds of political change will follow? In this chapter, we describe the demographic changes that have brought Texas to its current majority minority status and to the verge of a Hispanic majority.

Bragging Rights: Population Growth in Texas

Texas has grown more rapidly than the U.S. since the 1830s, a fact in which Texans take pride each time new census figures are announced. The 2010 census figures showed that Texas had grown by 21 percent since 2000, adding almost 4.5 million people, while the U.S. had grown by just 10 percent. Many Texans assume that their burgeoning population numbers reflect the state's dynamic economy when compared with an over taxed and regulated national economy. To some extent they do, but they reflect both the plusses and minuses of being a business-friendly, low wage, state. A few of the plusses are rapid population and job growth, but a few of the minuses are modest wages and benefits. It has always been a trade-off. Still, Texas has been putting up big numbers for a long time.

During the first half of the nineteenth century, the U.S. grew at a very robust 35 percent per decade. During the second half of the century, U.S. growth moderated a bit, to the still very solid 25 percent per decade. By 1900, the frontier was closed, the processes of urbanization and industrialization were well underway, and by the mid-twentieth century the U.S. was an advanced industrial society. Though immigration was limited from the mid-1920s through the mid-1960s, population still grew at the rate of about 15 percent per decade.

Not surprisingly, late arrivals on the periphery—Texas, California, and Florida—grew more rapidly than the nation, especially in their early decades. Once independence was secured in 1836, Texas experienced a 187 percent population increase in the 1840s, rising from 78,000 to 223,592, and in the 1850s growing by 170 percent from 223,592 to 604,215. The 1849 discovery of gold at Sutter's Mill near Sacramento drove a 310 percent population increase in California during the 1850s. Figure 3.1 shows that growth rates for Texas, California, and Florida remained well above the national average after 1860. California grew by almost 50 percent per decade for the next one hundred years. Florida grew by 39 percent per decade during the same period, while Texas grew at 33 percent per decade. In the past half century, since 1960, Florida has grown at 33 percent, Texas at 21.4 percent, and California at 19.2 percent. From 2000 to 2010, Florida grew at 25 percent, Texas grew at 21 percent, and California trailed off to just 10 percent, no better than the national average. Texans struggle not to celebrate the decline of California, but they also worry about what the future holds for them. There are reasons for concern.

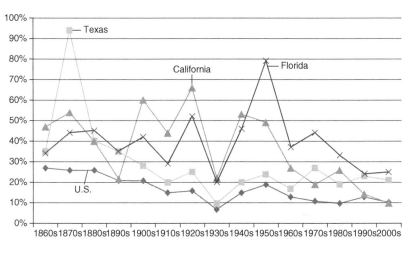

Figure 3.1 Population Increase by Decade in the U.S., Texas, California, and Florida.

Source: U.S. Census data, see www.census.gov/population/www/censusdata/ hiscendata.html.

Paul Burka's statement that "demographic change produces political change" was first and most colorfully stated by the nineteenth-century French philosopher Auguste Comte. Comte's declaration that "demography is destiny" has been much on Texas minds lately. Demography is the statistical study of the size, structure, growth, and distribution of human populations. Other social sciences, including economics, sociology, and political science, draw on the findings of demography to study variations in income, wealth, education, health, and the like by race and ethnicity. Many Texans are aware that broad demographic changes have been underway in the state for decades. Some wonder whether the ongoing demographic changes forecast for Texas—a shrinking Anglo population and an expanding Hispanic population—foretell a certain "destiny" for Texas (Table 3.1).

Texas's rapid population growth has masked some internal dynamics of the growth that will repay detailed attention. In 1800, there were probably fewer than 30,000 inhabitants in Texas and more than 85 percent of them were Indians. The rest were Spanish and Mexicans with just a few black slaves. In 1850, when Texas was first included in the U.S. Census, there were fewer than a quarter million people in the state, but most now were whites and their black slaves. Population took off from there, breaking one million in the early 1870s and three million by 1900. In 1900, Texas was an overwhelmingly Anglo republic. Whites were almost 80 percent of all inhabitants, the black population was falling, and Hispanics, though probably undercounted, were reported to be less than 5 percent of the population. Total population grew steadily through the twentieth century, breaking five million in the 1920s, ten million in the 1960s, twenty-five million by 2010, with projections of forty-one million by 2050. Prior to the 1980s, there was little suspicion that Texas's Anglo republic was threatened. Though Anglo Texans know that the demographic make-up of the state is changing, most probably do not realize that the Anglo population of Texas has grown slower than the national population since 1980

Table 3.1 Texas Population Growth by Decade, Race, and Ethnicity

Decade	Anglo	Black	Hispanic	Indian	Asian/Other	Total
1780		20	2,250	30,000		32,270
1790		40	3,169	27,500		30,709
1800		60	3,500	25,000		28,560
1810	250	80	4,000	22,500		26,830
1820	1,000	100	2,500	20,000		23,600
1830	20,000	2,000	4,000	17,000		43,000
1840	50,000	10,000	5,000	13,000		78,000
1850	145,537	58,555	8,500	11,000		223,595
1860	398,291	182,921	15,000	8,000		604,212
1870	534,004	253,475	25,000	6,100		818,579
1880	1,152,365	393,384	43,000	3,000		1,591,749
1890	1,685,356	488,171	60,000	2,000		2,235,527
1900	2,355,926	620,722	71,062	1,000		3,048,710
1910	3,080,722	690,049	125,069	702		3,896,542
1920	3,469,425	741,694	450,000	2,109		4,663,228
1930	4,285,069	854,964	683,681	1,001		5,824,715
1940	4,751,112	924,391	736,433	1,103	1,785	6,414,824
1950	5,727,045	977,458	1,000,000	2,736	3,955	7,711,194
1960	6,974,831	1,187,125	1,400,000	5,750	11,971	9,579,677
1970	7,950,575	1,399,092	1,840,648	17,231	62,640	11,196,730
1980	9,390,437	1,692,542	2,985,824	40,075	120,313	14,229,191
1990	10,284,909	1,976,360	4,339,905	65,877	319,459	16,986,510
2000	11,074,716	2,451,653	6,669,666	125,111	685,785	20,851,820
2010	11,397,345	2,886,825	9,460,921	220,000	1,180,470	25,145,561
2020	11,752,527	3,295,218	12,047,446	250,000	1,576,459	28,921,650
2030	11,850,199	3,658,975	15,106,347	295,000	2,016,724	32,927,245
2040	11,676,168	3,951,928	18,511,750	340,000	2,542,667	37,022,513
2050	11,376,567	4,182,147	22,270,859	410,000	3,071,648	41,311,221

Source: Tracing the racial and ethnic development of Texas is no easy task. Prior to 1850, we must depend on scattered Spanish, Mexican, and Texan enumerations and the educated guesswork of anthropologists and historians. Still, the numbers are small and there is a rough consensus. The U.S. Census of 1850 was the first to include Texas. Whites and blacks were carefully enumerated, but Hispanics were not separated from whites and one can reasonably assume that Hispanics were undercounted. Hispanic numbers have been estimated by historians and are subtracted from the census count of whites above. The data and projections for 2000 to 2050 are from the Texas State Data Center and Office of the State Demographer, 2012 Texas Population Projections.

(7.3 percent per decade compared to 11 percent). Moreover, the Texas State Demographer projects that the growth of the Anglo population over the next four decades will be—precisely—zero. While black population growth has outstripped Anglo growth since 1980, it is Hispanic growth that has been truly eye-popping. Over the past three decades, Hispanic population growth in Texas has averaged 45 percent per decade and is projected to grow at 25 percent per decade over the next four decades.

Between 1900 and 2000, the Hispanic share of the Texas population increased from less than 5 percent to 32 percent and by 2050 is expected to be 54 percent. Bluntly, the question now is—since Hispanic income and educational attainment are lower than Anglos—does this mean that an increasingly Hispanic Texas must be poorer, less educated, and less productive? The answer, some assure, is no; especially if Hispanics, or Texas, or some combination of the two, act to improve Hispanic educational attainment. Then Hispanic productivity and income will grow and Texas will continue to prosper. Others worry that demographic change is outrunning improvement in educational attainment. As Texas State Demographer Lloyd Potter said in early 2011, "A [Hispanic] population that isn't making enough money to fuel our economy, or ends up being a burden on the state—that is not indicative of having a higher quality of life in the future."[2]

Texas has two choices: it can either try to change these numbers or it can try to change the social and economic attributes of the coming Hispanic majority. Over the first century and more of the state's history, Texans and their political leaders took the first path: they tried to shape the racial and ethnic make-up of the state. During the coming decades, Texans and their political leaders will either commit to the second path, changing Hispanic social and economic attributes, or pay an unsustainably heavy price.

Shaping the Anglo Republic

Few states have seen the sweeping demographic changes experienced by Texas. As the American Revolution raged on the Atlantic Coast, there were no Anglo-Americans and very few blacks in what was then northern Mexico, now Texas. There were fewer than 2,500 Spanish, Mexican, and Mestizo settlers north of the Rio Grande and perhaps 30,000 to 50,000 Indians. While the Indian population sank to between 20,000 and 30,000 by 1820, the Mexican population rose to about 3,500 by 1800, before falling back toward 2,500 during the Mexican war for independence from 1810 to 1821. The first Anglo settlers did not arrive in Texas until about 1815 and then only in small numbers.

Prior to the first Anglo settlers, a few white men, almost always looking for trouble, wandered into Texas. One of the first was a persistent pest named Philip Nolan. Nolan entered Texas several times during the 1790s from what was then Spanish Louisiana. Though he bore a trade license from the Spanish authorities in New Orleans when he entered Texas in 1791, his goods were seized by Spanish authorities in San Antonio and he was jailed. He returned to New Orleans two years later with nothing to show for his efforts but a couple dozen mustangs. Nolan made two more trips into Texas, but his last trip was fatal. After spending the winter of 1800–1801 catching and trading for mustangs in Central Texas, Nolan awoke on the morning of March 22, 1801, to find his camp surrounded by Mexican cavalry. When Nolan approached the soldiers to plead his case, they opened fire and he was killed almost immediately.[3]

Anthony Glass was another early trader into Texas. Glass was a Mississippi plantation owner and Louisiana Indian trader who entered Texas in 1808 to trade with the Caddo, Wichita, and Comanche on the Red River and the Middle Colorado. Glass and ten colleagues, bearing passports and licenses from U.S. agent for Indian Affairs John Sibley of Natchitoches, Louisiana, crossed into Texas in July 1808 with sixteen horses packed with goods and three saddle horses per man. Glass's party successfully traded for mustangs over the fall and winter and returned to Louisiana in May 1809. The daily journal that Glass kept is one of the first Anglo reports of early nineteenth-century Texas. But traders were not the only Anglos in Texas during these years.

In the first two decades of the nineteenth century, especially once the Spanish and Mexicans were distracted by the Mexican war for independence (1810–1821), Anglo adventurers, called filibusterers, sought to seize some or all of Texas for themselves. The most famous Texas filibusterer was Natchez doctor and businessman James Long. In 1819, Long led about 300 armed men into East Texas, easily capturing Nacogdoches. Long then proceeded to Galveston Island hoping to strike an alliance with the pirate Jean Lafitte. In Long's absence, Spanish forces from San Antonio forced his men out of Nacogdoches and he escaped back to New Orleans. Long returned to Texas in 1820 with just fifty men and set up a camp called Fort Las Casas, at Point Bolivar on Galveston Bay. Long and several of the filibusterers were joined by their families. The leisurely pace of their planning meant that they did not select their target, La Bahia, and attack until September 1821. Again, Long's forces initially prevailed only to fall to a Spanish counterattack a few days later. Long was captured, sent to Mexico, jailed, and eventually killed. His wife, Jane, and daughter remained at Point Bolivar, eventually alone except for a slave girl, awaiting word on James Long's fate. Abandoned, her husband dead in Mexico, Jane Long delivered a baby she named Mary James Long on December 21, 1821, reported, incorrectly as it turned out, to be the first Anglo baby born in Texas. Though the baby died before she was two, Jane Long left Texas only briefly, returning as one of Stephen F. Austin's early settlers.[4]

Once Mexico secured its independence from Spain, Mexican authorities moved to rebuild their depopulated and dangerous northern frontier. They worried about both American expansion into the Mississippi Valley and Comanche raids out of Texas into northern Mexico. As early as 1818, Moses and Stephen Austin claimed land in Southwest Arkansas at Long Prairie on the Red River. On the other side of the Red River lay Mexican Texas. By late 1820, Moses Austin was in San Antonio seeking an empresario contract to bring settlers into Texas. By late June 1821, Moses was dead and Stephen was in Natchitoches, Louisiana, preparing to cross the Sabine into Texas to complete his father's plan. The Austin grant anticipated 300 families, willing to declare Catholicism and Mexican citizenship and to settle in South Central Texas between the Colorado and Brazos rivers. There were perhaps 1,000 Anglos in Texas when Stephen Austin arrived, 100 slaves, just about 2,500 Mexicans, and at least 20,000 Indians. Mexican trepidation about Anglo immigration is easy to understand. Just as Stephen F. Austin was in San Antonio negotiating the details of his first empresario contract, James Long was attacking La Bahia, 90 miles to the southeast.

By 1836, when Texas secured its independence from Mexico, the Anglo population had grown to nearly 30,000, almost eight times the 4,000 residents of Mexican extraction, 5,000 slaves, and perhaps 15,000 Indians.[5] University of Texas geographer and demographer Terry G. Jordan, working in the tradition of Wilbur Zelinsky's "first settlement" thesis, reported in an article entitled "A Century and a Half of Ethnic Change in Texas, 1836–1986," that "In Texas, the host/dominant group . . . consisted of old-stock Anglo-Americans of colonial eastern-seaboard ancestry. More precisely, *southern* Anglos . . . "[6] Billy D. Ledbetter's famous article, "White Over Black in Texas," used settlement patterns to explain the prevalence of southern racial attitudes in Texas, saying "Only four Northern states had contributed over 1,000 settlers to . . . [Texas], whereas all the Southern states that ultimately seceded from the Union, with the exception of Florida, were represented by over 9,000 settlers."[7]

Moreover, southerners in Texas thoroughly dominated the state's economy, society, and politics. Nearly three-quarters of Anglo heads of households in 1860 had southern roots as did fully 90 percent of slave-owners. Randolph B. Campbell's *An Empire for Slavery: The Peculiar Institution in Texas, 1821–1865*, concluded that "Antebellum Texas, . . . had all the characteristics of an advanced slaveholding society." Though only 27 percent of Anglo heads of household owned slaves as the Civil War approached in 1860, and just 3 percent held twenty or more slaves, they were the state's leadership elite. Campbell reports that slaveholders in 1860 owned 71 percent of the state's improved acreage, 73 percent of the state's wealth, and fully 91 percent of its cotton crop. Their economic dominance gave them social primacy and political control. In 1860, slave-owners held 68 percent of local, state, and federal offices.[8]

As we shall see below, though it will seem harsh in the viewing, "Anglo Texas racism against Mexicans, Indians, and Blacks defined and directed nineteenth-century Texas history."[9] Anglo Texans sought to remove both Indians and Mexicans from Texas. While slavery was legal, blacks were thought useful, even indispensable, but after slavery, attitudes changed.

Texas and the Indians

Scholars disagree about the number of Indians in North America generally and in Texas more specifically before Europeans arrived. David La Vere, author of *The Texas Indians* (2004), reviewed the scholarship and reported that estimates of the North American native population, once one to two million, had risen to seven to nine million, with some saying perhaps eighteen million. Population estimates for Texas in 1500 range from 50,000 to several hundred thousand to perhaps a million. Adopting the middle range of seven to nine million Indians on the continent and perhaps half a million in Texas in 1500 seems a reasonable guess, but it is only a guess. Still, La Vere reminds us that in 1500 "Indians lived in virtually every part of Texas . . . and a person could not travel far before they encountered Indians and often a considerable number of them."[10]

Precise numbers, even fairly general population estimates, are not possible for many reasons. First, some Indian tribes ranged in and out of Texas depending upon the seasons and the movement of the buffalo herds. Second, even the more fixed agricultural tribes, such as the Caddo, did not reside in one state. The Caddo spilled out of Northeast Texas into Louisiana and Arkansas. Third, and most importantly, Indians had no written languages and they took no surveys or census counts. Modern experts are dependent upon scattered reports from Spanish, French, and, later, American soldiers, traders, and travelers. Hence, David La Vere discusses the Caddo population from 1500 to 1700 and beyond as follows: "Much controversy exists over the size of the Caddo population at the beginning of the sixteenth century. Some scholars suggest . . . between 200,000 and 250,000 in 1500. Others say not nearly that many. In any event, by the late seventeenth century the Caddo population had dwindled to somewhere between 8,000 and 40,000 and was still falling." Similarly broad ranges are offered for the Coahuiltecan, the Wichita, and others.[11]

Whatever their numbers before the arrival of Europeans, Indians suffered steep population declines after contact. Contact occurred first in South and East Texas and only much later in West Texas, but once it occurred Indian numbers always fell quickly. The first Europeans in Texas were Alvar Nunez Cabeza de Vaca and about ninety of his shipmates. Initially shipwrecked in Florida, they built rafts and put back to sea, finally wrecking again on Galveston Island on November 6, 1528. Most soon died from their ordeal or were killed by Indians, but Cabeza de Vaca and a few colleagues were taken in by the Coco band of the Karankawa Indians. Soon "cholera hit the Indians and killed half of them."[12] Over the next three centuries, contacts between Europeans, Americans, and Texas Indians decimated the Indians. By the time that Anglo settlement of Texas began in earnest, around 1820, Indians in Texas numbered only 20,000 to 40,000. John Ewers translated a book by Jose Francisco Ruiz, entitled *Texas Indians in 1830*, that places the number near 40,000, but most historians, including T.R. Fehrenbach, place the number at 30,000 in 1820, while Randolph Campbell says 20,000.[13]

The precise number of Indians in Texas in the 1820s matters little, because in a few short decades they were virtually all gone and epidemics were not the only cause of their decline. Stephen F. Austin arrived in Texas convinced that "The Indians . . . may be called universal enemies of man. There will be no way of subduing them but extermination."[14] While Sam Houston, first President of the Republic of Texas, was sympathetic to the Indians and sought to treat with them, his successor, President Mirabeau B. Lamar, pursued a policy of removal or extermination.

Lamar's opening address to the Texas Congress in December 1838 made his intentions clear. He warned that, "If the wild cannibals of the woods will not desist from their massacres, if they will continue to war upon us with the ferocity of tigers and hyenas, it is time that we should retaliate their warfare. . . . " The goal, he said, was "their total extinction or total expulsion."[15]

In 1842, William Bollaert observed that, "Texas . . . is now fast becoming the grave of the tribes of Red Men."[16] Subsequent policies, equally brutal, had cleared North Texas by 1860. The final battles on the high plains against the once mighty Comanche occurred in the early and mid-1870s. The fundamental fact, however, is that by the time large numbers of Anglos arrived in Texas, the Indians were already broken, a shadow of their former selves, their numbers down 90 percent and falling. Despite the terror that a Comanche war party might still cause on the Texas plains in the early 1870s, they represented the chips and shards of long lost Indian nations. Within half a century of the establishment of Austin's colony, Anglo Texans had cleared the state of its native population.

Two stories, one concerning treaty negotiation and one concerning the establishment of reservations in Texas, highlight the Anglo attitude toward the Indians. Sam Houston had long mourned that Indians were easy prey for dishonest white traders and settlers. He sought to negotiate fair treaties to free some Indian land for white settlement while securing some land for permanent Indian use. The Texas Congress ratified few of Houston's treaties because nearly all Anglo Texans saw Indian land as wasted. When Lamar succeeded Houston as president in late 1838, he charted a far more popular course on Indian policy. Lamar shared in the widely held Anglo view that Indians lacked integrity and so could not be negotiated with in any meaningful sense. Indians likely thought the same about whites.

In 1840, chiefs of the Penatekas band of the Comanche rode into San Antonio to meet Texas authorities to discuss suspension of hostilities and the return of white hostages. The Indians brought few hostages, but one they did bring, sixteen-year-old Matilda Lockhart, bore obvious signs of torture and abuse. Texans moved to take the chiefs hostage as leverage for the return of all white captives and fighting broke out, leaving seven Anglo Texans and thirty-seven Indians, including twelve chiefs, dead and three dozen Indian women and children captive. The Comanche, with Kiowa and Mexican support, attacked Victoria, stealing 1,500 horses, and sacked Linnville. Texan volunteers intercepted the Indians at Plum Creek as they retreated north. A running battle left nearly 100 Comanche dead. In the fall, another battle near modern-day Ballinger saw Texans, supported by Lipan Apache and Tonkawa warriors and scouts, attack a Comanche village, kill 130 Indians, and retrieve much of the booty from Victoria and Linnville.

The story of Texas's short-lived Indian reservations is equally remarkable. Though most East Texas Indians had been pushed north of the Red River by 1840, conflict between advancing Anglos and Indian remnants, as well as raiding parties from the Oklahoma Indian Territory, continued into the early 1850s. Establishing an effective Indian policy after Texas accession to the U.S. was difficult because Indian policy was a federal government responsibility but Texas had retained control of all public lands within the state and most whites opposed leaving any of it to Indians. Houston famously said, "If I could build a wall from the Red River to the Rio Grande, so high that no Indian could scale it, the white people would go crazy trying to devise means to get beyond it."[17]

In what seemed a breakthrough, the Texas Legislature agreed in 1854 to provide land for two Indian reservations in North Texas.[18] One was called the Clear Fork Reserve, the other the Brazos Reserve. Anglo Texans never accepted the presence of the reservations and blamed any crime or mischief in their vicinity on the Indians. Anglo vigilantes, led by John R. Baylor, attacked the Brazos Reserve several times in 1859. Earlier Baylor had been an Indian agent to the Comanche at the Clear Fork Reserve. Baylor was fired by his supervisor, John Neighbors, when he accused the reserve Indians, perhaps correctly, of cooperating with nonreserve Indians in local raids. The final attack, in which Baylor led a ragged force of 250 Anglo residents of the area, convinced Neighbors to close the two Texas reserves and lead the Indians north into the Oklahoma Indian Territory. Historian David La Vere concluded that, "The removal of the Clear Fork and Brazos Reserve Indians was the culmination of the process begun by Mirabeau Lamar some twenty years earlier. By 1860 Texas found itself virtually denuded of Indian peoples."[19]

The respective fates of John Neighbors and John Baylor make the story even more poignant. When Neighbors returned to Texas after overseeing the Indians' removal, he was assassinated, killed by a shotgun blast to the back. John Baylor served, always controversially, as a Confederate army officer and congressman. He sought the Democratic Party nomination for Governor of Texas in 1873 before settling into the life of a prominent rancher near Uvalde. He died peacefully in 1894. Baylor County, immediately north of the reserves, was named for Baylor's brother Henry. The demise of the Indian population in Texas was no cause for Anglo mourning. John Wesley Wilbarger spoke for many Texas Anglos in his 691-page book, *Indian Depredations in Texas* (1889), when he wrote that, "We are glad . . . that there are no Indians now in Texas except 'good ones,' who are as dead as Julius Caesar."[20] Wilbarger was wrong, there were a few Indians left in Texas as the nineteenth century closed, but just a few. The U.S. Census of 1900 counted fewer than 1,000 (Figure 3.2).

Texas and the Mexicans

Texas Hispanics also suffered greatly in the wake of Texas independence. Stephen F. Austin described the Texas revolt as "a war of barbarism . . . waged by a mongrel Spanish-Indian and Negro race, against civilization and the Anglo-American race."[21] The Texian battle cry, "Remember the Alamo, Remember Goliad," was a blood reminder of Mexican savagery and Anglo bravery and sacrifice. As Leigh Clemons reminds us, "Tejanos living in the Republic of Texas after the Revolution were dispossessed of their property, harassed, and forced to flee or, in some cases, killed."[22]

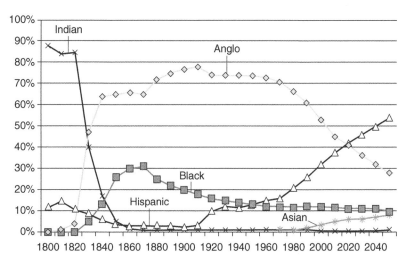

Figure 3.2 Shares of the Texas Population by Decade, Race, and Ethnicity.
Source: Percentage population shares derived from the data in Table 3.1.

Despite the fact that Tejanos fought for independence at the Alamo and San Jacinto, mistrust and greed put Anglos and Tejanos at odds. Lorenzo de Zavala was an accomplished Mexican diplomat and politician, appointed Governor of the state of Mexico, who resigned his positions and fled to Texas after denouncing Santa Anna as a tyrant. He signed the Texas Declaration of Independence and assisted in drafting the Republic of Texas Constitution before being elected *Interim* Vice President of Texas. He resigned due to ill-health and died in November 1836 before the tensions between Anglos and Tejanos grew ugly. Juan Seguin, perhaps the most famous Tejano participant in the Texas revolution, was not so fortunate.

Juan Seguin came from a prominent Tejano family in San Antonio. Seguin fought at the Alamo before Travis sent him through the Mexican lines with letters and instructions to bring back reinforcements. Seguin delivered the letters but returned with reinforcements too late; the Alamo had already fallen. Seguin then led cavalry covering the retreat east of Houston's ragged army and of Anglo families trying to outrun Santa Anna's advance. Seguin's cavalry detachment rejoined Houston's army at San Jacinto. As with the Indians, Houston was sensitive to the ambiguous place of the Tejanos in the fight for independence. On the eve of the decisive battle, Houston ordered Seguin and nineteen Tejanos to the rear with orders to guard the baggage train. Seguin protested and Houston relented, permitting the Tejanos to join the line only after they had placed distinctive markers on their hats so the Anglos could tell them from the enemy.

After independence was secured, Seguin retained his rank in the Texas army and in 1840 he was elected Mayor of San Antonio. As Texas filled with aggressive Anglo adventurers ignorant of the Tejanos service in the revolution, two Mexican invasions of South Texas in 1842 caused a spike in Anglo/Tejano tensions that brought Seguin down. In the first invasion, Seguin was ordered by Texas military officials to burn San Antonio to prevent its capture and use by the Mexicans. Seguin refused, abandoned the city, and then counter attacked, chasing the Mexicans from Texas, but both Texas officials and San Antonio Anglos accused him of cowardice, if not treason. Fearing for his life, Seguin fled to Mexico, to "seek refuge among my enemies." In Mexico, Seguin was arrested and impressed into the Mexican army where he fought during the U.S./Mexican War. Though Seguin returned briefly to Texas after the war, there was no place for him. He spent most of the rest of his long life—he died in 1890—in Nuevo Laredo, Tamaulipas, Mexico.

Anglo Texans made little effort to distinguish between Mexicans and Tejanos. Quite the contrary, some Texas leaders sought to equate Indians and Mexicans and urge the expulsion or extermination of both. Branch T. Archer, Texas Secretary of War, argued for the removal of Mexicans as well as Indians from Texas. Archer argued that Mexicans were worse than Indians, saying "The merciless Indian savage is, if possible, eclipsed in cruelty by our semi-barbarian Mexican foe; who are at this time engaged in the work of plunder and rapine, desolating in their bloody career, the fairest portion of our western frontier."[23] Others, perhaps the moderates of their day, urged discrimination rather than expulsion. A delegate to the Texas Constitutional Convention of 1845 reminded his colleagues that, "In their taste and social instincts, they [the Mexicans] approximated the African. . . . Notice how [the peons] meet [the slave] on an equality. They do not intermarry with the white population; they form their connections among the slaves."[24] Whether the Mexicans were more like the Indians or more like the Africans might be debated in early Texas, but they were not to be mistaken for citizens.

The Texan attitude toward Mexicans, Indians, and Africans was nicely captured by Joseph Eve, United States Chargé d'Affaires in a May 10, 1842, letter to Richard Southgate. Eve is quoted by Texas historian William Ransom Hogan, saying "most Texans were contemptuous of Mexicans, 'feble, dastardly, superstitious priest ridden race of mongrels, composed of spanish Indian and negro blood' and were 'always willing to fight them or the Indians five to one.'"[25] David Montejano, a prize-winning historian of Anglo–Mexican relations in Texas, noted that the "Anglos who settled in the Southwest brought with them a long history of dealing with Indians and blacks, while the experience of the Alamo and the Mexican War served to crystallize and affirm anti-Mexican prejudice. . . . Anglos and Mexicans stood as conquerors and conquered, as victors and vanquished."[26] By 1850, Hispanics and Indians each constituted about 5 percent of the population and both declined from there.

Moreover, Anglo Texans often resented Mexicans undercutting Anglo wages and sometimes used violence to stop it. In the famous "cart wars" of the late 1850s, Anglo haulers working the route between San Antonio and the coast killed seventy-five Mexicans because their rates were lower than the Anglos thought they needed to stay in business. The *Nueces Valley Weekly* spoke for moderate Anglo opinion. The paper editorialized that, "There is evidently a large amount of prejudice among our people against the greaser population, which often breaks out in acts of violence. . . . The fact of their being low in the scale of intelligence is no excuse for making them scapegoats."[27]

Mexicans fought back, but with no more than occasional and temporary success. Most famously, Juan Cortina was a borderlands legend from 1859 to 1875. After witnessing a Brownsville marshal pistol-whip a Mexican cowhand from his mother's ranch, Cortina intervened, shot the marshal in the shoulder, and carried the cowhand to safety. Anglo authorities pursued him; Cortina gathered Mexican supporters from both sides of the border and counterattacked, briefly capturing Brownsville in the fall of 1859. Cortina was eventually pushed south of the border but he continued to organize raids from Mexico. In the 1860s, he became a Mexican army general and later was governor of Tamaulipas.[28] As late as 1875, Mexican raiders identified with Cortina were stealing Texas cattle. The fact that Cortina harassed the Norte Americanos made him a Mexican hero, but Anglo Texans were not amused. Texas Rangers under the command of the famous Captain L.H. McNelly "caught a group of Mexican cattle banditos red-handed near the border and 'naturalized' thirteen of them."[29] Ranger violence toward Mexicans in South Texas eventually made them a cowering and subservient population. As Montejano notes, "By 1900 the Mexican upper class would become nonexistent except in a few border enclaves."[30] But change was coming.

In 1898, Robert Kleberg, scion of the fantastic King Ranch, discovered that deep wells on his Santa Gartrudis ranch tapped a huge aquifer. In 1905, entrepreneurs opened the 160-mile long St. Louis, Brownsville, and Mexico Railway between Brownsville and the Corpus Christi terminal of the Missouri–Pacific Railroad. By 1909, a spur had been run out into the Winter Garden counties of Dimmit, Zavala, Frio, and La Salle, linking the central valley to northern markets. As the economy of South Texas evolved from ranching to agriculture, the number of Mexicans grew rapidly and the relations between the Anglos and Mexicans changed. In the ranching society, the patron ruled over a relatively stable underclass of Mexican ranch-hands—vaqueros and rancheros—and their families. The farmers did not need permanent hands; they needed large numbers of transient, migratory, low-wage-laborers at harvest time.

The Mexican Revolution of 1910 to 1920 brought great instability to the border region. During and after the revolution, violence and poverty in Mexico sent streams of refugees north. Texas Governors Oscar Colquitt, James Ferguson, and William Hobby each called for a greater federal presence on the border. The Mexican-American population in Texas rose from less than 5 percent in 1910 to 12 percent in 1930. However, the Great Depression of the 1930s brought widespread unemployment and a wave of anti-immigrant rhetoric and policy. In 1935, Texas's arch-conservative Congressman Martin Dies called for a "relentless war without quarter and without cessation" on foreigners illegally in America "until the last one is driven from our shores. Either we are for or against our country."[31]

From the perspective of Anglo Texans, Mexicans were a mixed race, sharing with blacks and Indians many characteristics that required a place outside Anglo society. In 1925, Edward Everett Davis, Dean of the North Texas Agricultural College, now the University of Texas, Arlington, declared that, "All that has been said about the Negro regarding his low economic productivity, poor standards of living, and large family, . . . apply with equal validity to the Mexicans."[32] Nor was Dean Davis alone in his negative evaluation of Mexicans and other Texas minorities. Walter Prescott Webb, a leading Texas historian and author of the classic *The Texas Rangers: A Century of Frontier Defense* (1935), wrote, "There is a cruel streak in the Mexican nature, or so the history of Texas would lead one to believe. This cruelty . . . may, and doubtless should, be attributed to their Indian blood."[33] But Hispanic numbers continued to increase, so that by the late 1940s "persons of Hispanic ancestry surpassed blacks in number to become the largest ethnic minority in Texas." Terry G. Jordan argued persuasively that this seismic demographic shift, still on-going today, allowed the Anglo host culture to shift its self-image from southern to western. "Indeed, the widely held self-image of Anglo Texans as westerners rather than southerners may be linked in part to the displacement of blacks by Mexicans as the largest ethnic minority."[34] Both the rise of Hispanic numbers and the fall of black numbers over the course of Texas history are fascinating stories. We turn now to the evolving place of blacks in Texas history and society.

Black Texans in Slavery and Freedom

From Anglo first settlement through the end of the Civil War, Texas was an Anglo slave republic. Though Stephen F. Austin later claimed that he had resisted the idea of slavery in his colony, he soon concluded that, "Texas must be a slave country. Circumstances and unavoidable necessity compel it. It is the wish of the people there, and it is my duty to do all I can, prudently, in favor of it."[35] Austin's first empresario contract, calling for 300 families, was complete by 1825. By the fall of 1825, "sixty-nine families in Austin's colony owned slaves and the 443 bondsmen were nearly 25 percent of the total population of 1,800." [36]

Not surprisingly, history takes only slight and always ambivalent note of blacks in the Texas revolt. Though only two men were known to have survived the Alamo, one was the Tejano Brigido Guerrero and the other was William B. Travis's slave Joe, neither is included in the pantheon of Texas heroes. While William Travis gained eternal fame as co-commander, with Jim Bowie, of the Alamo and author of the letter "To the People of Texas and All Americans in the World," promising "Victory or Death," Joe is dismissed. During the final assault, Travis ordered Joe to get his gun and join him on the wall. Both men fired, but Travis was soon hit and fell backward inside the wall. The PBS documentary, *Remember the Alamo*, reports that "Joe, seeing his master fall, and the Mexicans coming over the wall . . . ran, and ensconced himself in a house." Though wounded in the later fighting, Joe survived, and even more remarkably, was taken before Santa Anna and ordered returned to Travis's heirs. Two years later, Joe stole two horses and escaped to freedom. Texas history has seemed more interested in counting Joe a coward and a thief than noting his presence at the Alamo or his subsequent flight to freedom.

History is even less certain what to make of Emily Morgan, sometimes known as Emily West, though legend has it that she aided in the decisive

Texan victory at San Jacinto. The legendary "Yellow Rose of Texas," Emily Morgan was reported to have been a mulatto slave who occupied or distracted Santa Anna in his tent on the afternoon of April 12, 1836. Houston and the Texans, attacking in the mid-afternoon, caught the Mexicans napping and destroyed them in just twenty minutes. Leigh Clemons reports that virtually all the details about Emily Morgan are in dispute: her name, her race, her status as slave or free, and how she came to be in Santa Anna's tent. Nonetheless, the legend renders her impure and, therefore, suspect. To have been in Santa Anna's tent, she must have been at least mulatto and a slave—no honor there.[37]

Section 9 of the Republic of Texas Constitution of 1836 "guaranteed that people held as slaves in Texas would remain in servitude and that future emigrants to the republic could bring slaves with them. Furthermore, no free black could live in Texas without the approval of Congress, and any slave freed without the approval of Congress had to leave the republic."[38] In every decade through the 1860s, the black slave population grew more rapidly in percentage terms than the Anglo population. The locus of the slave population in antebellum Texas was in the old Austin colony, along the lower Brazos and Colorado rivers, in East Texas centering on San Augustine, and near the Red River in far northeast Texas. By 1850, six counties in east central Texas and northeast Texas had black majorities. By 1860, the number of black majority counties had risen to thirteen.[39]

In 1860, Texas was 66 percent Anglo, 30 percent black slave, less than 5 percent Hispanic, and about 1 percent Indian. As General Sherman and the union armies swept through the South, some wealthy white southerners sent their families and slaves to the comparative safety of Texas. Estimates of the number of slaves sent to Texas range from under 50,000 to as many as 150,000.[40] Once the war was over and blacks were free, their presence, at least in Anglo eyes, became deeply problematic. The freedmen wanted real freedom; some whites wanted black labor under as close to the old terms as possible, while other whites simply wanted the blacks gone.[41]

In the wake of the Civil War, few Texas whites could envision a bi-racial society. The general assumption among Anglos was that blacks, unchecked by slavery, would run amuck, threatening white persons and property. Some turned immediately to violence to keep freedmen in their traditional roles, while others hoped for a black exodus from Texas. John H. Reagan, former Confederate Post-Master General and future congressman and U.S. Senator from Texas, 1875–1891, predicted that, "The negroes will, it is hoped, gradually diffuse themselves, . . . many of them will probably go to Mexico, and other countries, in search of social equality, and few or none of their race will be added . . . by accession from other countries."[42] Anglo hopes were realized in that the state's population became increasingly Anglo and decreasingly black in the final decades of the nineteenth century, while Hispanic numbers remained under 5 percent and Indian numbers fell to a fraction of 1 percent. By 1900, Anglos were 77 percent and blacks were 20 percent and continuing to decline.

For most of American history, certainly well into the twentieth century, migration paths led west. The upper Midwest was settled out of New England, the Ohio Valley out of the Middle Atlantic region, and Texas out of the South. The westward course of migration makes understanding the impact of migration on post-Civil War Texas quite challenging. As the westernmost southern state, Texas received migrants, white and black, from the Old South, while losing native Texans, white and black, to other states. After the Civil War, southerners, white and black, but mostly white, drifted west in search of new cotton lands. The largest numbers came, as they had before the war, from Alabama, Tennessee, Mississippi, Georgia, and Arkansas. The economist Neil Fligstein has reported that, "The major difference between black and white patterns is the fact that the net out-migration rates were almost always higher for blacks than whites."[43]

Texas historians explain the decline in the black share of the total population as a function of post-Civil War interstate migration patterns. T.R. Fehrenbach explained that, "Thousands upon thousands of Southern poor whites, seeing the hopeless landscape around them, determined to move to Texas. . . . The Negro population rapidly fell, since the new arrivals brought no slaves."[44] Randolph Campbell similarly reports that, "Most of the [post-Civil War] immigrants came from the states of the Old South to escape the ruin and stagnation left by the war. . . . blacks declined from 32 percent of all Texans in 1870 to 22 percent by 1890."[45]

While the broad story of rapid growth of the white population and a declining black share of total population is correct, it was more a product of intention and policy among both whites and blacks than is commonly understood. White entrepreneurs advertised the virtues of Texas throughout the South to attract dispossessed whites. They came in droves during the 1870s. The Anglo population in Texas increased by 116 percent during the 1870s, more than twice as fast as black population growth. In fact, during the 1870s, 230,700 more whites immigrated to Texas than emigrated from Texas, while 10,300 more blacks emigrated from Texas than immigrated to it from other states. Similar patterns held for the 1880s and 1890s; whites moved to Texas while blacks left (Table 3.2).

Despite the numbers involved and the decades over which it occurred, black migration out of Texas was no simple matter. Most freed slaves had no property or money income, most were illiterate, and most knew little of the broader world. Some blacks, especially those recently brought to Texas, returned east to search for home and family. Some Texas freedmen chose to try life in the North or West.[46] Most famously, the "Great Exodus" of 1879 saw about 6,000 blacks leave Texas, Louisiana, and Mississippi for Kansas.[47] Texas experienced a net out-migration of 10,300 blacks during the 1870s, so, obviously, Kansas was not the only destination. In

Table 3.2   Post-Civil War Net Migration by Decade for Texas Whites and Blacks

Decade	Native Whites	Blacks
1870–80	230,700	−10,300
1880–90	63,700	−16,700
1890–00	23,800	−12,800
1900–10	−62,500	−54,000
1910–20	−79,200	−15,600
1920–30	−2,700	−39,700
1930–40	−146,000	16,300
1940–50	305,485	−77,630
1950–60	321,435	−102,926
1960–70	339,729	−97,264

Source: Everett S. Lee, Ann Ratner Miller, Carol P. Brainerd, and Richard A. Easterlin, prepared under the direction of Simon Kuznets and Dorothy Swaine Thomas, Population Redistribution and Economic Growth, United States, 1870–1950, Philadelphia: American Philosophical Society, 1964, vol. 1, pp. 74–77 and 87–90. State-of-Birth Methodology. 1950 Census, Special Reports, 4A-16, Table 9, 1960 Census, Vol. II, Special Reports, 2A, State-of Birth, Table 13 and 14, 1970 Census, Vol. II, Series PC(2), Subject Reports, 2A, State-of-Birth, Tables 7, 8, and 9.

Net migration numbers are a sum of in-migration minus out-migration. If in-migration is greater than out-migration, net migration is a positive number, if in-migration is less than out-migration, net migration is a negative number. Readers should keep in mind that net migration underreports total migration for many reasons. Two obvious reasons are that a single person moving several times from one state to another is counted just once and a person moving from one state to another and back is not counted at all.

the 1880s, Texas experienced a net out-migration of 16,700 and another 12,800 left in the 1890s. Between 1870 and 1900, the Anglo population of Texas increased from 534,004 to 2,355,926, a total increase of 341 percent, while the black population increased from 253,475 to 620,722, a total increase of 149 percent. In 1870 blacks made up 31 percent of the Texas population; in 1900, just 20 percent.

Between 1900 and 1950, the Anglo population of Texas increased by an average of 20 percent per decade while the black population grew by less than 10 percent. During that period the black share of the total population of Texas fell from 20 percent to 13 percent. In the first decade of the twentieth century, 54,000 more blacks left Texas than arrived. In the second and third decades of the century, 55,300 more left and in the 1940s more than 77,000 left. Only in the 1930s, when Texas suffered less than many other states during the Depression, did more blacks, 16,300 more, come to Texas than left it. Nonetheless, once the economy began to rebound in the late 1930s, Texas blacks were on the move again.[48] During the three decades from 1940 to 1970, about 100,000 more blacks left Texas than arrived each decade.

The economist Gavin Wright provided the best study of the evolution of the southern economy in the twentieth century. Wright explained that, "blacks left the South at all ages and educational levels. Net out-migration became increasingly black over time, and the reason is evident; most new jobs in the South were reserved for whites." As the southern economic revival got under way in the 1940s, the black exodus gained momentum. Wright says that, "Between 1940 and 1960, the South thus presents us with an amazing economic spectacle. It was the most rapidly growing region in the country. . . . And yet all of this was occurring at the same time that job-hungry workers were leaving the region by the thousands."[49] Many blacks were simply in search of a less threatening social and economic environment.

In something of an understatement, the historian Numan Bartley observed that, "The sorry state of segregated black schools, the unavailability of on-the-job-training, and all the other hindrances that beset blacks left them at a disadvantage."[50] Hence, Wright concluded that despite the undeniable difficulties southern blacks faced in the North, they were better off than they would have been had they stayed in the South. He wrote that, "With all the suffering, the out-migration of blacks from the South after 1940 was the single greatest economic step forward in black history, and a major advance toward the integration of blacks into the mainstream of American life."[51] One hundred thousand blacks left Texas in the 1950s, many headed toward California.

The "Great Migration" continued through the 1960s even as early school desegregation and civil and voting rights victories convinced some blacks that change was actually coming. Over the course of the 1970s, a reverse migration began in which some blacks, facing deindustrialization in the North and a less threatening South, offering an expanding job market and the warmth of family ties, returned home. Nonetheless, the human costs of the "Great Migration" were high. Isabel Wilkerson, author of the Pulitzer prize-winning book *The Warmth of Other Suns: The Epic Story of America's Great Migration*, called it "Perhaps the single greatest act of family disruption and heartbreak among black Americans in the twentieth century."[52] When the Great Migration began, 90 percent of American blacks lived in the South. By 1970, only 53 percent lived in the South. That number has rebounded a bit as the 2010 census reported that 57 percent of American blacks lived in the South.[53] While the return of some blacks to the South is an interesting sociological phenomenon, the numbers are small and are not expected to alter the more powerful demographic processes underway in Texas and the nation.[54]

In 2010, Anglos accounted for less than half, about 45 percent of Texans, Hispanics for about 38 percent, blacks for about 11 percent, Asians, barely present until the 1980s, for about 5 percent, and Indians far less than 1 percent. Texas state population projections, taking the median projection, say that by 2050 Anglos will have fallen to 28 percent, blacks to 10 percent, Hispanics to 54 percent—a simple majority—Asians will be about 7.5 percent, and Indians will still be less than 1 percent. Will Texas in 2050 be a better place, a worse place, or just a different place?

Meeting the Challenges of the Coming Hispanic Majority

Half of children born in the United States in 2010 were born to minority parents. Minorities comprise 35 percent of the U.S. population: Hispanics account for 15 percent, blacks for 13 percent, Asians for almost 5 percent, and Native Americans for just under 1 percent. The Hispanic population is by far the fastest growing because it is young, fertile, and supplemented by larger immigration flows than other races and ethnicities. Of the Hispanic share of U.S. population increase in 2009–2010, two-thirds come from births and one-third from immigration. Strikingly, Hispanic births outstrip deaths by nine to one whereas white births and deaths balance at about one to one.[55] No wonder the sociologist Stewart Tolnay described fertility, mortality, and migration as "the traditional trinity of demographic processes."[56]

Several states, including California (2000) and Texas (2003), the nation's two most populous states, have already made the transition from majority Anglo to majority minority and the U.S. will follow sometime around 2040. The burgeoning minority population has triggered some Anglo trepidation. As early as 1978, California passed Proposition 13, limiting state property tax increases to no more than 2 percent per year and requiring a two-thirds vote in the state legislature to raise other taxes. Proposition 13 is blamed for having severely limited funding of public schools and other services. In the 1990s, California voters adopted propositions eliminating state affirmative action and bilingual education, as well as tightening laws against illegal immigration.[57] As the recipients of California's (once) generous public services and students in their (once) excellent public schools became increasingly minority, Anglo Californians tightened the purse strings. As we shall see below, political dynamics in Texas have been different because the purse strings in Texas were never loose to begin with.

Tight purse strings have generally made Texas Anglos more sanguine about the Hispanic presence than their California, or more recently Arizona, counterparts. If social services in Texas were more generous and, therefore, more expensive, Anglo Texans might share more of the Californian's skepticism. On the other hand, low wages and thin public services have left Texas Hispanics, both citizens and illegal aliens, poor, less educated, less competitive, and more vulnerable. As we shall see throughout this book, much will hinge on providing enough high-quality public services, especially in education and health care, to allow, even promote, Hispanic advancement.

The Hispanic Center of the Pew Research Center charts in detail the place and prospects of Hispanics in the U.S. and in each of the individual states. In 2010, Texas's 9.5 million Hispanic residents comprised 37.6 percent of the state's total population, behind only New Mexico (45 percent) and California (38 percent). Nearly one in five U.S. Hispanics resides in Texas. Two-thirds of Texas Hispanics are native-born U.S. citizens, while one-third are foreign-born and generally not U.S. citizens. Nearly nine in ten Texas Hispanics trace their origins to Mexico.

Texas Hispanics have annual personal earnings of $20,368, compared to $25,460 for Texas blacks, and $35,644 for whites. For comparison, California Hispanics make $22,405, blacks make $30,552, and whites make $40,737. Texas Hispanics make 80 percent of what Texas blacks make and only 57 percent of what Texas whites make. Not surprisingly then, poverty rates are high among both adult and young Texas Hispanics. Among Texas adults, 19 percent of Hispanics, 14 percent of blacks, and just 3 percent of whites live in poverty. Among Texans aged 17 and younger, 32 percent of Hispanics, 31 percent of blacks, and 9 percent of whites live in poverty. For comparison, poverty rates for all groups in California are lower. Among California adults, 15 percent of Hispanics, 10 percent of blacks, and just 2 percent of whites live in poverty. Among California young people, 25 percent of Hispanics, 26 percent of blacks, and 8 percent of whites live in poverty. Similarly, Texans struggle to afford health care. Thirty-eight percent of Hispanics in Texas and fully 61 percent of foreign-born Hispanics lack health insurance, compared to 23 percent of blacks and 14 percent of whites. For California, the comparable numbers show that 29 percent of Hispanics and 45 percent of foreign-born Hispanics lack health insurance, compared to 17 percent of blacks and 10 percent of whites.

Finally, age and fertility differences by ethnicity and race promise that Hispanic presence in the nation's population, as well as those of Texas and California, will continue to grow. The median age of the U.S. population is 36, while that of Hispanics is 27 and that of Hispanics of Mexican origin, just 25. In Texas, the median age of whites is 41, blacks 31, and Hispanics 26. Moreover, the median age of native-born Hispanics, two-thirds of all Hispanics in Texas, is just 19. For comparison, California whites are older, 44, and native-born Hispanics are younger, 17. The age profile of a population relates to family formation and fertility in ways both ominous and direct. In 2008, Hispanic women 15 to 44 comprised 17 percent of American women and had almost 22 percent of all babies. In Texas, Hispanic women in this age range had 46 percent of all births. Though 68 percent of Texas Hispanics are native born, they had only 58 percent of babies, while the 32 percent of foreign-born Hispanics had 42 percent of babies.

For Hispanics in Texas to enjoy greater economic success, they must first improve their educational attainment. Better jobs and higher incomes follow higher educational achievement. Richard Fry of the Pew Hispanic Center explains that Texas Hispanics underperform their Anglo and black counterparts at all levels of the educational system. Texas has higher high school drop-out rates than the nation as a whole, with Texas Hispanics having higher rates than Anglos and blacks. Texas also has lower college attendance rates than the nation as a whole, with Texas Hispanics having lower college attendance rates than Anglos and blacks. The Federal Reserve Bank of Dallas reports that, "Forty percent of Texas Latinos age 25 and older didn't graduate from high school, compared to 5 percent of non-Hispanic whites. Only 11 percent of Latinos earned college degrees, well below the 38 percent for non-Hispanic whites."[58] In 2008, 54 percent of the nation's white high school graduates went on to college, as did 48 percent of black graduates, and 43 percent of Hispanics. In Texas, the numbers were lower: 52 percent of whites, 45 percent of blacks, and 41 percent of Hispanic high school graduates went on to college.[59]

Inadequate education leaves many Texas Hispanics with few economic options. Emily Kerr, Pia Orrenius, and Madeline Zavodny of the Dallas Federal Reserve Bank find that, "Latino workers in Texas are on the short end of two pay gaps. They earn substantially lower wages than the state's non-Hispanic white workers. They also earn less than Latinos working in other parts of the U.S." They further find that low educational attainment "explains more than half of the Latino pay gap vis-à-vis non-Hispanic whites in the state and 20 percent of the gap vis-à-vis Latinos outside Texas." The remainder of the in-state gap between Hispanics and Anglos is likely explained by the relatively low cost-of-living in Texas, "the state's proximity to Mexico, long history of discrimination and relatively low minimum wage." While Kerr and her colleagues do not make policy recommendations, they do note that, "targeting educational outcomes would likely pay off in reducing occupational inequality and increasing Latino wages."[60] They do not say what they think the likelihood of such "targeting" is given the "long history of discrimination" in Texas, but one assumes they realize that it is very low.

Clearly, both the Federal Reserve Bank of Dallas and the Office of the State Demographer of Texas are keenly aware that, "The key issue facing Texas" in the coming decades "will be to reduce the economic and educational disparities prevalent among the state's ethnic groups as the population continues to grow and evolve."[61] As official agencies of government, neither has been eager to say exactly how difficult that will be, especially as Texas state government seems convinced that limiting expenditures on education and health care are necessary to balance the state's budget. In fact, the economic and educational disparities between Hispanics, blacks, and Anglos in Texas will grow inexorably unless effective action is taken.

Table 3.3 Components of Population Change in Texas, 1950–2010

Year	Population	Numerical Change	Natural Increase	Net Migration%	>	% from Natural Increase	% from Net Migration
1950	7,711,194						
1960	9,579,677	1,868,483	1,754,652	113,831	24.2	93.91	6.09
1970	11,196,730	1,617,053	1,402,683	214,370	16.9	86.74	13.26
1980	14,229,191	3,032,461	1,260,794	1,771,667	27.1	41.58	58.42
1990	16,986,510	2,757,319	1,815,670	941,649	19.9	65.85	34.15
2000	20,851,820	3,865,310	1,919,281	1,946,029	22.8	49.65	50.35
2010	25,145,561	4,293,741	2,358,981	1,934,760	20.6	54.94	45.06

Source: Derived from U.S. Bureau of the Census Estimates for dates indicated by the Texas State Data Center, University of Texas at San Antonio. All values for the decennial dates are for the indicated census year. Values for 2010 are for July 1 as estimated by the U.S. Bureau of the Census.

The population of Texas has grown rapidly since 1950, increasing from 7.7 million to more than 25 million in 2010. Moreover, the composition of Texas population growth since 1950 has changed dramatically and these changes will have a cumulative impact over the next several decades. Table 3.3, derived from U.S. Census data and employed by both the Dallas Federal Reserve Bank and the State Demographer, presents data on the contributions to the state's rapid population growth since 1950 from natural increase and net migration. Table 3.3 is updated from a February 2012 presentation by Lloyd B. Potter, Texas State Demographer, entitled, "Texas: Demographic Characteristics and Trends." The data show clearly that Texas population growth in the 1950s and 1960s was produced overwhelmingly, 94 percent and 87 percent, by natural increase—births to Texas residents. Since 1970, just slightly more than half of the state's population growth, 53 percent, has come from natural increase. The rest, 47 percent, came from net migration, both from other U.S. states to Texas and from other nations to Texas. High net migration is neither good nor bad. Its impact depends on who comes, how well-educated, trained, and talented they are or how well they are educated or trained once they arrive.

Net total migration to Texas, generally the number of persons migrating to Texas minus those migrating from Texas to other places, over the past decade totaled almost 1.8 million people: 33 percent Anglo, 40 percent Hispanic, 15 percent black, and 12 percent other (Table 3.4). Net total migration is composed of two flows, net domestic migration and net international migration. Net domestic migration during the first decade of the twenty-first century was about 48 percent of total migration. Net domestic migration reflects an Anglo plurality of 44 percent, Hispanic 28 percent, black 23 percent, and other 5 percent. Net international migration, 52 percent of total migration, was 50 percent Hispanic, 24 percent

Table 3.4 Estimates of Migrants to Texas between 2000 and 2009 by Race and Ethnicity

	White	*Hispanic*	*Black*	*Other*	*Total*
Net Domestic Migration					
Number of migrants	371,150	238,866	195,024	43,663	848,702
Percent of row total	44%	28%	23%	5%	48%
International Migration					
Number of migrants	224,820	469,591	73,140	165,532	933,083
Percent of row total	24%	50%	8%	18%	52%
Total Migration					
Number of migrants	595,970	708,457	268,163	209,195	1,781,785
Percent of row total	33%	40%	15%	12%	100%

Source: Percentages of domestic and international migrants by race and ethnicity derived from the 2006–2008. American Community Survey. Total numbers of domestic and international migrants between 2000 and 2009 are from Table 4, Cumulative Estimates of the Components of Residential Population Change for the United States, Regions, and Puerto Rico, April 1, 2000 to July 1, 2009. U.S. Census Bureau.

Anglo, 8 percent black, and 18 percent other. Unfortunately, international migrants tend to be less well educated than domestic migrants.

Finally, population projections from the Office of the Texas State Demographer for 2010 to 2040 suggest that 85 percent of the population growth in Texas will be in the Hispanic population, 9 percent will be among Asians and others, 6.6 percent will be among blacks, and 0 percent will be in the Anglo population (Figure 3.3). The point, made several times already, is that unless Hispanic educational attainment and earning power improve, Texas will inevitably become a less productive and poorer state. Hence, in Chapter 4 we look at the Texas economy, especially the job market and income levels in Texas. In Chapter 5 we look at public education in Texas because education and income are so closely connected.

A Concluding Exercise

Now, let's conclude with a simple, and to some extent implausible, but eye-opening, exercise. First, we analyze data on per capita income by race for Texas in 2010. Second, we analyze the same 2010 income data, but change the race and ethnicity data to those projected to be in place in 2040 to see what impact this change has on overall per capita income. We use per capita income figures, rather than median personal income, median household income, or median family income, because it accounts for differences in family size. Hispanics generally have larger families than Anglos, for example, and this means that income must be spread across more people. Nonetheless, all of these measures of income display the same general pattern as we see with per capita income.

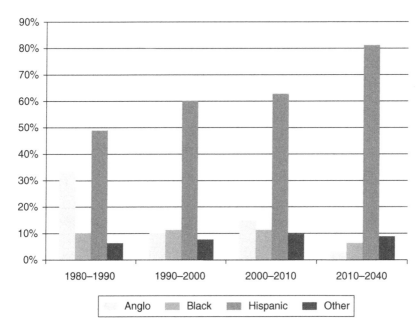

Figure 3.3 Percent of Texas Population Growth and Projected Population Growth by Race and Ethnicity.

Source: U.S. Census Counts, and the Texas State Data Center 2008 Population Projections, 0.5 Scenario.

In 2010, Anglos were 51.6 percent of the workforce and Anglo per capita income was $34,826 annually. Blacks were 10.2 percent of the workforce making about $18,418 per capita annually. Hispanics were 32.8 percent of the workforce making about $14,169 per capita annually. And Asians were about 3.5 percent of the workforce making $28,253. As Table 3.5 shows, multiplying the percentage of the workforce in each racial and ethnic group by their average annual per capita income and adding the four resulting numbers gives a per capita income for Texas in 2010 of $25,485.

To put an even sharper point on this, we can compare the per capita income of Texas Anglos to the per capita income of Anglos or whites in the other forty-nine states and do the same for blacks, Hispanics, and Asians. In 2012, Texas Anglo per capita income of $35,721 ranked 11th among Anglos in the fifty states. Texas Asians at $30,468 ranked 13th among the states, while blacks at $18,950 ranked 17th, and Hispanics at $14,950 ranked 28th among Hispanics in the fifty states. Texas Anglos have every reason to be satisfied, they make more than Anglos in three-quarters of the states and far more than Texas blacks and Hispanics. Today, Texas might be called an Anglo paradise, but trouble looms.

Table 3.5 Reason for Concern: Texas Per Capita Income by Race in 2000 with Projections to 2040

	2010			2040		
	% Workforce	*Per Capita Income*	*Income Share*	*% Workforce*	*Per Capita Income*	*Income Share*
Anglo	51.6 ×	$34,826 =	$17,970	25.2 ×	$34,826 =	$8,776
Black	10.2 ×	$18,418 =	$1,879	7.9 ×	$18,418 =	$1,455
Hispanic	32.8 ×	$14,169 =	$4,647	58.7 ×	$14,169 =	$8,317
Asian	3.5 ×	$28,253 =	$989	5.0 ×	$28,253 =	$1,413
Statewide Per Capita Income			$25,485			$19,961

Source: Texas State Data Center, http://txsdc.utsa.edu/subjindex/ (click on I, go to Income).

If we hold the average salary numbers at 2010 levels, but change the racial and ethnic make-up of the workforce to the composition projected for 2040, what happens to average per capita income in Texas? In 2040, the Anglo share of the workforce is projected to be 25.2 percent, the Hispanic share to be 58.7 percent, the black share to be 7.9 percent, and the Asian share to be 5 percent. If income by racial and ethnic groups does not change, average per capita income in Texas will be $19,961, down more than $5,500 and, shockingly, 22 percent.

These numbers, of course, are not set in stone, though some are firmer than others. The population projections are pretty firm and, if anything, have tended in past decades to underestimate the growth of the Hispanic population. The income numbers, on the other hand, could change if black and Hispanic earnings improve. We can hope that they will, but when we look for evidence suggesting that they will, we find little. Most analysts believe that improvements in Hispanic educational achievement, including better test scores, lower drop-out rates, and more attendance and success in college, will have to precede significant increases in Hispanic per capita income. Pointedly, if the proportion of high earners in the workforce (Anglos) falls and the proportion of low income earners in the workforce (Hispanics) rises, per capita income in Texas must fall and the Texas economy will fall with it. Succeeding chapters ask what Texas is doing to secure the future.

Notes

1 Paul Burka, "Capitol Affair," *Texas Monthly*, July, 2011, pp. 12–14.
2 Mercedes Olivera, "Census Will Show Scope of Hispanic Growth," *Dallas Morning News*, January 1, 2011, p. 3B.
3 Randolph B. Campbell, *Gone to Texas: A History of the Lone Star State*, New York: Oxford University Press, 2003, p. 85. See also Henderson K. Yoakum, *History of Texas*, New York: Redfield, 1856, pp. 111–115.

4   Ibid., pp. 95–96. See also Henry Stuart Foote, *Texas and the Texans*, Philadelphia: Thomas, Cowperthwaite and Co., 1841, pp. 201–217.

5   Stanley Siegel, *A Political History of the Texas Republic, 1836–1845*, Austin, TX: University of Texas Press, 1956, p. 39.

6   Terry G. Jordan, "A Century and a Half of Ethnic Change in Texas, 1836–1986," *Southwestern Historical Quarterly*, vol. 89, no. 4, April 1986, p. 386.

7   Billy D. Ledbetter, "White Over Black in Texas: Racial Attitudes in the Antebellum Period," *Phylon*, vol. 34, no. 4, 4th quarter, 1973, p. 406.

8   Randolph B. Campbell, *An Empire for Slavery: The Peculiar Institution in Texas, 1821–1865*, Baton Rouge, LA: Louisiana State University Press, 1989, pp. 209–210.

9   James McEnteer, *Deep in the Heart: The Texas Tendency in American Politics*, Westport, CT: Praeger, 2004, p. 31.

10   David La Vere, *The Texas Indians*, College Station, TX: Texas A&M University Press, 2004, p. 28.

11   Ibid., pp. 107, 64–65.

12   Ibid., p. 63.

13   T.R. Fehrenbach, *Lone Star: A History of Texas and the Texans*, New York: Macmillan, 1968, pp. 130–131; Campbell, *Gone to Texas*, p. 14.

14   Robert Perkinson, *Texas Tough: The Rise of America's Prison Empire*, New York: Metropolitan Books, 2010, p. 53.

15   Glenn Frankel, *The Searchers: The Making of an American Legend*, New York: Bloomsbury, 2013, p. 52.

16   William Bollaert, *William Bollaert's Texas*, Norman, OK: University of Oklahoma Press, 1956, p. 73.

17   La Vere, *The Texas Indians*, p. 187.

18   W.W. Newcomb Jr., *The Indians of Texas: From Prehistoric to Modern Times*, Austin, TX: University of Texas Press, 1961/1989, p. 354.

19   La Vere, *The Texas Indians*, p. 201.

20   Frankel, *The Searchers*, p. 151.

21   McEnteer, *Deep in the Heart*, p. 26.

22   Leigh Clemens, *Branding Texas: Performing Culture in the Lone Star State*, Austin, TX: University of Texas Press, 2008, p. 61. See also Glen Sample Ely, *Where the West Begins: Debating Texas Identity*, Lubbock: Texas Tech University Press, 2011, p. 76

23   McEnteer, *Deep in the Heart*, p. 31.

24   Quintard Taylor, *In Search of the Racial Frontier: African Americans in the American West, 1528–1990*, New York: W.W. Norton, 1998, p. 43.

25   Joseph Eve to Richard Southgate, May 10, 1842, "A LetterBook of Joseph Eve, United States Chargé d'Affaires to Texas," *Southwestern Historical Quarterly*, XLIII, 4, April 1940, p. 494. Quoted in William Ransom Hogan, *The Texas Republic*, Norman, OK: University of Oklahoma Press, 1946, p. 14.

26   David Montejano, *Anglos and Mexicans in the Making of Texas, 1836–1986*, Austin, TX: University of Texas Press, 1987, p. 5. See also Arnoldo De León, *The Tejano Community 1836–1900*, Albuqerque: University of New Mexico Press, 1982.

27   McEnteer, *Deep in the Heart*, p. 43.

28   Robert A. Calvert, Arnoldo De León, and Gregg Cantrell, *The History of Texas*, 4th edn, Wheeling, IL: Harlan Davidson, Inc., 2007, p. 125.

29   James Reston Jr., *The Lone Star: The Life of John Connally*, New York: Harper & Row, 1989, p. 7; Fehrenbach, *Lone Star*, pp. 575–579.

30   Montejano, *Anglos and Mexicans*, pp. 50, 183. See also Terry G. Jordan, "The Forgotten Texas State Census of 1887" *Southwestern Historical Quarterly*, vol. 85, no. 4, April 1982, pp. 401–408.

31   McEnteer, *Deep in the Heart*, p. 80.

32   Gene B. Preuss, *To Get a Better School System*, College Station, TX: Texas A&M University Press, 2009, p. 45.

33   Water Prescott Webb, *The Texas Rangers: A Century of Frontier Defense*, Boston: Houghton, Mifflin, 1935, p. 14.
34   Jordan, "A Century and a Half of Ethnic Change in Texas," pp. 392, 404.
35   Perkinson, *Texas Tough*, p. 51.
36   Campbell, *An Empire for Slavery*, p. 19.
37   Clemons, *Branding Texas*, pp. 55–57.
38   Campbell, *Gone to Texas*, p. 148.
39   Campbell, An Empire for Slavery, p. 57–58.
40   Calvert et al., *The History of Texas*, p. 148; David G. McComb, *Texas: A Modern History*, revised edition, Austin, TX: University of Texas Press, 2010, p. 72; Lawrence D. Rice, *The Negro in Texas, 1874–1900*, Baton Rouge, LA: Louisiana State University Press, 1971, p. 162.
41   Calvert et al., *The History of Texas*, p. 153.
42   Michael Phillips, *White Metropolis: Race, Ethnicity, and Religion in Dallas, 1841–2001*, Austin, TX: University of Texas Press, 2006, pp. 25–33, 37.
43   Neil Fligstein, *Going North: Migration of Black and Whites from the South, 1900–1950*, New York Academic Press, 1981, pp. 77.
44   Fehrenbach, *Lone Star*, p. 603.
45   Campbell, *Gone to Texas*, pp. 290–291.
46   Rice, *The Negro in Texas, 1874–1900*, p. 202.
47   Nell Irvin Painter, *Exodusters: Black Migration to Kansas After Reconstruction*, Lawrence, KS: University of Kansas Press, 1976.
48   Alwyn Barr, *Black Texans: A History of African Americans in Texas, 1528–1995*, 2nd edn, Norman, OK: University of Oklahoma Press, 1996, p. 154.
49   Gavin Wright, *Old South, New South: Revolutions in the Southern Economy Since the Civil War*, New York: Basic Books, 1986, pp. 255–257.
50   Numan V. Bartley, *The New South, 1945–1980*, Baton Rouge, LA: Louisiana State University Press, 1995, p. 118; see also Calvert et al., *The History of Texas*, p. 260.
51   Wright, *Old South, New South*, p. 237.
52   Isabel Wilkerson, *The Warmth of Other Suns: The Epic History of America's Great Migration*, New York: Random House, 2010, p. 238.
53   J. David Woodard, *The New Southern Politics*, Boulder, CO: Lynne Rienner Publishers, 2006, pp. 45, 52. See also, Sabrina Tavernise and Robert Gebeloff, "Wave of Blacks Moving South, Census Shows," *New York Times*, March 25, 2011, pp. A1, A3.
54   James N. Gregory, *American Exodus: The Dust Bowl Migration and Okie Culture in California*, New York: Oxford University Press, 1989, pp. 1–19.
55   Conor Dougherty, "U.S. Nears Racial Milestone," *Wall Street Journal*, June 11, 2010, A3.
56   Stewart E. Tolnay, "The African American 'Great Migration' and Beyond," *Annual Review of Sociology*, 29, 2003, pp. 209–232.
57   Gregory Rodriquez, "The White Anxiety Crisis," *Time*, March 22, 2010, pp. 52–54.
58   Emily Kerr, Pia Orrenius and Madeline Zavodny, "Texas's Latino Pay Gaps: Taking a Closer Look," Federal Reserve Bank of Dallas, *First Quarter 2010, Southwest Economy*, p. 10.
59   On the Record, A Conversation With Richard Fry, "Why Hispanic Education Deficits Persist," Federal Reserve Bank of Dallas, *First Quarter 2010, Southwest Economy*, pp. 8–9.
60   Kerr, Orrenius, and Zavodny, "Texas's Latino Pay Gaps," pp. 10–11, 13.
61   D'Ann Petersen and Laila Assanie, "The Changing Face of Texas: Population Projections and Implications," Federal Reserve Bank of Dallas, October 2005, p. 37.

Part II

The Reality Thus Far

4   Jobs, Income, and Wealth in Texas

> [T]he rankings of states by income have remained stable over the past century. . . . Thus, any discussion of rich and poor states is potentially as much about each state's history as peripheral and rural or as metropolitan and urban.
>
> (Andrew Gelman, 2008)[1]

Texas is frequently touted as the best job producing state in the nation and as the most business-friendly state in the nation. For example, in April 2009, *Forbes*, one of the nation's top business magazines, ranked the job producing prospects of 333 major metropolitan areas. *Forbes* reported that "the top five large metropolitan areas for job growth [are] all located in the Lone Star State. . . . Nine of the top twenty cities on Forbes' overall list are in Texas." In May 2014, *Chief Executive* reported a survey ranking the "Best and Worst States" for business. The best states for business were Texas, Florida, Tennessee, North Carolina, and South Carolina, while the worst were California, New York, Illinois, New Jersey, Massachusetts, Michigan, and Connecticut. Such reports are common. Texas has been ranked number one by *Chief Executive* every year since 2004. CNBC has conducted a similar ranking since 2007. Texas has finished either first or second every year.

Texas leaders treat such reports as unambiguously positive, declaring that they prove that Texas is a great place to work and do business. They rarely stop to ponder the fact that *Chief Executive*'s worst states for business are among the wealthiest states in the nation, with New York, New Jersey, Massachusetts, and Connecticut perennially among the five wealthiest. *Chief Executive*'s top five, including Texas, are all poorer states. Moreover, the reports are not new: similar reports are common back into the 1950s. But as the quotation at the start of this chapter, as well as Table 1.1 and Figure 2.1 in previous chapters show, Texas has not been making a rapid transition from poor state to rich state, from low-wage state to high-wage state. In fact, it has been holding its own, perhaps moving up slowly, in fits and starts, but it is not sprinting ahead of the pack and there is little reason to believe that it soon will. In addition to job creation, attention must also be directed to issues of productivity, income, unemployment, poverty, and inequality to get an accurate picture of how well or poorly the Texas economy is performing. But often boosterism overwhelms analysis.

Joel Kotkin declared in a November 15, 2010, *Newsweek* article, entitled "Greetings From Recoveryland," "For sheer economic promise, no place beats Texas. . . . Businesses have been flocking to Texas for a generation, and that trend is unlikely to slow soon. Texas now has more Fortune 500 companies—58—than any other state, including longtime corporate powerhouse New York."[2] "For a generation," of course, means since the late 1980s banking bust and real estate crisis in Texas. In another piece, this one written for *Forbes*, Kotkin offers a comparison of California and Texas that is decidedly in Texas's favor regarding population, job growth, and income gains. However, Kotkin notes but does not explore certain storm clouds in the Texas sky, writing "To be sure, Texas has its problems: a growing budget deficit, the need to expand infrastructure to service its rapid population growth and the presence of a large contingent of undereducated and uninsured poor people."[3]

Prior to World War II, the Texas economy was rarely described as booming. But since World War II, it frequently has been so described. Texas became urban and industrial in the 1940s and 1950s. Texas oil fueled the allied war machine, refineries and petrochemical plants sprang up along the Gulf coast, and the aerospace industry and other major defense contractors clustered in the Dallas-Fort Worth Metroplex. Texas cities continued to grow in the 1960s and in the 1970s and Exxon, Shell, and Gulf all moved their corporate headquarters to Texas. Demographically, migration to Texas and the broader sunbelt South and Southwest from the rust belt of New England and the Midwest picked up speed. Population and job growth went hand in hand. Texas "became the nation's strongest state economy for much of the 1960s and 1970s."[4]

As we shall see below, Texas led the South and Southwest in its post-World War II build-out. The formula for attracting new businesses to the region, once air conditioning was in place, was well known. Numan V. Bartley's important study, *The New South: 1945–1980*, reported that, "In a 1975 study of the 'business climate' of American states, that equated 'excellence' with 'low taxes, low levels of public assistance, restrictive labor legislation, and a low level of spending and debt'" Texas was placed number one.[5] For Texas, this meant steady as she goes. Champagne and Harpham noted that by the mid-1980s, Texas had "repeatedly been identified as offering either the best or second best 'business climate' (behind Florida) in the nation."[6] Texas's selling points were: (1) a mild climate, in the sunbelt, centrally located in the U.S.; (2) a low cost-of-living, including cheap land and housing; (3) a growing labor pool, with low wages, limited benefits, and weak unions; (4) small government, low taxes, thin social services, and light regulation.

Texans have been showered for decades with assurances of how well their state is doing in terms of opportunity, jobs, and wealth creation. The Texas economy is often described as hitting on all cylinders, creating widespread opportunity and great wealth. The economic collapse of the late 1980s and early 1990s halted and even reversed these developments and the bursting of the tech bubble in 2000, the recession that followed the 9/11 attacks, and the Great Recession of 2008–2009 hit Texas and the nation hard. As a result, while the boomer description of the Texas economy often is accurate, it is just as accurate to say that the Texas economy has performed no better than the national economy since 1950. The Texas economy has grown, jobs have been created, and some Texans have become wealthy. But growth since 1950 has occurred at about the national average, so Texas barely has advanced in the ranking of American states by income and wealth.

Moreover, Texas boosterism must always be held up to the mirror of demography.[7] The key question about the Texas economy is always—for whom is it great, for whom good, and for whom not so good. The answer today, as it has been throughout the state's history, is it's great for Anglo elites, good for Anglos in general, and not so good for most others.[8] Hence, Anglos praise the Texas economy because they generally do well, or at least better, in it, while others offer less praise because they do less well.

In this chapter, we systematically explore how Texas and Texans have fared economically in relation to the nation, to other states, and to each other. First, we confirm that Texas has been a prolific job creation machine. Second, we demonstrate that as far back as good data goes Texas workers have been more productive but less well paid than the average American worker. Third, we look at two general measures of economic well-being: per capita personal income and median family income. We find that Texas has lagged the national average since records have been kept and that the state's standing has not improved much since 1950. On key issues of wealth and poverty we look closely at differences by race and ethnicity. Fourth, we compare the unemployment rate and poverty rate in Texas to the national rates to see how poorer Texans are doing. We find that the unemployment rate in Texas is above the national rate about half the time and below about half the time while the poverty rate is always significantly above the national rate. Finally, we ask whether the gap between rich and poor in Texas is greater or smaller than the gap for the nation and the other states. We find that it is greater than the average for the nation and for about forty of the fifty states and is increasing. The fundamental dilemma highlighted in this chapter is that although Texas workers are more productive than American workers in general, they receive less pay for their labor and they face a thinner social safety net when they stumble. That is—bluntly—what it means to be a "business-friendly" state.

Job Creation in Texas

In Chapter 3 we saw that the Texas population has been increasing faster than the national rate of population growth since the state's inception. Population growth means more customers and rising demand for the state's businesses and those businesses are then required to hire more workers. For example, looking back just to 1940, the U.S. has increased jobs at a rate of 20.8 percent per decade, while Texas has increased jobs at a rate of 35.2 percent per decade. As in Chapter 3, we can also compare Texas to other large, fast-growing sunbelt states over this same period. Since 1940, California has increased jobs at 31.8 percent per decade, a bit slower than Texas, while Florida has increased jobs at an astounding 46.5 percent per decade (Table 4.1). If we look just at the last two decades, 1990–2011, Texas outperformed the U.S. and both Florida and California in job growth, convincingly so in the last decade. Since 2000, Texas employment has expanded by 11.6 percent, while Florida's grew by just 4 percent, the U.S. declined by .2, and California declined by -1.6 percent. Clearly, Texas has created more jobs than any other state over the past two decades and Texas politicians have celebrated this fact endlessly. In this instance, Texas leaders are right to note that most states would love to have both the population growth and the job growth that Texas has enjoyed throughout its history.

Californians have been, by turns, defensive and scornful. John Ellwood, a public policy professor at Berkeley (that would be the University of California, Berkeley), recently sniffed that the Texas "model is a low-wage economy with greater income inequality."[9] As we shall see, Professor Ellwood's characterization of the Texas economy is accurate, though perhaps incomplete. Evidence for the accuracy of the characterization comes from the Corporation for Enterprise Development, a Washington based non-profit that has been compiling a "Development Report Card for the States" since 1987. The report card compares the states on sixty-seven measures of their "business climate" and assigns rankings on each measure and an overall grade—in Texas's

Table 4.1 Job Growth by Decade in the U.S., Texas, and Selected States, 1940–2011

	U.S.	Texas	California	Florida
1940–49	35.3	63.5	59.9	54.8
1950–59	17.9	31.0	48.8	80.7
1960–69	29.9	41.6	41.6	56.7
1970–79	26.7	54.5	39.1	57.1
1980–89	19.3	16.9	24.3	47.1
1990–99	17.8	29.0	12.0	26.8
2000–09	-1.0	9.6	-2.8	2.6
2010–11	1.2	2.0	1.2	1.4
Average	20.8	35.2	31.8	46.5

Source: Bureau of Labor Statistics, Current Employment Statistics Survey, "Employment, Hours, and Earnings." See also U.S. Census, Statistical Abstract of the United States, various years, Labor Force, Employment, and Earnings, "Employees in Nonfarm Establishments, by States."

case, a D. The measure of most relevance here is the proportion of each state's jobs that are low-income jobs, defined as jobs that don't pay enough to keep a family of four above the federal poverty rate (about $22,314). Nationally, 21.0 percent of workers are low-wage, California ranked 17th at 17.2 percent, Florida ranked 38th at 25.8 percent, and Texas ranked 42nd at 27.8 percent.[10] In addition, more Texans work for wages at or below the federal minimum wage than in most other states. In 2010, Texas tied with Mississippi for the state having the highest proportion of minimum wage workers (9.5 percent) earning at or below the federal minimum of $7.25 an hour. Texas had more minimum wage workers, 550,000, than California, Florida, and Illinois combined. In 2013, Texas had the sixth highest percentage of minimum wage workers.[11] What explains the fact that though the Texas economy creates a great many jobs, many of them are low-wage jobs that will not support a family?

Worker Productivity in Texas

Worker productivity, usually thought of as the value created by a worker over some period of time, such as a year, is the basis of wealth creation and so a subject of consistent interest. Some early visitors and immigrants to Texas were quite scathing in their assessments of Texas workers, while others were highly laudatory. William Ransom Hogan's history of *The Texas Republic* presents an entertaining mix of both views. Not surprisingly, Europeans and New Englanders took a dim view of the work habits of early Texans. Hogan reports that, "In 1834 a young German, George Willich, Jr., wrote: 'So great is the indolence of the present inhabitants, that they hate everything that causes the least work like death, and they know no greater happiness than eating, drinking brandy, and sleeping.'" Similarly, "Francis L. Trask, a school teacher from Massachusetts, commented in a letter to her father written in the following summer: 'The white people if ever so poor, consider it degrading to work, and would rather stay at home in their dirt, and rags, than to do the first days work for another—this is one of the evils of slavery.'"[12] Others, arriving from the South, took a more positive view of Texan energy, entrepreneurship, and general work habits:

> As one man wrote shortly after his arrival in 1839: "This country is full of enterprising and persevering people. The timid and lazy generally return to the States." In 1846 a visitor found an economic basis for Texas independence, and concluded that "the Texans are the most independent people under the whole canopy of heaven the wealthy of the old states not excepted."[13]

On one reading, slavery made whites, rich and poor, unwilling to work and certainly unwilling to work for wages, while on another reading this reluctance was simply an admirable Texan independence. In any event, modern Texas workers, though most do work for others, are among the most productive workers in the nation.

For more than half a century, we have had good data comparing Texas workers to American workers in general. Worker productivity is calculated by dividing Gross Domestic Product (GDP), the value of goods and services produced in a year, by the number of workers required to produce them. This gives the value created by the average worker annually and this can be done both for Texas workers and for U.S. workers. Then the value created by the average Texas worker is divided into the value created by the average U.S. workers and that gives the value created by Texas workers as a percentage of the value created by U.S. workers. The top line in Figure 4.1 shows quite clearly that, except for a brief period in the mid-1960s, Texas workers have created more value annually than have U.S. workers in general. For example, by the late 1970s, Texas workers were producing 10 percent more value than their counterparts nationally. In the early 1980s, Texas productivity peaked at 20 percent more than the national average, and, after a steep decline in the late 1980s, has stayed modestly above the national average since.

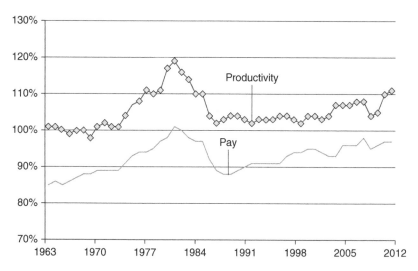

Figure 4.1 Worker Productivity and Worker Pay: Comparing the U.S. and Texas, 1963–2012.

Source: Productivity figures come from B-1. Employees on Nonfarm Payrolls, 1959 to date, ftp://ftp.bls.gov/pub/suppl/empsit.ceseeb1.txt; Gross Domestic Product by State, http://www.bea.gov/regional/gsp/ Pay figures come from U.S. Bureau of Economic Analysis, SA1–3–Per Capita Personal Income by States, 1929–2012, http://www.bea.gov/regional/spi/drill.cfm.

This simple chart paints an impressive picture of the productivity of Texas workers and the vibrancy of the Texas economy. It also suggests the outsized impact that the energy industry historically has had on the broader state economy. While the Texas economy was generally strong in the 1960s and early 1970s, Texas workers were just as productive as U.S. workers, sometimes a bit more productive and sometimes a bit less. The spike in oil prices produced by the Arab oil boycott in the early 1970s and the fall of the Shah of Iran in the late 1970s brought great wealth to Texas. High oil prices brought increased employment in the oil patch, though the value of Texas oil grew more rapidly than employment in the oil industry, so worker productivity (value created per year) spiked to 120 percent of U.S. worker productivity in 1980 and held above 110 percent from 1976 through 1985. Even after the price of oil peaked and started down, Texas worker productivity stabilized and held above the national average for the next two decades, averaging about 103 percent of the U.S. average, with a modest uptick from 2002 to 2008. The Great Recession of late 2008 and 2009 impacted Texas worker productivity because state GDP fell faster than employment, but the recovery after 2010 is clearly seen in Figure 4.1.

The lower line in Figure 4.1 presents Texas worker pay as a percentage of U.S. worker pay and is calculated from data provided by the U.S. Bureau of Economic Analysis. Obviously, the two lines track each other very closely, they rise and fall together, though we do see a couple of periods in which pay seems to rise toward productivity. The 1960s began with worker productivity a little over 100 percent of the U.S. average but pay only about 85 percent of the national average. By the early 1970s, productivity had remained pretty stable while worker pay had risen to almost 90 percent of the national average. As oil prices rose in the 1970s, both productivity and pay rose but the gap opened back up to about 15 percentage points. For example, in 1977 and 1978, Texas worker productivity was 110 percent of the national average while pay was 95 percent of the national average. In the early 1980s, the only time in this five decade period that Texas worker pay surpassed the national average, worker productivity reached 120 percent of the national average. The gap between productivity and pay remained at 12 to 15 points from the mid-1980s through the mid-1990s as the price of oil fell, property values fell, and the Texas banking and savings and loan industries collapsed. Texas did not restore its economic momentum until the mid-1990s. During the early 2000s, Texas worker productivity and pay trended up with only 8 to 10 percentage points between them. The 2008–2009 recession, in which Texas worker productivity turned down while pay held up, brought productivity and pay as close together, just five to seven points apart, as they had ever been, but as the recovery took hold in 2010 the gap opened to its traditional 12 to 15 points.

Now, what about that gap? After all, it represents money on the table and, inevitably, someone will claim it. Texas workers consistently produce value at a rate above the national average but draw pay at a rate consistently below the national average. Traditionally, the argument has been made that Texas has a cost-of-living about 10 percent below the national average, so Texas workers making 90 percent or more of average U.S. pay actually have the same or greater purchasing power than the average U.S. worker. This is true, of course, but it is true for both employers and employees: Texas has a low cost-of-living, but it also has a low cost-of-doing-business, low wages, cheap land, low taxes, light regulation. So what about that gap? It represents money on the table—but not for long as business sweeps it up. As it turns out, that—again—is what it means to be a "business-friendly" state.

Personal Income in Texas

The earliest reports on personal income in Texas suggest that money income was uncommon. Pioneer Noah Smithwick reported that when he arrived in 1827, "Money was as scarce as bread. . . . Pelts of any kind passed current and constituted the principal medium of exchange.[14] The Englishman William Bollaert reports that money was so scarce in 1843 that barter, "Cotton for sugar and coffee, and bacon for boots—corn for calomel quinine . . . beef for brandy" was the norm.[15] Within a few years a money economy emerged and some Texans were able to take their leisure. Wilhelm Steinert, writing in 1849, reported that, "Every American who can afford it keeps slaves and does no work at all. The women likewise only work if they cannot afford a slave woman. . . . As a rule, women then sit in their rocking chairs and smoke their pipes, or at most embroider a bedspread." Most Texans, of course, did not have slaves and had to work very hard, both men and women. Steinert reports that Texans who worked for others received modest pay: "Wages for day laborers are 50 cents on the average. A farmhand gets $10 to $15 per month plus board. . . . Girls get $4 to $8 per month."[16] The journalist Frederick Law Olmsted generally confirmed Steinert's numbers, writing in 1854 that, "Journeymen (late emigrants and rough hands) informed me that they were paid wages, $15 a month and upward, and found. Farm-laborers, $8 to $15, and found. Domestics (females), $5 to $8."[17]

By far the most thorough discussion of wealth-holding in antebellum Texas comes from Randolph B. Campbell and Richard G. Lowe and is entitled *Wealth and Power in Antebellum Texas*. They report that more than 75 percent of Texans in 1850 were directly involved in agriculture, of whom one-third were slave-owners and two-thirds were not and worked their own land. Slave-owners controlled between 60 percent and 70 percent of improved lands and produced about 90 percent of the valuable cotton crop. Finally, they report that slave-owners held ten times the net wealth of non-slave-owners.[18]

The outcome of the Civil War, obviously, brought great change. While Texas remained overwhelmingly agricultural, slavery was abolished and a new equilibrium in the labor market was slow in coming. Eventually, southern elites reestablished their control of agricultural wages, for both blacks and whites, and a new equilibrium emerged in which "the South was a low-wage region in a high-wage country." Gavin Wright explained in his classic *Old South, New South* that:

> Southern regional per capita income, though it stood at a level barely half of the U.S. average in 1880, nonetheless grew at about the national rate between 1880 and 1900, and faster than the national rate between 1900 and 1920. . . . But . . . the chaotic state of international trade stymied cotton demand . . . between 1920 and 1930. As a result, even before the Great Depression, the South lost virtually all of the relative income gains achieved by 1920.[19]

Texas was the wealthiest southern state, but in 1929 per capita income in Texas was only $474 annually, just 68 percent of the U.S. average.

From 1929 forward we have excellent annual data on Per Capita Personal Income (PCPI) for the United States and for the individual states. PCPI is a widely used general measure of comparative wealth and well-being which is derived by dividing total personal income by total population. Personal income includes all earned income including wages, self-employment income, interest, dividends, rent, social security, and other transfer payments.

The data in Figure 4.2 show that Texas has made real advances against U.S. PCPI, but they also show that most of those advances were made during the 1930s and 1940s. Texas survived the Great Depression of the 1930s better than most states, thanks to its dependence on agriculture and natural resources, as opposed to industry and finance, which were harder hit. Nonetheless, Texas agriculture and oil both suffered. The price of cotton, Texas's leading cash crop, dropped from 29 cents a pound to 6 cents from 1932 through mid-1933 before production limits produced a slow rebound in price. The oil industry, always boom and bust, gyrated wildly during the 1930s. "Dad" Joiner brought in the "Daisy Bradford 3" well in October 1930 to open up the great East Texas oil field. Within a matter of months the increased supply had driven the price from $1.30 to 10 cents a barrel in 1931 and, briefly, to 4 cents in 1933. Texas Governor Ross Sterling intervened, empowering the Texas Railroad Commission (TRC) to set production limits designed to bring supply back into balance with demand, and sending in the National Guard and Texas Rangers to shut down wells not abiding by the limits.[20] As agricultural and oil markets stabilized, Texas recovered somewhat faster than the rest of the nation.[21]

Texans are generally loath to admit that federal government programs and spending played a major role in the state's economic growth, but they certainly did in the 1930s and 1940s when Texas made most of its going against the national per capita income averages. Though the New Deal is most closely identified with President Franklin Roosevelt, Texans were deeply involved, especially during the early and mid-1930s. John Nance Garner of Uvalde was FDR's vice president, Sam Rayburn of Bonham was House Majority Leader, and Jesse Jones, a prominent Houston banker, was named by Roosevelt to head the powerful Reconstruction Finance Corporation (RFC). At the depth of the Depression, the RFC acted as a government bank to capitalize and resell bankrupt businesses, especially banks and railroads, fund relief programs such as the Works Progress Administration, and loan money to states to use in battling the Depression. Jones paid particular attention to Texas: "he turned on the spigot of federal funds from 1932 to 1945, and that infusion of capital transformed the state from a rural agrarian to an urban industrial society."[22] Texans benefited not just from federal relief projects but from dams and water projects, roads, and rural electrification.

In the 1940s, Texas was buoyed by war spending, which fueled both urbanization and industrialization. The wartime boom transformed a rural economy based on agriculture, ranching, and oil into an urban economy based not only on oil and natural gas, but also on energy services, petrochemicals, aerospace industries, and manufacturing in general. Texas historian David McComb noted that, "By 1945 the federal government had built thirty-five air fields, twelve army training camps, five naval

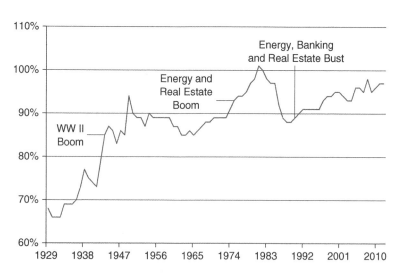

Figure 4.2 Texas Per Capita Personal Income as a Percent of U.S. Per Capita Personal Income, 1929–2012.

Source: U.S. Bureau of Economic Analysis, SA1–3–Per Capita Personal Income by States, 1929–2012, http://www.bea.gov/regional/spi/drill.cfm.

air stations, and eight hospitals—more than any other state." Moreover, "During the conflict government and business invested $600 million in petrochemical plants in the Houston area and added $300 million immediately thereafter. . . . What emerged in a 'golden triangle' of Houston to Freeport to Port Arthur-Orange was one of the . . . major petrochemical complexes in the nation."[23] Texas benefited greatly from the move from agriculture to the higher value added activities of manufacturing. Per capita personal income in Texas rose from 66 percent of the national average in 1930 to 74 percent in 1940. In fact, in two remarkable years, 1941 to 1943, Texas PCPI rose twelve points, from 73 percent of U.S. PCPI to 85 percent, before peaking at 94 percent of U.S. PCPI in 1949.

Texas wanted federal funds and the economic advances that they fueled, but it wanted them on Texas terms. As a result, public policymaking during the Depression and war years was a tug-of-war between national and state officials. Federal policies in regard to race, wages, social security, unemployment compensation, poor relief, and social welfare were all designed to challenge the traditional low-wage economy of the South. Despite the obvious need of the South, the nation's poorest region, by 1937 southern elites, including those in Texas, were in revolt against the New Deal.[24] The South's representatives in Congress sought to limit the New Deal's impact on southern race relations by, for example, excluding farmers and domestics from social security and unemployment compensation. Southern congressmen battled, but ultimately failed to stop, the 1938 Fair Labor Standards Act setting minimum wages and hours and limiting child labor.

As the southern support that Roosevelt had enjoyed during the early New Deal faded, he made a major push to explain to the South the benefits of a higher wage structure for the region. In June 1938, President Roosevelt assembled an expert panel charged to produce a "Report on the Economic Conditions of the South." The report was delivered to the president in July, declaring that, "Ever since the War between the States the South has been the poorest section of the Nation. The richest state in the South ranks lower in per capita income than the poorest state outside the region." The report also said, quite explicitly, that, "Differences in cost-of-living . . . are not great enough to justify the differentials in wages that exist."[25]

President Roosevelt barn-stormed West Texas in July, 1938, to defend the report and to campaign for liberal candidates in the upcoming midterm elections. In Fort Worth, Roosevelt tried to convince Texas elites of the merits of the Fair Labor Standards Act or minimum wage bill, saying "You need more industries in Texas, but I know you know the importance of not trying to get industries by the route of cheap wages for industrial workers."[26] Texas political and economic leaders were, of course, unmoved as low wages were precisely how they intended to attract new jobs and industries.

"By the end of 1947 a majority of the southern states—seven of the thirteen—had passed open shop laws. . . . By prohibiting union shops, the right-to-work states of Arkansas, Florida, Georgia, North Carolina, Tennessee, Texas, and Virginia" sought to preserve the region's traditional low-wage economy.[27] In 1950, as the nation recovered from the post-World War II economic slump, the South was on the move and Texas was the wealthiest of the southern states. Yet, for southern elites, the high wages required by the federal government remained a threat to the low wage, small government, low tax, thin social service model that had been the basis for their competitiveness. The rapid wage growth of the late 1930s and 1940s ended. For the next six decades and more, Texas averaged around 90 percent of U.S. PCPI, though it made two more runs at the national average, one in the early 1980s and another after 2005.[28]

The per capita income of Texans increased steadily after 1950, but so did income in the other states, so the ranking of Texas among the states did not change much. Texas was the highest-ranking southern state in per capita income in 1950, at 31st, while Florida ranked 34th and Virginia 37th. Louisiana, Georgia, Tennessee, and North Carolina followed at 41st through 44th, and the remaining southern states, Alabama, South Carolina, Arkansas, and Mississippi, held down the last four spots at 46th through 49th (D.C. is included but Alaska and Hawaii are not yet states). By 1962, both Florida and Virginia had surpassed Texas and would never fall behind again except very briefly in the oil boom of the early 1980s. Georgia surpassed Texas in 1987 and both North Carolina and Tennessee surpassed Texas in the mid-1990s before all three fell back in the late 1990s.

Between 1950 and 2012, Texas improved its ranking on per capita income, but five other southern states improved their rankings as much or more and several southern states improved considerably more. Texas moved up six places to 25th, while Florida moved up seven places to 27th, Oklahoma and Tennessee moved up seven, to 32nd and 34th respectively, Louisiana moved up twelve to 29th, and Virginia soared twenty-nine places to 8th.[29] Alabama, South Carolina, Arkansas, and Mississippi continued to hold down spaces in the bottom ten as they had a half century earlier. Texas remained below the national average for per capita income throughout the twentieth century and into the twenty-first century, except briefly in the early 1980s.

Figure 4.3 provides a comparison of PCPI for the U.S. and Texas between 1970 and 2012. Here we compare PCPI for the U.S. with that for Texas and later for several other states to get a more nuanced view of how Texans fared compared to other Americans. The answer as we shall see, unfortunately, is not so well: "The myth of the wealthy Texan to the contrary, Texas traditionally has lagged behind the U.S. average in per capita income."[30] The data show that, with the exception of a very brief period in the early 1980s, Texas PCPI has always tracked below the national average. It also shows once again that the progress that Texas made from the 1950s

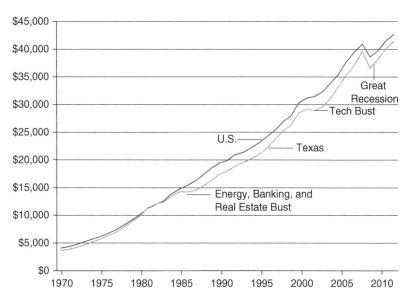

Figure 4.3 Per Per Capita Personal Income: Comparing the U.S. and Texas, 1970–2012.

Source: U.S. Bureau of Economic Analysis, SA1–3–Per Capita Personal Income by States, 1929–2012, http://www.bea.gov/regional/spi/drill.cfm.

through the early 1980s was lost in the devastating collapse of oil prices, property values, and the subsequent savings and loan debacle and banking crisis in the mid- to late 1980s.

During the 1970s and early 1980s, Texans regarded their economy as recession-proof. Agriculture and energy were thought to provide products with steadily rising markets. The oil boom began with the Arab oil embargo of 1973 and was fueled by shortages that followed the Shah of Iran's fall. These shortages drove oil prices from $3.50 a barrel to $35 by the early 1980s. The increase in oil and gas prices spurred domestic exploration and production and fueled a real-estate boom that made Texas one of the most rapidly growing states in the nation. While many Americans, particularly in the Northeast and Midwest, were hard pressed by rising energy prices, Texans reveled in their rising prosperity. Texas hats and boots were increasingly visible in the nation's airports and money centers, while back home "Drive 80 mph, Freeze a Yankee" bumper stickers became common. More importantly, the impression grew that the interests of the oil patch and of the nation were in conflict and Texans were unconcerned.[31]

Interestingly, good times, especially when not enjoyed elsewhere in the country, trigger a deep sense of superiority in Anglo Texans that grates on other Americans. Two generations earlier, in the classic Texas novel and movie *Giant*, this theme of Texas interests in conflict with broader

American interests is clear. Leslie Lynnton Benedict, played by Elizabeth Taylor in the movie, a Virginia socialite recently married to Texas rancher, Jordan "Bick" Benedict, played by Rock Hudson, has fled the dust and bluster of Texas for her Virginia family home. Bick has followed to win her back to the marriage and to Texas. As they try to get comfortable with each other again, Leslie notes, "Texas is booming. The rest of the country is flat. Is that good?" Bick's response is classic Texas bombast. He says, "Only good enough to make us the richest state in the whole country. We're a country within a country." Leslie, subject to yet another bathe of Texas braggadocio, cries "Again!" To which Bick responds, "Oil and beef and cotton. You can't stop it and you can't top it."[32] Maybe not, but two points come to mind. First, Bick's claim that Texas is or is on its way to becoming the richest state in the nation is just wrong—though it may feel true to Anglo elites. Second, good times come and good times go and when they go Texas and Texans can fall hard. Though eager to claim credit for good times, Texans almost always see hard times as fathered elsewhere, usually in Washington.

As the 1980s opened, "projections called for Texas, California, and Florida to be the three fastest-growing states in the country over the next several decades."[33] While this broad projection generally held, the mid-1980s proved to be extremely challenging for Texas. Texas prosperity in the 1970s and early 1980s hinged on the Arab oil embargo and on Saudi Arabia's willingness to limit its production to prop up the world price. Oil prices rose from $3 a barrel in 1970 to $21 in 1980. After peaking at $37 in 1981 it fell to $27 a barrel in late 1985. In early 1986, Saudi Arabia flooded the world oil market, driving the price below $10, to highlight to other producers the cost of global oil surpluses.[34] Oil exploration, services, and distribution ground to a halt and unemployment in Texas spiked to 10.3 percent by mid-year. As the Texas economy reeled under the collapse of oil prices, Congress passed the Tax Reform Act of 1986, one provision of which removed key tax benefits to investing in real estate. Commercial property values in Texas dropped by 30 to 40 percent.

The Texas Legislature tried to respond to the pressure that the collapsing energy and real-estate markets placed on the Texas economy by lifting long-standing restrictions on Texas financial institutions. The Texas Constitution of 1876 mandated community banking, precluding both branch banking (where one bank could have multiple bank locations or branches) and interstate banking (where a bank could operate in multiple states). Though the prohibition on branch banking was loosened in 1956 and 1970 to permit bank holding companies, the constraints on Texas banks were still real. As the Texas economy buckled in 1986, the legislature hurriedly approved both branch banking and interstate banking in the hopes of attracting money into the state. It worked, after a fashion. Texas's weakened banks were forced, one by one, to seek outside buyers. By the end of the decade, nine of Texas's ten largest banks had failed or been bought by out-of-state banks. In fact, 506 banks and 225 savings and loans failed in Texas between 1983 and 1992, far more than failed in any other state.

Bankers, financial regulators, and the Texas business community understood the gravity of what had happened, though they differed as to why it had happened and whether Texans were in any way to blame. Ben Love of Houston's Texas Commerce Bank (TCB) and Jody Grant of Fort Worth's Texas American Bank (TAB) both admitted that Texas bankers were overextended and that wrongdoing had been common in the state's savings and loan institutions, but they ultimately blamed Texas politicians and U.S. financial regulators for not easing the banks through the crisis. Ben Love lobbied the Texas Legislature to pass both branch banking and interstate banking for more than a decade, 1974 to 1986, to no avail.[35] As the Texas banks came under increasing pressure in late 1986, Jody Grant dispatched Texas American Bank's Bayard H. Friedman to seek help from Governor Bill Clements. Friedman reported that "the governor said that the banks were broke, they deserved to be broke, and he wasn't going to do a damn thing to help them." Grant describes the governor's "attitude as shocking and appalling: it was incomprehensible that the chief executive of the state had so little understanding of the economic fallout that would result from the bank's crippled status."[36] The governor later changed his mind and agreed to work with Texas banks, but it was too late.

Texas bankers complained most bitterly that the Federal Reserve, the Federal Deposit Insurance Corporation (FDIC), and the Comptroller of the Currency were biased against Texas banks. Bankers pleaded for forbearance from federal regulators to give them time to recapitalize their banks. Regulators listened but concluded that undercapitalized banks simply needed to be liquidated, by seizure or sale, before incurring further losses. Texas bankers were devastated and blamed the regulators for being too harsh. Al Casey of Dallas's First Republic Bank thought the FDIC should have accepted management's recapitalization plan. When the FDIC refused and forced the sale of the bank, Casey declared in a later deposition that he felt "a sense at the time of betrayal toward the FDIC."[37] Love writes that "In 1986, the Office of the Comptroller of the Currency regulators were transparently biased against Texas. In fact, the OCC examiners repeatedly demonstrated an anti-Texas bias, emphasizing that the Texas economy was faring worse than the major Texas banks believed."[38]

They were right, Bill Black of the Federal Home Loan Bank Board, which oversaw the savings and loan industry, said "Texas was at the top of the charts" in profitability in the early 1980s, "because more of its savings and loans engaged in accounting fraud than anywhere else. . . . Its state regulatory system was the worst in the nation and that's saying something."[39] Texas saw their small government, laissez-faire, regulatory system as advancing growth and entrepreneurship. Federal regulators like Black saw it as inviting fraud.

Ben Love described the shock felt among Texans when the Texas myth crumbled along with the energy and property markets. Love described a conversation he had with Bill Taylor, then chief-of-staff of the Federal Reserve Bank in Washington. Love thought the Texas banks might have weathered the storm if the regulators had been more flexible. Once Love had made his case, he reports that Bill Taylor said, "Ben, you Texans always think what you have in Texas is worth one hell of a lot more than any of the rest of us do." Taylor then went on to restate Fed policy, which we came to know again recently as "too big to fail." In the 1980s, the Texas banks were not too big to fail. Taylor told Love:

> The ten largest banks in this nation are not going to fail. As an element of federal government policy, the Federal Reserve will not let them fail. That's the way it is. But I will tell you one other thing: If we think it is proper, we *will* let any Texas bank fail because not one Texas bank is among the ten largest banks in the nation.[40]

Other bankers also looked somewhat askance at their Texas colleagues. Love reports a conversation with Bill Brown, head of the First National Bank of Boston, as Brown's bank fell under the gaze of the regulators. Brown said, "You know, Ben, I've heard you talk about how unfair the regulators were to Texas banks. I'm going to tell you, we're good friends, but I tended to dismiss what you were saying, thinking, Well, Ben's a Texan, and that's the way Texans are."[41] Love eventually brokered the sale of TCB to Chemical Bank of New York.

As the storm swept over Texas, financial analysts and observers recognized that the landscape would be different once it passed. The *Wall Street Journal* reported on December 17, 1986, that the demise of the Texas banks,

> brought an end to the era in which Texas controlled its own capital and, ultimately, its own economic destiny. Francis Tuggle, dean of the graduate business school at Rice, agreed. "There is a strong symbolic message in this," he said. "The notion of the Republic of Texas and the idea that we can do everything all by ourselves have gone by the boards, . . . Given the economics in the state, it's inevitable that we just can't go it alone any longer."[42]

Floyd Norris, the highly respected financial writer for the *New York Times*, saw the results of the Texas banking crash far differently than the Texas participants. Rather than adopting the local view—they hate us because we're Texans—Norris saw the federal government playing a more positive role that enabled Texas to stabilize rather quickly. Norris confirmed that, "The United States let the Texas banking industry collapse, with out-of-state banks picking up the pieces. . . . At the time, there was handwringing about how Texas could function without banks. Just fine, it turned out." Though Texas pride was dented by the loss of its big banks, banking services never missed a beat and "the national deposit insurance fund suffered substantial losses" in cleaning up the balance sheets of Texas banks so they could be sold. Though few Texas bankers would agree, Norris concluded that, "Texas greatly benefited from the fact that the American economy was integrated, with a central government that could and would help out."[43] Robert Bryce, author of *Cronies*, reported that federal bailout funds flowed to Texas totaling $4,775 per capita, while New Jersey citizens lost $1,047 per capita.[44] New Jersians apparently are not very entrepreneurial.

While the savings and loan scandal had a national impact, Texas was its epicenter and its impact in Texas was much more severe than it was nationally. Notice that the upward arc of the U.S. line in Figure 4.3 was unbroken through the late 1980s while the Texas line went sideways between 1985 and 1987. During those lost years Texas went from a PCPI at 100 percent of the national average in 1982 to just 88 percent in 1988 and 1989. Notice also that the national recession of 2001–2002 slowed growth of PCPI for both Texas and the U.S., but Texas was harder hit than the nation. Texas PCPI actually dropped from 2001 to 2002, while national PCPI growth merely slowed. By 2012 Texas had clawed its way back to 97 percent of U.S. PCPI.

And one must also say that others, just a few, have done better. Figure 4.4, adding Mississippi, Georgia, Florida, and Virginia to the U.S. and Texas provides a broader comparison. Mississippi tracks well below the U.S. PCPI and below the other four states. Mississippi is and has long been the poorest state in the union. But Texas, Georgia, Florida, and Virginia have varied interestingly around the national average. In 1950 Texas was the wealthiest of the five states, though all remained well below the national average. The U.S. PCPI in 1950 was $1,504, Texas was $1,360, Florida was $1,300, Virginia was $1,248, Georgia was $1,059, and Mississippi lagged at $765.

By 1980, as shown in Figure 4.4, Mississippi and Georgia still lagged, at $7,007 and $8,420 respectively, but the other three states were tightly clustered near the national average of $10,114: Texas at $9,880, Florida at $9,933, and Virginia at $10,144. Both Florida and Virginia had passed Texas, but the margins were tiny and all were within hailing distance of the national average. In 1981 Texas actually jumped ahead of Virginia, Florida, and the national average, though in 1982 Virginia moved back ahead of Texas, in 1983 Florida did likewise, and neither has looked back. When Texas faltered during the savings and loan and property crises of

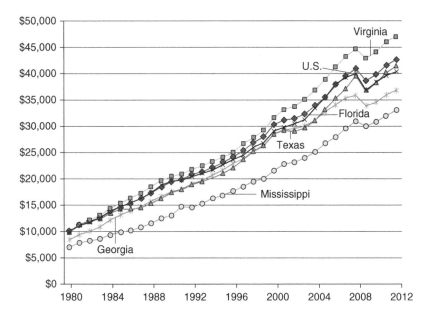

Figure 4.4 Per Capita Personal Income: Comparing the U.S., Texas, and Several Benchmark States, 1980–2012.

Source: U.S. Bureau of Economic Analysis, SA1–3–Per Capita Personal Income by States, 1929–2012, http://www.bea.gov/regional/spi/drill.cfm.

the mid-1980s, Georgia went by Texas for more than a decade, but never by much, while Florida and Virginia opened up significant margins. By 1989, Texas PCPI was $16,312, while Georgia was $16,701, Florida was $18,836, and Virginia was $19,740. Texas overtook Georgia and Florida, but Virginia has continued to move ahead. In 2012, the U.S.'s PCPI was $42,693, Virginia's was $47,082, Texas's was $41,471, Florida's was $40,344, Georgia's was $36,869, and Mississippi's was $33,073.

Median Family Income in Texas

Another way to compare the economic performance of Texas to the nation is in terms of median family income. Median family income, whether for the U.S. or for Texas, is the dollar income above which and below which are half of family incomes. Figure 4.5 compares U.S. and Texas median family income for 1959, 1969, 1979, 1989, 1999, and 2009. Texas has lagged uniformly behind the U.S. median family income at every period, except 1979, which was near the peak of the go-go years just before the crash of the mid-1980s.[45] At every other measurement, Texas ranked between 34th

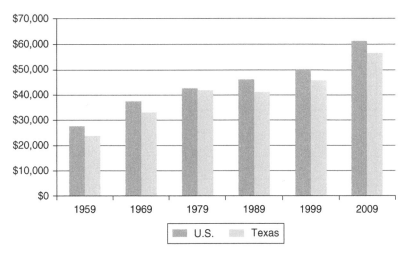

Figure 4.5 Median Family Income: Comparing the U.S. and Texas, 1959–2009.

Source: U.S. Census Bureau, Table S2, Median Family Income by State: 1959, 1969, 1979, 1989, and 1999, www.census.gov/hhes/www/income/histinc/state/ state2.html. 2009 is from U.S. Census Bureau, American FactFinder, GCT1902, Median Family Income, http://factfinder.census.gov/servlet/GCTTable?

and 36th among the fifty states and D.C. Essentially no improvement in Texas's standing among the states in median family income occurred in the half century between 1959 and 2009 (Texas ranked 34th in 2009). Texans got wealthier over this half century, but no faster than did their fellow Americans.

We get an even more sobering view of the distribution of median family income in Texas by looking at race and ethnicity. In the previous chapter, we described Texas as an "Anglo Republic" to highlight the fact that the state was founded and developed by Anglos for Anglos. To the extent that others, Native-Americans, blacks, and Hispanics, were present, they were tolerated only as they provided cheap and willing labor. Today's Texas leaders argue that these unfortunate truths are no longer relevant because all Texans enjoy equal opportunity and, hence, Anglos, blacks, and Hispanics are found throughout the state's social and economic structure—high and low. While it is true that there are wealthy blacks and Hispanics in Texas and that the black and Hispanic middle classes are growing, or were before the Great Recession, it is also true that there have long been stark and stable differences by race and ethnicity in median family income in Texas.

As we see in Figure 4.6, median family income in Texas varies dramatically by race and ethnicity and the gaps are changing only very slowly. The

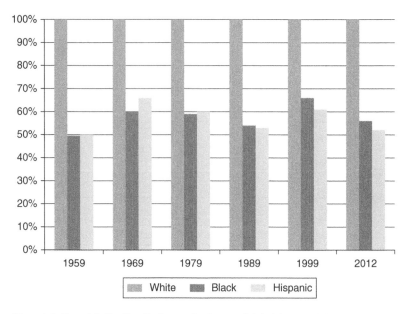

Figure 4.6 Texas Median Family Income by Race and Ethnicity, 1959–Present.

Source: United States Census, 1960, Texas, vol. 45:345; 1970, 45:451; 1980, 45:160; 1990, 45:178; 2000, Texas State Data Center, median family income by race, 2012, American Community Survey, median family income by race.

1960 census, reporting 1959 data, reported that non-white families made just less than half, 49.5 percent, of what white families made. In the 1970 and later censuses, non-whites were broken out in blacks and Hispanics, and in 1980 Asians were added (not reported in Figure 4.6 because the numbers were small). The 1970 census, reporting 1969 data, showed significant progress. Black families made 60 percent of what white families made and Hispanic families made 66 percent. In 1980, blacks slipped back to 59 percent and Hispanics to 60 percent of white family income. In 1990, blacks and Hispanics slipped further back, to 54 and 53 percent respectively, though in 2000, both rose with blacks making 66 percent of what white families made and Hispanics making 61 percent. The "Great Recession" of 2007–2009 knocked Texas minorities back yet again. The latest data, from the Census's 2012 American Community Survey, reported that Texas black families made 56 percent of what white families did and Hispanic families made 52 percent.

While most Texans of all races and ethnicities are better off than they were a half century ago, it is also true that minorities have made little progress against Anglo median family income—they still make about half. Texas blacks and Hispanics have provided a low-wage labor force throughout Texas history and that is changing only very slowly if it is changing at all.

Unemployment and Unemployment Compensation in Texas

One often hears that jobs are plentiful in Texas and that anyone truly wanting to work will find a job. In fact, Texas has had an interesting and even erratic relationship to the U.S. unemployment rate (Figure 4.7). Again, the early 1980s marked an important turning point. From 1970 through 1985 the Texas unemployment rate tracked well below, often between 1 and 2 percent below, the national unemployment rate. The Texas financial crisis of the mid-1980s sent the state's unemployment rate one and a half to two points above the national rate from 1986 through 1989. By the early 1990s, the Texas unemployment rate came down to about one-third to two-thirds of a point above the national rate, where it remained through 2006. The national recession that began in 2007 initially hit the nation harder than it hit Texas. In 2008, Texas was a full point under the national unemployment rate; and since 2009 Texas has been a point or a point and a half below the national rate.

Few events are as disruptive of individual and family life as the loss of a job and paycheck. Many people have enough savings to weather a job loss of modest duration, but few can manage longer-term unemployment.

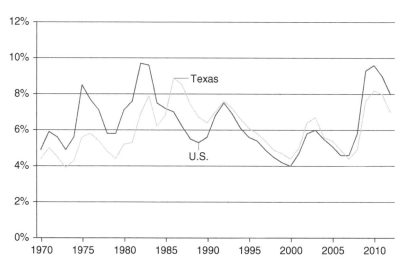

Figure 4.7 Unemployment Rate: Comparing the U.S. and Texas, 1970–2012.

Source: U.S. Bureau of Labor Statistics, Household Data Annual Averages, Table 1, Employment Status of the Civilian Non-institutional Population, 1940–date. Texas data from http://www.bls.gov/lau/staadata.txt.

Unemployment Compensation (UC) is a set of programs designed to assist workers who lose jobs through no fault of their own until they find new employment. But how generous the benefits are and how long they last might influence how hard an unemployed person looks for new work and what job they are willing to accept. Not surprisingly, Texas is a hard place to be unemployed. Texas has one of the stingiest unemployment insurance systems in the nation and Texas politicians are absolutely determined to keep it that way.

Not surprisingly, blacks and Hispanics in Texas are substantially more likely to be unemployed than are Anglos. Over the last three plus decades, the period for which we have good data for unemployment by race and ethnicity, black unemployment rates are usually twice or more Anglo rates, while Hispanic rates usually fall between Anglo and black rates. As Figure 4.8 makes clear, unemployment in Texas goes up and it goes down, but the racial pecking order from earlier periods in Texas history remains fixed.

Unemployment compensation in the U.S. is a joint federal state program with its origins in the New Deal. In fact, the Federal-State Unemployment Compensation Program was part of the Social Security Act of 1935. The federal government sets the general guidelines for UC and levies an unemployment tax through the Internal Revenue Service. The Federal Unemployment Tax Act of 1939 (FUTA) initiated the modern funding system. FUTA imposes a 6.2 percent tax on employers on the first $7,000 in salary paid to each covered worker. The states levy

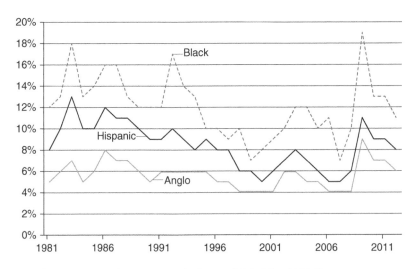

Figure 4.8 Texas Unemployment Rates by Race and Ethnicity, 1981–Present.

Source: Bureau of Labor Statistics, "Employment Status of the Civilian Non-institutional Population in States, by Sex, Race, Hispanic Ethnicity," http://www.bls.gov/lau/#ex14.

their own taxes and they determine eligibility requirements, weekly benefit amounts, and the number of weeks that those judged eligible may draw. If a state program is judged well-funded by the U.S. Secretary of Labor, state employers who are up to date on their state taxes get a 5.4 percent tax credit against their FUTA tax rate. The federal government keeps 0.8 of 1 percent to finance administration of the system, pay half of any extended benefits that might be approved, and to build up a loan fund from which states might borrow.

The Texas unemployment compensation system came in for particular scrutiny as unemployment rose in 2009. President Obama's $787 billion stimulus program, passed by Congress in early 2009, offered states a piece of $7 billion in new money if they would expand eligibility for unemployment compensation to cover various "part-time, low-income, and female workers." Texas's projected share of these monies was $556 million. Texas Governor Rick Perry responded, saying "If this money expands entitlements, we will not accept it. This is exactly how addicts get hooked on drugs."[46] Bill Hammond, head of the powerful Texas Association of Business, echoed the same theme, saying "It's like a drug dealer. The dealer gives you your first hit for free to get you hooked, and then you are addicted and are paying the consequences for a long, long time."[47] Perry ultimately rejected the $556 million, just as he said he would.

Governor Perry's point was that government support, even in difficult times, was simply not part of the Texas model. "People living in Texas are a heck of a lot better off than the vast majority of the other ones. My instinct is they'd whole lot rather have a good-paying job than they would unemployment insurance."[48] Probably so, but what if unemployment is high, as it often is in Texas, good-paying jobs are hard to find, and unemployment compensation is limited when it is available at all? "'This was pretty simple for us. Keep things going like they're going in Texas,' said the governor. . . . 'We can take care of ourselves. And we do not need any more strings from Washington attached to programs.'"[49]

What few appeared to realize during this debate was that Texas has always been very tight-fisted about access to unemployment compensation. The U.S. Department of Labor has good data on percentage of U.S. and Texas unemployed who draw on unemployment compensation, commonly referred to as the recipiency rate, going back to 1976. Between 1976 and 2012, the average recipiency rate for unemployed U.S. workers was 36 percent, while for Texas workers it was 22 percent. As we shall see, the coverage gap between the proportion of U.S. and Texas unemployed workers on unemployment compensation was very steady over this thirty-five-year period. Texas's average ranking among the states over this period—remember there are fifty-three programs—was 48th. Only a few states, and they are the normal suspects, regularly trail Texas.

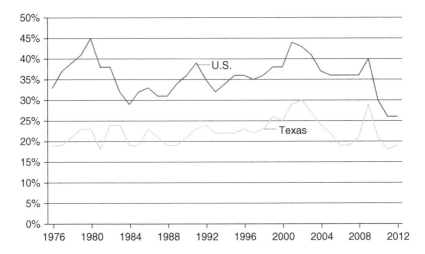

Figure 4.9 Unemployment Compensation Recipiency Rate: Comparing the U.S. and Texas, 1976–Present.

Source: U.S. Department of Labor, http://www.workforcesecurity.doleta.gov/unemploy/Chartbook.a13.asp.

"Texas covers the smallest percentage of unemployed workers of any state, said Don Baylor Jr., an analyst for the Center for Public Policy Priorities, an advocate for low income Texans. Four out of five laid off workers are not eligible for unemployment benefits, he noted."[50] Nationally, 36 percent of persons out of work draw unemployment insurance, while in Texas just 20 percent do. Only South Dakota covers fewer of its unemployed workers.[51] Whether Texas is last or next to last in coverage for the unemployed, or as in 2012 when five states, Florida, Georgia, South Dakota, Tennessee, and Virginia, had fewer unemployed receiving benefits, the idea that Texas does not want its unemployed to get too comfortable is clear. Not surprisingly, it has long been so.

Poverty in Texas

Poverty is another idea that fits uneasily with the Texas myth or the Texas model of small government. Some 20 to 25 percent of Americans lived in poverty until President Lyndon Johnson, following up on initiatives begun by John and Robert Kennedy, initiated a "War on Poverty" in the mid-1960s. By the early 1970s, poverty had dropped to 11 or 12 percent. In the early 1980s, President Ronald Reagan initiated "welfare reform" and poverty rates began to creep up, going to 15.2 percent in 1982 and holding in the 14 to 15 percent range until the late 1990s and around 12 percent thereafter.[52]

Texans experience poverty at a higher rate than do residents of most other states. Between 1980 and 2012, Texas had a higher poverty rate than

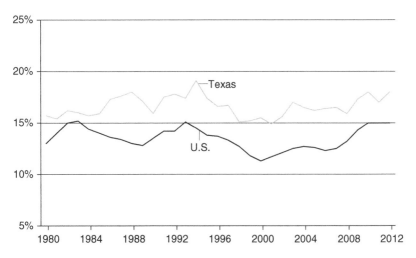

Figure 4.10 Poverty Rate: Comparing the U.S. and Texas, 1980–2012.

Source: For U.S. see, Historical Poverty Tables—People, Table 2, "Poverty Status," http://www.census.gov/hhes/www/poverty/histpov/hstpov2.xls.

For Texas see, Historical Poverty Tables—People, Table 21, "Poverty Rate by State, 1980–2010," http://www.census.gov/hhes/www/poverty/histpov/hstpov21.xls.

the nation every year (Figure 4.8). The Texas poverty rate ran an average of one or two points above the national average between 1980 and 1985 before popping up to four or five points above national average through the end of the decade. Texas poverty rates ran consistently two to four points above the national average throughout the 1990s and the first decade of the twenty-first century. For example, in 2000 the national average was 11.3 percent while Texas was 15.5 percent, and in 2012, the last year for which there is data, the U.S. rate was 15 percent while Texas was 17.6 percent.

In 2012, 4.5 million Texans, up from 4.3 million in 2009, lived in poverty. In percentage terms, Texans in poverty increased from 15.9 percent in 2009 to 17.6 percent in 2012. Texas had the seventh highest poverty rate in the nation in 2012. Among Texans aged 18 and younger the poverty rates were even higher. In 2011, 25.8 percent of young Texans lived in poverty, down from 27 percent in 2010. Among young Texans, the state had the fifth highest poverty rate in the nation.

As with median family income and unemployment, poverty rates among Texas families shown in Figure 4.11 vary dramatically by race and ethnicity. For more than forty years, as long as relevant data has been available, minority family poverty rates in Texas have been two and a half to nearly four times the Anglo rates. For example, in 1969, 12.4 percent of Anglo families in Texas lived in poverty, while more than 30 percent of black and Hispanic families did. In 1979, 1989, and 1999, minority family poverty rates were

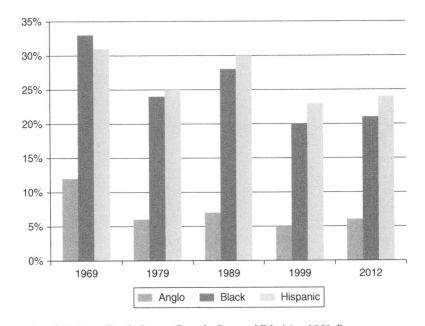

Figure 4.11 Texas Family Poverty Rates by Race and Ethnicity, 1969–Present.

Source: U.S. Census, 1970, General Social and Economic Characteristics, Texas, 45:451; 1980, 45:160; 1990, 45:178; 2000, Texas State Data Center, Tables 28b, 28d, 28h, and 28i; 2012, American Community Survey, American FactFinder, Table S1702.

four times Anglo rates, while in 2012, the latest data available, they fell back to about three and a half times Anglo rates. Again, not much progress here.

Measuring Income Inequality in Texas

The Gini Index is a widely used measure of income inequality. It is used to compare income inequality both between nations and between states within a nation such as the U.S. The Gini Index is a statistic that ranges between zero, when all households have the same income, and one, when a single household has all of the income and the others have none. Obviously, the tails of the range, near zero and near one, are unlikely distributions of income in the real world, so we expect actual measurements nearer the middle of the range. The Gini Index for nations rarely ranges above .65, usually for very poor African countries, like Lesotho and Swaziland, where just a few hold what little wealth there is, or .55 for Latin American countries such as Bolivia, Paraguay, and Guatemala, and .25 in quasi-socialist countries such as Sweden, Norway, Finland, and Germany.

The U.S., as a capitalist country in which competition for advantage is the rule, should have a Gini Index above Sweden but below Paraguay. In fact, that is exactly what we find, but that is not all we find (Figure 4.12). Over

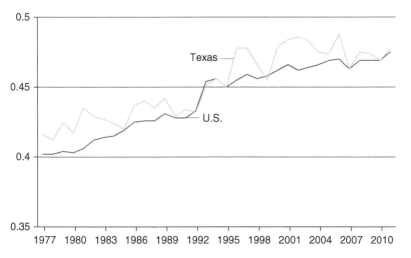

Figure 4.12 Gini Index of Household Income Inequality, 1977–2011.

Source: U.S. Census Bureau, Historical Income Tables—Households, Table H-4, "Gini Ratios for Households," http://www.census.gov/hhes/www.income.histinc/h04.html.

For Texas data see, U.S. Census Bureau, Current Population Survey, 1978 to 2011, Selected Measures of Household Income Distribution, Gini Index.

the past three decades, the Gini Index for the U.S. has steadily risen from .40 to .48 before falling a bit as the recession of 2007–2009 took hold.[53] The Gini Index for Texas is a bit more erratic but virtually always above the U.S. line. The Texas Gini Index was .42 in 1977 and had risen to .49 by 2002. Moreover, Texas's rank among the states has been high and quite steady. It has ranged between 35th and 50th with the overall average position of Texas among the states being 41st. In 2011 Texas ranked 43rd.

Conclusion

In the finest tradition of the Texas way, reports that laud Texas are accepted unquestioningly. The Small Business and Entrepreneurship Council's Business Tax Index 2013 ranked Texas first, followed by South Dakota, Nevada, and Wyoming—Texans smile, South Dakota, Nevada, and Wyoming! These three states together do not have 15 percent of Texas's population or GDP— who's the big dog. The index measured "taxes, government spending, health care mandates, crime rates and regulatory and energy costs. The non-profit advocacy group noted that the top six states have no personal income tax."[54] First, there are only seven states that do not have an income tax, so that single measure seems to be driving the rankings. Second, the Small Business and Entrepreneurship's measures all anticipate low taxes, low spending, minimal public services, and light regulation. They are intensely present-oriented. They do not anticipate, in fact they punish, future planning and investment for education, health and welfare, transportation, and the environment. Good for business today perhaps, but not so good for the state's future.

Also in the finest tradition of the Texas way, ambivalent or negative reports are rejected out of hand, even when they point to problems that we know are quite real. For example, the Marion Kauffman Foundation's "2010 State New Economy Index" placed Texas at 16th on innovation and competitiveness. The study was meant to measure how well states are managing toward an economic future based on education, knowledge, innovation, and entrepreneurship. Scored on twenty-six indicators, Texas ranked in the top ten in manufacturing value added, manufacturing and service exports, entrepreneurial activity, number of fast-growing firms, and number of initial public offerings. Texas ranked much lower, among the bottom ten, on educational preparation of the workforce and attraction of high-tech jobs. Rob Atkinson, who helped prepare the index for the Kauffman Foundation, said "The challenge for Texas is [to] make sure its strategy is driven toward a more knowledge- and innovation-based economy."[55] By 2012, Texas had slipped one spot to 17th.

Texans were either puzzled or offended by the findings. Brad Hancock, head of Texas Christian University's Neeley Enterprise Center, said "I would have thought we would have ranked higher," while others rejected the findings and criticisms outright. Jeremy Brandt, president of the Dallas chapter of the Entrepreneurs' Organization, said "I don't see some of those negatives. Texas and the Dallas-Fort Worth area have a very educated and strong workforce. The Dallas EO chapter is one of the largest in the world."[56] Two points. First, it is almost certain that, as Brandt said, Dallas has one of the biggest EO chapters in the world and that it reflects the broader entrepreneurial culture of Texas. Second, the very dominance of the EO culture may explain the bias toward individualism and small government that leaves Texas schools, colleges, and universities underfunded and underperforming. As we shall see in the next chapter, Texas funding of public schools and resulting test scores rank in the bottom third and Texas has a smaller proportion of its population with a B.A. or better than all but a very few other states.

Though Texans may resist, the telling point made by the Kauffman Foundation report is that the oil fueled industrial and manufacturing growth that pulled Texas out of the economic backwater between the 1940s and 1980s is fading. It is being replaced by an education fueled economy of knowledge, creativity, and experiment. Innovation and entrepreneurship will still be critically important, perhaps even more important than in the past, but Texas hustle, grit, and bluff will not be enough. The days of the Texas wildcatter with a sixth-grade education who struck it rich are gone.

We now turn to education in Texas and ask how we have been doing, both how much we have been investing in students and teachers, and, more importantly, how the students have been doing in comparison with students across the U.S.

Notes

1 Andrew Gelman, *Red State, Blue State, Rich State, Poor State: Why Americans Vote the Way They Do*, Princeton, NJ: Princeton University Press, 2008, pp. 62–63.
2 Joel Kotkin, "Greetings from Recoveryland," *Newsweek*, November 15, 2010, pp. 30–32.
3 Joel Kotkin, "California Suggests Suicide; Texas Asks: Can I Lend You a Knife?" *Forbes*, November 15, 2010. See also Joel Kotkin, "The Gulf Coast Is America's New Economy Powerhouse," *Dallas Morning News*, December, 7, 2012, 1P, 5P.
4 Sean P. Cunningham, *Cowboy Conservatism: Texas and the Rise of the Modern Right*, Lexington, KY: University of Kentucky Press, 2010, p. 240.
5 Numan V. Bartley, *The New South, 1945–1980*, Baton Rouge, LA: Louisiana State University Press, 1995, p. 403.
6 Anthony Champagne and Edward J. Harpham, *Texas at the Crossroads: People, Politics, and Policy*, College Station, TX: Texas A&M University Press, 1987, p. 46.
7 David Montejano, *Anglos and Mexicans in the Making of Texas, 1836–1986*, Austin, TX: University of Texas Press, 1987, p. 183.
8 Wilhelm Steinert, *North America, Particularly Texas in the Year 1849*, Dallas, TX: DeGolyer Library, 2003, p. 113.
9 Evan Halper, "Texas' Finances Not as Rosy as They Seemed," *Los Angeles Times*, February 7, 2011.
10 http://scorecard.assetsandopportunity.org/2014/state/tx
11 Bureau of Labor Statistics, Southwest Information Office, "Minimum Wage Workers in Texas, 2013," http://www.bls.gov/ro6/fax/minwage_tx.htm
12 William Ransom Hogan, *The Texas Republic*, Norman, OK: University of Oklahoma Press, 1946, pp. 108–109.
13 Ibid., pp. 267–268.
14 Noah Smithwick, *The Evolution of a State or Recollections of Old Texas Days*, Austin: University of Texas Press, 1983, p. 8.
15 William Bollaert, *William Bollaert's Texas*, Norman, OK: University of Oklahoma Press, 1956, p. 183. See also Anthony M. Orum, *Power, Money, and People: The Making of Modern Austin*, Eugene, OR: Resource Publishers, 1987, p. 16.
16 Steinert, *North America, Particularly Texas in the Year 1849*, pp. 117, 120.
17 Frederick Law Olmsted, *A Journey Through Texas*, Dallas, TX: DeGolyer Library, 2004, p. 116.
18 Randolph B. Campbell and Richard G. Lowe, *Wealth and Power in Antebellum Texas*, College Station, TX: Texas A&M University Press, 1977, pp. 29–30, 58, 63, 66–67, 88.
19 Gavin Wright, *Old South, New South: Revolutions in the Southern Economy Since the Civil War*, New York: Basic Books, 1986, pp. 12, 55–57. See also C. Vann Woodward, *The Burdens of Southern History*, New York: Vintage Books, 1940, p. 17; Michael Lind, *Land of Promise: An Economic History of the United States*, New York: Harper Collins, 2012, p. 344.
20 Bryan Burrough, *The Big Rich: The Rise and Fall of the Greatest Texas Oil Fortunes*, New York: Penguin Press, 2009, p. 77. See also Cunningham, *Cowboy Conservatism*, p. 19.
21 Randolph B. Campbell, *Gone to Texas: A History of the Lone Star State*, New York: Oxford University Press, 2003, p. 378.
22 James McEnteer, *Deep in the Heart: The Texas Tendency in American Politics*, Westport, CT: Praeger, 2004, p. 73.
23 David G. McComb, *Texas: A Modern History*, Austin, TX: University of Texas Press, p. 145.
24 Colin Woodard, *American Nations: A History of the Eleven Rival Regional Cultures of North America*, New York: Penguin Books, 2011, pp. 283, 302. See also Ira Katznelson, *Fear Itself: The New Deal and the Origins of Our Times*, New York, W.W. Norton, 2013.

25 Report on the Economic Conditions of the South, July 25, 1938, pp. 21, 38.
26 Lind, *Land of Promise*, p. 43.
27 Bartley, *The New South*, p. 49.
28 Ibid., pp. 145–146, 260, 430.
29 J. David Woodard, *The New Southern Politics*, Boulder, CO: Lynne Rienner Publishers, 2006, pp. 69–70. See also "Per Capita Personal Income, U.S. and All States, http://bber.unm.ed/econ/us-pci.htm
30 Champagne and Harpham, *Texas at the Crossroads*, p. 267.
31 Michael Lind, *Made in Texas: George W. Bush and the Southern Takeover of American Politics*, New York: Basic Books, 2003, pp. 83–89.
32 Edna Ferber, *Giant*, Garden City, NY: Doubleday and Company, 1952, p. 351.
33 Jody M. Grant, *The Great Texas Banking Crash: An Insider's Account*, Austin, TX: University of Texas Press, 1996, p. 11.
34 McComb, *Texas: A Modern History*, pp. 165–166.
35 Ben F. Love, *Ben Love: My Life in Texas Commerce*, College Station, TX: Texas A&M University Press, 2005, pp. 226–227.
36 Grant, *The Great Texas Banking Crash*, pp. 101, 238.
37 Ibid., p. 256.
38 Love, *Ben Love: My Life in Texas Commerce*, p. 232.
39 Gail Collins, As Texas Goes, New York: W.W. Norton, 2012, p.62.
40 Love, *Ben Love: My Life in Texas Commerce*, p. 236.
41 Ibid., p. 235.
42 Grant, *The Great Texas Banking Crash*, p. 73.
43 Floyd Norris, "The Texas Fix Is Unlikely for Ireland," *New York Times*, November 19, 2010, p. B1.
44 Collins, *As Texas Goes*, p. 65.
45 Champagne and Harpham, *Texas at the Crossroads*, p. 37.
46 Review & Outlook, "Governors v Congress: The Stimulus Sets a Long-Term Budget Trap for States," *Wall Street Journal*, February 23, 2009, A14.
47 Jason Embry, "Will Perry Reject Unemployment Piece of Stimulus Package?" in *First Reading* blog, February 24, 2009.
48 Todd Gillman, "Obama: Don't Put Politics Before Job Creation," *Dallas Morning News*, February 24, 2009, A8.
49 Christy Hoppe and Robert T. Garrett, "Perry Rejects Part of Stimulus," *Dallas Morning News*, March 13, 2009, A1, A14.
50 Christy Hoppe and Robert T. Garrett, "Perry Rejects Part of Stimulus," *Dallas Morning News*, March 13, 2009, A1, A14. See also Don Baylor Jr., "Modernizing Texas' Unemployment Insurance System," *Center for Public Policy Priorities*, March 10, 2009.
51 Catharine Rampell, "Stimulus Bill Would Bestow New Aid to Many Workers," *New York Times*, February 14, 2009, B1, B4.
52 Christine Nelson and John Lohmer, "An Old Battle Rejoined: States Are at the Front of a New Fight Against Poverty," *State Legislatures*, January 2009, pp. 30–33.
53 Gelman, *Red State, Blue State, Rich State, Poor State*, pp. 48, 58.
54 http://www.sbecouncil.org/2013/04/17/business-tax-index-2013.
55 Kauffman.org/snei2010.
56 Sheryl Jean, "Texas Improves Score on Economic Index," *Dallas Morning News*, November 18, 2010.

5   Public Education in Texas

> It is admitted by all, that [a] cultivated mind is the guardian genius of democracy, and, while guided and controlled by virtue, is the noblest attribute of man.
>
> (President Mirabeau B. Lamar, Republic of Texas, 1838)

In 2013, the U.S. Census reported that for the first time in U.S. history less than half of children under five were white. This transition to majority minority youth came to Texas more than a decade ago. In fact, the 2010 census reported that Hispanics accounted for 95 percent of child population growth in Texas since 2000 and that just 37.5 percent of children in Texas nursery, pre-school, and kindergarten programs were Anglo. In 2011, for the first time, half of all Texas public school students were Hispanic.[1] Only three states—Hawaii, New Mexico, and California—along with D.C., have smaller proportions of young Anglo students.[2]

What makes these numbers particularly intriguing is the near universal recognition that a good education, certainly a high school diploma and hopefully a college degree, is a prerequisite to a good job, a productive life, and a secure future. One cannot have a conversation about the future of the United States or Texas without the discussion turning quickly to education and the preparation of tomorrow's workforce. In today's Texas workforce, 40 percent of Hispanics lack a high school degree and, as we saw in the exercise that concluded Chapter 3, unless educational attainment among Texas Hispanics improves significantly in coming decades, Texas will be a less productive and poorer state.

Hence, we turn to an evaluation of Texas public schools. First, we provide a brief history of Texas public schools from their origins in the nineteenth century through the battle to desegregate them in the mid-twentieth century and to reform and adequately fund them in our own day. Second, we ask how well Texas has organized its public school system, funded its public schools, and paid its teachers since 1950. Finally, we evaluate the effectiveness of Texas public schools in terms of state and national exam results, high school completion, and college readiness.

We will, of course, be interested to see whether the educational attainment of minority students in general and Hispanic students in particular is improving as it must if Texas is to thrive in the coming decades.

A Brief History of Public Education in Texas

The Texas Declaration of Independence highlighted the failure of the Mexican government to establish public schools in Texas as one cause of the revolution. Prior to the revolution and after, Germans were quick to establish free public schools, but immigrants out of the American South were not. The planter class either left their younger children with relatives in the South to be educated or operated plantation schools for their children and those of neighboring plantation families. The older children of the wealthy, such as those of Stephen F. Austin's brother-in-law, the planter James F. Perry, were sent back to the U.S. for college. Perry's children went to Kenyon College in Ohio and Trinity College in Connecticut.[3] The children of the Anglo poor had few educational opportunities and other children had none.

Anglo Texans have always talked a better game on education than they have played. Texas's second president, Mirabeau B. Lamar (1838–1841), declared that "a cultivated mind is . . . the noblest attribute of man" and called upon the Congress of the Republic of Texas to set aside land in the public domain for the support of public education. He assured Congress that, "A suitable appropriation of lands to the purpose of general education, can be made at this time without inconvenience to the Government or the people."[4] In 1839 and 1841, Congress set aside four leagues of land (17,712 acres) in each county for public schools and fifty leagues (221,400 acres) for a state university, but in what would become typical Texas fashion, they allocated no money. But having called for state-supported public schools was enough to earn President Lamar the sobriquet of "Father of Education in Texas." The classic history of Texas education, *The Story of Texas Schools* (1955), by C.E. Evans, explained that, "There was no sentiment in the Republic of Texas for school taxation. . . . Any attempt at this time to establish public free schools . . . would have been condemned as tyranny."[5]

The Texas statehood Constitution of 1845 renewed Lamar's call for public schools. Article 10, section 1, read: "A general diffusion of knowledge being essential to the preservation of the rights and liberties of the people, it shall be the duty of the legislature of this State to make suitable provisions for the support and maintenance of public schools." Article 10, section 2, called for a statewide property tax to fund free public schools, as well as an annual appropriation of 10 percent of state revenues to build a permanent fund to support the schools. Few schools were actually started because Texas "courts held that . . . the assessment of general taxes for education, was unconstitutional."[6] In the absence of public schools, Texans who could afford to do so depended on private academies and tutors.

Wilhelm Steinert visited New Braunfels, the principal German settlement in central Texas, and wrote in 1849 that, "The schoolhouse was a small hut made of boards. . . . A group of some 15 students, boys and girls of different ages, sat in the small room. The open door let light into the room. Lessons consisted chiefly of reading, writing, and arithmetic." Steinert reported that, "people pay $2 per month per student" and many "would gladly have sent their children to school, but could not afford the tuition or lived too far from the school."[7]

The early 1850s brought an infusion of cash to Texas state government coffers and some of it was initially directed to education. Texas gave up claims to New Mexico in exchange for inclusion of El Paso and the Panhandle and $10 million in cash. After paying off war debts, Texas leaders had money remaining for transportation projects and another go at a public school system. Governor Elisha M. Peace signed a public schools bill on January 31, 1854, establishing a $2 million "Special School Fund," the annual interest from which was to pay operating expenses and teacher salaries. The fund generated $0.62 per student in 1854 and $1.50 in 1855, hardly enough to establish schools and pay teachers. Because state funding did not cover school expenses and teacher salaries, state law allowed tuition charges of up to 10 cents a day to cover the rest. Poor students would go to school during that portion of the year covered by state funds and drop out once tuition was required. Moreover, parents could take their pro rata share of state funds and enroll their children in a private academy or join with other parents to hire a teacher and start their own school. As Evans observed, "each parent claimed the right to give his children the kind and degree of education he thought wise, while the community insisted on the . . . right to manage its school in its own way."[8] Texas historian Randolph B. Campbell concluded that "public education remained only a much-talked-about dream in Texas before the Civil War."[9]

After the Civil War, funding black education was a major political issue. In response to the hunger of former slaves for education, the Freedman's Bureau established sixteen schools with more than 1,000 students in 1865. In early 1866, white conservatives met to draft a new state constitution in anticipation of being readmitted to the union. The Texas Constitution of 1866 acknowledged the end of slavery, but refused civil rights to blacks, including the right to attend and send their children to public schools. Instead, the Constitution called for separate white and black schools, with the black schools supported by taxes raised from black parents. Black parents—slaves just the year before—had no property or income to support schools for their children.[10] The U.S. Congress rejected the proposed Constitution and instituted Congressional or Radical Reconstruction and military occupation to insure black rights. Though the Freedman's Bureau education program soon grew to sixty-six schools with more than 3,000 students, white violence was a constant threat.

Congressional Reconstruction forced a new constitution. The Constitution of 1869 was highly centralized, including a powerful executive, annual meetings of the state legislature, racially mixed state militia and state police, and state-funded public schools for all children between the ages of six and eighteen. State funding was to come from public land sales, property taxes, poll taxes, and general revenues.[11] Republican Governor Edmund J. Davis set about implementing the Constitution's mandate. The Freedman's Bureau schools discontinued operation in 1871.[12] Soon 125,000 black and white students were enrolled in public schools, but white parents chaffed under the taxes, especially as part of the money was going to educate black children.[13] In September 1871, conservative white opponents of the Davis administration convened a "Tax Payers' Convention" in Galveston to protest "the taxes demanded of the people."[14]

When the Democrats returned to power in 1873, Anglo elites began to dismantle the system of free public schools. They immediately returned responsibility for the schools to parents and local governments and limited the power of local school boards to levy taxes.[15] When Reconstruction ended and a new state constitution was written in 1876, the job of dismantling the state's centralized school system was completed. The Constitution of 1876 provided in Article VII, section 1, that "A general diffusion of knowledge being essential to the preservation of the liberties and rights of the people, it shall be the duty of the Legislature . . . to establish and make suitable provision for . . . an efficient system of public free schools." Article I, section 3, provided that no more than one-quarter of state revenues could be dedicated to education, but did not require that any money, beyond a $1 poll tax, be provided. The Constitution also mandated in Article VII, section 7, that, "Separate schools shall be provided for white and colored children, and impartial provision shall be made for both."

Fights over state funding of the schools began almost immediately. As cotton prices fell, state revenues tightened and Governor Oran M. Roberts vetoed the school appropriation for 1879. The legislature had appropriated the full constitutional amount, one-quarter of state revenues, but the governor thought the revenue estimates inflated and demanded a "pay as you go" policy of spending only money on hand. As a result, the school appropriation, spending per pupil, and state enrollments all fell even though Texas was in the middle of a population boom.[16]

Texas ended the nineteenth century with its public schools under heavy pressure. In 1890, Texas per pupil expenditures were 63 percent of the U.S. average. The sharp economic contraction of the 1890s led Texas to cut per pupil expenditures to 56 percent of the national average in 1900.[17] Gene Preuss, a prominent historian of Texas schools, noted that in 1901, "Despite the fact that Texas spent more per child per diem than other southern states, it still ranked thirty-eighth in the nation in the number of children enrolled in school, thirty-seventh in per capita expenditures for education, and thirty-fifth in literacy."[18] These rankings are essentially unchanged today.

Not only were Texas schools poorly funded in general, there were vast differences between urban and rural schools and white and black schools. In 1900, urban schools were in session an average of 162 days a year and spent an average of $8.35 per student. Rural schools met only ninety-eight days a year and spent $3.34 per student. In 1910, school districts spent an average of $10 a year per white student and $5.74 per black student. Class sizes in black schools were about half again as large as they were in white schools.[19] UT professor Don Graham wrote that these schools, especially the rural schools, provided "functional literacy" and little more.[20]

Texas was slow to follow national educational advances during the first half of the twentieth century. Texas adopted compulsory school attendance in 1915, five years after neighboring Louisiana, and before only Georgia (1916) and Mississippi (1918).[21] In 1917, the U.S. Congress passed the Smith–Hughes Act, one of the first instances of federal funding of local schools, providing funds for the salaries of industrial arts and home economics teachers. Texas declined to come up with the matching funds required by the Act, so "only a small percent of the total funds available for Texas was used."[22] Sound familiar? The "Better Schools Campaign" of 1918–1920 did spur modest reforms. Free school text books were approved in 1918 and in 1919 voters considered a constitutional amendment allowing local districts to raise taxes to supplement state education funds. A poster used by the pro-reform campaign posed this challenge: Texas, "First in Size. First in Agricultural Products. First in Production of Cotton. Third in Production of Oil. Seventh in Wealth. Thirty-Ninth in Education. Shall Texas Keep this Rank?"[23] Though the Amendment prevailed by a two-to-one margin, Texas per capita spending on education rose no faster than the national average. Texas spent 63 percent of the national average per student in 1930 just as it had four decades earlier in 1890.

Frederick Eby, a noted historian of early twentieth-century Texas education, blamed an inattentive public and scheming politicians for the failure to do better. In an analysis that could just as well be made today, Eby reported that in the 1920s, "Flattered by the boasts of office-seeking politicians . . . [Texans] were firmly persuaded that their schools were among the best in the entire nation." Advocates of school reform found that it was "necessary to convince the people that these notions which had been boastfully asserted by provincial politicians were wholly erroneous" before they would listen to calls for change.[24] Though spending on public schools in Texas held up better than some other states during the Depression years of the 1930s, reaching 73 percent of the national average by 1940, the overblown claims of the politicians were embarrassingly exposed during World War II:

The National Education Association reported that Texas had one of the highest rejection rates for military service because of illiteracy.

With the national rejection rate for poor schooling at 12 percent, the Texas rejection rate was . . . almost 23 percent. This placed Texas among the twelve states with high educational deficiency rates. The report noted that only South Carolina, Louisiana, Georgia, Mississippi, Alabama, Arkansas, Virginia, and North Carolina had higher rejection rates than Texas. Tennessee, Arizona, and Florida fared better. The NEA report connected the results to the amount of money the states spent on education—the more money the state spent on education, the fewer military rejections.[25]

Remarkably, from this low point, Texas would soon undertake major educational reforms.

The Depression and World War II drove changes in industrialization, urbanization, immigration and migration. As the state's rural and agricultural economy became urban and industrial, attitudes toward education began to change as well. In 1949, the Texas Legislature passed and Governor Buford Jester signed the Gilmer–Aiken Laws. Named for Texas Representative Claude Gilmer and Senator A.M. Aiken, the Gilmer–Aiken Laws dramatically modernized both the organizational structure and the finances of Texas public schools. The package of three bills was introduced first in the Senate and passed by that body, as SB 115, 116, and 117, before being taken up in the House. The bills proposed to centralize the funding and administration of Texas public schools to a degree not seen since Reconstruction. SB 115 established "one Central Education Agency . . . [with] three main divisions: (1) a policy-forming State Board of Education elected by the people, (2) a professional Commissioner of Education appointed by the board to serve as its executive agent, and (3) a State Department of Education to serve as the professional and clerical staff of the commissioner and the board."[26] This structure remains in place today, except that in 1995 the legislature moved the power to appoint the Commissioner of Education from the State Board of Education to the governor. SB 116 created the Minimum Foundation Program to encourage consolidation and efficiency in school districts, set minimum standards for teacher pay, equalize school funding, and establish a nine-month school year and a twelve-grade school system. SB 117 took school funding out of the annual budget debate by mandating sufficient funds to fulfill the new Minimum Foundation Program requirements.[27]

But make no mistake, progress such as that represented in Gilmer–Aiken comes hard in Texas. Education reform was labeled socialism and declared to be an intrusion on local and parental rights and responsibilities. Dolph Briscoe, a future two-term governor, was in his first term in the

Texas house in 1949. In his 2008 autobiography, Briscoe noted that passage of the Gilmer–Aiken reforms was only achieved over strident opposition. "Opponents worked hard to prevent passage, even labeling the bills 'communistic.'"[28] Socialism and communism are terms that are frequently thrown around in Texas politics, especially in regard to "public" schools, which are, after all—public. Still, most parents were on-board this time. As we shall see below, 1950 was the highpoint for per pupil funding, teacher pay, and much more in Texas education.

During debate over the Gilmer–Aiken bills, proponents warned that failure to pass education reform might lead to federal intrusion in Texas public schools. Gilmer–Aiken passed but the federal intrusion came anyway. On December 1, 1953, one week before *Brown v. Board* came before the U.S. Supreme Court for re-argument, Governor Allen Shivers warned against accepting federal education money. With classic Texas bombast, Shivers declared, "We don't need [federal aid] and the federal money ought not to be taken into the school system because control follows the tax dollar."[29] On May 17, 1954, the Supreme Court declared in *Brown* that segregation of black and white students in public schools was an unconstitutional violation of the right of black students to the equal protection of the laws. Governor Shivers immediately trumpeted defiance, saying, "All my instincts, my political philosophy, my experiences and my common sense revolt against the Supreme Court decision. It is an unwarranted invasion of the constitutional rights of the states. . . . My administration has already told the local school districts that, as far as the state of Texas is concerned, there are no changes to be made."[30]

Two dynamics, a weak one toward compliance and a strong one toward resistance, competed in the two years after *Brown* was announced in May 1954 and implementation was mandated in May 1955. By 1956, sixty-five school districts, mostly in South and West Texas, where blacks were few, voluntarily moved toward integration, and, in 1957, sixty-nine more followed suit. These included districts in Austin, Corpus Christi, El Paso, Harlingen, Kerrville, San Antonio, and San Angelo. Both Dallas and Houston resisted integration as did all of East Texas, where the vast majority of Texas blacks lived.[31] The battle that turned the tide in favor of Governor Shivers and the segregationists occurred in the Tarrant County town of Mansfield.

Mansfield, about 15 miles southeast of Fort Worth, "was a small town on the western edge of what was considered the 'Deep South.'"[32] In October 1955, a suit was filed in the federal district court in Fort Worth on behalf of three black students wishing to attend the all-white high school in their home-town of Mansfield. As the date for the federal court ruling neared, an editorial in the *Mansfield News* announced, "We are not against the Negro, but we are against social equality. We think the Negroes are making great strides in improving their race and commend them for it, as long as they stick to their race."[33] On August 27, 1956, the federal district court ordered that Mansfield High be desegregated immediately. On the evening of August 28 and August 30, effigies were hung over main street and from the high school flagpole. On the day that the black students were to register for school, several hundred white protestors massed on school grounds to block their access. When parents and lawyers of the black students called on Governor Shivers for help, he responded, in part, "It is not my intention to permit the use of state officers or troops to shoot down or intimidate Texas citizens who are making orderly protest against a situation instigated and agitated by the National Association for the Advancement of Colored People."[34] Unable to safely register, the black students withdrew, returned to their all-black high school in Fort Worth, and Mansfield High remained segregated until 1965.

Governor Shivers sought to strengthen segregation by forcing three referenda onto the July 1956 Democratic Party primary election ballot: one exempted any child from compulsory attendance at an integrated school, another strengthened state laws against interracial marriage, and the third advocated "interposition" in cases of federal overreach. All passed by greater than three-to-one margins.[35] The Texas State Democratic Executive Committee backed the referenda, declaring "that Mansfield had been selected by the NAACP to promote the 'destruction of the southern way of life and Texas traditions.'" To limit the damage that the NAACP might cause to "Texas traditions," Judge Otis Dunagan of the East Texas community of Tyler issued a permanent injunction against further legal or political action in Texas by the NAACP. Judge Dunagan cautioned local newspapers against misunderstanding his order, saying, "Don't think this is a suit against the nigger people. . . . Actually, it isn't. It's true it [the NAACP] is an organization for the nigger people, but after all, three fourths of its directors are white people. . . . I ain't got nothing against the nigger people." Given these officials' attitudes and actions, it is not surprising that "Between August 1957 and May 1962, only ten school districts integrated in Texas. None of these were in East Texas."[36] It took the Civil Rights Acts of 1964 and 1965 and the Elementary and Secondary Education Act of 1965 to break the back of segregation in Texas and the South. In 1963, only 4.3 percent of black children were attending school with whites; this rose to 7.3 percent in 1964 and 17.2 percent in 1965, before jumping to 44.9 percent in 1966. By 1972, 92 percent of black children were attending school with white children. But the cost of the desegregation fight was high. During the fight, the legislature restricted state funding and many whites moved to the suburbs or placed their children in private schools.

By the late 1970s, issues of race began to recede and issues of educational quality began to come into focus. In the early 1980s, a "growing concern over deteriorating literacy among Texas's schoolchildren over two decades, reflected in students' scores on standardized tests," again prompted reform.[37] In 1983, Governor Mark White called upon Dallas businessman H. Ross Perot to head a "Select Committee on Public Education" to propose reforms intended to improve educational performance and quality. Other heavyweights on the committee were Lt. Gov. Bill Hobby, Speaker of the Texas House Gib Lewis, and Comptroller Bob Bullock.[38] The Perot Committee's recommendations formed the basis of legislation passed in a special session of the legislature in the summer of 1984. Those reforms sought to make teacher competence and student learning the twin engines of enhanced academic performance.

Teachers received pay raises in exchange for tougher credentialing standards and competency testing. Students were held to more stringent attendance and promotion standards. The Perot Commission's student reforms "abolished social promotion; established an extensive program of testing and remediation for students in the first, third, fifth, seventh, ninth, and twelfth grades; [and] introduced an 'exit test' for high school graduation."[39] Still, most attention was paid to the new "no pass–no play" rule that barred students from participating in extracurricular activities, including varsity sports, unless they passed their classes.[40]

Even as the Perot Committee and state government moved to buttress academic quality, opposition to how Texas funded schools moved toward center stage. In addition to the state's Minimum Foundation Program, Texas schools depended on local property tax revenues and these varied dramatically by the wealth or poverty of different cities and districts. School funding issues came before state and federal courts regularly through the 1970s and 1980s. San Antonio's Edgewood ISD was usually among the plaintiffs. In *Edgewood ISD v. Kirby* (1989), lawyers pointed out that, "Edgewood had $38,854 in property wealth per student while Alamo Heights . . . had $570,109."[41] The trial court found for the plaintiffs, the appeals court overturned the ruling, and the Texas Supreme Court overturned the appeals court, finding that the school finance system was "neither financially efficient" nor did it provide "for a 'general diffusion of knowledge' statewide, and therefore it violates Article VII, section 1, of the Texas Constitution."[42] During the early 1990s the Texas Legislature sought twice to patch the old system by providing more equalization funds, but the Texas Supreme Court rejected both attempts as insufficient.

In 1993, much against its will, the legislature passed the "Robin Hood" school funding bill in which revenues were "recaptured" from high property tax districts and reallocated to low property tax districts. Administrators and parents in property-rich districts complained bitterly that their students were being denied enrichment opportunities to fund activities in property-poor districts. Tensions grew through the next decade as more and more school districts, 690 of about 1,020 districts by 2003, bumped up against state property tax limits and saw their budgets stagnate. School districts, knowing that Texas rarely spends money unless it is ordered to do so by state or federal courts, recurred to the lawyers. In 2004, 300 school districts went to court in a case called *West Orange-Cove CISD v. Neeley*. The districts claimed that an underfunded public education system limited their ability to fulfill their constitutional mandate to promote a general diffusion of knowledge within the state.[43]

The school districts prevailed up through the Texas Supreme Court and the legislature reluctantly returned to the drawing board. Governor Perry and the legislature responded to the Court's demand for funding reform by lowering local property taxes by one-third, enacting a broad new business tax, called the margins tax, increasing the state cigarette tax from $0.41 to $1.41 a pack, and drawing on the state surplus. With the new school funding plan in place, the state's share of funding, which had dropped from 80 percent in 1949 to 35 percent, rose to 50 percent, the localities share dropped from 55 percent to 40 percent, and the federal share stayed at about 10 percent. State revenues from the margins tax came in lower than expected and school budgets again tightened. The 2009 state legislature increased school budgets by a minuscule $120 per student, but in 2011 tight budgets again led to deep cuts in school budgets. Both legislators and school superintendents assumed their traditional stances and the lawyers filed their briefs.

Texas is again enmeshed in a lawsuit over the equity of school finance, its tenth since 1984. Texas lost eight of the first nine and has lost the opening stages of the tenth as well. But the Texas Supreme Court can only find that the state is again in violation of its Constitution, it cannot order the legislature to appropriate a specific level of funding. Nonetheless, when the legislature cut $5.4 billion from public education in 2011 and added back just $3.4 billion in 2013, ignoring the fact that 170,000 students had been added to the system in the meantime, it further reduced its credibility with the court.

The problems facing Texas public schools are immense. Of five million public school students, nearly 3 million, or 60 percent, come from low-income households. Higher standards, less money, and a needy student body convinced two-thirds of Texas school districts, teaching three-quarters of the state's students, to sue the state of Texas in District Judge John Dietz's court. Testimony before Judge Dietz showed that the top 10 percent of Texas school districts enjoyed $7,998 per student while the bottom 10 percent got $5,616 per student. After twelve weeks of testimony, Judge Dietz ruled that Texas was not providing enough money for schools to meet their constitutional responsibilities. The judge declared that, "there is no free lunch. We either want increased standards and are willing to pay the price, or we don't. However, there is a cost to acting, namely a tax increase. And there is a cost to not acting, namely the loss of our competitive position as a state."

Judge Dietz estimated that an additional $10 to 11 billion might be required to fund the schools at constitutionally acceptable levels. Since the legislature was in session when he ruled, Judge Dietz suspended the ruling to allow the legislature time to respond. The legislature responded in two ways, by reducing the number of high-stakes, end of course, tests from 15 to 5 and by restoring part of the 2011 funding cuts. Judge Dietz agreed to hear new arguments from the plaintiffs and the state. Predictably, the plaintiffs complained that the legislature's responses were insufficient and the state congratulated itself on its generosity.

Average Spending Per Pupil in the U.S. and Texas, 1950 to Present

Before taking a close look at Texas school funding, we must take note of a broader point. Two well-known Harvard economists, Claudia Goldin and Lawrence F. Katz, published a book in 2008, entitled *The Race Between Education and Technology*. The thesis of this important book is that the U.S. led the world in technological innovation and wealth creation throughout most of its history because it also led the world in education. They also make a narrower point that is directly relevant to the history of education funding in Texas. They note that education funding is not just a question of economic means, but also of a sense of community and a willingness to spend money on the education of all of the community's children. Goldin and Katz note that, "the wider the distribution of income . . . the less support there will be for public education, since the rich can opt out and the poor will have a lower demand."[44]

Texas school administrators have been in a 150-year-long tug-of-war with Texas politicians over school funding. Almost always the politicians have won and the school administrators and the students they serve have lost. So far, Texas parents have most often sided with the politicians, rising consistently to the promise of no new taxes, to the detriment of public education and their own children. As we shall see in detail below, the academic performance of Texas school children has reflected the state's limited willingness to invest in them.

Political observers and academics have long been aware that Texans are ambivalent about their schools. As Nelson Dometrius wrote in his chapter on education policy in Gerry Riposa's *Texas Public Policy* more than a quarter century ago, "Texans value education in the abstract. . . . At the same time, Texans manifest a cultural attitude that educators are incompetent, underworked and wasteful of public funds. These competing themes lead to a boom and bust cycle in education policy, years of ignoring educational needs, followed by a sudden realization that problems have developed requiring a massive infusion of funds."[45] This excellent description is correct right up to the closing phrase—"a massive infusion of funds"—though perhaps it merely means that any increase in school funding feels massive to tight-fisted Texas legislators and taxpayers.

In only one year, 1950, the year after the passage of the Gilmer–Aiken education reform and finance laws, did Texas spend more than the national average on its students. In 1950, Texas spent $208.88 per student compared to a national average of $208.83. Perhaps chagrined that they had wasted that nickel, Texas politicians tightened students' belts for most of the next six decades. Though Texas never got back to the national average expenditure per student, it did make a couple of runs. One was in response to the findings of the Perot Commission in the mid-1980s, and another was in response to the court mandates of the late 1990s. Yet, each funding surge was pitifully short-lived, reflecting the commitment of just one, or at most two, legislative sessions, before lethargy, charges of wasteful spending, or other pressing demands sapped or diverted attention.

Since 1950, Texas has spent an average of 84 percent of U.S. spending per pupil for elementary and secondary schools. Over that six decade period, Texas has never been in the upper half, the top twenty-five states, in educational expenditures. Texas did briefly reach the 26th spot in 1998, but generally Texas has lagged in the thirties and forties, reaching a low of 48th (meaning only two states spent less per pupil than Texas) in 1972 and 47th in 1976. Texas's average position among the states from 1950 to the present has been 36th.[46] Texas has slipped badly since 2000, falling from 28th in 2000 to 49th in 2012. In fact, over the past decade, state and local funding of public schools in Texas has been flat after accounting for population growth and inflation. Remarkably, in 2002 the state appropriation per student was $8,366 and in 2012 it was $8,400.[47] Still, as Figure 5.1 so clearly shows, spending has dipped sharply in the wake of the recent Great Recession.

Passions flow when discussion focuses on school funding: it is the largest expenditure of state government and it involves children, their future, and that of the state itself. As the 2011 Texas Legislature prepared to impose deep budget cuts, former Texas Lt. Governor Bill Hobby charged that, "A huge majority of public school students in Texas are . . . black and brown. . . . I think Republicans don't like public education because they are educating black children and brown children. That's the inevitable conclusion."[48] Governor Hobby's charge is not wrong, race has played a major role in school funding decisions, but it is way too narrow. While minority children have frequently been short-changed, it is also true that neither Republicans nor Democrats have shown much interest in the education of Texas public school children—whatever their color.

Figure 5.1 presents average annual spending per pupil for the U.S. and Texas and it shows the familiar picture of Texas tracking along below the national average. The pattern in the early years is indistinct because the numbers are small and the lines are compressed but the pattern becomes clear as the numbers get larger in the later years. For example, in 1965 Texas

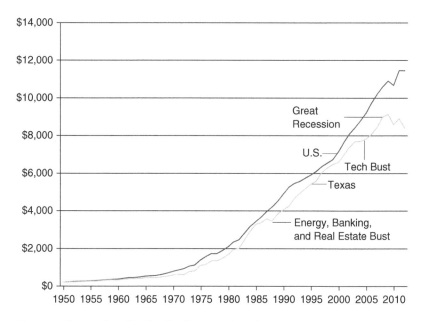

Figure 5.1 Average Spending Per Pupil in the U.S. and Texas, 1950–Present.

Source: U.S. Census Bureau, Statistical Abstract of the United States, each year from 1950 through 2012, http://www.census.gov/compendia/statab/past_years.html Various figure and table numbers, generally titled Average current expenditures per pupil in average daily attendance by states. See NEA, Ranking and Estimates, December 2012, Summary Table K, p. 96.

spent $449 per pupil, or 84 percent, of the U.S. average expenditure of $532, though this significant difference is hard to see on the graph. But we do again see the familiar pattern of Texas going sideways in the late 1980s as it is hard hit by the oil, property, banking, and S&L crises. Texas gathered itself to close on the national average again in the boom period of the late 1990s, only to fall back in the first decade of the new century and seriously so in the last few years.

Figure 5.2 presents Texas's expenditures as a percentage of U.S. expenditures and the data present a stark picture. Passage of the Gilmer–Aiken laws in 1949 brought per capita education expenditures in Texas to 100 percent of the national average in the early 1950s. Commitment to education spending sputtered in the mid-1950s and then went into a steep decline, reaching just 65 percent of the national average by 1972. Texas resisted the demand of the U.S. Supreme Court in *Brown v. Board of Education* (1954) that schools be desegregated and resisted the threat of the U.S. Congress in the Elementary and Secondary Education Act (1965) that federal funds would be withheld unless desegregated proceeded. By the early 1970s, Texas succumbed and desegregation of public schools did occur. However, between 1955 and 1972 one of the key ways that Texas resisted desegregation was to limit funding to its public schools. Once racial issues retreated from center stage, Texans began again to think about educational quality.

The broad arc of Texas school funding since 1950 shows three distinct peaks, highpoints identified with passage of the Gilmer–Aiken Laws in 1949, adoption of the Perot Committee's recommendations in the mid-1980s, and the adoption of the Robin Hood school funding program in the mid-1990s. But it shows more than that. To Texas's detriment it shows that each monumental effort, each historic success in dealing with school funding, was followed by a sense that the problem has been addressed, attention wandered, and the gains leaked away. On the other hand, and to Texas's credit, it shows that as the gains leaked away, attention returned, politicians tried and to some extent did respond, but those responses are only partial until the big push—Gilmer–Aiken, the Perot Committee, Robin Hood—put Texas schools back on track. Inevitably though, the low-tax, low-service model that has governed Texas politics from its earliest days reasserts itself and Texas students suffer. Even more troubling, there is an aggressive ignorance at work that sees virtually all public spending as bad, even evil. In 2003, yes 2003, Republican state representative Debbie Riddle (R-Houston) asked, "Where did this idea come from that everybody deserves free education, free medical care, free whatever?" In answer to her own question, she declared, "It comes from Moscow, from Russia. It comes straight out of the pit of hell."[49]

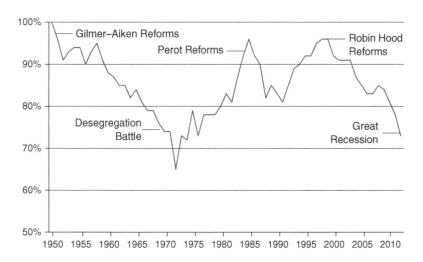

Figure 5.2 Texas Spending Per Pupil as a Percent of U.S. Spending Per Pupil, 1950–Present.

Source: U.S. Census Bureau, Statistical Abstract of the United States, each year from 1950 through 2012, http://www.census.gov/compendia/statab/past_years.html Various figure and table numbers, generally titled Average current expenditures per pupil in average daily attendance by states.

The current situation of school funding in Texas is dire. Texas historian David McComb noted that, "In 2005, after the state decreased funding, Texas ranked fortieth in the nation [on student funding] while its students placed forty-ninth in verbal skills and forty-sixth on the SAT."[50] Texas slipped to 42nd in 2006, 2007, and 2008, 44th in 2009 and 49th in 2012.

The 2011 Texas Legislature not only cut school funding by $4 billion, they changed the legal requirement to fund the Minimum Foundation Program, in place since the Gilmer–Aiken reforms of 1949, to a discretionary allocation set by the legislature each biennium. Chillingly, State Senator Dan Patrick (R-Houston) said, "I think it's a change we needed as we move forward. We have to have real cuts. . . . [This is] a true cut in an entitlement."[51] The 2011 cuts ultimately totaled more than $500 per student, or about 7 percent, from the preceding biennium.[52] Texans came late to seeing education as, yes, an entitlement, and now that commitment may be slipping away.

Teachers' Salaries in the U.S. and Texas, 1950 to Present

Not surprisingly, since school funding and teachers' salaries are set by the same people (the state's politicians), at the same time (in the biennial legislative session), very similar patterns pertain. Texas teachers in the immediate wake of Gilmer–Aiken's passage in 1949 were paid $3,122 in 1950, fully 104 percent of the national average teacher pay of $3,010. Texas teacher pay beat the national average only once more, in 1954. Texas teacher pay has trailed the national average in every year from 1955 to the present. During the boom years of the 1970s and early 1980s, the Briscoe and Clements administrations were able to increase teacher pay without raising taxes, of which they were quite proud. But these were high inflation years and other states were raising teacher pay too, so Texas teachers made only modest progress against national averages.[53] The Perot Committee reforms brought Texas teacher pay back near the national average in the mid-1980s ($22,600 compared to $23,500 in 1985 for example), but the gap quickly reopened as economic turmoil engulfed Texas in the late 1980s (Figure 5.3). Texas teacher pay ranked 18th in the nation in 1950 and 1954 and generally held in the twenties through the early 1960s and has bounced around in the twenties and thirties since. Texas's average ranking among the states since 1950 has been 29th.

As with per pupil funding, Figure 5.4 depicting Texas teacher pay as a percentage of U.S. teacher pay is very informative. Again, the high points following Gilmer–Aiken and the Perot Committee are obvious, but the impact of Robin Hood and the tax swap on teacher pay was more modest. Nonetheless, Texas teacher pay has held up more consistently over the decades than has per pupil funding. From 1950 to the present, Texas teacher pay has averaged 90 percent of U.S. teacher pay and has rarely fallen below 85 percent. It rests today at 85 percent.

Another way to think about the adequacy of teacher pay is to ask how it compares to private sector pay. A recent study by Professor Ed Fuller of the Department of Educational Administration at the University of Texas, Austin, reported that shortages of math and science teachers had grown. The reason was not far to seek as "secondary math and science teachers continue to earn substantially less than their peers in the private sector, even after adjusting for summers off. Teachers made, on average, between $23,000 and $40,000 less than individuals in nonteaching careers in math and science. The average salary in 2007 for math and science teachers was about $47,000." Texas Senator Florence Shapiro, chair of the Senate Education Committee, suggested that the way to deal with the teacher shortages might be to trim the math and science requirements for high school graduation, saying "There would still be math and science requirements, but we would not have as many students taking higher level courses such as calculus and physics."[54] Feel better now? Probably not, but lagging teacher salaries may help explain why half of new Texas teachers leave the profession in their first five years.[55]

Budget cuts imposed by the state legislature in 2011 cost 10,717 teacher jobs in the 2011–2012 school year. Class sizes increased and average

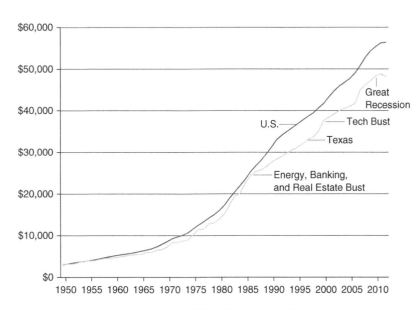

Figure 5.3 Average Teacher Pay in the U.S. and Texas, 1950–Present.

Source: U.S. Census Bureau, Statistical Abstract of the United States, each year 1950 through 2012. Public Elementary and Secondary Schools—Numbers and Salaries of Teachers, by state, various figure and table numbers, http://www.census.gov/compendia/statab/past_years.html See NEA, Rankings and Estimates, December 2012, Summary Table G, p. 92.

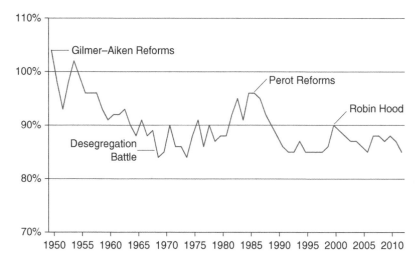

Figure 5.4 Texas Teacher Pay as a Percent of U.S. Teacher Pay, 1950–Present.

Source: U.S. Census Bureau, Statistical Abstract of the United States, each year 1950 through 2012. Public Elementary and Secondary Schools—Numbers and Salaries of Teachers, by state, various figure and table numbers, http://www.census.gov/compendia/statab/past_years.html

teacher pay in the state fell by $263 to $48,110, 36th in the nation. To make ends meet, many teachers take second and third jobs. The Associated Press reported Department of Education National Center for Education Statistics data showing that teacher moonlighting nationally had increased from 10 percent in 1981 to 20 percent in 2011. In Texas, teacher moonlighting rose from 22 percent in 1980 to 41 percent in 2011, the highest in the nation.[56]

Accountability and Performance in Texas Public Schools

The Texas Legislature passed an extensive school accountability bill in 2009. It was lightly revised for the 2012–2013 school year. The accountability bill was a mixed bag at best. To start on the positive side of the ledger, the Texas Legislature maintained the basic 4×4 design of the core curriculum. As Table 5.1 shows, each Texas high school student must take four years of four basic subjects: English, Math, Science, and Social Studies. The requirement that students take two years of a foreign language also was maintained. Additional requirements that students take two semesters of computer technology and a semester of health education were eliminated and the P.E. requirement was reduced from three semesters to two. The reductions were intended to allow students to pursue their interests by taking almost twice as many elective courses as they could under the old system.

Table 5.1 The Texas Recommended High School Program, 2012

Subject	Previous Credit Requirements	New Credit Requirements
English	4	4
Math	4	4
Science	4	4
Social Studies	4	4
Foreign Language	2	2
Physical Education	1.5	1
Fine Arts	1	1
Health	.5	0
Speech	.5	.5
Technology	1	0
Electives	3.5	5.5
Total	26	26

Source: Texas Education Agency.

Soon after the school accountability bill was passed, State Education Commissioner Robert Scott declared that all high school students, not just freshmen, were eligible to proceed under the new curriculum requirements. Representative Rob Eissler (R-The Woodlands), chair of the House Education Committee, proudly explained that, "If a kid chooses a course, he or she is more likely to be interested in it and probably will do better in it. That was one of the goals of the legislation, to make our course requirements a little more market-friendly for students."[57] Within weeks it became evident that neither the legislators who drafted the bill nor Commissioner Scott understood exactly how student friendly were the new graduation requirements. Critics soon pointed out that students could load up on P.E. or P.E. substitutes such as football, band, and cheerleading for six and one-half credits, more than a quarter of what they needed to graduate.

Representative Eissler, of course, dismissed the prospect that students would try to game the graduation requirements by taking lots of P.E. and cheerleading. Eissler said, "I don't think it's going to happen. And if a bunch of kids tried to do that, local school officials could step in and adjust their course requirements. That's what we call local control." Maybe so, but others were less sanguine. Geraldine Miller (R-Dallas), a member of the State Board of Education, said "Kids are kids, and we know this could become an option for some. We need safeguards to prevent any abuses like this." State Board of Education staff were ordered to draft rules limiting how students could use their elective hours.[58] In late 2009, the State Board of Education closed the P.E. loophole by lowering the limit to four credits. The board arrived at the four credit limit under heavy lobbying by the Texas High School Coaches Association. Board member Don McLeroy observed, absurdly, that, "The argument for counting four years of athletics toward graduation is pretty persuasive now that the state requires four years of math, science, English, and social studies to graduate."[59]

In the meanwhile, Texas has worked hard to maintain its own state assessment standards and avoid involvement in national assessment standards. Texas claims that this is so they can have strict standards, but critics are dismissive. For example, when Congress allocated $4.35 billion in stimulus funds to the Department of Education (DOE) for its "Race to the Top" educational reform program, Texas officials crowed that they had long been at work on educational reform, which was to some extent true, and were well-positioned to win one of the grants and to serve as a model for others. Some of those others were skeptical. Bill Slotnik, executive director of Boston-based Community Training and Assistance Center, which consults nationally on education reform, said "Just being from Texas is not going to carry the weight that it did in the previous [Bush] administration." The Obama DOE will ask, "Are the things you are doing reaching the classroom in a way that is demonstrably benefiting students?" Arne Duncan, Secretary of the U.S. Department of Education, was just as blunt, "we want to reward those states that are willing to lead the country where we need to go and are willing to push this reform agenda very, very hard. And the states that don't have the stomach or the political will, unfortunately, they're going to lose out."[60]

Just weeks before applications were due, Governor Perry instructed Texas Commissioner of Education Robert Scott not to commit to adoption of national education standards, thereby compromising any Race to the Top application. Perry claimed that:

> Texas is already ahead of most other states in setting college and career-ready standards in our schools. The citizens of Texas, not the federal government, know what is best for our children. As the federal government continues its sweeping expansion of federal authority from the financial, energy and health care systems, it is now attempting to increase their intrusion into Texas classrooms.[61]

Scott Hochberg, a Democrat from Houston and a leader of the Texas House Education Committee, observed that, "the governor is throwing up the white flag and admitting that they're not willing to compete."[62]

Texas does its own educational assessment, but its findings are suspect. One of the great problems with educational assessment in Texas is that it changes so often that it is difficult to establish and assess trends. Since 1979, Texas has had four major statewide testing regimes. Each took several years to develop, test, and implement and then each was in place for just a few years. The Texas Assessment of Basic Skills (TABS) was in place from 1979 to 1984, the Texas Educational Assessment of Minimum Skills (TEAMS) was in place from 1984 to 1990, the Texas Assessment of Academic Skills (TAAS) was in place from 1990 to 1999, and the Texas Assessment of Knowledge and Skills (TAKS) began development in 1999. TAKS was to be discontinued in 2011, but delays in launching its successor briefly extanded its life. If you wanted to make accurate assessment next to impossible, the best way to do it, short of abandoning testing altogether, would be to frequently change the testing regime.

There is some data to analyze from the TAAS assessment regime of 1994 to 2002 and the TAKS regime of 2003 to 2012 (Table 5.2). Both exams test minimum standards for competency rather than complete command of the subjects tested. Both exams appear to register extraordinary educational achievement and steady progress year to year. The Texas Education Agency (TEA) reports that in 2011, 86 percent of rising seniors passed all four TAKS exams. Unfortunately, the failure rate on the TAKS test in 2012, even after retesting, was about 5 percent. This means that almost 15,000 students completing their senior year in 2012 did not receive a diploma. Moreover, black and Hispanic failure rates are about three times the failure rate for Anglo and Asian students.[63] As if the extraordinarily high pass rates were not enough, in 2009 the state changed the criteria by which a school could earn the top exemplary rating. In 2009, the "Texas Projection Measure" was implemented which allowed schools to count a student as passing not just if they really did pass but if the new measure predicted that they would pass in a future year.[64] The proportion of Texas schools receiving an exemplary rating jumped from 13.3 percent in 2008, to 28.2 percent in 2009, and 33.9 percent in 2010. Uproarious laughter followed this maneuver and it subsequently was discontinued. In 2011, 15.5 percent of schools were labeled exemplary.

Beginning with the 2011–2012 school year, Texas introduced the new State of Texas Assessments of Academic Readiness, or STARR, exam. Like TAKS, STARR tests students from third grade through high school, with high school students taking twelve end of course exams, three each in English, math, science, and social studies, beginning with 9th graders in 2011–2012. TEA officials claim that STARR will "again raise the bar for Texas education" and that the exams will be benchmarked to national and international standards to insure rigor.[65]

The rough roll-out of STARR was immediately followed by its rollback. Signs of assessment fatigue were clear in early 2011 when Robert Scott, then Texas Education Agency Commissioner, told 4,000 school administrators that state testing had become a "perversion of its original intent." School testing had been accountability religion in Texas since 1993, especially after Governor George W. Bush took it national with his No Child Left Behind presidential initiative. Scott's comments fed into a debate within school districts about whether STARR could be

Table 5.2 Texas Annual Academic Testing, TAAS and TAKS: Pass Rates, 1994–2013

	Total	White	Black	Hispanic
TAAS				
1994	56	69	33	41
1995	61	75	38	46
1996	67	80	47	54
1997	73	85	56	62
1998	78	88	63	68
1999	78	88	64	70
2000	80	89	68	72
2001	82	90	72	76
2002	85	93	77	80
TAKS				
2003	49	59	33	38
2004	72	83	58	61
2005	68	82	52	56
2006	64	79	45	52
2007	69	83	52	57
2008	71	83	55	61
2009	75	86	61	67
2010	82	91	73	76
2011	84	92	76	80
2012	86	92	78	83
2013	86	92	78	83

Source: TAAS at Texas Education Agency, Academic Excellence Indicator System, http://ritter.tea. state.tx.us/perfreport/aeis/hist/stateold.html. TAKS at http://ritter.tea.state.tx.us/perfreport/pocked/ 2010/pocked2010.pdf.

implemented at all after the 2011 legislature cut $4 billion in school funding. Scott predicted, correctly, that the 2013 legislature would reassess and likely scale back testing in Texas.

Within weeks, key Texas state senators, led by the Senate education chair, Florence Shapiro (R-Plano), called for slowing down implementation of STARR. In June 2012, Texas 9th graders took end of course STARR exams for the first time. With passing standards set as low as 37 percent for Algebra I and biology and as high as 68 percent for reading, 87 percent passed biology, but only 55 percent passed English I reading. With passing standards set to rise in 2014 and again in 2016, students, parents, educators, and legislators expressed frustration with the number of end-of-course exams required—15—and the fact that the exams were mandated to comprise 15 percent of final course grades.

Defenders of Texas's test-heavy school accountability regime, led by the Texas Association of Business's Bill Hammond, declared that, "What we are seeing today is a full-frontal assault on school accountability."[66] Commissioner Scott announced that he would step down in July 2012, but the fat was in the fire. By November, both the State Board of Education and Governor Perry had called for suspending the requirement that end-of-course exams count for 15 percent of course grades. With the legislature scheduled to convene in January 2013, accountability advocates feared even more fundamental changes. In fact, new legislation resulted in a major roll-back of high stakes testing in Texas. End-of-course exams were slashed from 15 to 5 and they no longer needed to be factored into final grades.

STARR test results for 2012–13 were reported on the day Governor Perry signed the new education law. Again, almost half of high school freshmen and sophomores failed the writing exams and historic differences by race and ethnicity were again present. Sixty-nine percent of Anglos passed the writing exams, but just 43 percent of black students and 45 percent of Hispanic students passed.[67] In classic Texas fashion, some political leaders blamed the test to avoid blaming the quality of education offered by the state. Senator Dan Patrick (R-Houston), chair of the Senate Education Committee, said, "I have great concerns about the validity of the tests. Either these tests are right, and we are in far worse shape than we imagine, or the tests just aren't testing what our kids are learning."[68]

Setting educational standards in Texas has long been as much, and often more, about religious and ideological control of the curriculum than it has been about the integrity of academic standards.[69] A century ago, in 1913, the John Bell Hood chapter of the United Confederate Veterans mounted a campaign to remove anti-southern content, including a photo of Abraham Lincoln, from the state's history texts. The state textbook board sided with the veterans, but Governor Oscar Colquitt brought the scuffle to a halt by declaring, "I want the truth of history taught. . . . I had rather resign the Governor's office of Texas than to have my children studying a textbook in the public schools of Texas with Abe Lincoln's picture left out of it, and I am a son of a Confederate soldier."[70] Recent governors and state leaders have been less bold. Two decades ago the State Board of Education (SBOE) declared that Texas science teachers explore both the "strengths and weaknesses" of the theories they teach. The SBOE was particularly interested in assuring that evolution, Charles Darwin's theory of biological change, be presented as unproven, incomplete, and likely flawed. In 2009, a teacher advisory panel recommended that the "strengths and weaknesses" language be changed to instruct science teachers to "analyze and evaluate scientific explanations using empirical data." SBOE chairman Don McLeroy, who described himself as a "Darwin skeptic," led a seven-member minority of the fifteen-member board in a long and contentious fight to maintain the "strengths and weaknesses" language for another ten years. McLeroy failed but was able to get language approved advising teachers to inform their students "about aspects of the fossil record that do not neatly fit with the idea of species gradually changing over time."[71] Scientists were, of course, appalled.

When the Texas Senate refused to renew Don McLeroy as chair of the SBOE, Governor Perry named Gail Lowe, another Christian social conservative to the position.[72] As Lowe took the helm of the SBOE, the board had just turned to reviewing the social studies standards. The board had already appointed a six-member expert panel to advise on the upcoming revision. Three of the six members were Texas educators and social studies experts, while the other three, named by the board's conservative members, were Christian fundamentalists and ideologues. One of the conservative members created a stir in summer 2009 when he recommended that Cesar Chavez and Thurgood Marshall be removed from Texas social studies texts. Chavez, the prominent Hispanic and farm labor activist, and Marshall, the famous NAACP lawyer and first black member of the U.S. Supreme Court, were thought too radical to provide useful examples of democratic citizenship to Texas students.[73]

The role of ideology in Texas public schools is nowhere more evident than in sex education. While comprehensive sex education has become more and more common around the country, Texas doggedly adheres to an "abstinence only" program. Abstinence only makes the incontrovertible point that if young people abstain from sex before marriage, they will not get pregnant, while ignoring the equally incontrovertible fact that many do have sex and do get pregnant. A 2009 study by Professor David Wiley and others at Texas State University found that 94 percent of Texas school districts taught abstinence only, 2 percent taught no sex ed, and about 4 percent taught a more comprehensive program dealing with sexual health and safety in addition to abstinence.[74] The U.S. has a national teen pregnancy rate of 34.2 per 1,000 young women. The rate in Texas is 52.2 cases per 1,000; only Mississippi, Arkansas, and New Mexico are higher. If facts mattered, changes would be made. They don't.[75]

High School Graduation Rates and College Readiness

Texas puts less money into its schools than do most American states. That fact is worrisome but not dispositive, what really matters is how well Texas students are educated. Two measures are available. Perhaps the best information we have on the educational attainment of the population over 25 comes from the U.S. Census. These data include students who graduate on time, return to school to graduate late, or get a General Educational Development (GED) degree later in life. These data also report educational attainment by race and ethnicity.

From the 1950s through the 1970s, Texas educational attainment trailed the U.S. rates by three or four percentage points; since the 1980s that gap has been more often in the six to eight point range. However, in both the U.S. and Texas, the gap between black and white educational attainment rates has closed while the gap between Hispanic and black and white rates has remained disturbingly large. Table 5.3 shows that U.S. educational attainment rates, measured as the share of adults over age 25 holding a high school diploma, have increased from 34 percent in 1950 to 87 percent in 2010, while Texas rates have increased from 30 percent in 1950 to 80 percent in 2010. White educational attainment rates remain about ten points ahead of black rates and about thirty points ahead of Hispanic rates.

Are those who graduate from high school in Texas ready for college? The Scholastic Aptitude Test (SAT) is the principal college placement exam taken by Texas high school seniors. About 60 percent of the class of 2012, nearly 172,802 students, took the SATs. We can compare the mean score achieved by Texas high school seniors with the mean score achieved by high school seniors nationally since 1987. Figure 5.5 shows that in every year from 1987 through 2012 Texas seniors trailed their peers nationally by anywhere from fourteen to thirty-seven points. Texas picked up some ground on the national average SAT scores in the early 1990s, closing the gap from twenty-nine points in 1987 to just fourteen points in 1995. But the gap widened to thirty-four points in both 2001 and 2004, and fully thirty-seven points by 2012. Once again, year after year, Texas is striving to get to the national average and never quite making it.

Table 5.4 allows us to look more closely at differences in performance on the SAT by ethnic groups nationally and in Texas. Average SAT scores for the U.S. and Texas improved from 1987 through 2005 in the case of the U.S. and 2007 for Texas. In the past several years the bottom has fallen out of U.S. and Texas SAT scores. In both cases they have slipped back to 1987

Table 5.3 Educational Attainment in the U.S. and Texas, Percent of High School Graduates, 1950–2010

	U.S.				Texas			
	Total	*White*	*Black*	*Hisp.*	*Total*	*White*	*Black*	*Hisp.*
1950	34	36	14		30	33	12	
1960	41	43	20		40	42	21	
1970	55	57	36		47	50	39	
1980	69	72	51	45	64	68	55	
1990	78	81	66	51	75	76	66	45
2000	84	88	79	57	76	80	76	49
2010	87	88	84	63	80	91	84	57

Source: U.S. Census Bureau, Statistical Abstract of the United States, each year 1950–2011, "Persons 25 and Over, Years of School Completed by States," www.census.gov/compendia/statab/past_years. html and http://nces.ed.gov/programs/digest/d10/tables/dt10_012.asp. Texas in 1950 is Census, 43: 402; 1960 is Census, 45: 716.

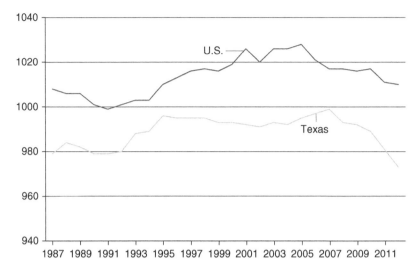

Figure 5.5 Scholastic Aptitude Test (SAT) Scores for the U.S. and Texas High School Seniors, 1987–2012.

Source: Texas Education Agency, "Results of College Admissions Testing in Texas for 1997–98 Graduating Seniors," Table 1-A, p. 23; "College Admissions Testing of Graduating Seniors in Texas High Schools, Class of 2009," Table 22, p. 51. See http://ritter.tea.state.tx.us/research/pdfs/98act.pdf and http://ritter.tea.state.tx.us/research/pdfs/sat-act_2009.pdf.

levels. In the late 1980s, the average Texas SAT score trailed the national average by about twenty to thirty points and every major Texas ethnic group—whites, blacks, and Hispanics—trailed their respective national groups. Texas whites trailed national whites by about twenty points, Texas blacks trailed national blacks by about a dozen points, and Texas Hispanics trailed national Hispanics by single digits. By the late 1990s, all of these deficits had been cut to ten points or fewer and though they increased in the early 2000s for blacks and Hispanics. By 2007 Texas Anglos and blacks passed their national peers, though Texas Hispanics still trail theirs.

In 2013, Texas whites scored 1064 on the SAT compared to 1061 for U.S. whites, Texas blacks very nearly matched U.S. blacks by 859 to 860, and Texas Hispanics trailed their peers nationally by 899 to 911. How can it be, when two of three of Texas's major racial and ethnic groups beat or match their national peers, that Texas still trails the overall SAT national average by thirty-four points. The answer is in the comparative ethnic make-up of the test groups nationally and in Texas. Nationally about 17 percent of SAT-takers are Hispanic and in Texas the number is about 36 percent. In 2013, Hispanic test-takers averaged about 165 points less than white test-takers in Texas, hence, with the Texas test group composed of

Table 5.4 Scholastic Aptitude Test (SAT) Scores for U.S. and Texas High School Seniors, 1987–2013

	U.S.				Texas			
	Total	*White*	*Black*	*Hisp.*	*Total*	*White*	*Black*	*Hisp.*
1987	1008	1038	839	908	979	1016	821	901
1988	1006	1036	847	910	984	1020	840	909
1989	1006	1038	849	919	982	1021	841	910
1990	1001	1034	847	911	979	1019	842	906
1991	999	1031	846	909	979	1022	842	904
1992	1001	1034	847	908	980	1025	835	902
1993	1003	1037	850	910	988	1034	845	911
1994	1003	1039	849	909	989	1038	843	913
1995	1010	1046	854	916	996	1043	853	917
1996	1013	1049	856	918	995	1044	852	912
1997	1016	1052	857	917	995	1046	848	911
1998	1017	1054	860	916	995	1048	850	910
1999	1016	1055	856	915	993	1047	847	906
2000	1019	1058	860	918	993	1051	850	904
2001	1026	1060	859	915	992	1051	846	900
2002	1020	1060	857	911	991	1052	840	896
2003	1026	1053	857	912	993	1054	841	894
2004	1026	1059	857	916	992	1050	843	897
2005	1028	1068	864	923	995	1061	853	905
2006	1021	1063	863	919	997	1063	861	907
2007	1017	1061	862	921	999	1062	868	916
2008	1017	1065	856	916	993	1065	861	910
2009	1016	1064	855	914	992	1069	862	908
2010	1017	1064	857	918	989	1068	861	910
2011	1011	1063	855	913	981	1062	861	902
2012	1010	1063	856	909	973	1062	857	897
2013	1010	1061	860	911	976	1064	859	899

Source: Texas Education Agency, "Results of College Admissions Testing in Texas for 1997–98 Graduating Seniors," Table 1-A, p. 23; "College Admissions Testing of Graduating Seniors in Texas High Schools, Class of 2008," Table 22, p. 55–56. See http://ritter.tea.state.tx.us/research/pdfs/98act. pdf and http://ritter.tea.state.tx.us/research/pdfs/sat-act_2008.pdf.

fewer white test-takers and more Hispanic test-takers than the national test group, the Texas average is lower than the national average. 2013 was the first year that more Texas Hispanics than Anglos took the SAT.

The American College Testing (ACT) exam is also taken by a large number of Texas high school students preparing for college, more than 109,841 in 2013. ACT scores show the same pattern of the slow movement toward the national average that we saw with the SAT scores. Again, in recent years Texas whites and blacks have outperformed their national peers while Texas Hispanics still trail their Hispanic peers nationally. Because the number of Hispanics, the lowest scoring group, in Texas schools is growing and the number of Anglos, the highest scoring group, is shrinking, it is unlikely that Texas SAT and ACT scores will surpass the national average. If anything, Texas is likely to fall back.

Conclusion

Texas was late to establish public schools, slow to make attendance mandatory, and unwilling for decades to fund minority schools at the level of Anglo schools. Though some important reforms were undertaken in the first half of the twentieth century, other states were reforming as well, so Texas's ranking among the states barely changed. Only after World War II, with the state rapidly urbanizing and industrializing, did Texas turn its attention to modernizing its school system. The Gilmer–Aiken reforms of 1949 actually did make Texas a model for educational reform in the other southern states. But like the other southern states, Texas's school system was segregated by race and many of the benefits of reform were lost to a fifteen-year struggle to maintain segregation.

Texas has consistently trailed national averages for per capita educational spending, teacher pay, high school graduation rates, and college preparation as measured by SAT and ACT scores. Over the past six decades, Texas educational expenditures have averaged 84 percent of the national average for state expenditures. Texas has ranked 36th among the fifty states and D.C. since 1950, but has fallen far back in recent years—to 49th in 2012. Texas has done somewhat better on teacher pay, though we slipped to 85 percent of the national average in the most recent data and our average rank among the states since 1950 has been 29th. There have been some improvements by Anglo and black students, but Hispanic students in Texas have continued to lag.

These facts highlight the importance of student effort and teacher effectiveness, but they also highlight the importance of effective public policy. To be perfectly clear, the future of Texas depends upon minority educational achievement. There were 5 million children in Texas public schools in 2011–2012 and two-thirds of them were minority students: 50.8 percent were Hispanic, 12.8 percent were black, 30.5 percent were Anglo, 3.6 percent were Asian, and about 2 percent were others. By 2040, Anglo children will be just 20 percent of Texas school children and the rest will be what historically have been called minority children. Anglo elites, who still control the state and likely will for decades to come, must fund high-quality public education for minority children. Funding equalization between wealthier and poorer schools, even channeling funding toward the poorer schools, seems imperative. Forcing poorer schools to engage in yet another lawsuit to get the funds they need is to fiddle while Rome, or Texas in this case, burns.

Notes

1   Morgan Smith, "At Some Schools, The Demographic Future Is Now," *New York Times*, August 13, 2012, pp. A21A–A22Z.
2   William H. Frey, "A Demographic Tipping Point Among America's Three-Year-Olds," Brookings Institution, February 7, 2011.
3   William Ransom Hogan, *The Texas Republic*, Norman, OK: University of Oklahoma Press, 1946, p. 146.
4   *Journal of the House of Representatives of the Republic of Texas*, Third Congress, pp. 168–170.
5   C.E. Evans, *The Story of Texas Schools*, Austin, TX: The Steck Company, 1955, p. 52. See Noah Smithwick, *The Evolution of a State*, Austin: University of Texas Press, 1983 p. 169 for an unvarnished view of Texas education during the Republic.
6   T.R. Fehrenbach, *Lone Star: A History of Texas and the Texans*, New York: Macmillan, 1968, p. 303.
7   Wilhelm Steinert, *North America: Particularly Texas in the Year 1849*, Dallas, TX: DeGolyer Library, 2003, pp. 47, 72, 124.
8   Evans, *The Story of Texas Schools*, p. 68. See also George P. Garrison, *Texas: A Contest of Civilizations*, Boston: Houghton-Mifflin, 1903, pp. 277–278.
9   Randolph B. Campbell, *Gone To Texas: A History of the Lone Star State*, New York: Oxford University Press, 2003, pp. 228–230.
10   Alwyn Barr, *Black Texans: A History of African Americans in Texas, 1528–1995*, Norman, OK: University of Oklahoma Press, 1973/1996, p. 23.
11   Fehrenbach, *Lone Star*, pp. 411, 419; Gene B. Preuss, *To Get A Better School System*, College Station, TX: Texas A&M University Press, 2009, p. 10.
12   Preuss, *To Get A Better School System*, p. 9.
13   Carl H. Moneyhon, *Republicanism in Reconstruction Texas*, Austin, TX: University of Texas Press, 1980, pp. 172–174, 183–184.
14   Preuss, *To Get A Better School System*, pp. 11–12. See also Evans, *The Story of Texas Schools*, p. 87.
15   Thad Sitton and Milam C. Rowold, *Ringing the Children In: Texas Country Schools*, College Station: Texas A&M University Press, 1987, p. 7.
16   Preuss, *To Get a Better School System*, pp. 13–14. See also Evans, *The Story of Texas Schools*, pp. 99–100.
17   Gavin Wright, *Old South, New South: Revolutions in the Southern Economy Since the Civil War*, New York: Basic Books, 1986, p. 80.
18   Preuss, *To Get A Better School System*, p. 15.
19   Sitten and Rowold, *Ringing the Children In*, p. 206.
20   Don Graham, *State of Minds: Texas Culture and Its Discontents*, Austin, TX: University of Texas Press, 2011, p. 27.
21   Frederick Eby, *The Development of Education in Texas*, New York: Macmillan, 1925, p. 51.
22   Evans, *The Story of Texas Schools*, p. 122.
23   Preuss, *To Get A Better School System*, pp. 27–28.
24   Eby, *Development of Education in Texas*, p. 218.
25   Preuss, *To Get A Better School System*, p. 69.
26   Rae Files Still, *The Gilmer-Aiken Bill: A Study in the Legislative Process*, Austin, TX: The Steck Company, 1950, p. 2.
27   Numan V. Bartley, *The New South, 1945–1980*, Baton Rouge, LA: Louisiana State University Press, 1995, pp. 149–151.
28   Dolph Briscoe, *Dolph Briscoe: My Life in Texas Ranching and Politics*, Austin, TX: University of Texas Press, 2008, p. 99.
29   Richard Morehead, *50 Years in Texas Politics*, Burnet, TX: Eakin Press, 1982, p. 110. See also Ricky F. Dobbs, *Yellow Dogs and Republicans: Allan Shivers and Texas Two-Party*

Politics, College Station, TX: Texas A&M University, 2005, pp. 108–111 and Sam Kinch and Stuart Long, *Allen Shivers: The Pied Piper of Texas Politics*, Austin, TX: Shoal Creek Publishers, 1973, p. 157.

30 Robyn Duff Ladino, *Desegregating Texas Schools: Eisenhower, Shivers, and the Crisis at Mansfield High*, Austin, TX: University of Texas Press, 1996, pp. 37–38.

31 Sean P. Cunningham, *Cowboy Conservatism: Texas and the Rise of the Modern Right*, Lexington, KY: University of Kentucky Press, 2010, p. 101.

32 Ladino, *Desegregating Texas Schools*, p. 48.

33 Ibid., p. 5, editorial dated August 6, 1956.

34 Ibid., pp. 93–96, 102.

35 Cox and Phillips, *The House Will Come to Order*, Austin, TX: University of Texas Press, 2010, p. 75.

36 Ladino, *Desegregating Texas Schools*, pp. 130, 137, 140.

37 *Texas Almanac, 2008–09*, published by *Dallas Morning News*, distributed by College Station, TX: Texas A&M University Press Consortium, 2008, p. 582.

38 W. Gardner Selby, "Twenty-Five Summers Ago, a Special Session Touched Off Changes in Public Schools," *Austin American-Statesman*, July 2, 2009.

39 Anthony Champagne and Edward J. Harpham, *Texas at the Crossroads: People, Politics, and Policy*, College Station, TX: Texas A&M University Press, 1987, p. 162.

40 Michael Lind, *Made in Texas: George W. Bush and the Southern Takeover of American Politics*, New York: Basic Books, 2003, p. 125.

41 Bill Hobby, *How Things Really Work: Lessons From a Life in Politics*, Austin, TX: University of Texas Press, 2010, p. 98.

42 J. Steven Farr and Mark Trachtenberg, "The Edgewood Drama: An Epic Quest for Education Equality," *Yale Law and Policy Review*, 17, 2, 1999, pp. 607–727.

43 E. Jane Irons and Sandra Harris, *The Challenge of No Child Left Behind*, New York: Rowman and Littlefield, 2007, p. 118.

44 Claudia Goldin and Lawrence F. Katz, *The Race Between Education and Technology*, Cambridge, Mass: Harvard University Press, 2008, p. 208.

45 Nelson Dometrius, "Education Policy," in Gerry Riposa (ed.), *Texas Public Policy*, Dubuque, IO: Kendall/Hunt, 1987, p. 45.

46 Goldin and Katz, *The Race Between Education and Technology*, p. 345.

47 Robert T. Garrett, "White, Shami Bash Perry on Education," *Dallas Morning News*, February 8, 2010, A1.

48 Robert T. Garrett and Christy Hoppe, "Political Veterans Dissect Budget," *Dallas Morning News*, January 23, 2011, A1.

49 Erica Grieder, *Big, Hot, Cheap, and Right*, New York: Public Affairs, 2013, p. 59.

50 David G. McComb, *Texas: A Modern History*, Austin, TX: University of Texas Press, 2010, p. 190.

51 Kate Alexander, "On School Funding, 'no guarantee' Anymore," *Austin American-Statesman*, June 1, 2011; see also, Patti Kilday Hart, "Public Schools About to Take a Backseat," *Houston Chronicle*, June 4, 2011.

52 "The-Truth-O-Meter Says," *Austin American-Statesman*, March 24, 2012.

53 Briscoe, *Dolph Briscoe: My Life in Texas Ranching and Politics*, pp. 240, 249, 253.

54 Terrence Stutz, "Texas Teacher Shortage in Math, Science Worsens," *Dallas Morning News*, February 10, 2009, p. 4A.

55 National Center on Teacher Quality, "State Teacher Policy Yearbook: What States Can Do to Retain Effective New Teachers, Texas, 2008," pp. 1–2; Tony Wagner, *The Global Achievement Gap*, New York: Basic Books, 2008, p. 14.

56 Christine Armario, Associated Press, "More Teachers Are Moonlighting," *Dallas Morning News*, November, 12, 2011, p. 619.

57 Terrence Stutz, "Texas Adds Electives, Scales Back Required Classes in High School," *Dallas Morning News*, July 7, 2009, A1, A6.

58   Terrence Stutz, "Education Board Seeks Limits on PE Classes," *Dallas Morning News*, August 15, 2009, p. 3A.

59   Terrence Stutz, "Board Changes Rules So Students Can't Load Up On PE Classes," *Dallas Morning News*, November 21, 2009, A1.

60   Kate Alexander, "How Will Texas Compete in Race to the Top?" *Austin American-Statesman*, June 29, 2009.

61   Office of the Governor, press release, http://governor.state.tx.us/news/press- release/13982/.

62   Kate Alexander, "Texas Will Not Compete for Federal Education Grants," *Austin American-Statesman*, January 13, 2010.

63   Terrence Stutz, "9th Graders Beat Lower STARR Expectations," *Dallas Morning News*, June 9, 2012, A1, A2.

64   Holly K. Hacker, "New Rule Boosts Schools to Top of the Ratings," *Dallas Morning News*, August 3, 2009, pp. 1B, 7B.

65   Terrence Stutz, "State's New Tests to be Tougher, Longer," *Dallas Morning News*, December 2, 2010, A3.

66   Kate Alexander, "House Member Get Careful On STARR," *Austin American-Statesman*, June 19, 2012.

67   Terrence Stutz , "New Tests, Same Troubles," *Dallas Morning News*, June 11, 2013, A1, A9.

68   Jeffrey Weiss, "After 3 Decades, A Rollback On Testing," *Dallas Morning News*, June 17,2013, A1, A6.

69   George Norris Green, *The Establishment in Texas Politics: The Primitive Years, 1938–1957*, Norman, OK: University of Oklahoma Press, 1984, pp. 59, 64.

70   Gregg Cantrell, "The Bones of Stephen F. Austin: History and Memory in Progressive-Era Texas," *Southwestern Historical Quarterly*, vol. 65, no. 2, October, 2004, p. 176.

71   James C. McKinley Jr., "Split Outcome in Texas Battle on Teaching of Evolution," *New York Times*, January 24, 2009, A12.

72   Paul Burka, "Lowe and Behold," *Texas Monthly*, September 2009, pp. 8–10.

73   Russell Shorto, "Founding Father?" *The New York Times Magazine*, February 14, 2010, pp. 30–45.

74   David Wiley and Kelly Wilson, "Just Say Don't Know: Sexuality Education in Texas Public Schools," Texas Freedom Network Education Fund, January 2009, pp. 1–76.

75   Christy Hoppe and Danielle Abril, "Sex Ed Is Latest Culture Battle," *Dallas Morning News*, March 10, 2013, A1, A4.

6   Health and Human Services in Texas

> As Texans, we always take care of the least among us. . . . We will pro-
> tect them, . . . but cannot risk the future of millions of taxpayers in the
> process. We must cut spending to keep our economic engine on track.
>
> (Rick Perry, Inaugural Address, 2011)

The Texas political culture highlights independence and individualism and so has little patience with dependency. As with Governor Perry in the quotation above, Texas leaders claim to care about the needy and the afflicted, but they adopt constitutions, pass laws, and allocate funds in a manner that limits actual support for them to a minimum. The tragic consequences of the Texas way regularly come to light, sometimes as a result of official inquiry and action, but more commonly as a result of all too predictable tragedy. To live in Texas is to be subject to a numbing barrage of media reports on underfunded and poorly managed state institutions and programs supposedly designed to serve the poor and the disabled. Texas rarely responds to the needs of the poor and disabled without the intervention of the federal courts and some of these cases go on for decades.

Texas officials are deeply resistant to spending state funds on social services, but they are also resistant to spending federal money, especially when the feds expect more than minimal matching funds. Hence, the 2014–2015 biennial budget allocated $30.8 billion of state general funds to health and human services—a lot of money. But the federal government put up even more: $43.1 billion or nearly 60 percent of total health and human services spending in Texas. Finally, Texas restricts access to health and social welfare programs to keep costs down and leaves federal money on the table when taking it would require matching funds or commit-ments to increase future state spending. Texas is ever wary of the entan-gling "strings" that come attached to federal monies.

Minimal public service is a key component of a "business-friendly" cli-mate in Texas. Persons with access to public support for income, health care, and retirement services might be less willing to work for low pay, while persons without such access will have no choice. Social services raise the cost of doing business by increasing wages and, more importantly, benefits and taxes. Texas's conservative elite, addicted to low taxes, low services, and low wages—though not for themselves of course—even resist spending federal money because they fear it may make the workforce more secure and, therefore, less compliant.

A Brief History of Health Care and Social Services in Texas

Texas has always ranked among the most reluctant states when it comes to social service provision. This has been so since the Republic and remains so today. Every travel account of early Texas is replete with complaints of the "auge," chills, fever, and days lost to slow recovery. East Texas and the Gulf Coast were southern lowlands, to which white labor was thought unfitted and only black labor, held to the task by the whip, could profitably be employed. Still, we know less than one might think about the diseases of early Texas. As the Texas historian T.R. Fehrenbach noted, "The actual incidence of dread diseases, cholera, typhus, and yellow fever, is hard to determine, because Texas newspapers vigorously suppressed such news."[1] Texans did not want to scare away potential immigrants, customers, buyers, or clients, with unfortunate reports about illness and disease.

But we do know that Texans dealt with the incidence of disease and its treatment in the Texas way. Wealthy Texans sought out the best health care available, oftentimes traveling to the United States, while most Texans had to depend upon the little health care available locally. Stanley Siegel's *The Political History of the Texas Republic* explained that in late 1840, "President [Mirabeau B.] Lamar, completely worn down by the cares of state and suffering from an intestinal disorder, asked Congress for a leave of absence to journey to the United States for treatment." President Lamar returned to Austin two months later, "his health restored."[2] The president's decision to seek medical treatment outside Texas was well-made, but not an option open to most of his fellow citizens. Chapter 9 in William Ransom Hogan's *The Texas Republic*, entitled "These Racking Fever Chills," described the medical and political uncertainties of health care in early Texas. Hogan observed that,

> The existence of a few crude hospitals did little to relieve human suffering. . . . For several years the small tax on incoming passengers from foreign ports was the source of support for the Galveston hospital, described by an Englishman as "that shell of misery, that great coffin of the unburied dead." In the summer of 1843 a court ruled that there was no provision for the tax in the city charter and that consequently it was illegal. In commenting on the finding of the court a local editor wrote: "The burden must now fall upon the charity of the people."[3]

Beyond the culture of elite rule, small government, low taxes, and personal responsibility, lay the domain of slavery and the demand for unquestioned discretion in dealing with one's property. Most slave-owner wealth was bound up in slaves, not land, and so slave-owners protected their investment by providing medical care, as they thought appropriate, to their slaves.[4] They cared for their own family and others dependent upon them, again, as they thought appropriate, but they had no incentive to participate in providing care to others. Robert Perkinson has noted that, "Out of the cauldron of slavery, with the endemic violence and dehumanization, emerged a political culture [in which] . . . leading southerners fought vigorously against intrusive government and all types of humanitarian initiatives, which they feared led inexorably to abolitionism."[5]

After slavery, Anglo Texas elites had few incentives to provide special services to the poor, whatever their color. Little changed until the early decades of the twentieth century, especially the 1930s and later, and again only in the Texas way. During the first three decades of the century, governors such as Tom Campbell, the Fergusons, Pat Neff, and Dan Moody campaigned on a more active state government, but every time the legislature considered new appropriations or the people considered referenda to provide new revenues, they pulled back. As Fehrenbach noted, "Public services of all kinds in Texas . . . were calculated to a grudging minimum in almost every case."[6]

When the Great Depression hit, the Hoover administration argued that poor relief was the responsibility of local communities, churches, civic groups, and state government where needed. These resources were soon overwhelmed and when the Roosevelt administration came into office in March 1933, they moved to supplement state efforts. Texas did so little in poor relief that the federal government threatened to stop aid unless the state did more. In response, the Texas Legislature, with Governor Jim Ferguson's strong backing, submitted a proposal to the voters for $20 million in "bread bonds" to provide welfare benefits to poor Texans. Though the bonds were approved in August 1933, as late as November 1937 the average state welfare benefit was just $15 a month paid to about 140,000 recipients.[7]

Franklin Roosevelt's aggressive action to confront the Great Depression had many Texas supporters, including Vice President John Nance "Cactus Jack" Garner, Majority Leader and then Speaker Sam Rayburn, and a young Lyndon Johnson. But by 1940, Vice President Garner's distaste for the big, powerful, and expensive government of the New Deal provoked him to stand against FDR for the presidency. Rayburn supported Garner, but LBJ stuck with the president. Texans divided over the contest and great bitterness followed Roosevelt's easy defeat of Garner.[8] The Texas Democratic Party split into liberal and conservative wings with conservative Democrats dominating until the Republicans took over, except for the one-term governorships of Mark White in the early 1980s and Ann Richards in the early 1990s.

For decades, Texas conservative Democrats were well to the right of national Republicans. In January 1969, newly elected Governor Preston Smith used his inaugural address to promise "that he would cope fairly and justly with 'problems of the young, of the old, of racial minorities, of disadvantages economic groups, problems of the sick, the afflicted, and the mentally ill.'" A few months later, when the governor was called to Washington to be briefed on a new Nixon administration initiative on slum clearance, he listened, and then immediately declared his opposition to the program. Governor Smith explained that a similar program had been tried in his hometown of Lubbock. One slum neighborhood had been cleared, but displaced residents just moved to another slum across town. Smith concluded that "some people just like to live in slums."[9]

The Texas way early found a dominant political strategy in regard to social services—keep taxes low, depend on federal money where possible, but do not threaten the traditional compliance of Texas workers. A 1962 study by the non-partisan Texas Research League caught part of this, saying, "Texas has traditionally followed a policy of appropriating the minimum amount of state money necessary to get the maximum amount of federal money available."[10] As we shall see throughout this chapter, the modest but sensible strategy described by the Texas Research League has changed over the past half century. For decades now it has been quite common for Texas to leave large amounts of federal money on the table because it is unwilling to raise and spend the required matching funds.

No one disputes that Texas has long been one of the most tight-fisted states when it comes to public assistance broadly defined. There is, however, lively debate over why this is so and whether it is good or bad. Texas has long touted individualism and personal responsibility and disdained big, expensive, and intrusive government. Texas-elected officials frequently argue that overly generous government programs, whether administered from the national or state levels or jointly, might sap a person's willingness to work. They have moved forcefully to see that that does not happen. Of most direct relevance to the substance of this chapter, Article III, section 51a, of the Texas Constitution, an amendment approved in 1945, declared that, "The maximum amount paid out of state funds for assistance grants to or on behalf of needy dependent children and their caretakers shall not exceed one percent of the state budget." The Great Recession of 2008 and 2009 laid bare the need in Texas but did little to shake the commitment of the state's political elite to small government.

In 2009, the *New York Times* highlighted the state's tight-fistedness on social spending. In a front-page story on May 10, 2009, the *Times*'s economic writer, Jason DeParle, surveyed the fifty states and D.C. on six social welfare programs: cash assistance, unemployment compensation, housing assistance, food stamps, and assistance with health care for both poor children and poor adults.[11] On each of the six measures, states were ranked by what proportion of the needy population was being served and then a general ranking was done across all six measures. Texas ranked 50 out of 51, only Colorado ranked lower, and Texas ranked in the bottom ten on four of the six measures and in the top ten on none. Even more strikingly, in 2012 the federal Agency for Health Care Research and Quality rated Texas worst in the nation, dead last, in health care services and delivery. Texas rated low in nine of twelve major areas of comparison, including quality of home health care services, about which more below, preventive acute and chronic care, limited Medicaid services, and access to health insurance.[12] So was Governor Perry right that Texas protects its most vulnerable citizens even while keeping taxes very low? Or does the priority on low taxes preclude the possibility of protecting the poor in Texas?

Does Texas Care for Its Most Vulnerable?

We answer with a long sad tale about Texas and its most dependent citizens, the mentally challenged. Throughout 2009 the *Dallas Morning News*, one of the state's leading conservative papers, ran a series entitled "State of Neglect," referring both to the state of Texas and to the poor social services that it provides. One focus of this series was the condition of state institutions and programs to serve the mentally challenged. Stories such as these have run regularly in Texas newspapers for decades.

Throughout the middle decades of the twentieth century, Texas consistently ranked near the bottom on state funding for care of those then called the mentally retarded. When Governor Buford Jester died unexpectedly on July 11, 1949, the sad state of Texas's mental hospitals had already been on the agenda for a decade. Allan Shivers, the state's new governor, toured the state facilities and in early 1950 called a special session of the legislature to deal with what he found. Shivers was a staunch conservative, wealthy businessman, and, through his wife, owner of the famous Sharyland ranching properties in South Texas. Nonetheless, Shivers decried the fact that, "Texas—the proud Lone Star State—first in oil— forty eighth in mental hospitals. First in cotton—worst in tuberculosis. First in raising goats— last in caring for state wards."[13] Just as it had three decades earlier with education, challenging the state's pride by mocking its low ranking on services carried the day, at least temporarily. Shivers got increased appropriations for the state's mental institutions, improvements were made, but soon other emergencies arose, attention drifted away, and the old status quo reemerged.

In late 1974, a quarter century after the Shivers reforms, the Dallas Legal Services Foundation sued the Texas Department of Mental Health and Mental Retardation (TDMHMR), in a case called *Lelsz v. Kavanaugh*, charging that "the state institutions were little more than barren and dreary warehouses for mentally retarded persons where, rather than receiving treatment, the residents were being subjected to chronic abuse and neglect amid deplorable conditions."[14] The suit dragged on for nearly a decade until in 1983 Texas Attorney General Jim Maddox pressured TDMHMR to agree to a settlement guaranteeing the mentally challenged the right to individualized care, often in community settings instead of large state institutions. Part of the settlement involved hiring an expert consultant, Linda R. O'Neall, to oversee implementation. O'Neall worried that "What you have in Texas is a great propensity to institutionalize people," and that once institutions are built, they become part of the political resistance to change.[15]

Yet, another quarter century on, Texas spends less on assistance to the mentally challenged than virtually any other state and houses more people in large state institutions, and politicians preen at their still modest accomplishments. The most recent data (2012) show that Texas ranks 50th among the fifty states and D.C. on state mental health spending. The national average for state spending on per capita mental health services is $125 while Texas spends just $39.[16] Before passing on too quickly, let your mind dwell on those numbers and then consider the following. By 2010, more than a quarter century after the state agreed to provide community care for the mentally challenged, 40,000 Texans with mental disabilities remained on waiting lists for home and community-based treatment.

Under new pressure from a four-year investigation by the federal Department of Justice, which found civil rights violations across the thirteen state institutions for the mentally challenged, Governor Perry declared the state schools a legislative emergency in early 2009. Texas Senator Steve Ogden (R-Bryan), chair of the Senate budget committee said, as if echoing Linda O'Neall's comments from twenty-five years earlier, "My view is that it is politically impossible to close a state school, but we can manage the size of the state schools. There's always a constituency out there in support of each individual state school, and they can usually muster enough political firepower to prevent us from closing any state school." One of the state's major newspapers then noted, rather laconically, that "Nationally, there's a trend for states to move away from institutionalizing people with mental retardation, but Texas hasn't kept pace: The Lone Star State has a higher institutionalization rate than the nation as a whole and has more people living in state schools than any other state."[17]

Then in March 2009, as legislators debated, video surfaced of state mental health facility employees organizing late-night "fight clubs" by pairing off patients and forcing them to fight. As the footage aired on national and international news outlets, Texas officials had no choice but to move. By mid-May, Texas reached an agreement with the Justice Department requiring that the state spend $112 million over five years to hire 1,000 workers to improve staffing ratios, increase monitoring and oversight, and enhance care. Assuming that the money is spent and conditions improve, federal oversight would be lifted at the end of the five-year period. State

Senator Jane Nelson (R-Flower Mound), chair of the committee that oversees the state's health and human services agencies, declared that "We are all ready for a new beginning in our efforts to take care of and protect Texans with disabilities."[18] Skepticism is still advised, though the legislature initially did more than required by the Justice Department agreement. They allocated an additional $200 million (for a grand total of new and old money of $507 million) to provide community-based care to 8,000 people on the state's waiting lists. If long-standing patterns hold, good intentions (and embarrassment) will fade, new crises will arise in other underfunded programs, and the mentally disabled will again fade from view. As Mimi Swartz noted in a *Texas Monthly* article dedicated to the shortcomings of Texas mental institutions, "It is a measure of how bad things are . . . that some who fought for the increased appropriation and accompanying reforms are grateful for what they got."[19]

Texas politicians, mental health professionals, and citizens know that the next morning's paper might bring reports of another tragedy. Despite the most recent settlement with the federal government, many go unserved until it is too late. In July 2009, Otty Sanchez, a schizophrenic institutionalized for two weeks in 2008, suffering from post-partum psychosis, sought admission to Houston's Metropolitan Methodist Hospital's psychiatric unit. She was denied admission as neither suicidal nor homicidal. Less than a week later, she decapitated her infant son.[20] Just as tragically, in the summer of 2007, Steven Guillory, a schizophrenic released from the Psychiatric Center of the Harris County Jail, threatened his mother with a knife. She called "911" and the police responded. Steven was in the yard waving a length of pipe when they arrived. He menaced them with the pipe and they shot him dead.[21]

Inadequate mental health treatment facilities produce tragedies of various kinds. One tragedy is that adults with mental health problems that might be treated instead end up in prisons and jails ill-equipped to handle them. "Already, the Harris County Jail is the largest mental health ward in the state, treating some 2,500 inmates for mental health conditions."[22] Just as sadly, Texas youth with mental health conditions must, by law, be released from Texas Youth Commission facilities that are not equipped to treat them. One such youth, unnamed because of his age, killed Todd Henry, his special education teacher at John Tyler High School in Tyler, with a butcher knife.[23] The deep budget cuts enacted for the 2012–2013 biennium made Texas state mental health services even less available, with predictable consequences.

The 2013 legislative session added $240 million to state mental health funding. This is good to be sure, but in a state that has ranked 49th or 50th for a decade, all the time touting its renewed commitment to addressing the needs of the most vulnerable, it is pitifully little. When the next set of comparative state figures come out, Texas will still rank near the very bottom.

Texas Health Care Practitioners and Expenditures

Texas has always had fewer doctors per 100,000 of population than most other states and the nation in general. Excellent data on doctors per 100,000 of population go back more than half a century and show that Texas had just 75 percent of the national average of doctors per 100,000 of population between 1955 and 1970 and about 80 percent since. Though the number of doctors per 100,000 of population has doubled in both the U.S. and Texas in the past half century, from 133 to 274 for the U.S. and from 102 to 218 in Texas, Texas has lagged behind the entire time and has made up little ground over time. Today, Texas ranks 39th among the fifty states (Figure 6.1). The doctor shortage is particularly acute in rural Texas. In 2012, more than half of Texas's 254 counties were designated by the federal government as primary-care (regular family doctors) shortage areas. Twenty-six counties had no doctors at all.[24] Data on nurses actively working in health care are sketchier, showing a similar but even lower trajectory. Through the 1960s, Texas has less than 60 percent of the national average of nurses per 100,000 and has generally been in the 70 percent range since, reaching 80 percent only in the mid-1990s and since 2006. Moreover, Texas's physician and nursing force is aging. More than 40 percent of doctors and 35 percent of nurses are over 50 years of age and, hence, approaching retirement over this same period.[25]

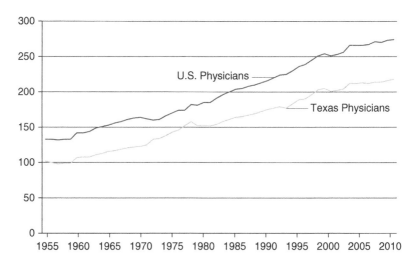

Figure 6.1 Number of U.S. and Texas Physicians Per 100,000 of Population, 1955–Present.

Source: U.S. Census Bureau, Statistical Abstract of the United States, each year 1955 to present, Health and Nutrition, Health Care Resources, Active Physicians and Nurses by State.

One might assume, rightly, as it turns out, that a tight supply of doctors and nurses would drive up the price of health care in Texas. Texas hospitals are more expensive than U.S. hospitals in general, and so Texans respond by spending less time in them. In 1970, the average daily cost of a hospital stay in Texas was 90 percent of the average U.S. cost, $73 compared to $81, while the average cost of a multiday stay was just 79 percent, $525 compared to $664 nationally. A decade later, in 1980, the cost per day was still just 90 percent of the national average, $252 compared to $281, while the average cost of a multiday hospital stay was still 78 percent, $1,661 compared to $2,126 nationally. By 1985, the average per day cost in Texas had eclipsed the national average, though the per stay cost remained at just 86 percent of the national average. By 1990, the average per day cost ballooned to 109 percent of the national average, $752 compared to $687, while the per stay cost had also risen, but just to 94 percent of the national average, $4,463 compared to $4,947. This pattern continues to hold today. The data in Figure 6.2 show Texans paying more for each day's hospital stay but staying fewer days in the hospital than do their fellow citizens nationally.

Another factor driving up the cost of care in Texas is the number of persons without health insurance. Persons without health insurance tend not to seek care until they are truly ill and then to seek it in the most expensive venue—the emergency room. Texas has for many years had among the

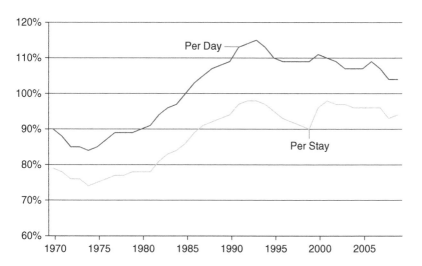

Figure 6.2 Average Cost Per Day and Per Stay of Texas Community Hospitals as a Percent of U.S. Costs, 1970–Present.

Source: U.S. Census Bureau, Statistical Abstract of the United States, Health and Nutrition, Health Care Resources, Average Cost of Community Hospitals by State. See also Kaiser State Health Facts.

highest proportion of uninsured residents in the country, and in recent years, Texas never ranked better than 48th. Over the past two decades, about 15 percent of U.S. residents and 25 percent of Texas residents have not had health insurance. Among children the numbers of uninsured are slightly lower, but Texas still has 8 percent more uninsured children than the U.S. in general. About 6.4 million Texas residents did not have health insurance in 2012 (Figure 6.3).

The large number of uninsured in Texas drive up insurance premiums and health care costs for those who do have insurance. Families USA issued a major study in 2009 showing that average annual health insurance premiums in Texas rose from $6,638 in 2000 to $12,721 in 2009, an increase of 92 percent. Over that same period of time, workers' median income rose less than 20 percent.[26] The Center for American Progress reported that "cost-shifting" from the uninsured to the insured added $1,800 or 13 percent in premiums to every insured family plan. Finally, more of the uninsured in Texas are employed than is the case nationally. Texas is a low-wage economy that depends heavily on small businesses for jobs. Only 51.1 percent of the state's residents were covered by employer-sponsored insurance 2009–2010, compared to 58.6 percent nationally, the Census Bureau reported. The low rate for Texas reflects the fact that 75 percent of companies are small businesses, with under fifty employees, and less than one-third of them offer insurance. Fully 82 percent of uninsured Texans are in working families.[27]

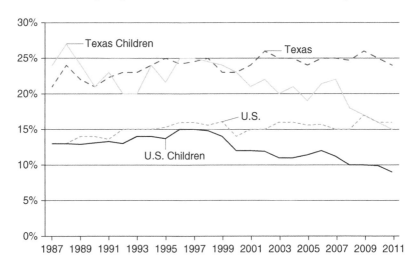

Figure 6.3 Percent of Persons without Health Insurance in Texas and the U.S., 1987–Present.

Source: U.S. Census Bureau, Historical Health Insurance Tables, Table H1–4 and Table H1–5, http://www.census.gov/hhes/www/hlthins/historic/hlthin05/hihistt4.html.

(Data source contains health insurance rates by race.)

Conservatives, especially Texas conservatives, argue that medical malpractice reform, often referred to simply as tort reform, is a critical element of reducing or at least slowing the rise of health care costs. Thirty states have enacted some version of medical malpractice reform, with Texas being among the most comprehensive. In 2003, Texas capped medical malpractice non-economic damages, for what is often described as pain and suffering, at $250,000. Doctors are still liable for loss of earnings and medical expenses, but the prospect of being on the hook for additional millions has been removed. As a result, medical malpractice suits fell by 70 percent, doctors' medical malpractice premiums fell by nearly half, but medical costs in Texas continued to rise at rates faster than the national average. Advocates of the reform claim that the number of doctors in Texas and particularly the number of emergency room physicians has increased, though, as we saw above, the overall numbers have not budged. In 2003, Texas had 80 percent of the physicians the U.S. had per 100,000 of population (212 vs. 266) and, in 2010, Texas had the same 80 percent (218 vs. 271).

A study by Northwestern University's Kellogg School of Management involving 10 million Americans covered by employer-sponsored health plans found that nationwide tort reform might lower health care costs by up to 2.3 percent. A 2004 study by the Congressional Budget Office reported that less than 2 percent of medical expenses could be attributed to malpractice awards and defensive medicine.[28] Studies of Texas Medicare spending between 2002 and 2009, led by UT law professor Charles Silver, found no reduction in doctor's fees and no influx of doctors into the state following tort reform.[29] Therefore, one must ask, if medical malpractice reform does not affect the cost of health care to the consumer, then what is the justification for limiting consumers' rights to legal redress for medical injury? Better than malpractice reform alone would be reforms that tackled both medical negligence and the uncertainty and expense doctors incur in insuring against it.

Medicare, Medicaid, and CHIP in the U.S. and Texas

Social Security was passed in 1935, during the Great Depression, to cushion the elderly from the loss of income when they were no longer able to work. Medicare and Medicaid were passed in 1965 to add pre-paid health care for the elderly and other eligible groups (Medicare) and free health care for the poor (Medicaid). Medicare was established as an adjunct to Social Security, organized and funded similarly, through payroll taxes paid by workers and their employers. Like Social Security, Medicare is administered and funded by the federal government. Medicaid is a joint federal/state program wherein the federal government establishes the broad design and provides base funding for the program and each state defines eligibility criteria and provides additional funding to reach the benefit levels that they have set. Some states add generously to the base federal funding for Medicaid and some states do not. Medicare and Medicaid, one run on federal money and one run on base federal funding and state matching funds, provide insight into Texas's attitude toward public services and their financial support.

Medicare is essentially a bottomless pool of federal money. Medicare negotiates reimbursement rates for health care services provided by doctors, hospitals, medical laboratories, medical equipment providers, home health care providers, and others and then reimburses providers at those rates for services delivered to eligible Medicare patients. Rates vary somewhat by region according to the historic and traditional costs of service delivery in that region. Once a provider is in the Medicare system as an eligible provider, there is little oversight of the millions of individual health care transactions, from office visits, to medical tests, hospital and out-patient procedures, and prescriptions.

Texans, both patients and service providers, have been among the nation's most enthusiastic users of Medicare services. Moreover, Texas's use of the Medicare system and the costs of that usage have increased dramatically in recent decades and especially in recent years. Medicare was established in 1965 and we have very good data on national and state usage beginning in 1967 (Figure 6.4). Between 1967 and 1981, Medicare costs per enrollee in Texas averaged about 95 percent of costs nationally. In the early 1980s, costs rose as high as 106 percent in 1984, before moderating later in the decade. By the mid-1990s, Texas Medicare costs jumped from 95 percent of the national average to 119 percent and have run between 110 and 115 percent since. As late as 1991, twenty states had average per enrollee Medicare costs greater than Texas. By 1995 only three states (Massachusetts, Florida, and Louisiana) had higher costs per enrollee, by 1996 only two states (Massachusetts and Louisiana) did, and by 1997 only Louisiana had higher rates. Though per enrollee costs moderated a little after 1997, from 1995 through 2010, Texas averaged 112 percent of the national average for expenditures per Medicare enrollee, placing Texas 5th highest among the fifty states during that period. In 2010, the latest year for which we have complete data, the average cost per Medicare enrollee in the U.S. was $9,347 while in Texas it was $10,694 per enrollee.

Explanations for the dramatic increase in Medicare spending in Texas over the last twenty years vary. Some point to the fact that Texas provides little health care to its nonelderly poor and so they arrive at Medicare eligible age with more problems than do their counterparts in other states. This is undoubtedly true, but there is more to it than that. A major study by the Dartmouth Institute for Health Policy and Clinical Practice, released in February 2009 and based on intensive analysis of two decades of data, declared that "Medicare beneficiaries in high-spending regions do not

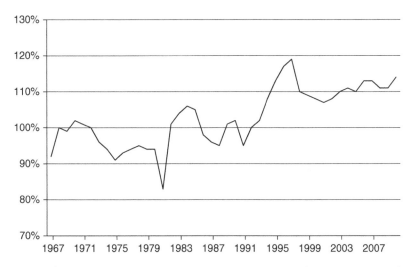

Figure 6.4 Texas Medicare Payments Per Enrollee as a Percent of U.S. Payments, 1967–
Present.

Source: U.S. Census Bureau, Statistical Abstract of the United States, each year, Table entitled
Medicare—Summary, by State." See also AARP Public Policy Institute, "Texas Quick Health Facts
2010," Leigh Purvis, 202-434-3890.

receive more 'effective care.' . . . Patients in high-spending regions are
hospitalized more frequently, spend more time in the ICU, see physicians
more frequently, and get more diagnostic tests than identical patients in
lower-spending regions."[30] The Dartmouth study confirmed what many
health professionals and experts already knew, that high cost, absent
improved health outcomes, suggested substantial inefficiency and waste.

Medical studies, even on critical topics, rarely become the topic of
national conversation. The Dartmouth study did when a provocative article, "The Cost Conundrum: What a Texas Town Can Teach Us About
Health Care," appeared in the June 1, 2009, issue of *The New Yorker*. The
author of the *New Yorker* piece, a medical doctor named Atul Gawande,
particularized the issue of regional disparities in Medicare costs by asking
how McAllen, Texas, hard on the Mexican border in Hidalgo County, one
of the poorest counties in the nation, became one of the most expensive
health care markets in the nation. Plausible reasons exist to believe that
health care might be expensive in McAllen—poverty, lack of health insurance, the prevalence of heavy drinking, and high obesity rates obviously
produce health consequences. But as Gawande noted, El Paso, Texas, eight
hundred miles up the Rio Grande and also on the Mexican border, had a
very similar social, economic, and demographic profile. Medicare expenses

per enrollee in McAllen in 2006 were $15,000 while they were half that, about $7,500, in El Paso.

McAllen did not have more doctors, more specialists, or better equipment and facilities. Gawande concluded that overutilization of medical services, driven by and for the benefit of local doctors, hospitals, and other medical service providers, was the distinguishing driver of soaring costs: "Compared with patients in El Paso and nationwide, patients in McAllen got more of pretty much everything—more diagnostic testing, more hospital treatment, more surgery, more home care."[31] Gawande noted that "In 1992, in the McAllen market, the average cost per Medicare enrollee was $4,891, almost exactly the national average. But since then, year after year, McAllen's health costs have grown faster than any other market in the country, ultimately soaring by more than ten thousand dollars per person."[32] But McAllen is by no means alone in Texas. The Medicare market in Texas generally began to heat up in the early 1990s and has made Texas among the most expensive Medicare states. McAllen is just a particularly egregious example and was called out for it nationally.

Not surprisingly, the Dartmouth Study and the Gawande article have not gone unchallenged. Urban hospitals in particular have made the strong case that they serve patients that are sicker and poorer.[33] Despite the criticism, two points—that costs have risen much more rapidly in some areas than others and that higher costs do not necessarily mean better health care results—are now entrenched. For example, in late 2009, the Medicare Payments Advisory Commission released a study, entitled "Measuring Regional Variations in Service Use," in which five Texas metropolitan areas, including Houston and Dallas-Fort Worth, were among the fifteen most expensive areas of 404 studied.[34] Dartmouth and the Medicare Payments Advisory Commission both highlight comparisons such as that between Sacramento and Dallas between 1994 and 2006. In 1994, Sacramento and Dallas were both near the national average for Medicare expenditures per patient at about $4,500. By 2006, Sacramento had risen to $7,324, the national average had risen to $8,304, and Dallas had soared to $10,103.[35] Sacramento held down costs by coordinating and integrating care, bringing together doctors, nurses, and hospitals and other caregivers around patient service and quality.

Increasingly, discussions of the high cost of health care in Texas cite the state's "entrepreneurial tradition." This is not a compliment; rather, it suggests a health care community built around provider profit more than around patient care. A glaring example of Texas entrepreneurialism that has drawn recent attention is Medicare-funded home health care. Home health care is an important service as the frail elderly often have difficulty getting to the doctor's office or the hospital. But even important services can be abused: "Texas has more home health agencies billing Medicare and more Medicare home health patients than any other state. It also ranks near the bottom in Medicare home health quality ratings and near the top in suspected waste and fraud." This is obviously problematic, but it gets much worse. In a near feeding frenzy between 2002 and 2006, Texas saw a 102 percent increase in the number of home health agencies billing Medicare and a 144 percent increase in home health care spending. In 2007, each Texan served by home health care cost Medicare $7,761, the highest cost in the nation, 41 percent per patient higher than California and 53 percent higher than the national average of $5,064.[36]

In 2010, according to AARP, Texas had more Medicare recipients receiving home health care than the national average (12.3 percent, compared to 7.4 percent), being visited more frequently (sixty times a year compared to thirty-seven), by more home health care providers. Remarkably, by 2010 more than 20 percent of Medicare certified home health care agencies in the U.S. were in Texas, fully 2,114 of 10,135 nationally.[37] By 2013, the number of home health care agencies in Texas was up to 2,949. It seems that Texans discovered that the honey pot was essentially unguarded and that you could dip into it with a bucket as easily as you could with a cup.

In early 2012, federal investigators moved against "a massive health care fraud scheme" in which Dallas area Dr. Jacques Roy, working with several dozen home health care companies recruited clients, including in homeless shelters, and then billed Medicare and Medicaid for nearly $375 million in services. Roy's practice became the largest in the nation between 2006 and 2011 as he and others "certified 11,000 Medicare beneficiaries for more than 500 home health services."[38] Investigators found and froze $4 million of an estimated $19 million of Dr. Roy's illicit charges and 78 Dallas area home health companies were suspended as approved Medicare and Medicaid providers.

Dr. Roy was by no means alone. In August 2012, the nation's top health care inspector called for a moratorium on new home health care agencies. He found that 80 percent of suspicious billing cases came from just four states—Texas, Florida, Michigan, and California—and 40 percent came from Texas alone. One reason that Texas has so many home health care agencies filing so many claims is that, unlike in many states, Texas does not require new home health care businesses to file a "statement of need" for their services—entrepreneurship and limited regulation you see!

Finally, a 2012 study by the Commonwealth Fund, entitled "Rising to the Challenge," ranked 306 hospital referral regions around the nation. High costs and large numbers of uninsured placed Dallas 264th, Houston 283rd, and Beaumont 303rd of 306. Even more strikingly, on health insurance coverage, fully 16 of the bottom 30 cities were Texas cities. Newspaper reports noted that these "findings were in line with other scorecards done by Washington's Brookings Institution and the Dartmouth Institute for Health Policy and Clinical Practice."[39]

One reason that the lid is off the honey pot in Texas is that state government has outsourced much of its health and human services claims processing and service delivery to private contractors. Privatization allows the passing through of federal funds to contractors with few state employees required for service delivery or oversight of programs. Newspaper reports in early 2009 explained that, "Government outsourcing in Texas expanded dramatically with 2003 legislation that crunched twelve health and human service agencies into five . . . and replaced state workers with private contractors. . . . This year's [2009] health and human services budget is $29.3 billion. . . . nearly $25 billion was for contracts, including payments to doctors, pharmacies, hospitals and private companies."[40] If state government is undermanned, as it surely is in Texas, who is watching the private interests of both contractors and service providers?

Unlike Medicare, which is a federal program generally serving the retired elderly, Medicaid is a joint federal/state program serving poor children. Although the federal government establishes the general guidelines for the program, states set the eligibility rules and payment levels. When the program was passed by Congress in 1965, it was designed to be the insurer of last resort for the society's most needy. States were initially required to serve families who qualified for Aid to Families with Dependent Children (AFDC, about which more below) and elderly and disabled who qualified for Supplemental Security Income. In the 1980s, Congress began to require states to broaden and deepen eligibility, adding children of low income families, pregnant women with children aged under 6 whose family income was below 133 percent of the poverty rate, children aged 6 to 19 whose family income was up to 100 percent of the poverty rate, and several other groups. States were encouraged to make still other categories of people eligible, such as poor adults without children, and to raise the income levels below which persons become eligible. Texas's response to the expansion of Medicaid, beginning in the mid-1980s, was to cut to a bare bones program. Unfortunately, good data on the Texas Medicaid program goes back just to 1979.

From 1979 through 1982, Texas limited the number of persons eligible for Medicaid services but built on federal Medicaid contributions. Texas Medicaid expenses per enrollee averaged 123 percent of the national average. But as the Texas economy began to stall in the mid-1980s, Texas held the number of Medicaid recipients steady while cutting back on state contributions to Medicaid. Medicaid expenses per enrollee in Texas did not increase between 1983 and 1990, they were $1,935 per enrollee in 1983 and $1,929 in 1990. By 1990 Texas was spending just 72 percent of the national average, $2,695 vs. $1,929, per Medicaid enrollee. Texas spending per enrollee averaged 75 percent until the late 1990s, before rising back to 90 percent in 2000 and 2001. It has declined to 84 percent in the most recent data (Figure 6.5).

Texas will spend almost $60 billion, more than one-quarter of its $200 billion biennial budget, on Medicaid during the 2012–2013 biennium.

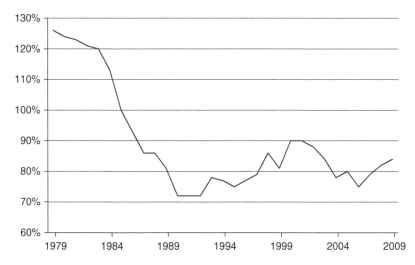

Figure 6.5 Texas Medicaid Payments Per Enrollee as a Percent of U.S. Payments, 1979–
Present.

Source: U.S. Census Bureau, Statistical Abstract of the United States, Health and Nutrition section,
"Medicaid—Summary by State."

Of this, $25 billion, slightly over 42 percent, will be Texas funds and the
remainder, $35 billion, will come from the federal government. Again, Texas
limits its Medicaid expenses by setting tight eligibility and reimbursement
limits, rather than by close monitoring and regulation of the program. The
average state's Medicaid spending is 40 percent on mandatory services and
60 percent on optional and expanded services. In Texas, it is the other way
around, 60 percent of funds go to mandatory services and 40 percent go to
optional and expanded services.[41] To limit expenses, Texas Medicaid rules
bar able-bodied adults who make more than $188 a month (26 percent of
the federal poverty rate) and are not pregnant from coverage. Seventy-six
percent of Texas's 3.6 million Medicaid enrollees are children and younger
adults and the remaining 34 percent are elderly and disabled. Sixty percent
of Medicaid expenditures go to care of the elderly and disabled because they
need more and more intensive health care than children. Even services to the
56,000 frail elderly in Texas nursing homes are tightly limited. The Texas
Medicaid program reimburses nursing homes $125.68 per enrollee per day,
30 percent below the national average of $177.55 per enrollee per day. Texas
ranks 49th, less than a dollar a day ahead of last place Illinois.[42]

Despite the fact that 42 percent of Medicaid funding is Texas dollars,
oversight is remarkably lax. A December 2010 report from the *Fort Worth
Star-Telegram* said, "With little oversight and apparent carte blanche,
a relative handful of Texas physicians wrote $47 million in Medicaid

prescriptions for powerful anti-psychotic and anti-anxiety drugs over the past two years. . . . Most of the drugs have gone to children and adolescents." Under a single doctor's prescription number, 44,138 prescriptions for anti-psychotic drugs, including 27,000 for the anti-anxiety medication Xanax, were written in 2009 and 2010 at a cost to Medicaid of $6.4 million. Clearly, more oversight is warranted.[43]

Not surprisingly, Texas has been deeply concerned about proposals to expand Medicaid as part of national health care reform. Despite the fact that Texas has more uninsured citizens than any other state, twenty-three of thirty-four Texas members of the U.S. House and Senate voted against the Democrats' health reform bill in 2010. Texas authorities immediately assaulted the bill, claiming that it would cost Texas an extra $27 billion over the next decade and that the state might be forced to pull out of Medicaid entirely, managing its own indigent health care system, to avoid the extra cost. When it became clear that withdrawing from Medicaid would halt nearly $15 billion a year in federal Medicaid funds to Texas, talk of withdrawing ceased but grumbling did not.

In 2012, though the Supreme Court found Obamacare constitutional, they declared that states could not be compelled to expand their Medicaid programs. Texas officials were immensely relieved and quickly declined to expand the state's Medicaid program despite the prospect of $100 billion in federal money over ten years in exchange for a $15 billion match from Texas. Obamacare encourages states to expand their Medicaid programs to healthy adults making up to 133 percent of the federal poverty line, $14,856 for a childless adult and $30,657 for a family of four, by promising to pay 100 percent of the cost for 2014–16, sliding down to 90 percent in 2020 and beyond. Governor Perry and other conservatives argue that "Medicaid is broken" so it is unconscionable to add so many new beneficiaries, and, they claim, it is a bait-and-switch scheme in which federal deficits will lead Congress to cut its promised support, leaving states holding the financial bag. But Texas has never supported expansive public services, even with federal money—because it saps individualism, personal responsibility, and the willingness, in fact, the need, to work.

In 2012 and 2013, another battle between Texas conservatives and progressives played out over the state's management of the Women's Health Program within Medicaid. Texas conservatives, or at least Texas conservative elected officials, abhor Planned Parenthood, the progressive women's health care advocacy and services group. Texas receives $35.4 million in Federal money, for a $3.9 million state match, to deliver contraceptives and cancer screenings to poor women. Planned Parenthood provided 44 percent of these services to 130,000 Texas women. Conservatives moved in 2011 and then more successfully in 2013 to bar Planned Parenthood from the program on the argument that dollars are fungible and some Planned Parenthood affiliates provided abortion services.

The federal government required that women be able to select their health care providers, while Texas officials claimed that Medicaid rules allow them to define qualified, and unqualified, providers. When Texas would not relent, the federal government suspended its funding. Governor Perry promised that the state would run the program, sans Planned Parenthood, with its own money, though it struggled to do so. Once again, Texas demonstrated a willingness to leave federal money on the table, even in the case of a nine-to-one match, to both adhere to its values and limit services to the poor.

The Children's Health Insurance Program (CHIP) was enacted in 1997 to cover children in working families that earn too much to qualify for Medicaid but not enough to afford private health insurance. Although the federal government pays most of the costs, states set the eligibility rules and must decide how much of their own money they are willing to put up to attract the federal match. In general, the federal government pays 65 percent of the cost of state CHIP programs, but because Texas is a relatively poor state with high levels of uninsured, the federal government pays 71 percent. This means that Texas puts up only 29 cents of every dollar spent on CHIP in Texas, or, described another way, Texas gets $2.50 in federal dollars for every dollar it puts up. This is one of the truly good deals in U.S. federal relations, but Texas has long been skeptical. In fact, Texas has been more than ready to cut its own funding to CHIP, thereby sacrificing $2.50 for every dollar it cuts, when its budget gets tight.

Texas historian Robert Calvert noted that, "Between 2000 and 2005, the state lost some $832 million in federal funding for CHIP because it refused to appropriate the required matching funds."[44] In 2003, facing a $10 billion deficit, Texas trimmed CHIP and cut completely its dental, vision, and mental health benefits. It also reduced the assets that a family could have and still be eligible for CHIP, changed the continuous enrollment period from one year to six months, and trimmed provider payment rates. As a result, CHIP enrollment dropped from 507,000 to under 309,000. As budgets loosened, many of these changes were reversed—dental and vision benefits were restored in 2005 and eligibility rules were relaxed in 2007—but the number of children in the program did not return to 2003 levels until 2008. Nonetheless, Texas remains tight-fisted. In early 2009, President Obama signed a five-year extension of CHIP that included substantial increases in funding and raised the cap below which families were eligible for CHIP from 250 percent of the federal poverty rate to 300 percent.[45] Texas kept its eligibility cap at 200 percent of the poverty rate.[46]

Assistance to the Poor: TANF and Food Stamps

Prior to the Great Depression most social welfare policy was made by state and local government and most charity was actually administered by churches and civic groups. In 1933, four years into the Depression, "only 20 of 254 Texas counties offered mothers' aid, and the number dropped as the Depression deepened—to 8 by 1935 . . . and the average monthly grant of $12.07 was only half the national average and below even the average ($14.06) of the southern states." Texas politicians were worried about the socialist elements of public aid undermining the state's traditional commitment to personal responsibility. After the Social Security Act was passed in 1935, with Aid For Families with Dependent Children (AFDC) one of its major components, Texas "limited its contribution to not more than $8 for one child or $12 per family and set the cut-off age at fourteen, even though the federal government, which contributed one-third of ADC grants, permitted a maximum of $18 for the first child and $12 for each additional child under sixteen."[47]

Still today, Texas participates, if only barely, in federal government programs designed to assist the poor through cash grants and food aid. From the Great Depression through the welfare reform of the mid-1990s, Aid for Families with Dependent Children (AFDC) provided cash grants to poor families as a matter of right, usually where the adults were unemployed. AFDC grew rapidly in the Great Society years of the 1960s, doubling its number of recipients from five to ten million between 1967 and 1971, before it came under the downward pressure of more conservative administrations in the 1970s and 1980s. As with other federal/state social programs, the federal government provides about 60 percent of the funding and lays out broad rules. The states set more specific eligibility rules and payment levels. Writing a quarter of a century ago, Champagne and Harpham noted that, "Texas officials have used this power to make the AFDC program in Texas one of the most miserly in terms of payments and one of the most difficult for which to become and remain eligible.[48] Texas AFDC payment levels ranked 46th among the fifty states and D.C. in 1986.

In 1996, President Bill Clinton and the Republican Congress led by House Speaker Newt Gingrich passed a major welfare reform program. A key element of this reform was to change the focus of AFDC from provision of cash assistance to the nonworking poor to work support through a revised program named Temporary Assistance to Needy Families (TANF). TANF still provides cash assistance to poor families, but the aid is limited to five years and adults must actively prepare for self-support through work. As a result, the number of beneficiaries drawing on AFDC/TANF has declined sharply since 1996 and, of course, more sharply in Texas than nationally. Robert Calvert noted, "These results were largely the product of the state's unwillingness to allocate matching funds in order to receive federal money."[49] In 1996, 684,000 Texans drew TANF support; by 2010 that number had declined to 100,000, most of them children. Texas has held down participation in the program by setting very low limits on assets one can have and still be eligible for the program and on earnings one can

have while in the program. Only two states, Georgia and Delaware, have
a lower asset limit than Texas ($1,000 and an auto worth no more than
$4,650) and only five, Alabama, Arkansas, Florida, Indiana, and Louisiana,
have lower earnings limits than Texas's $401 a month. Thirteen states
allow more than $1,000 a month.

AFDC/TANF payments have always been modest, especially in Texas
(Figure 6.6). Average monthly payments nationally did not break $100 until
1957, $200 until 1974, $300 until 1984, and $400 until 2007. In Texas,
AFDC/TANF payments never broke $170 and have been flat since 1985. In
fact, only the Connally administration in the 1960s and the White administration in the early to mid-1980s made meaningful commitments to AFDC.
Texas cash assistance payments were about 75 percent of the national average
in the mid-1950s but have been on a steady downward trajectory, steeply since
the early 1970s, and are just 42 percent in the latest figures. This is among
the very lowest rates in the nation. From 2005 to 2007, only four states—
Alabama, Florida, Georgia, and South Carolina—had a smaller proportion
of their population on assistance than Texas (North Carolina and Wisconsin
had the same proportion). And only three states—Arkansas, Mississippi, and
Tennessee—paid those on the program less than Texas did. In 2010, the average monthly TANF payment for a family with two children nationally was
$412, while the maximum monthly benefit in Texas was $175.

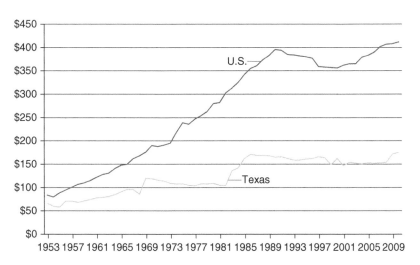

Figure 6.6 AFDC/TANF Average Monthly Benefits Per Family, U.S. and Texas, 1953–
          Present.

Source: United States Census Bureau, Statistical Abstract of the United States, Social Insurance and
Human Services section, AFDC table prior to 1996, TANF tables thereafter, various years. See also
Department of Health and Human Services, Administration for Children and Families, http://www.
acf.hhs.gov/programs/ofa/character/index.html Table 41, Families with two children.

Strikingly, Texas allows fewer people into its TANF program than most other states and then pays these fortunate few less than all but a few other states pay their beneficiaries (Figure 6.7). As Champagne and Harpham noted in the mid-1980s, and it is even truer today, "Welfare is an issue that is not popular in Texas. Poverty. The dole. Dependency. All appear to fly in the face of the reality and the myth which is Texas."[50] Texas has many poor and has made the policy judgment that assistance to them should be exceedingly meager.

The Food Stamp program, whose name was changed in 2008 to the Supplemental Nutrition Assistance Program (SNAP), has for decades provided poor families with food stamps, now a benefit card, to supplement their food budget. The $6 billion annual cost of the program in Texas is born by the federal government while the program is run by the state and administrative costs of $250 million are split 50/50 by the federal and state governments. So how do you suppose Texas approaches such a program? The benefit amount is capped at about $350 a month for a family of three, so no feeding frenzy, but Texas, as a poor state, does draw on the program at rates higher than the national average, 9.5 percent of households as opposed to 8.6 percent nationally. Moreover, the high unemployment of 2009 and 2012 pushed recipients from 2.3 million in 2008, to 2.8 million

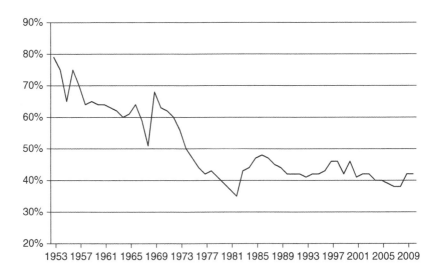

Figure 6.7 AFDC/TANF Average Monthly Benefits in Texas as a Percent of U.S. Monthly Benefits, 1953–Present.

Source: United States Census Bureau, Statistical Abstract of the United States, Social Insurance and Human Services section, AFDC table prior to 1996, TANF tables thereafter, various years. See also Department of Health and Human Services, Administration for Children and Families, http://www. acf.hhs.gov/programs/ofa/character/index.html Table 41, Families with two children.

in 2009, 3.6 million in 2010, and 4 million in 2011 and 2012, a 75 percent increase over just three years. Not surprisingly, program administration has been a problem. The Food Stamp program in Texas, like all of its social service programs, is understaffed even when things are going smoothly. When demand for services build, as they inevitably do during bad times, the staff are quickly overwhelmed. Federal rules require that food stamp applications be processed within thirty days. In 2009, Texas failed to meet that deadline on one-third of applications and ranked 52nd among the fifty states, D.C., Guam, and the Virgin Islands.[51] Texas finished just behind Guam. A big part of the problem in this and other Texas social service programs is low pay, high pressure, and the resulting staff turnover. In 2004, only 8.4 percent of staff had less than two years' experience, while in 2009 more than half of state food stamp workers had less than two years' experience. As a result, the error rate on handling applications, as measured by the state itself, rose from 2.8 percent in 2004 to 21.4 percent in 2008.[52]

In August 2009 Texas was sued in federal court by the Texas Legal Services Center and the National Center for Law and Economic Justice to try to force compliance with federal requirements on processing applications. In 2000, Texas had 10,400 state workers processing eligibility applications, a decade later they had 7,400. In the interim, the state undertook a major outsourcing effort involving private call centers to handle the initial screening of applicants. These call centers have had major problems, but they are not the sole source of problems. In late 2009, the federal agency that oversees the Food Stamp program suggested that to save time and money Texas eliminate an asset test and stop fingerprinting applicants. Texas is one of only three states that require fingerprinting, which Texas officials claim discourages fraud, such as double registering under assumed names, but it does at least suggest that Texas views poor food stamp applicants as potential criminals. In 2010, after being assessed a $4 million fine for slow and inaccurate handling of applications and renewals, Texas added 850 new caseworkers and cleared out the backlogged applications. Moreover, error rates declined to well below the national average.[53]

Beyond the specific issue of food stamps is the broader issue of what the U.S. Department of Agriculture calls "food insecurity." During 2010–2012, 14.7 percent of U.S. households and 25 percent of minority households had difficulty keeping adequate food on the table. Among the states, Texas ranked third worst, behind only Arkansas and Mississippi, with 18.4 percent of its families food insecure.[54] In the face of serious food insecurity, what does Texas do? Texas Agriculture Commissioner Todd Staples in 2010 drew attention to the fact that only 15 percent of children eligible for summer food programs actually take part. In 2009, Staples said the federal government reimbursed his department $46 million for summer food programs and more was available if participation could be increased.

Sounds good, right? But the story reporting Commissioner Staples's efforts also noted that, "No supplemental funding comes from the state."[55]

The Costs of Negligence: Teen Pregnancy, Obesity, and Diabetes

Teen pregnancy and child bearing is costly in many ways, not only to both the teenage mothers and child, but also to the state and community. Not surprisingly, Texas has been well above the national average for teen pregnancy, often by 3 or 4 percentage points, for as long as records have been kept. Since the mid-1980s, Texas has risen from the mid-thirties to the mid-forties among the states in the teen pregnancy lists. In 1998 and 1999, Texas ranked 50th, surpassed only by Utah. From 2007 through 2010, Texas ranked between 44th and 46th.

Though teen pregnancy and birth rates nationally have fallen by nearly a third since the early 1990s, it is still the case that nearly a third of girls get pregnant before they are 20 and 80 percent of them are unmarried. Teenage births in Texas have also fallen, but just 19 percent between 1991 and 2010. An analysis by the National Campaign to Prevent Teen Pregnancy reports that nearly three-quarters of a million teen births occurred in Texas from 1991 to 2004, costing $15.1 billion over that period, mostly in social services such as Medicaid and CHIP.[56] In 2010, Texas had the fifth highest teen birth rate in the nation, an improvement on its third highest in the nation finish in 2008 and highest in the nation finish in 2007 (Figure 6.8).

Texas's approach to the problem of teen pregnancy is more ideological than medical. As noted in Chapter 5, Texas is one of the few states in the nation to run an "abstinence only" sex education program in its public schools.[57] In addition, Texas and Utah were the only two states in 2009 that barred unmarried teenage girls from accessing contraceptives without their parents' permission and one of four states that prohibits CHIP from providing contraceptives. In 2013, Senator Ken Paxton (R-McKinney) offered SB521, a bill to ban planned parent speakers and materials from Texas public schools.

Another key health problem facing Texans is the increasing rate of obesity. Less than 20 years ago, the rate of adult obesity in the U.S. and Texas, while worrisome, was identical at 15.9 percent of the population. Texas moved slightly ahead of the U.S. average in 1996 and never looked back. The latest figures, for 2011, show that the rate of obesity in the U.S. has increased to 27 percent while the rate in Texas has increased to 30.4 percent. Colorado was best, with just 20.7 percent obese, Mississippi was worst at 34.9 percent, while Texas's 30.4 percent ranked tenth most obese. But before we celebrate one more time at Mississippi's expense, Texas State Demographer Lloyd Potter and the Texas Health Institute estimate that the obesity rate in Texas will be 42.6 percent by 2040 unless major changes in personal habits and public policy are undertaken.[58]

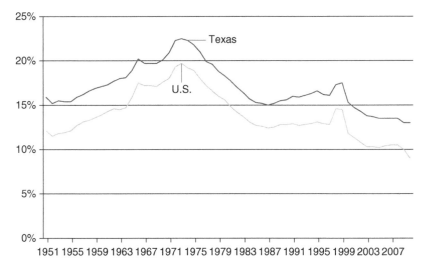

Figure 6.8 Teen Births as a Percent of Total Live Births in the U.S. and Texas, 1951–Present.

Source: United States Census Bureau, Statistical Abstract of the United States, "Low Weight and Births to Teenage Mothers and to Unmarried Women, by States, present to 1985; prior to 1985, United States Department of Health and Human Services, National Center for Health Statistics, Vital Statistics of the United States, vol. 1, Table 1–62.

One of the most dangerous medical conditions related to obesity is diabetes. According to a recent report, about two million Texans are currently diagnosed as diabetic, with another half a million likely diabetic but undiagnosed. The report, by the Texas Health Institute, the State Demographer's Office, and the Methodist Health Care Ministries of South Texas, predicts that the number with diabetes will nearly quadruple to nine million over the next three decades. Moreover, the burgeoning Hispanic population in Texas is particularly given to obesity and diabetes. The population of diabetic Hispanics is expected to rise from 855,000 in 2010 to 4.7 million by 2040. One in ten health care dollars now goes to manage diabetes and that share of health spending is bound to rise.[59]

Conclusion

The Texas way envisions small government, low taxes, deregulation, and personal responsibility. This model works very well to protect the assets, opportunities, and choices of the well-off. It does less well for those who have little to protect and many needs to fulfill. Some of those needs include access to adequate health care for themselves and their children as well as income and nutritional support during particularly difficult times. Texas elites have always understood that need, even the fear of need, makes the working and lower classes more tractable, more willing to work, even for modest pay and benefits, and more fearful of losing work.

Hence, we see distinctive patterns in the provision of health care and other social service support in Texas. In Medicare, where only federal money is involved, particularly in discretionary aspects of the program such as home health care, usage will be high tending toward abusive. For the last two decades, Medicare costs in Texas per recipient have been about 110 percent of the national average. Patterns of usage and abuse in Texas cities such as McAllen and Dallas have drawn scrutiny and new approaches to uncovering Medicare abuse have been piloted in Texas. The specialized home health care program within Medicare cost 53 percent more than the national average per recipient in 2007 and fully 20 percent of the nation's home health care providers were in Texas. The lid is off the honey pot.

Where federal and state money are involved, as with Medicaid and CHIP health care programs, usage is restricted and payments are low. Even though the federal government pays more than 60 percent of the cost, Texas officials complain endlessly about the expense and inflexibility of Medicaid. Texas limits access to Medicaid mainly to poor children and the elderly and disabled. Treatment of elderly Texans under Medicare provides a good comparison to the discussion above about lavish spending on home health care under Medicare. Texas nursing homes housing elderly Medicaid recipients receive $125.68 a day compared to a national average reimbursement of $177.55 a day. Texas ranks 49th. For elderly Texans, if it's federal money, nothing is too good, if it's state money, too good is a dream and barely good enough is the norm.

If possible, Texas is even more tight-fisted with the remnants of what used to be called welfare programs. In the AFDC/TANF program, which provides income support to needy families with children, the national average monthly stipend is $412, compared to Texas's $175, 42 percent of the national average. The Food Stamp program distributes federal dollars, but states are required to share administrative expenses 50/50. Texas responds to these incentives by shortchanging the administrative elements of the program. As a result, it has among the highest proportion of applications handled late or erroneously.

Notes

1 T.R. Fehrenbach, *Lone Star: A History of Texas and the Texans*, New York: Macmillan, 1968, p. 598. See also Grieder, *Big, Hot, Cheap, and Right*, New York: Public Affairs, 2013, p. 99.

2 Stanley Siegel, *A Political History of the Texas Republic, 1836–1845*, Austin, TX: University of Texas Press, 1956, pp. 147–148, 151.

3 William Ransom Hogan, *The Texas Republic*, Norman, OK: University of Oklahoma Press, 1946, p. 241.

4 Randolph B. Campbell, *An Empire for Slavery: The Peculiar Institution in Texas, 1821–1865*, Baton Rouge, LA: Louisiana State University Press, 1989, pp. 141–142.

5   Robert Perkinson, *Texas Tough: The Rise of America's Prison Empire*, New York: Metropolitan Books, 2010, p. 71.

6   Fehrenbach, *Lone Star*, pp. 649, 651.

7   Richard Morehead, *50 Years in Texas Politics*, Burnet, TX: Eakin Press, 1984, pp. 15, 23.

8   James Reston Jr., *The Lone Star: The Life of John Connally*, New York: Harper and Row, 1989, pp. 39–41, 92–93; D.B. Hardeman and Donald C. Bacon, *Rayburn: A Biography*, New York: Madison Books, 1987, pp. 232–233.

9   Sam Kinch Jr. and Ben Proctor, *Texas Under a Cloud*, Austin, TX: Jenkins Publishing Co., 1972, p. 61.

10   Anthony Champagne and Edward J. Harpham, *Texas at the Crossroads: People, Politics, and Policy*, College Station, TX: Texas A&M University Press, 1987, p. 275.

11   Jason DeParle, "For Recession Victims, Patchwork State Aid," *New York Times*, May 10, 2009, pp. A1, A18.

12   See http://statesnapshots.ahrq.gov/snaps11/overall_quality.jsp

13   Ricky F. Dobbs, *Yellow Dogs and Republicans: Allan Shivers and Texas Two-Party Politics*, College Station, TX: Texas A&M University Press, 2005, p. 54.

14   Frank R. Kemerer, *William Wayne Justice: A Judicial Biography*, Austin, TX: University of Texas Press, 1991/2008, p. 316.

15   Ibid., p. 325.

16   Kaiser State Health Facts, http://statehealthfacts.kff.org/comparable.jsp.

17   Corrie MacLaggan, "Lawmakers Poised to Write New Chapter in State School Saga," *Austin American-Statesman*, February 6, 2009.

18   Emily Ramshaw, "Agency to Boost Staff, Conditions," *Dallas Morning News*, May 23, 2009, A4.

19   Mimi Swartz, "Failing Darla," *Texas Monthly*, July 2009, pp. 8–10. See also Andrea Ball, "Despite Decades of Scrutiny, State-Run Disability Residences Still Cannot Pass Muster," *Austin American-Statesman*, March 21, 2012.

20   Dave Mann, "Gone, Baby, Gone," *Texas Observer*, January 8, 2010, pp. 13–17.

21   Patricia Kilday Hart, "Cop Drama," *Texas Monthly*, August 2010, pp. 68–76.

22   Bob Moser, "Goodbye Government," *Texas Observer*, November 12, 2010, p. 28; see also Brandi Grissom, "As Mental Health Cuts Mount, Psychiatric Cases Fill Jails," *New York Times*, February 25, 2011, A21A.

23   AP, "Repeat Offenses in Texas Raise Questions Over Release of Mentally Ill Juveniles," *New York Times*, December 21, 2009, A16.

24   Corrie MacLaggan, "As Nation Discusses Health Care, Texas Doctor Shortage Expected to Worsen," *Austin American-Statesman*, September 6, 2009.

25   Steve Jacob, editorial, "Texans Need More Doctors and Nurses," *Dallas Morning News*, July 15, 2010, p. A19.

26   Families USA, "Costly Coverage: Premiums Outpace Paychecks in Texas," September 2009, www.familiesusa.org/resources/publications/reports/costly-coverage.html.

27   Jason Roberson, "Industry Groups Back Health Care Bills," *Dallas Morning News*, March 25, 2009, D5.

28   Catharine Arnst, "A Second Opinion on Malpractice," *Businessweek*, September 28, 2009, p. 30.

29   Mary Ann Roser, "New Study: Tort Reform Has Not Reduced Health Care Costs in Texas," *Austin American-Statesman*, June 20, 2012.

30   Elliott Fisher, MD, MPH, David Goodman, MD, MS, Jonathan Skinner, PhD, and Kristen Bronner, MA, "Health Care Spending, Quality, and Outcomes: More Isn't Always Better," The Dartmouth Institute, February 27, 2009, p. 2.

31   Atul Gawande, "The Cost Conundrum: What a Texas Town Can Teach Us About Health Care," *The New Yorker*, June 1, 2009, p. 38.

32   Ibid., pp. 37–38.

33   Reed Abelson and Gardiner Harris, "Study Cited for Health-Care Cuts Overstated Its Upside, Critics Say," *New York Times*, June 3, 2010, pp. A1, A8.

34 Jim Landers, "Texas, Take Heed if Medicare Commission Gains Muscle," *Dallas Morning News*, December 8, 2009, pp. D1, D5.

35 Jim Landers, "Getting In Sync, Saving Money," *Dallas Morning News*, December 27, 2009, A1, A29.

36 Gregg Jones, "A Critical Component or Avenue for Fraud," *Dallas Morning News*, September 23, 2009, A1, A12.

37 AARP, Quick Health Facts 2010, Texas, http://aarp.org/research/ppi.

38 Nomaan Merchant, "7 Accused of Bilking $375M from Medicare, Medicaid," *Austin American-Statesman*, February 28, 2012.

39 Jim Landers, "Dallas Health Care Lags," *Dallas Morning News*, March 15, 2012, A1, A13.

40 Gregg Jones, "Health Care Law Had Revolving Door Spinning," *Dallas Morning News*, January 5, 2009, A1, A14; see also Daniel L. Hatcher, "Poverty Revenue: The Subversion of Fiscal Federalism," *Arizona Law Review*, 52, 2010, pp. 675–726.

41 The Kaiser Commission on Medicaid and the Uninsured, Table 4a, p. 22.

42 Bob Moos, "Nursing Homes in a Tight Fix," *Dallas Morning News*, March 4, 2009, pp. 1D, 12D.

43 Darren Barbee, "Some Doctors Handing Out Prescriptions to Kids for Potent Medications," *Fort Worth Star-Telegram*, December 11, 2010, B1. See also, Gardiner Harris, "Talk Doesn't Pay, So Psychiatry Turns Instead to Drug Therapy," *New York Times*, March 6, 2011, A1, A21.

44 Robert A. Calvert, Arnoldo De León, and Gregg Cantrell, *The History of Texas*, 4th edn, Wheeling, IL: Harlan Davidson, Inc., 2007, p. 419.

45 Kevin Sack, "Defying Slump, 13 States Insure More Children," *New York Times*, July 19, 2009, A1, A20.

46 Kaiser Family Foundation, State Health Facts, "Federal Matching Rate for CHIP," http://statehealthfacts.kff.org/comparetable.jsp?ind=239&cat=4.

47 Judith N. McArthur and Harold L. Smith, Texas through Women's Eyes, Austin, TX: University of Texas Press, 2010, p. 90.

48 Champagne and Harpham, *Texas at the Crossroads*, p. 264.

49 Calvert et al., *The History of Texas*, p. 419.

50 Champagne and Harpham, *Texas at the Crossroads*, p. 262. See also Grieder, *Big, Hot*, pp. 121–122.

51 www.fns.usda.gov/snap/government/program-improvement.htm.

52 Corrie MacLaggan, "Backlog, Processing Errors Bedevil Food Stamp Program," *Austin American-Statesman*, September 24, 2009.

53 Robert T. Garrett, "State Praised for Better Handling of Food-Stamp Cases," *Dallas Morning News*, June 17, 2011, p. 3A.

54 U.S. Department of Agriculture, Economic Research Service, *Food Security in the U.S.*

55 Jessica Meyers, "Trying to Feed More Kids," *Dallas Morning News*, June 3, 2010, p. A2.

56 The National Campaign to Prevent Teen Pregnancy, "By the Numbers: The Public Costs of Teen Childbearing," www.teenpregnancy.org/costs.

57 O. Ricardo Pimentel, "Urgency Lacking on Teen Pregnancy," *San Antonio Express-News*, June 2, 2011.

58 For the Eschbach study, see www.texashealthinstitute.org/files/Key_ findings_obesity_ Eschbach.pdf.

59 Jim Landers, "Obesity Weighs Heavily on State," *Dallas Morning News*, September 4, 2012, 10, 80.

7 Crime and Punishment in Texas

> In your dealings with Texans of the American extraction you must take care not to provoke them. The consequence might be a bullet in your head, and nobody would take any notice of it.
>
> (Wilhelm Steinert, 1849)[1]

To the modern mind, society's response to crime involves police, courts, and prisons. It was not always so. In early Texas, government was a wispy presence at best. Individual citizens assumed responsibility for their own defense. Those with much to defend used government and law to authorize action at discretion and those who could not defend their own autonomy were dealt with summarily. Local jails held most offenders for brief periods, serious criminals were generally warned away with a pistol butt to the skull or hanged, while only the most fortunate white criminals saw the inside of a prison. For rebellious slaves, it was the whip and shackles.

Interpersonal conflicts tended to be settled directly. The Texas pioneer Noah Smithwick, remembering San Felipe de Austin in the late 1820s, the days of "the Old Three Hundred," wrote, "There was a certain doctor who, when under the 'influence,' was always belligerent. He had a falling out with Colonel DeWitt and challenged him. 'You can have your choice of weapons,' said the doctor. 'All right,' said the colonel, 'I accept your challenge, and this is my weapon.' And with that, he raised his cane and gave the bellicose medico a drubbing that cured him of dueling."[2] The Colonel did not think to call upon the authorities for assistance. Yankees and foreigners found this sort of swift dispute resolution to be disconcerting.

Wilhelm Steinert, a thirty-year-old German school teacher sent to Texas in 1849 to scout it out for potential immigrants, advised his countrymen to mind their tongues as Texans of American extraction were dangerous when provoked. Probably not coincidentally, 1849 was the year that the Texas state prison at Huntsville, soon known as "the Walls," opened its doors. The Huntsville prison had 225 cells at a spacious 7×5×7 feet, but just three prisoners on opening day. In 1850, when the prison population had reached sixteen, the legislature held their first hearings into how to defer the costs of incarceration. Inmate labor seemed the obvious answer. From the beginning, inmates grew their food and performed all of the carpentry, brickwork, and smithing required by the prison and its staff. In 1854, a cotton mill was constructed on prison grounds where inmates produced cloth for their own clothing and for local sale. The cotton mill was the prison's first profit-making enterprise. For the first century and more of their history, Texas prisons were expected to hold inmates at as little cost to the public as possible.[3]

Douglas A. Blackmon, winner of the Pulitzer Prize for his masterful 2008 study, *Slavery by Another Name*, reminds us that, "Prior to the Civil War, all of government in the region, at every level, was unimaginably sparse by modern standards. . . . Incarceration was an expensive and impractical outcome in a society where cash rarely changed hands."[4] Francis C. Sheridan, visiting Texas in 1839, made the same point to his journal, noting "that laws may be said to be received only on sufferance by the people, for the government have not the power or means to enforce them."[5]

The Texas political culture shaped the state's criminal law and penal system. The dominant traditionalism of the older and more thickly populated sections of the state used law and prisons to protect and serve the interests of the state's propertied Anglo elite. Texas sociologists and criminologists Chad R. Trulson and James M. Marquart wrote that, "In the antebellum Texas prison system . . . Only the most serious white criminals . . . were confined in the . . . penitentiary."[6] Often the formal apparatus of law and courts, much less prisons, were not thought necessary to doing justice, even to white outlaws. Steinert noted in the late summer of 1849 that, "thieves had made the vicinity of Mill Creek [near LaGrange] unsafe. Then 300 citizens caught and hanged 18 of the accused thieves." For his European readers, Steinert explained, "This is called 'lynch law.'"[7] Texans, of course, knew about lynch law and generally approved the efficiency.

Black slaves who ran afoul of white social expectations might be managed in a number of ways. Formally, Texas law gave slaves the right to a jury trial for all major crimes, but as Randolph Campbell noted, "many slaves were punished by their masters without regard to the law."[8] And in some cases, the law had to be forcefully pushed aside before the master's justice could be applied.

> Francis C. Sheridan told of a Negro who had run away from his master and later stolen a stranger's horse. After being apprehended by the horse's owner, the Negro was tried and sentenced to hang. His master heard about the affair and, unwilling to lose valuable property to the gallows, rode with a friend to the town where the Negro was held. 'At night, they very easily extracted him from the jail, mounted him on a spare horse, and galloped away.'[9]

After slavery, both law and lawlessness were directed at controlling the place and role of blacks in Texas society. Trulson and Marquart point to both phenomena. They note that, "From 1865 to 1883, the Texas prisoner population grew from 165 to 2,301 prisoners, more than half of which were freed slaves." And many black men coming to the adverse notice of whites never made it to prison. Extra-legal racial violence from the petty to the deadly was common. "Between 1885 and 1942, there were 468 lynching victims in Texas, and of these 339 were African-American, 77 were white, 53 were Hispanic, and 1 was Native American . . . Lynchings . . . [were] regarded by many whites at the time as a necessary form of social control."[10] As Robert Perkinson noted in *Texas Tough*, "The strong arm of the law has regularly been deployed not only to protect public safety but to preserve privilege, bolster political fortunes, and, most of all, to discipline those on the social margins, especially African-Americans."[11]

Studies of crime and prisons in Texas highlight the traditional political culture that we have discussed throughout this book. As argued in earlier chapters, Texas was established as an "Anglo Republic," Indians and Mexicans were exclude and blacks were enslaved. Texas criminologists James Marquart, Sheldon Ekland-Olson, and Jonathan R. Sorenson apply this broad logic to criminal justice by describing "a cultural tradition of exclusion."[12] People of color were "excluded" from the Anglo understanding of society except as they were useful in subservient roles. After slavery and as the Hispanic population began to increase in the early decades of the twentieth century, segregation maintained racial and ethnic exclusion. Exclusion from social, political, and economic opportunity left Texas minorities with unattractive options and results. Anglo political control allowed use of the state's criminal justice and penal systems to secure Anglo persons, property, and social control against outsiders, whether those outsiders lived among them or not.

As we shall see throughout this chapter, the focus of Texas law, courts, and prisons on minorities, especially blacks, is long-standing. The 3.5 times overrepresentation of blacks at the end of late nineteenth- and early twentieth-century lynch mob ropes and the 2.5 times overrepresentation of blacks in early twentieth-century Texas prisons is present in today's criminal justice statistics. Texas's historic use of law, courts, and prisons as tools of social order and control still stands, as do the effects of the Texas way on the state's poor and minority populations.[13] In Texas prisons today, 36 percent of inmates are black, three times their presence in the population, while 33 percent are Hispanic, and 31 percent are white.

A Brief History of Crime and Punishment in Texas

Nineteenth-century Texas was such a breathtakingly violent place that "Can you top this?" stories became commonplace. The Englishman William Bollaert's diary entry for September 20, 1842, explained that, "[if] a *friend* tells you he will shoot you, or it is intimated by another friend that s^d *friend* intends to have a *difficulty* with you—if you wish to save your own life you must kill s^d *friend* as soon as you can—a jury will find a verdict of not guilty."[14] New York journalist and landscape architect Frederick Law Olmsted, after touring Texas in 1854, confirmed Bollaert's shoot on first frown advice. Olmsted described the regular course taken by personal disputes in Texas; "More often than otherwise, the parties meet upon the plaza by chance, and each, on catching sight of his enemy, draws a revolver, and fires away. As the actors are under more or less excitement, their aim is not apt to be of the most careful and sure, consequently it is, not seldom, the passers-by who suffer."[15]

In fact, as Bollaert and Olmsted well understood, the willingness of offended parties to shoot on sight, even on a public plaza, was dependent upon the understanding nature of Texas juries. Juries were often willing to overlook the unintended injury to persons in the wrong place at the wrong time as, well, unintended. Even military men found the violence of early Texas disconcerting. Albert Sidney Johnston, a West Point graduate and regular U.S. Army officer before moving to Texas in 1834, rose from private to major during the Texas Revolution and, by 1838, was Secretary of War in President Sam Houston's cabinet. Johnston rejoined the U.S. Army during the Mexican War and by 1855 he was in command, with Robert E. Lee as his second in command, of the U.S. Second Cavalry fighting Indians on the Texas frontier. Johnston was responsible for preparing his non-Texan officers for what they might face not just from the Indians in front of them but from the Texans to the rear. Johnston's *Reminiscences* relate, "a story in which a man, after due deliberation, decided to kill his neighbor. He went to his door, rang the bell, and plunged his Bowie knife into his breast. . . . Subsequently he realized that he had killed the wrong man. The coroner's jury acquitted him on the grounds that the man had died by an accident."[16] In mid-nineteenth-century Texas, a jury of one's peers was a true blessing as everyone went armed and knew the danger of recognizing an enemy too late. Yet, when the army is warned to be careful of the civilians, you can be pretty sure you are in a violent place.

With juries as understanding and lenient as these, Texas judges could assume that those actually convicted of serious crimes were really dangerous. The following story, based on a composite of the real-life misfortunes of John Quick and David Jones, executed for murder in Houston in 1838, is probably apocryphal but was told and retold in Texas and beyond for decades. The *Mississippi Free Trader and Natchez Gazette* rendered the story this way in January 1843:

> A very learned and compassionate judge in Texas, on passing sentence on one John Jones, who had been convicted of murder, concluded his remarks as follows:—The fact is, Jones, that the court did not intend

to order you to be executed before next spring, but the weather is very cold—our jail, unfortunately, is in a very bad condition—much of the glass in the windows is broken . . . ; besides, owing to the great number of prisoners, not more than one blanket can be allowed to each; to sleep soundly and comfortably, therefore, will be out of the question. In consideration of these circumstances, and wishing to lessen your suffering as much as possible, the Court, in the exercise of its humanity and compassion, do hereby order you to be executed tomorrow morning, as soon after breakfast as may be convenient to the Sheriff and agreeable to you.[17]

Since not everyone could be hanged in the morning, other ways to limit the number of prisoners and the cost of holding them had to be found. The prison population at Huntsville grew in the 1850s but declined during the Civil War—authorities undoubtedly figuring, if these men want to fight, let's send them to the war—from 211 in 1861, to 157 in 1863, and 134 in 1866. In the wake of the Civil War, the 13th Amendment to the U.S. Constitution freed the slaves, presenting white Texans with the critical issue of how to hold free black labor to its traditional agricultural tasks. Share cropping was the general solution, but prisons provided a source of "enslaved" labor. In 1866, the legislature created the Board of Public Labor and charged it to contract with private interests, mostly plantations, to employ the convict labor.[18] In an 1875 report to the governor, the super-intendent of prisons explained that "The greater number of persons who have incurred Penitentiary punishment for lesser offenses, since liberty was bestowed upon our uneducated population, are unfitted for other than agricultural employment. . . . Many of these convicts are now at work on plantations."[19]

The initial prisoner lease system was so brutal because, unlike the antebellum slave owners, the leasors into whose hands the prisoners were placed had no economic reason to concern themselves with their life or health. Initial reforms put prison officials in charge of leased prisoners at their work sites. Still, between 1876 and 1899, fully 2,142 prisoners died and 3,075 escaped. In 1876 alone, 16 percent of all convicts escaped. Over the first two decades of the twentieth century, Texas slowly abandoned convict leasing in favor of prison farms.[20] These new prison farms not only were located in the old East Texas plantation belt, they were organized and run like plantations, principally with black field labor.

The prison at Huntsville housed 503 in 1870, just under 1,700 in 1876, and 2,301 in 1883. There were about 4,000 prisoners in 1909 and 4,800 in 1929. Prison population grew during the Great Depression decade of the 1930s, reaching 7,000 by 1939, before falling during World War II to just 3,000 in 1946. Blacks initially formed a majority of prisoners, falling from about 60 percent in the late nineteenth century to 40 percent in the

1930s. Whites accounted for 30 to 40 percent and Hispanics for about 10 percent.[21] Racial segregation was a mainstay of the Texas prison system. Anglo, black, and Hispanic prisoners were segregated on separate farm units into the mid-twentieth century. During the third quarter of the twentieth century, the Texas prison system grew slowly under incredibly stable leadership. That leadership was given a free hand so long as it kept scandals out of the press and costs low. H.H. Coffield was chair of the prison board from 1948 to 1977 and only three men served as director of Texas prisons between 1947 and 1983. They were O.B. Ellis (1947–1961), George Beto (1961–1972), and W.J. Estelle (1972–1983). This was the heyday of the Texas prison system; Ellis commonly gets credit for successfully reforming the Texas prison system, Beto gets credit for refining the classic "corrections model" of hold them securely and cheap, while Estelle gets the blame for the fact that he stood unblinking as it all came apart. Mid-twentieth-century Texas prisons were run by no nonsense characters such as Warden Carl L. "Beartrack" McAdams of the Wynne unit and Warden James V. "Wildcat" Anderson of the Ramsey I unit.

Even as Texas Department of Corrections (TDC) officials boasted that their system was "one of the best in the nation," the nation's corrections community was entering a period of dramatic change. Beginning in the 1960s, the U.S. Department of Justice and the federal courts reflected an evolving national consensus concerning the civil and individual rights of prisoners in which Texas and much of the South did not share. In 1968, the federal courts held in *Lee v. Washington* that Alabama's segregation of its jails and prisons was a violation of the 14th Amendment guarantee of "equal protection." In the early 1970s, the Arkansas and Mississippi prison systems, both organized around prison farms and featuring both official and prisoner violence to maintain order, were found by federal courts to be in violation of 8th Amendment guarantees against "cruel and unusual punishment." Texas officials girded for a fight.

On October 17, 1972, Allen L. Lamar, a black TDC inmate, filed a lawsuit claiming that segregation in Texas prisons constituted a denial of his and other prisoners' civil rights. In May 1973, the U.S. Department of Justice (DOJ) intervened on behalf of Lamar and against the state of Texas and its TDC. Once consolidated with related cases, *Allen L. Lamar v. H.H. Coffield* became one of the most important civil rights cases in the history of the Texas prison system. *Lamar v. Coffield*, and the even more prominent *Ruiz v. Estelle*, discussed in more detail below, moved in tandem through the federal court system over the course of two decades, from the early 1970s through the early 1990s. Their results transformed the Texas prison system in many ways, some good, some bad.

Lamar challenged segregation by race in Texas prisons from intake and prisoner classification, to assignment to particular prisons and work details, to segregation in social settings such as prison barber shops, day rooms, and mess halls, to cell block and single cell assignments. Texas lost and by October 1978 had signed a consent decree to desegregate, though full compliance took another decade. With the consent decree in *Lamar* signed, attention shifted to the *Ruiz* case where no consent decree could be reached.

On June 29, 1972, David Ruiz, a Hispanic inmate in the maximum security Eastham Unit, filed a broad prisoner rights case, which became *David Ruiz v. W.J. Estelle. Ruiz v. Estelle* was filed in Judge William Wayne Justice's federal courtroom in Tyler, Texas. Once consolidated with several similar cases, *Ruiz* went to trial in 1979. "Ruiz quickly developed into the most comprehensive prison reform case in legal history."[22] Judge Justice ruled in December 1980 that underfunding and overcrowding produced constitutional deficiencies in the TDC. Justice wrote that "Over crowding at TDC exercises a malignant effect on all aspects of prison life." He also found that underfunding compromised prison security and led to an over-reliance on force. "TDC compensated for its chronic shortages of civilian security personnel by using inmates to perform security functions." "Staff brutality, Justice wrote, was 'widespread' and 'nothing short of routine.'"[23] Texas resisted doggedly. Finally, in 1987 Judge Justice held Texas in contempt of court because its progress had been so slow. Only then did Texas begin to comply with the court's orders. Judge Justice did not release the Texas prison system from federal oversight until 2002, almost thirty years after *Ruiz v. Estelle* was initiated. Needless to say, over this period of time, the great nicknames of Texas prison wardens disappeared. When you are being hauled into federal court for prisoner abuse, it does not help to be called "beartrack" or "wildcat."

This remarkable battle between the State of Texas and Judge Justice, and behind him the U.S. Department of Justice and the U.S. Constitution, turned on different and incompatible models of criminal justice and penology. Texas held consistently to a correctional model in which "Their primary responsibility was to the public, and as they saw it, the public in Texas asked only that offenders be held securely and that they work to defray the cost of their incarceration." Hence, as the case played out and Judge Justice found guard brutality and abuse of the system of building tenders, Governor Bill Clements declared that "our department of corrections is one of the finest in the country and I am confident that we will prevail in the higher courts."[24] The State of Texas opened its 1981 appeal of Justice's ruling before the Fifth Circuit Court of Appeals by declaring, in fine Texas fashion, that the TDC administers "the largest prison system in the U.S." and that "the eighteen separate prison units operated by the TDC [are] among the best penal facilities in the country."[25]

Texas Attorney General Mark White (1979–1983), later Governor Mark White (1983–1987), a Democrat, was steadfastly supportive of TDC. As

Attorney General, even after the Fifth Circuit affirmed Justice's finding that the Texas prison system was unconstitutional and that his court could oversee remedies through a Special Master, "White claimed that the ruling gave 'the state of Texas a sweep on the issues that were before the court. . . . It gives us a much stronger negotiating point. We have the hold cards and they don't.'" Unfortunately for White and for Texas, more and more information supporting Justice's findings on the pervasiveness of the prison tender system and of excessive violence by guards continued to pour out. Finally, White was forced to observe that "It does very little good to try to . . . punish a prisoner, if members of the officials appointed there are violating the law. I hope they weren't. I trust they weren't. If they were, they're going to be dealt with harshly." Yet, as White was leaving the governorship in early 1987, he went out of his way to visit a TDC prison to declare his view that Texas operated "constitutional prisons."

White's successor, Governor Bill Clements, a Republican, used his State of the State address to the opening of the 70th legislative session to declare that the battle over Texas prisons was lost. Clements said, "Let me state clearly the facts of the Ruiz case. The lawsuit is over. . . . We must get in compliance as quickly as possible. We have no choice." Still, the chairman of the TDC board wondered "how we are ever going to get the judge to believe us, after we lied to him for ten years."[26] Fortunately, by 1990, Judge Justice was almost as eager as Governor Clements and the recently renamed Texas Department of Criminal Justice (TDCJ) for the case to be concluded. "Judge Justice issued an order in 1990 phasing out the Office of Special Master and ordering the parties to negotiate a comprehensive settlement. In 1992, he approved the settlement in a final judgment consent decree that returned day-to-day control of the system to the Texas Department of Criminal Justice."[27] Judge Justice died in 2009 at age 89.[28]

In 1972, when the Ruiz case was filed, the Texas prison population was just under 17,000. In 1988, as Texas began to move seriously to comply with the court's orders in Ruiz, the Texas prison population was still under 40,000.[29] Over the next two decades, even as crime rates nationwide and in Texas peaked and began a long decline, Texas spent billions of dollars improving and expanding its prison system. The population of Texas prisons more than tripled between 1990 and 1999, rising from 50,042 to 163,190. At its peak in 2008, Texas had 172,000 prisoners distributed among fifty-two state prisons, seven contract prisons, and sixty state jails, transfer facilities, boot camps, and hospital facilities. Moreover, unlike most of the policy areas that we have surveyed in previous chapters, the cost of prisons is paid in Texas tax dollars; less than 6 percent comes from the federal government.[30]

The Fiscal Year 2012 Statistical Report of the Texas Department of Criminal Justice reports that of the 152,303 state prisoners (Texas federal prisoners are not included in the report), 54,313 are black (36 percent),

47,274 are white (31 percent), and 49,940 are Hispanic (33 percent). Recall that the population of Texas in 2010 was 47 percent white, 38 percent Hispanic, and 12 percent black, so blacks are overrepresented in Texas prisons by a factor of three, while whites and Hispanics are underrepresented. Texas prisons are no longer segregated, but they are still used for social control.

Crime and Crime Rates in the U.S. and Texas

Texas has often had more crime than the domesticated parts of the country, but reliable numbers go back only to 1960. The FBI collects data on violent crime, which include murder, rape, robbery, and aggravated assault, and property crime, which include burglary, larceny, and auto theft. Both violent crime and property crime increased dramatically in the U.S. and Texas from 1960 into the early 1990s before it began a steady decline. Annual crime rates are generally reported as the number of crimes per 100,000 of population.

Figure 7.1 shows violent crime in the U.S. and Texas from 1960 to the present. The levels of violent crime in the U.S. and Texas were identical in 1960 at 161 violent crimes per 100,000 of population. For the next quarter century, violent crime rates nearly quadrupled, to 557 in the U.S. and 550 in Texas in 1985, with Texas numbers at or often trailing U.S. numbers. But since 1986 it has been a different story. Violent crime rates in Texas

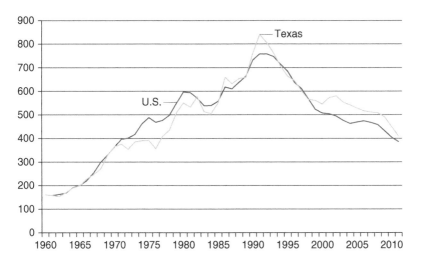

Figure 7.1 Violent Crime Rates in the U.S. and Texas, 1960–Present.

Source: U.S. Department of Justice, Office of Justice Programs, Bureau of Justice Statistics, Reported crime in the U.S. and for Texas, violent crime, http://bjsdata. ojp.usdoj.gov/dataonline/Search/Crime/State/RunCrimeStatebyState.cfm.

surpassed those in the U.S. in 1986, peaking in 1991 at 840 in Texas and 758 in the U.S. Since the early 1990s, violent crime rates in Texas and the U.S. have fallen, to 386 in the U.S. and 409 in Texas in 2011, but Texas rates have run ahead of the national average in eighteen of the twenty-one years between 1991 and 2011. In summary, violent crime rates in Texas ran ahead of the U.S. rates in twenty-five of the fifty-two years between 1960 and 2011.

Property crime rates in Texas run consistently ahead of U.S. rates and often well ahead (Figure 7.2). During the 1960s and the first half of the 1970s, property crime in the U.S. and Texas rose steadily with Texas usually just marginally ahead of the U.S. That changed in the mid-1970s as U.S. property crime slowed, plateaued from the late 1970s to the early 1990s, and then began a steady decline. The property crime rate continued to rise in Texas through the early 1980s, then saw a dramatic rise from the early 1980s through the early 1990s, before it began its decline, but from much higher levels. For example, in 1980, property crime in Texas registered 5,593 per 100,000, while the national rate was 5,353, lower, but not appreciably. By 1988, the national rate had fallen to 5,027 while the Texas rate had surged to 7,365. The Texas numbers came down in the 1990s, but since 2000 they have remained 20 to 30 percent above the national average.

We can get another view of how Texas violent and property crime rates compare to those in the U.S. by showing Texas as a percentage of the U.S.

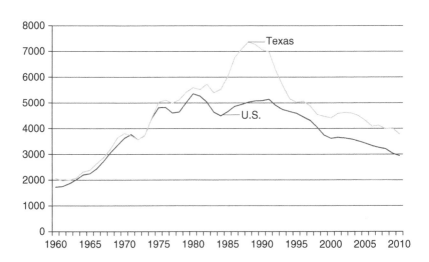

Figure 7.2 Property Crime Rates in the U.S. and Texas, 1960–Present.

Source: U.S. Department of Justice, Office of Justice Programs, Bureau of Justice Statistics, Reported crime in the U.S. and for Texas, property crime, http://bjsdata.ojp.usdoj.gov/dataonline/Search/Crime/State/RunCrimeStatebyState.cfm.

rates since 1960 (Figure 7.3). Prior to 1985, Texas usually trailed the U.S. in violent crime but surpassed it in property crime. Since 1985, Texas has generally been above the national average in both violent crime and property crime though it has led in property crime by much more. Still, the most striking aspect of this figure is the dramatic surge in property crime in Texas during the 1980s and early 1990s. As we shall see below, the nation's war on drugs, fought with special gusto in Texas, swelled the prisons. In 2011, Texas violent crime was 106 percent of the U.S. average while property crime was 119 percent of the U.S. average.

Figures 7.1 and 7.2 show that crime rates have been falling in the U.S. and Texas since the early 1990s. Falling crime rates are obviously a good thing, though criminologists and other experts have a hard time explaining why the rates are falling. Some cite new police methods, including the "broken window" theory and CompStat system introduced in New York City in the early 1990s, while others cite the burgeoning prison population. The broken window theory of fighting minor crimes, such as graffiti and vandalism, so that a permissive environment conducive to more serious crime does not develop is undoubtedly part of it. So is CompStat which is a system for tracking crime rates block-by-block so pockets of crime can be flooded with police assets as soon as they arise. But crime rates began to fall in New York City a few years before police methods changed and crime rates fell both in cities that followed the New York model and in cities that did not. Moreover, larger prison populations might reduce crime rates by

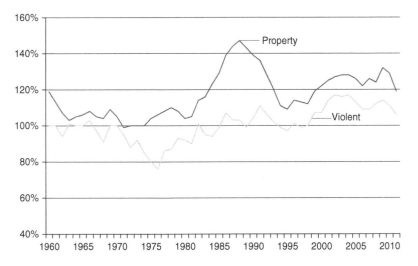

Figure 7.3 Texas Crime Rates as a Percent of U.S. Rates, 1960–Present.

Source: U.S. Department of Justice, Office of Justice Programs, Bureau of Justice Statistics, Reported crime in the U.S. and for Texas, violent crime, http://bjsdata.ojp.usdoj.gov/dataonline/Search/Crime/State/RunCrimeStatebyState.cfm.

taking more criminals off the street, but Canada experienced falling crime rates without a rise in prison populations.[31]

Again, falling crime rates are obviously a good thing, even when you are not entirely clear on why they are falling. But Robert Perkinson points out with particular relevance to Texas that crime rates and prison populations "correlate only weakly." As we have seen, crime rates in Texas have been falling since the early 1990s, but as we shall see next, Texas prison populations grew, in fact skyrocketed, during these same years. Perhaps there are reasons other than rising crime rates for rising prison populations in the U.S. and, more specifically, Texas. Perkinson points out that, "the rise of imprisonment since the seventies has been concentrated overwhelmingly among young African American men, a trend unexplainable by criminal offense data."[32]

Prisons and Incarceration in the U.S. and Texas

The prison population in the U.S. and in the states is generally discussed both in raw numbers (how many people are in prison) and in incarceration rates (the number of prisoners per 100,000 of population). First, the number of persons imprisoned in the U.S. from 1950 to 2009 increased more than ten-fold—from 148,362 in 1950 to 1,615,487 in 2009. A three year decline, beginning in 2010, left the U.S. prison population at 1,571,013 in 2012. In Texas, the rise in imprisonment has been even steeper, soaring from 6,424 in 1950 to 172,224 in 2011, a nearly twenty-seven-fold increase. Texas saw a decline to 166,372 prisoner in 2012, though this is still by far the largest prison population among the states and is falling late and slowly. Strikingly, the U.S. prison population grew moderately from 1950 into the mid-1970s and then much faster through the late 1990s before leveling off. In Texas, the growth was faster from 1950 into the mid-1970s than it was in the U.S. in general, but not dramatically so, before it absolutely exploded through the rest of the century, slowing thereafter.

The social instability of the 1960s convinced many Americans that "law and order" was in danger. President Nixon advocated adoption of mandatory sentencing provisions for drug crimes at both federal and state levels. In 1973, New York's Governor Nelson Rockefeller pushed through a set of stiff mandatory sentences for drug crimes. Many states followed suit and the nation's prison population began to grow. California and Texas were eager participants. Texas Governor Dolph Briscoe used the 1973 and 1977 legislative sessions to enhance the state's anti-drug laws and penalties. In 1973, he supported stiffer penalties for drugs from speed to heroin, and in 1977, he supported stricter rules on probation and parole. Republican Governor Bill Clements, first elected in 1978, continued the anti-drug, tough on crime campaign. Long-time Texas Lieutenant Governor Bill Hobby (1973–1991) has written that, "The Texas war on drugs . . . created new crimes, set higher penalties for old ones, and made it harder to get parole." As a result, "Texas has the largest prison system in the United States."[33]

The U.S. Justice Department's Bureau of Justice Statistics, which collects and organizes most of our national justice statistics, described the general pattern in a study entitled "The Prevalence of Imprisonment." The Bureau wrote that "In the 1960s, while crime soared, prison populations declined. What followed in the 1970s was a marked shift in national opinion: increasingly, the public began to demand that the justice system get tough with criminals. The response of the justice system seemed immediate."[34] The U.S. prison population grew by 25 percent in the 1950s, dropped by 7 percent in the 1960s, grew again by 58 percent in the 1970s, 115 percent in the 1980s, 99 percent in the 1990s, before slowing to 21 between 2000 and 2009 (Figure 7.4). Over the entire fifty-nine-year period, the U.S. prison population grew 870 percent while the total population merely doubled. A slow decline in the nation's prison population began in 2010.

Texas's contribution to prison growth in the U.S. was Herculean. As we discussed above, the Texas prison case of *Ruiz v. Estelle* was filed in 1972, went to trial in 1978, was decided against Texas in 1983, and the federal courts did not release Texas prisons from direct supervision until 1992. Texas's response to the intervention of the federal courts was to build more prisons. In 1950, Texas held just 6,424 prisoners in Huntville and a handful of smaller facilities. By the end of the 1970s, the Texas prison system comprised eighteen prisons holding about 25,000 inmates. During the 1980s, Texas struggled to hold down the prison population, comply with Judge Justice's ruling, and build prisons for the

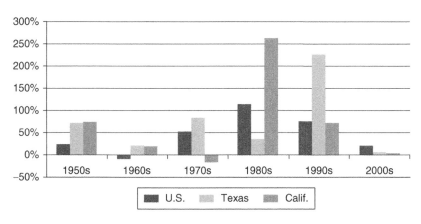

Figure 7.4 Percent Growth in Prison Population by Decade, 1950–Present.

Source: U.S. Census Bureau, Statistical Abstract of the United States, Law Enforcement, Courts, and Prisons, Prisoners Under Jurisdiction of State or Federal Correctional Authorities, Summary by State, various years, www.census. gov/compendia/statab/tables/09s0333.pdf.

day when they no longer answered to the judge: "In the late 1980s and early 1990s, the state built eighty-nine more prisons that could house 140,000 more inmates."[35]

As the U.S. prison population burgeoned in the last quarter of the twentieth century, not all states grew at the same rate or began their growth at the same time. Figures 7.4 and 7.5 show this clearly. In the 1950s, Texas expanded its prison population by 73 percent while California expanded by 75 percent; in the 1960s, Texas grew by 21 percent, California by 20; in the 1970s, Texas grew by 85 percent while California shrank by 15 percent. But California was just taking a breather to build more prisons. In the 1980s, Texas's prison population grew by just 36 percent while California's skyrocketed by 263 percent. Not to be outdone, Texas expanded by 226 percent in the 1990s, compared to California's 76 percent. Both slowed between 2000 and 2009, to 8 percent for Texas and 5 percent for California. The federal courts have demanded reductions in California's prison population while Texas's has declined more slowly due to financial pressures.

Figure 7.5 shows that the prison population of some states, California and Texas, grew dramatically, Florida and New York grew steadily but moderately, while Virginia and Georgia obviously worked to hold down growth. New York is particularly interesting. New York in 1950 had the nation's largest prison population, though it had fallen behind California in terms of population. But New York held its prison population steady for

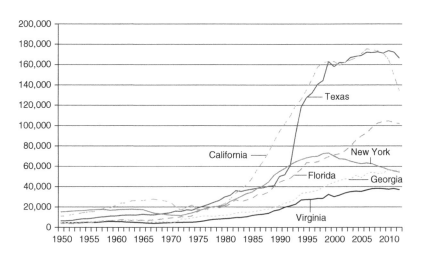

Figure 7.5 Prisoners Held in Texas and Other Large States, 1950–Present.

Source: U.S. Census Bureau, Statistical Abstract of the United States, Law Enforcement, Courts, and Prisons, Prisoners Under Jurisdiction of State or Federal Correctional Authorities, Summary by State, various years, http://www.census.gov/compendia/statab/tables/09s0333.pdf

the next quarter century, until the Rockefeller drug laws more than quadrupled it between 1973 and 1999. California surpassed New York by the late 1950s and, except for a brief period in the late 1970s, has held twice as many prisoners as New York. Figure 7.5 clearly shows, as the bar chart did, that the California prison population took off nearly a full decade before Texas's truly began to soar. Under federal court mandate, California's prison population began a steep decline in 2010. Florida's prison population grew steadily beginning around 1980, but never as dramatically as California and Texas. New York tracked Florida's steady rise through the 1980s and 1990s, but its numbers declined over 19 percent between 2000 and 2010. Georgia and Virginia have held their prison populations down throughout.

Another way to look at imprisonment in the U.S., Texas, and other states is to move from the raw number of prisoners to incarceration rates. Incarceration rates control for population growth by measuring imprisonment as the number of prisoners per 100,000 of population. Incarceration rates paint a remarkable picture, especially in regard to Texas. Interestingly, in 1950 Texas had a lower incarceration rate (at 83) than the U.S. (109) or any of the states, California (104), New York (103), Virginia (134), Florida (143), and Georgia (132), that we have been using to put Texas in context.

Looking more closely at the pattern of growth in the U.S. incarceration rate, we see that it rose modestly between 1950 and 1961, from 109 to 119, before falling slowly through the 1960s to a low of 93 in 1972. A slow rise through the 1970s put the incarceration rate at 133 in 1979. Looking across the period 1950 to 1979, we see a modest rise of just 22 percent, or less than 1 percent per year. Growth rates increased dramatically during the 1980s, almost exactly doubling from 139 in 1980 to 276 in 1989. Incarceration rates increased another 60 percent during the 1990s, rising from 297 in 1990 to 476 in 1999, before slowing to 5 percent for the period 2000 to 2009. Incarceration rates have declined modestly since 2009.

Glancing briefly back at Figure 7.5, which depicts prison population by state, the figure suggests that both California and Texas expanded dramatically in the 1980s and 1990s. Figure 7.6 tells a different and more accurate story. California's incarceration rate was 104 per 100,000 of population in 1950, rose to the 140s for most of the 1960s, before falling to a low of 80 by 1977. In fact, California's incarceration rate dropped by 11 percent, from 104 to 93, well below the national average, during the three decades from 1950 to 1979. California's incarceration rate increased by 196 percent, effectively tripling, during the 1980s. In 1980, California's incarceration rate stood at 98 per 100,000 of population and in 1989 it stood at 290. Nonetheless, because California's population was so large and growing so fast, its incarceration rate never went much above the national average. During the 1990s it increased to 481 before dropping slightly thereafter. A court enforced reduction in the state's prison population sent its incarceration rate from 458 in 2009 to 351 in 2012.

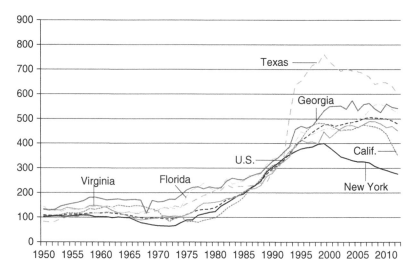

Figure 7.6 Federal and State Incarceration Rates, 1950–Present.

Source: The U.S. incarceration rates come from the U.S. Census Bureau, Statistical Abstract of the United States, Mini-Historical Statistics, No. HS-24, Federal and State Prisoners, 1925–2001. See also Bureau of Justice Statistics, Incarceration rates, 1980–2007, http://www.ojp.usdoj.gov/bjs/glance/tables/incrttab.htm. State rates come from the Bureau of Justice Statistics, filename corpop25.csv, Incarceration Rates for Prisoners Under Federal and State Jurisdiction, per 100,000 residents, 1977–1998, http://www.ojp.usdoj.gov/bjs/data/corpop25.csv. Author calculation for states, 1950–1976: resident population divided by 100,000 (if resident population is expressed in thousands, divide that number by 100), and then divide the resulting number into the number of prisoners in the state.

The pattern for Texas in Figure 7.6 is much more striking. In 1950, Texas had an incarceration rate, at 83 per 100,000 of population, that was just 76 percent of the national rate (109). The Texas rate rose faster than the national rate during the 1950s until Texas tied with the U.S. in 1959 and 1960 at 117. The 1960s saw very moderate growth, just 4 percent, in Texas. The 1970s and 1980s saw somewhat faster, but still fairly moderate growth, 87.5 percent over two decades, from 128 to 240 per 100,000 of population, compared to 187.5 for the nation. In fact, as late as 1987 Texas and the U.S. were tied at 231 and from 1988 through 1991, the incarceration rate in Texas was below the national rate. The years 1993–1994 changed everything as the incarceration rate in Texas jumped from 385 per 100,000 in 1993 to 636 in 1994 and then kept going through the remainder of the decade, peaking at 762 in 1999. It has since fallen to 601, fifth highest in the nation behind Louisiana (at an astonishing 893), Mississippi (717), Alabama (650), and Oklahoma (648).

Figure 7.6 highlights the impact of *Ruiz v. Estelle* on incarceration rates in Texas. Prior to Ruiz, rates increased a bit in the 1950s and fell a bit in the 1960s, but they remained in a fairly narrow band. Incarceration rates picked up in the 1970s, growing by 39 percent nationally and 53 percent in Texas, but Texas remained in the middle of the pack. Briefly, in the late 1980s, as the court orders issued by Judge Justice in *Ruiz v. Estelle* took effect, Texas fell behind the national average and behind all of our comparison states. However, as dramatically increased expenditures brought new capacity online, Texas incarceration rates leapt. In 1992, the U.S. and all six states in our chart had nearly identical incarceration rates, ranging from Virginia's low of 327 to Georgia's high of 365, with the U.S. average at 332 and Texas at 344. Over the next two years, Texas jumped to 511 and then to 636, a jump highlighted in the chart.

Figure 7.7 provides the clearest perspective yet on Texas's evolving proclivity to imprison. Figure 7.7 compares Texas's share of the total U.S. population with Texas's share of the total U.S. prison population. In 1950, Texas accounted for 5.1 percent of the total U.S. population and 4.3 percent of its prison population. By 1959 the population and prison number had met at 5.3 percent of both population and prisoners. Over the next two decades, the tumultuous 1960s and the more conservative 1970s, Texas sought stability in an expanded prison system. In 1980, Texas accounted for 6.3 percent of the U.S. population and 9.5 percent of its prisoners.

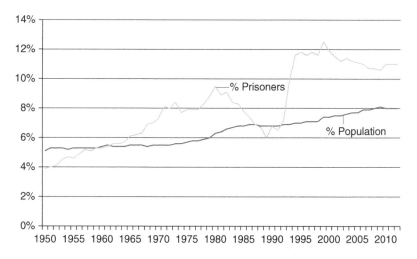

Figure 7.7 Texas Population and Prisoners as a Percent of U.S. Population and Prisoners, 1950–Present.

Source: U.S. Census Bureau, Statistical Abstract of the United States, various years, Population section and Law Enforcement, Courts, and Prisons section.

However, as Judge Justice pushed toward a final resolution of the *Ruiz v. Estelle* lawsuit, overcrowding of Texas prisons was a major point of contention. In early 1982, 4,000 Texas prisoners were housed in tents. In spring 1982, the corrections board ordered the prison system not to accept any more prisoners. Before long 30,000 state prisoners were backlogged in county jails. Texas's response was a prison-building program. Texas added 108,000 beds after 1983 at a cost of $2.3 billion, but in the short term it was forced to bring its inmate population down. By 1989, Texas had 6.8 percent of population and just 6 percent of prisoners. But just as soon as Judge Justice relinquished day-to-day control of the prisons and new prison capacity came online, the Texas prison population shot to unprecedented heights. By 1999, Texas accounted for 7.4 percent of the total U.S. population and 12.5 percent of prison inmates. By 2012, Texas accounted for 8.3 percent of the U.S. population and 10.6 percent of inmates.

Figure 7.7 suggests that, absent Judge Justice's control of the Texas prison system in the late 1970s and 1980s, its response to the cultural revolution of the 1960s would have been a rapid build out from the 1960s through the 1990s. The cultural panic spawned in Texas by the civil rights revolution, the anti-war movement, the women's movement, and rising crime rates produced the state's gargantuan prison system. Issues of race and gender are still with us, but crime rates began abating more than two decades ago. Nonetheless, the Texas prison population did not stop growing until 2011 and now the state is saddled with a bloated prison system and unsustainable prison costs. Only a few Texas politicians have begun to think about new directions.

In 2007, led by Senator John Whitmire, chair of the Senate Criminal Justice Committee, and Representative Jerry Madden, chair of the House Corrections Committee, the Texas Legislature decided it could afford no more new prisons. Texas prisons were near capacity and the state was looking at another $503 million in additional construction costs over the next five years. Instead, working with the U.S. Department of Justice and the Pew Charitable Trusts' Center on the States, the 2007 legislative session diverted about half of those funds from new prison construction to programs for prison diversion, more effective use of probation and parole, and community residential and addiction treatment facilities.[36]

By 2009, growth of the Texas prison system had slowed markedly. Officials claimed that they had 2,000 empty prison beds and that no new prisons would be needed for at least five years. Representative Madden noted that, "the research showed that our prisons were being overwhelmed by those who could receive alternative treatment to incarceration and therefore preserve our resources for the dangerous violent offender." Madden neglected to say that these insights had come to other state prison authorities a decade or more ago. Instead, he simply noted that Texans are, "a proud people who don't like to change. But now being tough and smart on crime is a better utilization of the taxpayer dollar."[37] Despite the official crowing, inmates in Texas numbered 172,116 in 2006 and 172,224 in 2011, though the number did drop to 166,372 in 2012.

Correctional Employment and Expenditures in the U.S. and Texas

Looking at correctional employment in Texas and the U.S. provides another interesting insight into the effect on the Texas prison system of Judge Justice's handling of *Ruiz v. Estelle*. In his testimony at the Ruiz trial, Director W.J. Estelle (1972–1983) reported that staff-to-inmate ratios in Texas were among the lowest in the nation during his tenure. At the time of trial, October 1978 through June 1979, the average guard-to-prisoner ratio nationwide was one to five, while in Texas it was one to 12.45. Estelle also testified that turnover ratios among lower level staff ran at 60 to 70 percent annually.[38] Judge Justice found that overcrowding and insufficient staffing led to an unconstitutional denial of prisoner rights. When Judge Justice issued his final decree in April 1981, he ordered that the staff-to-prisoner ratio be reduced from one to twelve to one to six. Texas appealed the overcrowding and staffing findings, which were modified by the Fifth Circuit Court of Appeals in June 1982, but not before the TDC Board closed Texas prisons to new admissions in May. In a June Special Session, the legislature authorized $58 million in new expenditures for prison construction and additional staffing. Nonetheless, as we have seen above, the Texas prison population went sideways during the 1980s, awaiting new prisons and more staff. Between 1979 and 1985, corrections staff expanded from 2,500 to 9,000.[39]

Still, Texas responded only as it had to and only in its traditional fashion. Texas increased prison spending and hiring, but continued to spend less per capita on prisoners and guards than the rest of the nation. State appropriations for prisons rose from $50 million in 1975, to $300 million in 1980, $1 billion in 1985, $1.7 billion in 1996, $2.3 billion in 2001, and $3 billion in 2012. Texas also increased its corrections staff. In 1982, Texas had 110 corrections staff per 100,000 of population compared to 130 nationally. By 1985, Texas had surpassed the U.S. average by 150 to 140 and by 1995 Texas had 340 correctional staff for every 100,000 of population while the U.S. averaged 240. As Figure 7.8 shows, the U.S. has remained at about 240 while Texas has just fallen below 300.

Despite decades of increased prison funding, Texas continued to lag on expenditures per prisoner and on pay for corrections officers. Data on annual cost per prisoner in the U.S. and Texas is scattered but quite consistent. In 1974, Texas spent just under $1,100 annually per prisoner. As *Ruiz v. Estelle* was about to be decided in 1980, Texas spent $2,679 annually, in 1983 it spent $6,951, in 1985 it spent $10,950, and in 1988 it

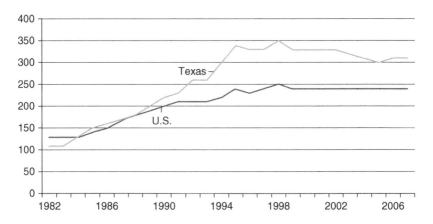

Figure 7.8 Correctional Staff in the U.S. and Texas Per 100,000 of Population, 1982–Present.

Source: Bureau of Justice Statistics, Criminal Justice Expenditure and Employment Extracts, Table 8, www.ojp.usdoj.gov/bjs/eande.htm#selected.

spent $12,500. By comparison, California spent $22,597 per prisoner in 1988 and in 1990 the U.S. average per prisoner was $18,400.[40] In 1996 and 2001, the Bureau of Justice Statistics' "State Prison Expenditures," the only really systematic comparison of state prisoner expenditures per year, showed Texas lagging far behind. In 1996, Texas spent $12,215 per prisoner, compared to the U.S. average of $20,142 and California's $21,385. Texas ranked 47th among the states, trailing only Alabama, Mississippi, and Oklahoma. In 2001, Texas spent $13,808, compared to the U.S. average of $22,650 and California's $25,053. Texas ranked 46th among the states, trailing only Alabama, Louisiana, Mississippi, and Missouri. A recent study by the highly respected Pew Charitable Trust, "One in 31: The Long Reach of American Corrections," using 2008 data, shows a national cost per prisoner of $28,817 to Texas's $15,527. Finally, the Vera Institute of Justice did a study, using 2010 data from 40 states, that included incarceration costs outside the traditional corrections budget. The Vera study reported an average cost per prisoner of $31,286, compared to Texas's annual cost of $21,390—68 percent of the national average.[41]

Perhaps even more telling is the comparison between the annual salary of corrections officers in the U.S. and in Texas. Recall that Director Estelle testified in the Ruiz trial that he had a turnover ratio of 60 to 70 percent annually among his lower level guards. Even today, we can immediately see why that would be so. We have good data only for 1993 through 2006, but it is telling. In 1993, Texas prison guards made 82 percent as much as their peers nationally, $24,252 vs. $29,556. In 2010, Texas prison guards made just 70 percent as much as their national peers, $34,188 vs. $48,552—and surprise turnover remained high. By 2013, guards were leaving in droves to take jobs in the oil and gas fields and guard pay had slipped to 47th in the nation. Texas has a higher proportion of its state workforce in corrections (16.9 percent) than any other state.[42] Texas has 45,000 correctional employees serving in the state's 111 prisons.

The Death Penalty in the U.S. and Texas

One of the more puzzling aspects of Texas's approach to crime and punishment has been its relatively recent but fervid commitment to the death penalty. For most of the state's history, the death penalty was used regularly, at somewhat higher rates than the nation as a whole, but not at rates disproportionate to the South as a region. Like the rest of the South, Texas used the death penalty predominantly against minorities until the U.S. Supreme Court stepped in to demand change. First, we will look at the broad sweep of Texas history to show that the death penalty was, in fact, used largely against minorities. Second, we will compare use of the death penalty in Texas to that in other major states and the nation from 1950 to the present. Finally, we will look at the exoneration movement nationally and in Texas.

First, from 1819 to 1974, 62 percent of the persons executed in Texas were black, 28 percent were white, 10 percent were Hispanic, and a small number were unidentified by race.[43] Simple inconsistency in how the death penalty was applied in the U.S. led the Supreme Court, in a series of decisions beginning with *Robinson v. California* (1962) and culminating in *Furman v. Georgia* and *Branch v. Texas*, both in 1972, to find the death penalty as then applied unconstitutional in light of the 8th and 14th Amendments provisions regarding "cruel and unusual punishment" and "equal protection of the laws." The court noted racial disparities in the application of the death penalty but did not cite them as the basis for unconstitutionality.

Interestingly, when the death penalty came under judicial scrutiny in the Robinson case, Texas, though not directly involved, suspended its use of the death penalty in 1965. The U.S. Supreme court suspended the death penalty nationally in 1972 and after a four-year moratorium, states that had reformed their death penalty statutes and standards to insure that they were employed consistently were permitted to reinstate the death penalty. Even states that did reinstate the death penalty were cautious in using it. Texas did not begin using the death penalty again until 1982. But by the early 1990s Texas was using the death penalty much more than it ever had before and much more than any other state.

The debate in the Texas legislature over whether and in what form to reinstitute the death penalty was both interesting and entertaining. The outcome was not really in doubt as all of the southern states eventually reinstituted the death penalty, but there was opposition. It was quelled by an appeal to Texas commonsense. Arguing in favor of the death penalty, a combative San Antonio attorney named Fred A. Semann made the point that while civilized states like Minnesota might get away without the death penalty, Texas could not. When first-term Texas House member Craig Washington (D-Houston) asked him whether he thought Texans were more violent than others, he answered yes, saying, "I don't think in Maine, New Hampshire, Vermont and those states people go to a beer joint the way some people do in Texas—sit there and drink beer, and because somebody goes up and puts a nickel in a jukebox and plays a tune that somebody else don't like, kill him for it. That's been done here!"[44] The logic was irrefutable; Texas House Bill 200 was approved (114 to 30 in the House and 27 to 4 in the Senate) and went into effect on June 14, 1973. Texas was one of the first states to reinstitute the death penalty, though it did not use it for nearly a decade.

Death penalty convictions in the U.S. peaked at 315 in 1996 and have since fallen, steeply until 2001 and more steadily since, to 178 in 2012. Texas averaged thirty-four death sentences a year throughout the 1990s, but just nine in 2012. Most analysts point to the passage in Texas in 2005 of the "life without parole" option to the death penalty. Since 2005, Texas has averaged only ten death sentences annually. Still, Texas death row is backed up and executions, though also down, have still run at twenty a year since 2005.

Figure 7.9, covering the 1830s to the 2000s, shows the high proportion of minority executions prior to the 1970s and the somewhat smaller proportion following the Supreme Court's rulings in *Furman v. Georgia*

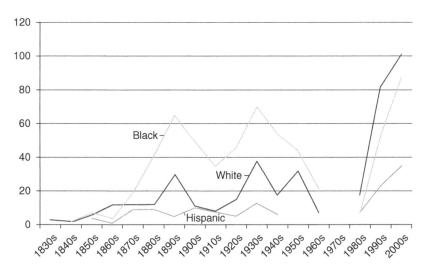

Figure 7.9 Texas Executions by Decade and Race, 1830s–Present.

Source: Death Penalty Information, the Espy file and the Executions by state file. See www.deathpenaltyinfo.org/number-executions-state-and-region-1976.

and *Branch v. Texas.* Before the Civil War, blacks as property were rarely executed. After the Civil War, and, more particularly, after Reconstruction when whites were employing all tools to reestablish unchallenged sway, blacks were sent to the gallows and, after 1924, the electric chair, in numbers that did not begin to taper off until the 1950s. By the time Texas returned to execution in early 1982, lethal injection had replaced electrocution as the method of execution. The total number of executions soared, though for the first time since Reconstruction slightly more whites were executed than blacks. From 1982 through mid-2013, Texas executed 500 persons: 36 percent black, 45 percent white, and 17 percent Hispanic. Nonetheless, while whites and Hispanics were executed at rates lower than their presence in the population, blacks were executed at a stunning three times the rate that their presence in the population would suggest.

Figure 7.10 highlights Texas's modern avidity for the death penalty. The third quarter of the twentieth century saw widespread questioning of the death penalty, at least in its application if not in its fundamental legitimacy. The number of executions in the U.S. came steadily down while a series of legal challenges to the implementation of the death penalty, its fundamental fairness, and its constitutionality made their way through the nation's courts. Though the Supreme Court did not declare a legal moratorium until 1972 and then began to lift the moratorium on a state by state basis in 1976, virtually all states halted use of the death penalty by the mid-1960s and did not return to it until the early 1980s. Texas

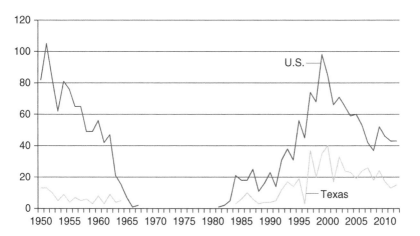

Figure 7.10 Number of Executions Nationally and in Texas, 1950–Present.

Source: U.S. execution numbers, 1930-2010, Bureau of Justice Statistics, http://www.ojp.usdoj.gov/ bjs/glance/tables/exetab.htm See also Death Penalty Information Center, Executions by State, http:// www.deathpenaltyinfo.org and the U.S. Census Bureau, Statistical Abstract of the United States, Law Enforcement, Courts, and Prisons section, "Prisoners Executed Under Civil Authority by States, various years.

carried out no executions between 1965 and 1981. In fact, executions in Texas remained generally in single digits into the early 1990s. However, from 1991 through 2012, Texas averaged twenty-one executions per year, fully 39 percent of all of the executions carried out in the U.S. during that period. While the death penalty is under review in some states, it is not in Texas. Eighteen states and D.C. no longer have the death penalty and fifteen more have used it ten or fewer times since 1976.[45] Since the death penalty was reinstated in 1976, six states—New York in 2004, New Jersey in 2007, New Mexico in 2009, Illinois in 2011 Connecticut in 2012, and Maryland in 2013—have abolished the death penalty.[46] About three-quarters of Texans support the death penalty and candidates for office generally voice full-throated support.

Exoneration in the U.S. and Texas

Many Americans and more Texans think of some crimes, horrific murders being the most obvious example, as worthy of the death penalty. Still, virtually all supporters of the death penalty presume that only the worst will be sentenced to death and that extraordinary care will be taken to assure that innocents are not mistakenly caught up in this terrible process. But many now wonder whether there is some even remote possibility that an innocent person might be convicted, sentenced to death, and executed. Since 1973, 138 men who were tried, convicted, and sentenced to death have had their convictions reversed—they have been exonerated—and been released. Other men and women have been convicted of lesser crimes, later found innocent and released, but most of the attention revolves around those sentenced to death and later released because in these cases the state had come closest to irreversible error—executing an innocent person.

The posthumous pardon of Timothy Cole in March 2010 comes perilously close to the execution of an innocent man. Timothy Cole was convicted of raping a fellow Texas Tech student in 1985. He protested his innocence at trial and throughout his eleven years in prison. He died in prison of an asthma-induced heart attack in 1999. Meanwhile, another Texas inmate, Jerry Wayne Johnson, began admitting to various rapes and in 2007, unaware that Cole had died, wrote to Cole's mother admitting to that rape. Subsequent DNA testing confirmed Cole's innocence and Johnson's guilt. Governor Perry issued the state's first posthumous pardon, clearing Cole's name nearly two decades after his conviction and a decade after his death. Had Timothy Cole gone on to graduate from Texas Tech, rather than being wrongly imprisoned for more than a decade, it is highly unlikely that he would have died of complications from asthma.

Despite the posthumous pardon of Timothy Cole, Texas officials have remained resistant to the very idea of judicial error. Texas has so many people on death row, 300, and has executed so many people since 1976, 500, that most state officials are reluctant to allow even for the possibility that the death penalty has been used mistakenly. While Texas has executed 37.4 percent (500 of 1,338) of the persons executed in the U.S. over the past four decades, less than 9 percent (12 of 138) of the death row inmates exonerated in the U.S. have been in Texas. Alternatively, Florida, which has more people on death row, 398, but has executed fewer, seventy-seven, has exonerated and released twenty-four people. Either Florida was much sloppier than Texas to begin with, sending people to death row who they later had to release, or they are being much more careful now. California provides another model. California has more people on death row, 727, and executed far fewer of them, just thirteen since 1976, but has exonerated only three. California has not exonerated many people, but they are much less likely than Texas to make a mistake they cannot correct. Table 7.1 indicates that Florida and California are not alone in being more careful than Texas. Everyone is more careful. Ominously, Texas ranks 50th among the fifty states and D.C. in providing legal assistance to indigent defendants.

We close with the ongoing controversy surrounding the execution of Cameron Todd Willingham. Willingham was executed by the state of Texas in 2004 for the 1991 house fire, judged to be arson by the initial investigation and at trial, that killed his three young children.

Table 7.1 Death Row Inmates, Executions, and Exonerations

States	Death Row, 2012	Executions since 1976	Exonerations since 1973	Exonerations as % of Executions
California	727	13	3	23%
Texas	300	500	12	2%
Florida	413	77	24	31%
Pennsylvania	202	3	6	200%
Alabama	198	55	5	9%
Ohio	147	51	6	12%
North Carolina	161	43	7	16%
Arizona	127	34	8	24%
Georgia	97	53	5	9%
Oklahoma	60	105	10	10%
Louisiana	88	28	8	29%
South Carolina	53	43	2	5%

Source: Death Penalty Information Center, www.deathpenaltyinfo.org.

Willingham professed his innocence throughout and subsequent review of the evidence upon which he was convicted, sentenced, and executed has called much of it into question. Specifically, three separate reviews of the forensic evidence by a total of seven of the nation's leading arson experts led them to question whether arson had in fact occurred. If the house fire was not arson, then the children's deaths were not murder and the execution was unwarranted.

The controversy around the Willingham execution had been percolating since before his execution on February 17, 2004, but did not become a national story until 2009.[47] As Willingham awaited execution in 2004, a nationally acclaimed fire expert named Gerald Hurst reexamined the trial evidence and declared that the fire had been accidental—not arson. Hurst wrote a report outlining his conclusions and submitted them to Governor Perry's office and the state Board of Pardons and Paroles. Neither took explicit note of his findings. As the execution date approached, Hurst said that "the most distressing thing is the state of Texas will kill an innocent man and doesn't care they're making a mistake."[48] The execution was carried out as scheduled. Hurst subsequently told the *Chicago Tribune* that "there's nothing to suggest to any reasonable arson investigator that this was an arson fire. It was just a fire."[49]

In 2009, Craig Beyler, another renowned arson investigator, compiled a report for the Texas Forensic Science Commission (TFSC), again finding no evidence of arson. Governor Rick Perry responded that he was "familiar with the latter-day supposed experts on the arson side of it. . . . I have not seen anything that would cause me to think that the decision that was made by the courts of the state of Texas was not correct."[50] Still, even jaded long-time political observers were stunned when Governor Perry abruptly replaced three members of the TFSC, including the chairman, just two days before the Commission was set to examine Beyler's findings. The new chairman, District Attorney John Bradley of Williamson County, promptly cancelled the meeting arguing that he and his new colleagues needed time to get up to speed on the case. Newspapers from Chicago to Houston, spurred by charges of cover-up issued by Barry Scheck of the Innocence Project, cried foul. The outgoing chairman, Sam Bassett, who Perry had named to his post two years earlier, said "In my view, we should not fail to investigate important forensic issues in cases simply because there might be political ramifications." And Senator Kay Bailey Hutchison, Perry's opponent for the Republican gubernatorial nomination in 2010, stirred the pot by asking, "Why you wouldn't at least have the hearing that the former member suggested, to find out what the facts are, when a man has been executed and now the facts are in dispute?" She closed, covering her Texas political bases, by declaring, "I am strongly for the death penalty, but always with the absolute assurance that you have the ability to be sure—with the technology that we have—that a person is guilty."[51] Governor Perry then sent the conspiracy theorists into further paroxysms of outrage when he refused to release the documents that were provided for his review (some question whether the documents really were closely reviewed) in the hours before Willingham was executed.

In the days following the reorganization the TFSC, Sam Bassett, the ousted chair, told the *Chicago Tribune* that top legal aides to the governor had tried to pressure him over the direction of the Willingham review. Bassett had been called to two meetings with lawyers from the governor's general counsel's office and representatives of that office had been attending the Commission's meetings. Bassett expressed concern for the future of the TFSC, saying "It's clear to me that the Willingham investigation is a lightning rod for the future of the commission. I'll never, ever say we shouldn't have taken on that investigation."[52] Beyler, the fire expert, called Perry "unethical." Beyler argued that "the governor had a conflict of interest because he approved the execution of Cameron Todd Willingham of Corsicana. His failure to recuse himself is both unethical and injurious to the cause of justice." Perry responded by forcefully declaring that Willingham was "a monster." "This was a guy that murdered his three children, who tried to beat his wife into an abortion—person after person has stood up and testified to the facts of this case that, quite frankly, you guys aren't covering," Perry said to the media. "This was a bad man."[53]

The state's newspapers were unsatisfied by Governor Perry's increasing emotional protestations. Lisa Falkenberg wrote a commentary in the *Houston Chronicle* noting that "being a bad man isn't a crime punishable by death, even in Texas." Falkenberg went on to say that,

> the fact that he was a "bad man," that he beat his pregnant wife, that he'd been convicted of low-level crimes, that he was fond of expletives, might have been enough, even a month ago to sow doubt about his innocence or simply deflect attention from the case of such an unsympathetic figure. But the story isn't about Willingham anymore. It isn't just about guilt or innocence. It isn't even about whether Perry did his homework before allowing Willingham's 2004 execution. It's about whether Perry is purposely trying to subvert the law in Willingham's case, and potentially obstruct justice in countless other arson cases that could benefit from the commission's review, all for political gain during a hotly contested primary.[54]

Governor Perry's newly named commission chair declared in early 2010 that the Commission's procedures for handling complex cases such as Willingham's needed to be refined before the case responsibly could be considered. Critics howled, but the process went underground for much of the year. Governor Perry easily survived the March 2010 Republican primary, beating Senator Kay Bailey Hutchison by twenty points, and then cruising to re-election later in the year. Just weeks prior to the general election, Chairman Bradley offered the Commission a draft report clearing arson investigators of any fault in the Willingham case. The Commission rejected the draft and members declared their intention to interview arson experts about the state of fire investigation science in 1994 and whether the investigators in the Willingham case appeared to have understood the science and applied it correctly. In other words, Perry's maneuver and Chairman Bradley's stalling left the Commission right where it had been a year earlier, needing to interview fire investigation experts. This did not go unnoticed. When Governor Perry nominated Bradley in 2011 for a full term as commission chair, the overwhelmingly Republican Texas Senate rejected the nomination. Perry's next nominee, Dr. Nizam Peerwani, the highly respected Chief Medical Examiner for Tarrant County, would have been expected to bring the Willingham case to a public resolution. Grizzled old veterans of Texas politics smiled when Texas Attorney General Greg Abbott declared in mid-2011 that the TFSC had no legal authority to investigate fires before the date of its founding in 2005. The TFSC did eventually issue a final report, but it took no position on Willingham's guilt or innocence. When Perry declared in 2013 that he would not seek re-election as governor, Abbott immediately declared for governor—the Willingham case is well and thoroughly buried.

Nonetheless, the travails of the TFSC did spur change elsewhere in Texas state government. Since 2012, the Texas State Fire Marshal, Chris Connealy, has been working with the Texas Innocence Project and leading arson investigators to identify old cases in which outdated fire science might have led to wrongful convictions. One case, similar to the Willingham case in many respects, involved Ed Graf, convicted in 1988 of setting a fire in which his two step-sons were killed. Graf has spent 26 years in prison, protesting his innocence, and may well get a new trial as a result of the new inquiries. Change comes slowly.

Conclusion

Texas A&M sociology professor Ben Crouch, a close observer of the Texas prison system since the 1970s, noted that, "Institutionalized sanctions of serious criminal offenders mirror the society in which they are applied. . . . In turn, citizens whose behavior and lifestyle least reflect these values are invariably those most often subject to criminal sanctions."[55] Crouch's observations clearly apply to Texas; throughout the state's history, its traditional political culture bore most heavily on African Americans and Hispanics, but particularly African Americans. Once the Civil War ended slavery, blacks quickly became the majority of prisoners and have always, then to now, been represented in the prison population at two to three times their presence in the state's population. Still, the fact that Texas has always been particularly watchful of its minority populations does not fully explain the extraordinary rise of the state's prison population, incarceration rate, and use of the death penalty.

The 1960s were a period of social tumult that thrilled some and terrorized others. Many of those others were in Texas and they moved decisively to limit social change where they could. Between 1968 and 2005 the Texas prison system expanded by 1,350 percent, nearly twice as much as all U.S. prison systems. Robert Perkinson has noted that, "While the white prisoner population has increased eightfold since 1968, the African-American prisoner population has grown fourteen-fold; the Mexican-American prisoner population has jumped even faster, increasing twenty-five fold."[56] Sentences grew longer, early release harder to achieve, and cost rose from less than $30 million to $4.9 billion.

Though the growth of the Texas prison system peaked around 2010 at over 172,000 and has fallen by a few thousand in recent years, it has not fallen at anything like the fall in the crime rate. Violent crime in Texas peaked in 1991 and has fallen by more than half since then. During precisely these years, the Texas prison system grew from 52,000 to 172,000 inmates. As a result, Texas is saddled with an overbuilt prison establishment that we have only begun to unwind. Texas officials congratulated themselves on closing the first prison in the state's history—the 102-year-old Central Unit in Sugar Land, in 2011—but there is much more to be done. Michelle Alexander of the Ohio State University has written of the U.S. prison system—and it applies to Texas in spades:

> If our nation [and Texas] were to return to the rates of incarceration we had in the 1970s, we would have to release 4 out of 5 people behind bars. A million people employed by the criminal justice system could lose their jobs . . . This system is now so deeply rooted in our social, political, and economic structures that it is not going to fade away without a major shift in public consciousness.[57]

Notes

1 Wilhelm Steinert, *North America, Particularly Texas, in the Year 1849*, Dallas, TX: DeGolyer Library, 2003, pp. 121–122.

2 Noah Smithwick, *The Evolution of a State*, Austin, TX: University of Texas Press, 1983, p. 54.

3 Ben M. Crouch and James W. Marquart, *An Appeal to Justice: Litigated Reform of Texas Prisons*, Austin, TX, University of Texas Press 1989, p. 13.

4 Douglas A. Blackmon, *Slavery by Another Name*, New York: Anchor Books, 2008, pp. 61–62.

5 Marilyn McAdams Sibley, *Travelers in Texas*, 1761–1860, Austin, TX: University of Texas Press, 1967, p. 120.

6 Chad R. Trulson and James M. Marquart, *First Available Cell: Desegregation of the Texas Prison System*, Austin, TX: University of Texas Press, 2009, p. 78.

7   Steinert, *North America, Particularly Texas*, p. 93.
8   Randolph B. Campbell, *An Empire for Slavery*, Baton Rouge, LA: Louisiana State University Press, 1989, p. 104.
9   Sibley, *Travelers in Texas*, pp. 128–129.
10   Trulson and Marquart, *First Available Cell*, pp. 78, 29.
11   Robert Perkinson, *Texas Tough: The Rise of America's Prison Empire*, New York: Metropolitan Books, 2010, p. 8.
12   James W. Marquart, Sheldon Ekland-Olson, Jonathan R. Sorensen, *The Rope, the Chair and the Needle*, Austin, TX: University of Texas Press, 1984, pp. x– xi.
13   Vesla M. Weaver and Amy L. Lerman, "Political Consequences of the Carceral State," *American Political Science Review*, 104, 4, November 2010, pp. 817–833.
14   William Bollaert, *William Bollaert's Texas*, Norman, OK: University of Oklahoma Press, 1956, p. 146.
15   Frederick Law Olmsted, *A Journey Through Texas*, Dallas, TX: DeGolyer Library, 2004, p. 105.
16   James R. Arnold, *Jeff Davis's Own: Cavalry, Comanches, and the Battle for the Texas Frontier*, Edison, NJ: Castle Books, 2000, p. 50.
17   William Ransom Hogan, *The Texas Republic*, Norman, OK: University of Oklahoma Press, 1946, p. 255.
18   Marquart, et.al., *The Rope*, p. 2. See also Blackmon, *Slavery by Another Name*, p. 54.
19   Steve J. Martin and Sheldon Ekland-Olson, *Texas Prisons: The Walls Came Tumbling Down*, Austin, TX: Texas Monthly Press, 1987, p. 5.
20   Crouch and Marquart, *An Appeal to Justice*, p. 14.
21   Trulson and Marquart, *First Available Cell*, p. 78; Martin and Ekland-Olson, *Texas Prisons*, p. 12.
22   Frank R. Kemerer, *William Wayne Justice: A Judicial Biography*, Austin, TX: University of Texas Press, 1991/2008, p. 356.
23   Martin and Ekland-Olson, *Texas Prisons*, pp. 169–171.
24   Kemerer, *William Wayne Justice*, p. 379.
25   Martin and Ekland-Olson, *Texas Prisons*, pp. 113, 187.
26   Ibid., pp. 217, 232, 244–246.
27   Kemerer, *William Wayne Justice*, p. 416.
28   Douglas Martin, "William Wayne Justice, Judge Who Remade Texas, Dies at 89," *New York Times*, October 16, 2009, B11.
29   James R. Parrish, *Two-Headed Monster: Crime and Texas Prisons*, Austin, TX: Eakin Press, 1989, p. 32.
30   Texas Legislative Budget Board, *Fiscal Size-Up 2010–11*, pp. 62–63, 306, 313–321.
31   David Von Drehle, "Why Crime Went Away," *Time*, February 22, 2010, pp. 32–35.
32   Mike Shea, "Previews + Reviews: Books, Robert Perkinson," *Texas Monthly*, March 2010, pp. 60–62.
33   Bill Hobby, *How Things Really Work: Lessons From a Life in Politics*, Austin, TX: University of Texas Press, 2010, pp. 149–150.
34   Parrish, *Two-Headed Monster*, p. 32.
35   Hobby, *How Things Really Work*, p. 150.
36   Justice Center, the Council on State Governments, Justice Reinvestment State Brief: Texas, www.pewcenteronthestates.org/uploadedFiles/TX%20State%20Brief.pdf. See also Cindy Horswell, "Texas Says Rise in Paroles Gives State Bragging Rights," Houston Chronicle, August 15, 2012.
37   Cindy Horswell, "Texas Cuts Costs Amid Prison Reforms," *Houston Chronicle*, December 15, 2009.
38   Kemerer, *William Wayne Justice*, pp. 370–371; see also Martin and Ekland- Olson, *Texas Prisons*, p. 141.

39 Crouch and Marquart, *An Appeal to Justice*, p. 155.
40 Martin and Ekland-Olson, *Texas Prisons*, p. 238; Kemerer, *William Wayne Justice*, p. 396.
41 Veva Institute of Justice, "The Price of Prisons: What Incarceration Costs Taxpayers," January 2012, Updated July 20, 2012.
42 The Pew Center on the States, "One in 100: Behind Bars in America," 2008, p. 33.
43 Marquart, Ekland-Olson and Sorensen, *The Rope*, pp. 12, 23.
44 Jon Sorensen and Rocky Leann Pilgrim, *Lethal Injection: Capital Punishment in Texas During the Modern Era*, Austin, TX: University of Texas Press, 2006, p. 22.
45 Death Penalty Information Center, "Facts About the Death Penalty," as of March 9, 2011.
46 "Death Penalty Under Examination," *State Legislatures*, June 2009, p. 10.
47 David Grann, "Trial By Fire: Did Texas Execute an Innocent Man?" *The New Yorker*, September 7, 2009, pp. 42–63.
48 Dahlia Lithwick, "Innocent Until Executed: We Have No Right to Exoneration," *Newsweek*, September 14, 2009, p. 29.
49 Steve Mills and Maurice Possley, "Man Executed on Disproved Forensics," *Chicago Tribune*, December 9, 2004.
50 Todd J. Gillman, "Governor Defends Disputed Execution," *Dallas Morning News*, September 19, 2009, pp. A1, A2.
51 Christy Hoppe, "Perry Ousts Officials Before Arson Hearing," *Dallas Morning News*, October 1, 2009, A1, A2.
52 Steve Mills, "Cameron Todd Willingham: Former Head of the Texas Forensics Panel Probing 1991 Fire Says He Felt Pressured by Gov. Perry Aides," *Chicago Tribune*, October 12, 2009.
53 Christy Hoppe, "Fire Expert Calls Perry 'Unethical,'" *Dallas Morning News*, October 15, 2009, A1, A3.
54 Lisa Falkenberg, "Commentary: Execution Controversy About More Than 'Bad Man,'" *Houston Chronicle*, October 14, 2009.
55 Trulson and Marquart, *First Available Cell*, "Foreword," p. ix.
56 Perkinson, *Texas Tough*, p. 365.
57 Michelle Alexander, "Opinion: In Prison Reform, Money Trumps Civil Rights," *New York Times*, May 15, 2011, p. Wk 9.

8 Good Roads, Highways,and Transportation in Texas

> I reached some plains so vast, that I did not find their limit . . . [It was as] if we had been swallowed up by the sea. . . . there was not a stone, nor bit of rising ground, nor a tree, nor a shrub, nor anything to go by.
>
> (Francisco Vazquez de Coronado to the
> King of Spain, October 20, 1541)

The first Europeans into Texas were struck by the massive distances that spread out before them. The very first, Alvar Nunez Cabeza de Vaca, saw a great deal of Texas. Cabeza de Vaca was a member of a Spanish party of exploration that first came to grief in Florida before setting to sea in makeshift rafts which eventually came ashore on Galveston Island in late 1528. Soon Cabeza de Vaca was one of a handful of survivors and a captive slave of Indians. He remained in the Galveston area for four years before linking up with three other survivors and setting out on a journey that led him through South Texas and into northern Mexico and as far west as the Mexican Pacific coast before the tattered band showed up in Mexico City in 1536. Cabeza de Vaca's claim to have seen golden cities on his journey intrigued Antonio de Mendoza, the Spanish Viceroy of New Spain.

After further inquiries seemed to confirm Cabeza de Vaca's claim, Mendoza dispatched the Conquistador Captain Francisco Vazquez de Coronado with a force of 1,500 Spanish and Indians to find the seven cities of Cibola and their riches. What Coronado found when he crossed out of what is now New Mexico and into Texas was terrifying to most of his men if not to the captain himself. In the spring of 1541, Coronado's force descended onto the "stockade plain" of the Llano Estacado. The rimrock that marked the edge of the plain reminded the Spaniards of a stockade wall, but it was the 30,000 square miles of flat, virtually featureless, grasslands stretching out beyond the horizon that left them awestruck. Anglos later mistranslated Coronado's descriptive phrase as "staked plains" and that name stuck. Once out on the plain, nothing but grass as far as the eye could see in every direction, the Spaniards were reduced to navigating as if they were at sea.[1]

For the next three centuries, Anglos, whether Europeans or eventually Americans, found traversing Texas a challenge. Indians had regular travel routes but these did not constitute what Anglos recognized as roads. At best, Indian routes might be footpaths "deepened somewhat by the poles dragged by the Indian's canine beasts of burden. When the Indians acquired horses, the old footpaths became wider, deeper tracks routed through less dense timber and, in West Texas, running from water hole to water hole. The first American explorers and settlers followed these same tracks."[2] Oftentimes, however, there were no tracks to follow. The Reverend Daniel Baker, an early evangelist in Texas, became lost in 1831. Baker wrote that, "Bewildered in the wild and trackless prairie, I was lost, *lost*, LOST! After wandering about in every direction . . . I began seriously to think that I should at last have to lie down and die in this untraveled wilderness, far away from my family and the habitation of men, without a friend to close my eyes, or dig my grave!"[3]

A Brief History of Texas Transportation

When Moses Austin crossed the Sabine into Texas in the fall of 1820, there were few roads. The Camino Real, or King's Road, began in Mexico City, passed through Monclova, crossed the Rio Grande at San Juan Bautista, ran north to San Antonio, and then northeast to Nacogdoches and Louisiana beyond. While the Camino Real was the most traveled route in Texas and Austin followed it into San Antonio, it was little more than a cart path across the prairie. The La Bahia road ran parallel to the Camino Real to the south. It ran from Monterrey, Mexico, crossing the Rio Grande at Laredo, then north and northeast through La Bahia to the Sabine. Most of the first settlers came overland by horse or wagon from Arkansas or Louisiana or they came by sea to Galveston. Those coming from the east by land, such as the planter Jared E. Groce from Alabama, guided their parties along the Camino Real before turning southwest across open land to the Austin colony.[4] Anglos soon came to call the Camino Real the Old San Antonio Road and the La Bahia Road came to be called the Opelousas Trail.

William Ransom Hogan's *The Texas Republic* includes a chapter on early roads entitled "Roads of Mud and Slush." Hogan reports that in early 1838 the new republic's distinguished president, Sam Houston, "wrote that he was unable to start on an intended trip from Houston to Nacogdoches because 'at this time the roads are most terrible and impossible in this section of the country.'"[5] The Texas republic struggled financially through out its decade-long history and so had no revenues to assist with road building or even improvement.

One of the most striking themes in the journal writing of the early Anglo immigrants and visitors to Texas is the difficulty and danger of simply trying to move around the state. The Englishman William Bollaert, traveling west from Houston to Columbus on the Colorado River, described the roads along Buffalo Bayou as treacherous. "During and after heavy rains,"

Bollaert wrote, "these creeks are not fordable and in some parts of the low country, what with the water in the bottoms swamps and creeks, the roads are rendered impassable for weeks." Not surprisingly, those who depended on the roads for their livelihood did not take the delays as gracefully as President Houston seemed to. Bollaert records that, "to swear like a bullock driver when bogged . . . is the concentrated essence of blasphemy."[6]

Wilhelm Steinert described the road from Fredericksburg to Austin in 1849 as "nothing more than field paths or tracks." After visiting Bastrop, La Grange, and Industry, Steinert reported that "we started for Columbus. The road went through meadows for many miles, broke up later in side roads, and gradually stopped altogether." Rain turned rutted wagon trails into axel deep mud and hard rain turned rivers and creeks into torrents that could not be crossed, occasionally requiring teamsters to camp by rivers for days, sometimes weeks, waiting for the water to recede. Steinert concluded that "Broken wagon parts lying along the roads give the best evidence of their condition."[7]

Every traveler commented on the lack of well-marked roads. In East Texas in the early 1850s, Frederick Law Olmsted reported that:

> The road could hardly be called a road. It was only a way where people had passed along before. Each man had taken such a path as suited him, turning aside to avoid, on high ground, the sand, on low ground, the mud. We chose, generally, the untrodden elastic pavement of pine leaves, at a little distance from the main track.

Similarly, on the broad, flat lowlands near the Texas Gulf, Olmsted again reported that "The road was a mere collection of straggling wagon-ruts, extending for more than a quarter of a mile in width, from outside to outside, it being desirable, in this part of the country, rather to avoid a road than to follow it." Finally, the Olmsteds were not simply eastern naïfs wandering aimlessly across Texas, they had a competent guide. Nonetheless, they frequently reported following the wrong cattle path or wagon track: "On the way from Trinity to Centreville. . . . At some fork in the indistinct road we have gone wrong, and are to the northward of our regular course. . . . Our road was little better than a cow-track, and once we followed a worn cattle-path for some two or three miles, and were obliged to follow it back again." On another occasion, "The road was very indistinct, and we followed some wagon tracks, at twilight, two hours out of our way."[8]

Even the army complained about the quality, really the absence, of Texas roads in the 1850s. With a string of frontier posts from Fort Belknap west of Dallas to Fort Clark just north of the Rio Grande, the army struggled with both troop movements and resupply. "The surgeon general complained that Texas's rough roads destroyed medicines and surgical instruments before the wagons delivered supplies to the garrisons. One passenger aboard an Overland Mail wagon reported that his coach overturned three times in the vicinity of Fort Belknap alone."[9] T.R. Fehrenbach reports that "Only a few miles of roadway in the entire state in 1860 were graded; exactly twenty miles in all was planked or similarly improved."[10]

Throughout the nineteenth century, first the Congress of the Republic of Texas and then the Texas state legislature made road building and maintenance a county responsibility. Robert Calvert has written that, "The state government entrusted internal improvements to the counties, but inadequate resources compelled local authorities to let bad roads languish. Besides the sorry shape of the roads, few bridges existed."[11] Counties were empowered to lay out and maintain roads and to authorize ferries and toll bridges. They were encouraged, but not required, to coordinate with adjoining jurisdictions. Counties also were empowered to require ten days of labor each year from every male resident between eighteen and forty-five and every slave between sixteen and fifty, though the political culture exempted wealthy whites and discouraged bothering citizens at all.[12] As late as 1879, the Texas Legislature renewed these county powers, adding exemptions for citizens willing to hire a substitute or pay a tax of a dollar a day up to their ten-day obligation. By the end of the nineteenth century, counties were authorized to levy property taxes to support road building and maintenance, but, again, they did so only rarely. Richard Morehead writes that in 1900 "Texas roads bore no semblance to an integrated system."[13]

Texas in the mid-nineteenth century was money poor and land rich. While the state could not fund road building, it could fund railroad construction with land grants. In 1854 and again in 1876, the legislature offered railroads a subsidy of sixteen sections of public land, 10,240 acres, for every mile of mainline track it laid. Thin population and light demand outside the early cotton belt slowed construction. By 1860, less than 400 miles of track connected Galveston and Houston to the plantations along the Brazos, Colorado, and Trinity rivers. By 1870, the rail system had grown to just 583 miles, but a boom was building. Between 1876 and 1883, forty railroad companies were awarded more than thirty-two million acres of public land in exchange for nearly 3,000 miles of new track. By the end of the century, Texas had nearly 10,000 miles of track, more than any other state.

Between 1875 and 1885, railroads connected Galveston and Houston to Corpus Christi, San Antonio, El Paso, Dallas, and Fort Worth. Unlike most public roads, railroads were owned and operated as private, profitmaking corporations. Texas farmers were concerned from the beginning that railroads favored big customers with lower rates and rebates while gouging the small shipper. The railroads also gave stock and free passes to legislators and other political friends to limit taxes, regulations, and oversight. Public outrage over the predations of the railroads led Attorney

General James Stephen Hogg to force the return of 1.5 million acres of public land by the railroads and to break up a railroad price-fixing scheme. In 1890, Hogg was elected governor and in the 1891 legislative session he sought and won approval of the Texas Railroad Commission (TRC). Texas was just the second state to form a regulatory commission to oversee railroad rates and services.[14]

The railroads that came to Texas after the Civil War helped, but roads, particularly farm to market roads in the vast rural reaches of the state, would wait another half century. Through the first quarter of the twentieth century, it was common for Texas farmers to face a 100 mile wagon ride over unimproved dirt roads to get their crops to market. Historians Thad Sitton and Milam Rowold write that, "Rural transportation in Texas during the first three decades of the twentieth century was extremely primitive . . . Roads were usually just raw tracks across the land, unimproved by gravel or asphalt, and in certain seasons so deep in the mud that travelers had to take to nearby fields or fence rows."

Though the automobile came late to Texas, its arrival changed everything. States in the east, led by Massachusetts and New Jersey, began providing state aid for road construction in the early 1890s. By 1915, all but three states—Indiana, South Carolina, and, you guessed it, Texas—had passed laws providing state funds to assist road building. Then Congress passed the Federal-Aid Highway Act of 1916 providing for sharing the cost of highway construction between the states and the federal government. Texas, Indiana, and South Carolina all passed state highway funding laws in 1917 so that they would be eligible for the federal matching funds. On April 4, 1917, Governor James Ferguson signed the bill creating the Texas Highway Department (THD) and the three-member Texas Highway Commission (THC) to oversee it. The THD assumed responsibility for road maintenance and arterial construction from the counties. By the end of the year, the THC had registered 194,720 vehicles, developed a plan for 8,865 miles of improved roadways, and raised the speed limit to 25 miles per hour. In 1923, the THD gained a dependable revenue stream when the legislature dedicated a fuels tax to fund highway construction. A decade later, when Texas adopted its first Drivers' License Law in 1935, "three million applicants received legal authority to operate motor vehicles." Despite the fact that the law required no exam to qualify for a license, "many Texans considered it an infringement on their independence and refused to obtain licenses."[16] Texans who needed no license to ride a horse or drive a wagon bristled at mandatory state licenses to drive motor vehicles.

Despite the creation of the THD and passage of the fuels tax, state funding of roads passed slowly from counties to the state over the course of fifteen years. During their three terms as governor, James (Pa) and Miriam (Ma) Ferguson joined the county commissioners courts and rural legislators to oppose centralized or state control of road building. In 1932, the state assumed primary responsibility for funding and the legislature passed the State Assumption Act to pay off outstanding county road bonds but the struggle continued into the mid-1940s. The first farm-to-market road was completed in Texas in 1937 and in 1949 the Colson–Briscoe Act mandated an annual $15 million appropriation for farm-to-market and ranch-to-market roads. Though the Texas Legislature remained tight with the dollar, it did recognize that a large state of mostly scattered rural communities needed roads and it spent money to provide them.

Two men are predominantly credited with making the THD of the mid-twentieth century a national model. Gibb Gilchrist established the THD as an agency above politics, but not without a fight. Gilchrist took an engineering degree at the University of Texas in 1909 and served in the U.S. Army Corps of Engineers in World War I before joining the THD. In 1924, he was briefly state highway engineer, the department's top job, before resigning over political interference by the Fergusons. Gilchrist returned to lead the department from 1927 to 1937 before leaving to become Dean of Engineering at Texas A&M. Gilchrist is credited with shaping the THD into a highly professional organization.

DeWitt Greer became chief highway engineer and head of the THD in 1940 and built on the solid foundation that Gilchrist had left behind. Greer, a Texas A&M graduate, spent fifty-five years with the THD. Greer was head of the highway department from 1940 to 1972, when he moved over to spend another decade, 1972 to 1981, as a member of the THC. When Greer took over in 1940, Texas had 22,207 miles of road and when he finally retired in 1981 it had 72,945 miles. Fifty thousand miles of new Texas roads had been built under Greer's watchful eye. Gilchrist and Greer made the THD among the very best in the nation, but that position began to deteriorate in the late 1970s and early 1980s. The current TxDOT headquarters on East 11th street in Austin is named in honor of DeWitt Greer.

The halcyon days of U.S. and Texas highway building were the late 1940s, 1950s, and 1960s and Texas led the way. Congress and the state highway departments began intensive planning for a national highway building program during World War II. In 1943, Congress passed a $1.7 billion highway bill that required state matching money. Greer's THD was ready with the plans and matching money in place when federal funds began to flow, receiving $30 million three years running from the initial allocation. In 1946, Texas passed the famous "Good Roads Amendment" to guarantee ongoing state revenues. The Good Roads Amendment, now Article VIII, section 7-a of the Texas Constitution, guaranteed that three-quarters of all road-user fees, including the gas tax, drivers' license fees, and vehicle registration fees, would go to roads, while the other quarter would go to education.[17]

The taxes and fees guaranteed to roads, with modest adjustments, kept the THD a pay-as-you-go operation into the late 1970s. Texas Governor

Coke Stevenson (1941–1947), one of the most conservative and tight-fisted men ever to occupy the governor's mansion, demanded a balanced budget for roads. But DeWitt Greer shared his view. Greer believed that planning a massive road-building effort required stable funding flows not subject to the vagaries of political manipulation. Only dedicated funds would suffice. Sam Waldrop, an Abilene businessman who served on the THC with Greer, observed that his "philosophy was that bonding and such were political traps. The politicians can spend a lot of money and vote a lot of expenses, but he doesn't have the courage to support the taxes necessary for this funding. The statesman does."[18]

By the late 1940s, "the Texas Highway Department emerged in the vanguard of states seeking federal assistance for massive road-building projects. Texas, in short, embraced federal policy in a way it would not in any other domestic policy area."[19] Fehrenbach notes that, "some Texas counties got their first paved roads in the 1940s—by the 1950s even the rural, farm-to-market roads in the underpopulated areas were superior to most U.S. highways in the East."[20] Finally, in 1962 at a ceremony celebrating DeWitt Greer's thirty-fifth anniversary with THD, THC member Charles Hawn declared, "We are so far ahead of other state highway departments, there is no comparison. . . . That sounds like Texas brag but it's on the record. . . . At the same time our average cost is way, way down . . . we get more for our tax dollar in our highway system than in most any other system or department."[21] Even adjusting just a bit for the standard hyperbole, Texas was making serious investments in roads by the mid-twentieth century, but, as with education and much else, it fell off thereafter.

THD bustled through the 1960s, but the 1970s, with Arab oil boycotts, a movement to smaller cars with higher gas mileage, 55 mile per hour speed limits, and double-digit domestic inflation brought tough times. THD reached an all-time high of 20,500 employees in 1972. By the end of the decade, gas tax revenues were still largely flat and THD employment was under 14,500, down 29 percent. Gas taxes were raised from 5 cents to 10 cents a gallon in 1984 and 15 cents a gallon in 1987, but by then the oil boom had collapsed and the state's property markets and banks had swooned as well. Texas's highway building and maintenance programs never recovered.

The Pace of Texas Population Growth, Road Building, and Vehicle Registration

In 1950, Texas was the nation's sixth most populous state, with 7.74 million residents, or 5.1 percent, of the nation's 151.87 million residents. In that same year, Texas had 196,426 miles of road, or 6.6 percent of the nation's 2.99 million miles of road. Texas is a big state with lots of lightly populated rural territory, so one would expect a higher proportion of road miles to population than the average state. By 2011, Texas was the nation's second most populous state, with 25.7 million residents, or 8.2 percent of the nation's 311.6 million residents. But in that same year, Texas had 312,910 miles of road, or 7.7 percent of the nation's 4.08 million miles of road. Since 1950, the population of Texas has increased by 230 percent while the road base has increased by just 59 percent. While the population of Texas has grown inexorably since 1950, its road building has lagged and lagged badly in recent years. Figure 8.1 highlights the steady growth of population and slower and slowing growth of roads.

Though Texas contains vast, lightly populated, rural areas, it has been a majority urban state since the 1940s. Hence, for decades Texas focused its road money on the economically critical urban road system within the triangle connecting Dallas-Fort Worth, Houston, and San Antonio. In the early 1950s, Texas matched the national average for percent urban population at about 55 percent and then quickly pulled away. By 1960, Texas was 75 percent urban while the national average was 70 percent. That margin held remarkably steady at four to six points for more than half a century. The 2010 census showed Texas as 86 percent urban and the nation as 82 percent urban. From the early 1950s through the economic travails of the late 1980s, Texas maintained a greater share of urban roads than did the nation as a whole and the Texas proportion of urban roads grew faster. In the late 1980s, Texas urban road building faltered, at least as a percent of total state roads, and it has remained stagnant since.

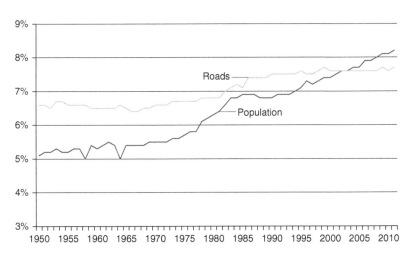

Figure 8.1 Texas Population and Road Mileage as a Percent of U.S. Population and Road Mileage, 1950–Present.

Source: U.S. Census Bureau, *Statistical Abstract of the United States*, Population section, various years, 1950 to present; Transportation section; "Highway Mileage by State—Functional Systems and Urban/ Rural," various years, 1950 to present.

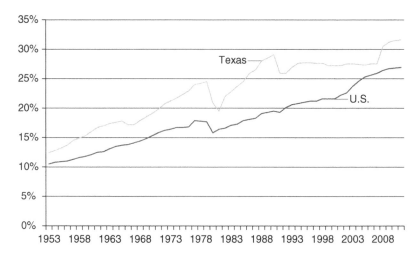

Figure 8.2 Urban Roads as a Percent of Total Roads in the U.S. and Texas, 1953–Present.

Source: U.S. Census Bureau, Statistical Abstract of the United States, Transportation section; various years, 1953 to present. The decreases, especially evident in the Texas data, reflect definitional changes. In 1976, the definition of an urban place was raised from 2,500 to 5,000, and in 1991 new legislation again adjusted the traditional definitions. Between 2007 and 2008 about 9,000 miles of Texas roads were reclassified from rural to urban.

As Figure 8.2 shows, in 1953 (the first year for which we have data) 12.4 percent of Texas roads were urban compared to 10.5 percent of U.S. roads. By 1960, 16 percent of Texas roads and 12.1 percent of U.S. roads were urban. By 1980, 20.9 percent of Texas roads were urban while just 15.8 percent of U.S. roads were urban. From 1991 through 2007, while the U.S. has continued to add to its urban road system, Texas has been absolutely flat. In 1991, the percent of U.S. roads that were urban stood at 19 percent, and in 2007, it stood at 26. In 1991, the percent of Texas roads that were urban stood at 25.9, and in 2007, it stood at 27.5. In 2008, Texas reclassified about 9,000 miles of rural roads as urban roads and jumped three full percentage points, to 30.5 percent. In 2011, Texas urban roads stood at 31.6 percent of total roads.

The results of Texas's underinvestment in roads is clear when we see that road building has not kept up with the number of vehicles on the roads. The road system in Texas is described in terms of both road miles and lane miles because, obviously, some roads are multilane. Widening a road from two lanes to four would double lane miles but would not increase road miles. Between 1950 and 2011 the road system in Texas grew from 196,426 road miles to 312,910 road miles, an increase of 59 percent. Over that same period, the number of vehicles on Texas roads rose from just under three million (2,968,143) to over nineteen million

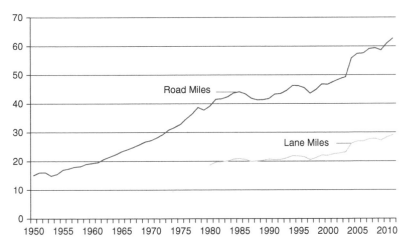

Figure 8.3 Licensed Vehicles Per Road Mile and Lane Mile in Texas, 1950–Present.

Source: Department of Transportation, Highway Statistics Publications, 1950–Present, http://www. fhwa.dot.gov/policy/ohpi/hss/hsspubs.cfm. The slight dip in 2009 is artificial. Texas reported an increase in road and lane miles in 2009 but no increase in licensed drivers.

(19,617,055), an increase of 561 percent. As a result, between 1950 and 2011, the number of vehicles per road mile increased from 15 to 63, an increase of 320 percent (Figure 8.3).

The data on lane miles go back only to 1980, so to get a good comparison of vehicle loads in relation both to road miles and to lane miles, we will need to look at both for the period 1980 to 2011. Road miles in Texas increased from 267,500 in 1980 to 312,910 in 2011, an increase of 17 percent. The number of vehicles on the roads increased from about 10.5 million (10,474,816) in 1980 to over nineteen million (19,617,055) in 2011, an increase of 87 percent. And the number of vehicles per road mile increased from thirty-nine in 1980 to sixty-two in 2011, an increase of 59 percent.

The number of lane miles in Texas increased from 561,408 in 1980 to 674,296 in 2011, an increase of 20 percent. The number of vehicles on the road, as we saw above, rose 73 percent. And the number of vehicles per lane mile increased from 18.66 in 1980 to 29.09 in 2011, an increase of 56 percent. Clearly, whether you look at road miles or lane miles, the number of vehicles per mile on Texas roads has increased by 55 to 60 percent over the last three decades. Texas has been losing the battle to provide adequate transportation infrastructure at least since the mid-1990s.

As with so many other policy areas, the fundamental fact is that Texas spends less of its own money, fewer state funds, on roads than do other states. Between 1950 and 2006, Texas per capita expenditure on roads from state funds amounted to just 86.3 percent of the national average for all of the states (Figure 8.4). As we have seen elsewhere, Texas was near the national average in 1950, spending $23.17 per capita on roads while the national average was $23.43. In 1959 and 1960, Texas exceeded the national average and for the entire decade of the 1950s Texas spent 94.2 percent of the national average for per capita road expenditures. In the 1960s, Texas spent 88.1 percent of the national average; in the 1970s, 74 percent; in the 1980s, 85.6 percent; in the 1990s, 78.1 percent; and from 2000 through 2004, Texas spent just 82.4 percent of the national average for per capita road expenditures. In 2005 and 2006, Texas matched the national average, and in 2007 and 2008, it was 128 and 143 percent of the national average before dropping back, probably because of debt exhaustion, to more historical averages of 85 percent of U.S. per capita highway spending in 2009 and 79 percent in 2010. From 1917, when Texas established the THD, until 2001 it ran a pay-as-you-go highway department. Roads were built and maintained as funds became available. In 2001, Governor Perry and the legislature approved borrowing for road construction for the first time. Texas's credit card was smoking there for a while.

Looking at per capita spending on roads from an annual perspective, as we do in Figure 8.5, shows Texas struggling unsuccessfully to fund its road system. As with education and so many other policy areas, Texas

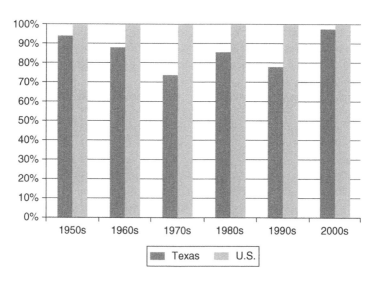

Figure 8.4 U.S. and Texas Per Capita Expenditures for Roads by Decade, 1950–Present.

Source: U.S. Census Bureau, Statistical Abstract of the United States, Population section, various years, 1950 to present; Transportation section; Highway Financing, "State Disbursements for Highways by States," various years, 1950 to present.

leaders in the immediate post-World War II era felt the state's growth and momentum and moved decisively to build a solid infrastructure under it. If growth outruns infrastructure, growth must slow, but keeping infrastructure up with population and economic growth is not easy because funding flows follow rather than lead growth. In the late 1950s, Texas's spending on roads began to fall behind and stayed in decline until 1970. The saw tooth pattern of per capita expenditures between 1970 and 1990 shows politicians struggling, ultimately unsuccessfully, to keep up with the growth-driven demand for transportation improvements. The subdued saw tooth pattern between 1990 and the early 2000s suggests capitulation. Per capita spending fell and stayed low but new revenues, new solutions to the state's growing traffic woes, did not come to hand. In 2001, all that changed. Texas moved away from pay-as-you-go to borrow, toll, and bluster. Texas per capita spending on roads increased dramatically after 2001, but it was all debt fueled. Authorized debt limits began bumping against their legal caps in 2008 and spending has fallen back to more normal levels. Unfortunately, these levels will barely fund repair of existing roads.

There are, of course, many practical results to inadequate funding of road maintenance and construction. In 2012, TRIP, a national transportation research group, reported that "Issues including traffic congestion, damage to vehicles from roads needing repair, and costs incurred in accidents caused by insufficient safety features on roadways cost drivers in Texas $23 billion annually."[22] Let that number, $23 billion annually, sink in—it is twice the annual budget of TXDOT. That means Texans are paying for excellent roads, $23 billion worth, but just are not getting them. The Texas response to congestion and inadequately maintained roads, typically enough, was to raise the state's maximum speed limit to 85 mph. Traffic engineers will determine which highways can handle the higher speeds. Only Texas and Utah have speeds over 75 mph. The 2011 legislature also removed all lower night and truck speed limits. Hilariously, House Transportation Committee chair Larry Phillips (R-Sherman) explained the changes as a delicate "balance between protecting citizen's rights and their individual freedoms and protecting our citizen's on our roadways."[23] Just off the top of your head—do you think they got the balance right?

Financing Texas Roads: The Federal and State Gas Tax

States fund their roads from a number of revenue streams, but the bulk of the funds traditionally have come from gas tax revenues they collect and from remittances to the states of gas taxes collected by the federal government. The federal government distributes gas tax funds to the states based on data that the states provide concerning motor fuel use.[24] States receive funds from federal gas taxes based on a formula that includes the

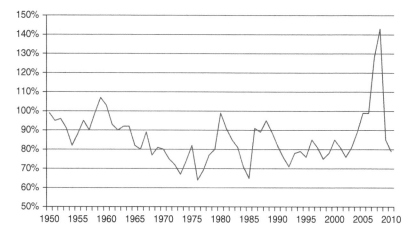

Figure 8.5 Texas Per Capita Expenditures for Roads as a Percent of Average U.S. Expenditures, 1950–Present.

Source: U.S. Census Bureau, Statistical Abstract of the United States, Population section, various years, 1950 to present; Transportation section; Highway Financing, "State Disbursements for Highways by State," various years, 1950 to present.

cost of road building and maintenance, so that Alaska and Wisconsin, where winters are harsh and roads break up, receive proportionately more than states such as Texas where wear and tear on roads is less. Texas and other "donor" states wail incessantly about receiving less than their fair share of federal highway dollars.

Since 1950, the gas tax charged by the federal government, Texas, and the average state gas tax have all risen from the low to mid-single digits to about 20 cents per gallon. The gas tax has been raised by different amounts at different times by the federal government and by each of the states including Texas (Figure 8.6). The federal gas tax of 1.5 cents per gallon in 1950 and 1951 was raised to 2 cents in 1952, 3 cents in 1957, and 4 cents in 1960, where it remained through 1982. In 1983, the gas tax was more than doubled to 9 cents a gallon, before being raised to 9.1 cents in 1987, 14.1 cents in 1990, and 18.4 cents in 1993, where it has remained ever since.

The U.S. Department of Transportation's Federal Highway Administration reports each year on how much of the Federal Highway Trust Fund is attributed to each state and how much each state is allocated from the fund. Congress supplements the Trust Fund with general fund dollars, so that most states come out ahead. For example, in 2011 no state received less than it put in and overall the Trust Fund paid out 132 percent of what it took in. Between 1956 and 2011, the Trust Fund paid out 116 percent of what it took in and fully forty-one states received more than

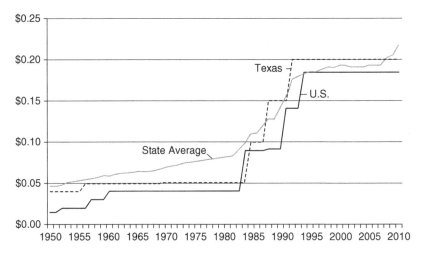

Figure 8.6 Federal Gas Tax Compared to Texas and Average State Gas Taxes, 1950–Present.

Source: U.S. Census Bureau, Statistical Abstract of the United States, 1950 to Present, "Federal and State Gasoline Tax, by states," www.census.gov/compendia/statab. See also Department of Transportation, Federal Highway Administration, Highway Statistics, various years, www.fhwa.dot. gov/policy/ohpi/hss/hsspubs.cfm.

they contributed. Seven states have received less than they put in and Texas has the lowest return of any state. Between 1956 and 2011, Texas paid in a total of $64.53 billion dollars and received allocations totaling $60.61 billion dollars; for every Texas dollar into the Trust Fund Texas gets 94 cents out. The next lowest states are Indiana and North Carolina at 96, and South Carolina at 97. Many of the federal funds made available to the states require matching funds and often Texas is reluctant.[25]

Champagne and Harpham argue that, "For over half a century, highway policy . . . stood as an exemplar of successful public policy in Texas."[26] Texas held its gas tax lower than most states for longer than most. Texas lagged the forty-eight-state (later fifty-state) average from 1950 through 1983, charging an average over that thirty-four-year period of 4.82 cents per gallon, compared to the fifty-state average of 6.69 cents per gallon. That may not sound like much of a difference, but in percentage terms it means that Texas charged just 72 percent of the fifty-state average. Since 1984, Texas has charged slightly more than the national average, 17.92 cents compared to 17.11 cents.

The Texas Legislature set the gas tax at 1 cent per gallon in 1923. It was raised to 2 cents in 1929, 4 cents in 1934, 5 cents in 1956, and then held there for almost thirty years. By 1983, the Texas gas tax, at 5 cents, was just over half the fifty-state average gas tax of 9.75 cents. In 1984, Texas raised its gas tax to 10 cents, still below the national average of 10.6 cents, and in 1987 they raised it again, to 15 cents, above the national average of 12.75. Texas fell behind the national average of 15.5 cents in 1990, though only briefly. In 1991, Texas reorganized THD, renaming it the Texas Department of Transportation (TxDOT), and raised the state gas tax to 20 cents per gallon, marginally above the national average, where it has remained ever since. Some states, though not Texas, have added to their road funds by charging a sales tax on gasoline (in addition to the gas tax itself) and by allowing local governments to add their own gas taxes. These additional motor fuel taxes and fees averaged 9 cents per gallon across the fifty states and D.C. in 2011. Tables 8.1 and 8.2 help make these points. They also show Texas at 40th in gas taxes per gallon.[27] Hence, with both the Texas and federal gas taxes stable since the early 1990s, inflation has steadily eaten away the buying power of those funds and road building in Texas has stagnated.[28]

Table 8.1 State Gasoline Motor Fuel Taxes by Region (cents per gallon)

Region	Basic Motor Fuel Tax	Other Motor Fuel Taxes	Total Sate Motor Fuel Taxes
Northeast	23.0	7.8	30.9
Mid-Atlantic	13.0	20.0	33.0
South Atlantic	14.1	15.6	29.7
Midwest	22.5	7.3	29.8
South	19.3	0.8	20.1
Mountain	23.6	0.2	23.7
West	34.6	10.1	44.8
U.S.	21.4	9.7	31.1

Source: American Petroleum Institute, http://www.api.org/statistics/fueltaxes

Table 8.2 State Gas Taxes and Related Fees

California	53.5	W. Virginia	34.7	Idaho	25.0	Alabama	20.9
Hawaii	50.6	Pennsylvania	32.3	Kansas	25.0	Louisiana	20.0
New York	49.8	Kentucky	32.3	Utah	24.5	**Texas**	**20.0**
Connecticut	49.3	Vermont	32.2	Wyoming	24.0	New Hamp.	19.6
Michigan	39.5	Maine	31.5	Massachusetts	23.5	Arizona	19.0
Illinois	39.1	Oregon	31.1	D.C.	23.5	New Mexico	18.9
Indiana	38.9	U.S. Aver.	31.1	Delaware	23.0	Mississippi	18.8
N. Carolina	37.9	Maryland	30.5	N. Dakota	23.0	Virginia	17.3
Washington	37.5	Minnesota	28.6	S. Dakota	22.0	Missouri	17.3
Florida	35.4	Georgia	28.5	Colorado	22.0	Oklahoma	17.0
Nevada	33.1	Ohio	28.0	Iowa	22.0	S. Carolina	16.8
Rhode Island	33.0	Montana	27.8	Arkansas	21.8	New Jersey	14.5
Wisconsin	32.9	Nebraska	27.2	Tennessee	21.4	Alaska	8.0

Source: American Petroleum Institute, http://www.api.org/statistics/fueltaxes

Though Texas gas taxes are among the nation's lowest, few Texas politicians have called for increasing them. Rather, Texas's former U.S. Senator, Kay Bailey Hutchison (R-Dallas), introduced a bill to allow each state to retain 100 percent of the federal gas taxes raised in that state. Demonstrating Texas's characteristic denial of federalism, Senator Hutchison declared that "It's time for every state to be able to be on its own. We are very underfunded because we're a high growth state, and we need to be able to use our dollars in a more efficient way." This is extremely unlikely to happen, since only about one-quarter of the states represented in Congress would benefit by the proposal, and, more importantly, it would help only at the margins. Even Texas Transportation Commissioner Ned Holmes, a Perry appointee who supported Hutchison in the 2010 governor's race, declared "If all we are doing is keeping the funding the same and pulling it from one state and giving it to another, then that is a pretty rough game to play. There needs to be more funding period. This is not just a big state, high growth state problem."[29] Hutchison lost the election and Holmes's term ended. He was not reappointed.

The deep recession of 2008–2009 depressed both the federal and Texas state gas taxes as Texas drivers cut back to save money. In late 2008 and early 2009, Texas state gas taxes were down 2.9 percent while the TxDOT budget had presumed a 1.5 percent increase. Worse, because federal gas tax revenues were lagging too, the state faced reduced funding in the coming years. Hence, some politicians, including Texas State Senator John Carona (R-Dallas), suggested the need to increase state gas taxes. Senator Carona introduced proposals to increase the gas tax in both the 2007 and the 2009 legislative sessions, to no avail. In late 2009, Carona told a Senate Transportation Committee meeting in El Paso that "We are in the critical position in this state where we are growing and will need more roads. But we have no money to build them and no more debt that we can issue." Absent new revenues, state Transportation Department executive director Amadeo Saenz has said "We'd be able to finish the projects that have already been funded, but no new dollars for construction will come our way."[30]

Transportation funding was discussed in the 2013 legislative session and in several special sessions that followed. Unfortunately, in the regular session, Governor Perry and many conservatives opposed raising taxes or fees, including gas taxes, transportation related sales taxes, or vehicle registration fees, to fund new road building. Mass transit and high speed rail were not even on the agenda. With no new revenues on the table, discussion flagged. In the special sessions, some forward momentum built around timid proposals to rechannel about $1.2 billion annually from the rainy day fund (more about the rainy day fund in Chapter 10) to transportation. The Texas House and Senate sought the political cover of a statewide ballot measure to approve or disapprove the spending.

Even if citizens approve an additional $1.2 billion a year to fund new road construction, TXDOT says it needs $4 billion in new money annually to catch up and keep up with the state's growth. Transportation funding will again be on the agenda when the 2015 legislative session rolls around, but no permanent solution will be found in merely redirecting current revenues—new revenues will be required.[31]

The Resort to Toll Roads and Debt

Toll roads, bridges, and ferries were not uncommon in nineteenth-century Texas. Tolls are a user fee, paid by those using the road, bridge, or ferry, and so attractive to those opposed to more general taxes. Once the automobile came into wide use and THD took over road building and maintenance, federal and state gas taxes and drivers' license and auto registration fees provided the bulk of the revenues. However, as early as 1954, toll fees were introduced to supplement gas taxes and to speed up the pace of road building. Between 1954 and 1957, the section of I-30 between Dallas and Fort Worth was constructed as a toll road. Once the costs of construction were paid off in 1977 and the tolls were removed, the road became, like most other roads, free to motorists.

More recently, "system financing" envisions permanent toll roads in which tolls from the system, including stretches no longer paying off bonds, remain tolled with revenues going to pay for new roads or to back new bonds for more toll roads. Victor Vandergriff, until recently Chairman of the North Texas Tollway Authority, put the matter succinctly: "Tolling is the only way we are getting any new roads built at this point in time. Funding from the state of Texas is not available for roads."[32] This represents dramatic change from the post-World War II period when Texas built the nation's most extensive road system on a pay-as-you-go basis to a system where borrow and toll seem the only tools available.

For more than a decade, Governor Perry has sought to meet the state's transportation needs through a number of devices that would add capacity but still allow him to claim that he had not raised taxes. The state constitution and statutes until 2001 severely limited the issuance of bonds to fund transportation projects. No transportation bonds were issued in the 1950s. The 1960s saw a single issue of $33.65 million, while the 1970s saw two issues totaling $111.2 million. Since the early 1980s, almost every legislative session has approved transportation bonds and in ever increasing amounts. In the 1980s, there were four issues totaling nearly $706 million.[33] Moreover, since dollars are fungible, money raised in general obligation bonds freed up money for roads without directly violating the constitutional and legal limits. As late as 1999, state and federal motor fuel taxes made up 76 percent of the State Highway Fund.

In 2001, Governor Perry and the Texas Legislature instituted a dramatic change in Texas's traditional pay-as-you-go system. Though this system had been under stress since at least the mid-1980s, Texas turned it on its head in 2001, making the state and federal gas tax revenues merely supplementary to the new revenue sources from bonds, private investors, and tolls. In 2001, Governor Perry proposed and the legislature approved the Texas Mobility Fund (TMF). The TMF went into effect when voters approved Proposition 15, adding Article 3, section 49k, to the Texas Constitution. TMF permitted the Texas Transportation Commission (TTC), for the first time, to issue bonds on its own authority, though within limits established by statute, to fund construction and maintenance of the state highway system. By the end of 2012, $6.3 in TMF bonds had been issued.

In 2003, Governor Perry and the legislature increased its dependence on debt financing by again amending the Texas Constitution and Transportation Code to allow the TTC to issue bonds and related forms of public debt secured by the State Highway Fund. In 2007, the legislature set $6 billion as the aggregate bonding limit available to TTC in its State Highway Fund account. By 2008, the percentage of road building and maintenance funded from federal and state gas taxes was down to just 39 percent while the remaining 61 percent came from new sources, including bonds, tolls, and public/private comprehensive development agreements (CDAs).[34] The TTC's aggressive borrowing, tolling, and comprehensive development agreement activities fueled legislative concern and a dramatic political split between Governor Perry and the legislature in 2009. Transportation legislation in the 2009 regular legislative session, including renewal of TxDOT's legal mandate, as well as TTC's bonding and CDA authority, were held up until late in the session and then lost in the last minute scramble before adjournment. Governor Perry was forced to call a special session in July 2009 to salvage his transportation agenda.

In the 2009 special session, the legal mandate of TxDOT was renewed but the department's authority to negotiate CDAs was repealed. Governor Perry pushed hard for an extension but the legislature was adamantly opposed. CDA agreements allow public/private deals in which the private entity, usually a multinational construction company, puts up some or all of the money to build a road in exchange for the right to charge tolls for use of the road for up to fifty years. The state lays out modest amounts of money, a road gets built, Texans pay tolls, often rising at rapid rates, in perpetuity, but—and this is the best part—politicians get to claim that the road was free and no tax monies were required. TTC, knowing that the tide had turned against them, ordered that existing bonding authority be encumbered immediately. Texas also received $2.8 billion in highway-related federal stimulus money in 2009, so road building continued. While these monies were rapidly running out, a panel of experts appointed by the Texas Transportation Commission estimated that the state will need an astounding $448 billion over the next twenty years to make up for past underinvestment and to meet the maintenance and new road construction needs of this rapidly growing state.

Noting the legislature's action in suspending CDAs, Michael A. Lindenberger, the *Dallas Morning News's* transportation reporter, said "Texas spent the past six years leading the nation in its pursuit of private toll roads. . . . Perry's policies, first given life by the legislature in 2003, have meant both billions of dollars in new highways constructed and ever higher tolls for millions of Texans. . . . Now, it looks to be among the first to call a timeout." Moreover, the timeout is likely to last for awhile, despite Governor Perry's commitment to private toll roads. James H. Brunley, Secretary of Transportation under Ronald Reagan, has argued that the economic climate that allowed CDAs is gone, at least in the near term. Brunley said "Virtually all of the public-private deals that have been seriously discussed in the last decade have involved significant leverage [large amounts of borrowed money]. As we return to a more normal economy those kinds of deals will be attractive again. But lenders [may] continue to be more conservative for many years to come, reducing availability of capital for infrastructure."[35]

Texas is not alone in struggling to pay for road building and maintenance. Many states are in the same boat, costs are rising fast and traditional funding mechanisms struggle to keep up. But Texas has more room to maneuver than others do, if it will take advantage of it. For example, as noted above, Texas collects about 10 cents per gallon less in gas and related taxes than does the average state. Some legislators have proposed increasing the state gas tax by as much as 10 cents, but that proposal has been rejected in the last three legislative sessions. Moreover, proposals by Regional Transportation Council leaders for a local option to allow cities, counties, and regions to raise funds for transportation improvement have been side-tracked in recent legislative sessions. Urban officials, particularly in Houston and Dallas-Fort Worth (DFW), feel a special urgency due to both traffic congestion and air pollution. In 2009, the local option tax provision was designed to allow regional transportation authorities to raise up to $25 billion by 2030 for transportation improvements. North Texas legislators hoped that as much as $10 billion might be raised to keep traffic moving and to extend the region's light rail system. Other areas of the state would also have been authorized to approach voters for more transportation money. Late in the session, Governor Perry, never a fan of allowing tax increases even by local option, opposed the bill, calling it a "big huge monstrosity with lots of taxes and lots of areas of the state" involved.[36]

In the 2011 legislative session, Senator Tommy Williams (R-The Woodlands), chair of the Senate Transportation Committee, proposed debt service funding for the last $1 billion in bonds authorized in 2009 and $3 billion in new bonding authority for the 2012–2013 biennium. The new bonds allowed TxDOT contracting levels to remain above $4 billion annually for the next biennium.[37] By 2012, TxDOT had sold $17.3 billion in bonds for four major road building programs. Those bonds require annual loan payments of nearly $715 million, which will rise to $800 million by 2015. Legislators know that road debt is prohibitively expensive over the long term. One major project, the $2.7 billion reconstruction of the LBJ Expressway and I-35 in Dallas, is being funded with $2.2 billion in private funding from Centra, a Spanish construction firm. Centra also will maintain the project through 2061. Cool, right, Centra picks up 80 percent of the initial cost and project maintenance for half a century. Not so cool—in exchange, Centra gets a share of the toll revenues estimated by TXDOT at $18.1 over the life of the contract.[38]

Legislators seemed to approach the 2013 legislative session with new determination and new leadership. The third new Senate Transportation Committee chair in the last three sessions, Senator Robert Nichols (R-Jacksonville), said, "We don't need to use more debt to solve our transportation problem. We need to identify a long-term, predictable revenue source so TXDOT can actually plan."[39] Since this predictable new revenue source cannot be from taxes or fees, one wonders where the revenues will come from—fairies maybe!

Urban Transit and High-Speed Rail in Texas

The dire problems faced by Texas's urban areas are worse than they first appear because not only have we fallen behind in road building, we have done even worse in regard to mass transit and high speed rail. Texas railroads have always been commercial carriers little interested in passengers. Private railroad passenger service to Dallas stopped in 1969 and to Houston in 1974.[40] Since the 1980s only the federally subsidized Amtrak system has carried passengers in Texas. The Heartland Flier makes the short trip from Oklahoma City to Fort Worth. The Sunset Limited goes from New Orleans to Los Angeles via Houston, San Antonio, and El Paso. And the Texas Eagle originates in Chicago, stops in Dallas and San Antonio, before heading west to Los Angeles.

Even while borrowing heavily to build roads, Texas largely has ignored alternative transportation modes and funding sources. Over the past quarter century, the Urban Mass Transportation Administration (UMTA), now the Federal Transit Administration (FTA), has funded urban bus, subway, light rail, and trolleys. The national average for per capita funding was $17 per year. Some states did much better: California received more than $22 annually per capita, New York, not surprisingly, got the most with almost $40 annually. Other states did worse than the national average: Florida got about $11, while Texas got just $9.45. Again, most federal programs involve matching funds, so energetic state programs, such as those in New York and California, draw generous matches while sleepy state programs draw much less.

Similarly, when the federal government offered $8 billion, with $5 billion more to follow over the next five years, in 2009 for high-speed rail as part of the fiscal stimulus package, Texas was caught flat-footed. The first $8 billion was to go to high-speed rail projects that were ready to build or had completed feasibility and environmental studies so that federal funds could reasonably be committed. Texas has had some high-speed rail proposals on the table for years but has never funded the initial evaluations that would make them ready to go. Amadeo Saenz, executive director of the TTC in 2009, admitted that "Texas is really behind everyone else because we have not done the studies to see if high-speed rail corridors are feasible."[41] Making the same point, the *Dallas Morning News* editorial page admitted that "Texas has been neglectful in not exploring and advocating improved passenger rail as an intercity option. California has been at it for a while, investing its own money in planning a bullet train route along the coast. Trying to get up to speed, Texas lawmakers passed a bill [in 2011] calling for a passenger-rail strategy. It's about time."[42] The phrase "investing its own money" is key here: Texas rarely invests its own money to get ahead of the game, in fact, it only grudgingly puts up enough of its own money to leverage a federal match when that is available. Texas is likely to be left behind on high-speed rail as it has been on public transportation in general.

Texas is home to three of the nation's ten largest cities, spaced far enough apart across ideal terrain to make high-speed rail clearly feasible. But because none of the planning that would have made Texas competitive for these federal grants had been done, Texas laid down a double-thick smoke screen. As Governor Perry's spokeswoman, Alison Castle, explained, TxDOT had requested federal funds for a study to "tell us the costs, benefits, use, etc. of HSR in the state—all of which are necessary before even deciding to pursue public or private investment in HSR." States best positioned to get federal awards had, of course, already completed feasibility studies on their own dime. To cover what everyone expected would be a denial of funds to Texas and awards to the better-prepared states, Castle said, "Perry isn't holding his breath, . . . Texas is routinely overlooked in federal transportation spending."[43] So the explanation of Texas being passed over was not that we were unprepared to compete, it was, once again, they hate us because we are a successful red state.

When the first round awards were made in early 2010, the big prizes went to Florida, Illinois, and California. Florida subsequently withdrew due to state budgetary constraints, but the other programs are proceeding. Texas got scraps, a mere $11 million, or about 1.3 percent of the funds available, for improvements to existing rail lines, but not for new high-speed rail. In the meanwhile, Texas appointed a new rail division chief within TxDOT, Bill Glavin, but remains in the early planning stages. In March 2010, *Fiscal Notes*, a publication of Texas Comptroller Susan

Combs's office, wrote: "According to state rail officials, to attract significant high speed rail funding, Texas needs a unified rail plan supported by officials from all levels of government. Many other states, including those that received the rail stimulus funds, are far ahead of Texas in this process."[44] In August 2010, Texas submitted requests for a number of small rail projects in the second round of the competition.

In late 2012, using $9 million in federal grant funds and $1.4 million in state money (i.e., 87 percent federal money), TXDOT initiated a two-year feasibility study on rail service, perhaps high speed rail, between Oklahoma City and Houston. Other plans are underway that would connect Austin and San Antonio to a rejuvenated rail grid. Bill Glavin said, "This is to define the parameters of what can be done." A bit more forthcoming, perhaps accidentally, was Jennifer Moczygemba, rail system sector director for TXDOT. She said, "What it does is it gets Texas caught up, as far as our planning level studies . . . that would put us in line for future funding."[45]

Conclusion

Transportation analysts suggest that while Texas is at the end of the "highway centric" phase of its development, it has not yet embraced the subsequent stage of urban mass transit and high-speed rail. Some argue that another possibility is to foster job growth in suburban and exurban areas so that people can more conveniently live and work outside the state's major urban centers and, therefore, not have to spend so much time on the roads. This would, they suggest, limit costs by reducing demand on the most expensive controlled access, high-speed roads—the freeways that have shaped modern Texas.

While urban mass transit and high-speed rail between the major urban centers of Houston, San Antonio, Austin, and DFW seem the most plausible, both are nearly as expensive as new freeways and, just as importantly, they fly in the face of Texan independence and individualism. Growing jobs in outlying areas is certainly an option and has to some extent been happening since the 1970s, but it misses the fact that modern Texas is intensely urban. The 2010 census declared that fully 86 percent of Texans live in urban settings and a related study by the *Dallas Morning News* found that two-thirds of Texans live within 20 miles of Interstate Highways 10, 35, and 45 that connect Houston, San Antonio, Austin, and the DFW Metroplex. Most transportation analysts in Texas, and in the nation for that matter, argue that the money to build huge new free roads on the model of the current interstate highway system is simply not there anymore. This, of course, begs the question—why not?[46]

Most pointedly, the Texas gas tax has been set at 20 cents per gallon since 1991. In the two decades between 1991 and 2011, cumulative inflation totaled 64.1 percent, meaning that goods purchased for $100 in

1991 would cost $164.10 in 2011. Road building and maintenance costs have risen faster than general inflation over this period. As a result, Texas's transportation revenues in 2011 almost equal the state's road maintenance costs with essentially no revenue for new road construction. One of the few elected officials to call for an increase in the gas tax during the 2009 legislative session was Senator John Carona (R-Dallas). Carona also called for ending diversion of transportation funds for other purposes, permitting local and regional referenda on increased funding options, and streamlining TxDOT management. For his trouble, Corona was removed as chairman of the Senate Transportation Committee for the 2011 regular session. Though Lt. Gov. Dewhurst and the new Transportation Committee chair, Robert Nichols, both talked in the early days of the session about an increased vehicle registration fee, no new fees were passed.

Unfortunately, the state's conservative leaders tend to ignore strong conservative arguments in favor of improved transportation systems. Transportation systems are designed, one hopes, to improve mobility in general—but specifically, mobility allowing people efficiently to get to work where they create value and earn wages and income upon which they pay taxes. The better the roads and the less time spent in gridlocked traffic, the more time spent on the job creating value. One clear sense of how costs to economic efficiency can rise is shown in commuter time lost to congestion presented by the Texas Transportation Institute (TTI) at Texas A&M University. TTI's "Annual Urban Mobility" study covers the period 1982 to the present. Over that nearly three-decade-long period, lost commuter time in Dallas increased from 7 hours per year in 1982 to 45 hours per year in 2011. Forty-five hours is the equivalent of a long work week lost to traffic congestion each year.[47]

In late 2011, the Texas Transportation Commission appointed Phil Wilson as executive director of TxDOT, relpacing Amadeo Saenz. Wilson, a Perry appointee as Secretary of State and former aide to the governor, is the first non-engineer to lead TxDOT. Wilson's salary of $292,500, about $100,000 more than Saenz had been paid, caused some legislative alarm, as did his appointment of a "director of innovative finance and debt management at $250,000 a year."[48] The long history of the Texas Department of Transportation as a professional agency, above politics, is clearly over.

Notes

1   Randolph B. Campbell, *Gone to Texas: A History of the Lone Star State*, New York: Oxford University Press, 2003, pp. 28–33. See also T.R. Fehrenbach, *Lone Star: A History of Texas and the Texans*, New York: Macmillan, 1968, pp. 25–27.

2   James R. Arnold, *Jeff Davis's Own: Cavalry, Comanches, and the Battle for the Texas Frontier*, Edison, NJ: Castle Books, 2007, p. 183.

3   Marilyn McAdams Sibley, *Travelers in Texas, 1761–1860*, Austin, TX: University of Texas Press, 1967, p. 51.

4 Campbell, *Gone to Texas*, pp. 46, 80. See also Henderson K. Yoakum, *History of Texas*, New York: Redfield, 1856, p. 66.

5 William Ransom Hogan, *The Texas Republic*, Norman, OK: University of Oklahoma Press, 1946, p. 53.

6 William Bollaert, *William Bollaert's Texas*, Norman, OK: University of Oklahoma Press, 1956, pp. 180, 340.

7 Wilhelm Steinert, *North America, Particularly Texas in the Year 1849*, Dallas, TX: DeGolyer Library, 2003, pp. 41, 54, 70, 79, 116.

8 Frederick Law Olmsted, *A Journey Through Texas*, Dallas, TX: DeGolyer Library, 2004, pp. 54, 150, 72, 80.

9 Arnold, *Jeff Davis's Own*, p. 184.

10 Fehrenbach, *Lone Star*, p. 319. See also, David B. McComb, *Texas: A Modern History*, Austin TX: University of Texas Press, 2010, p. 113.

11 Robert A. Calvert, Arnoldo De León, and Gregg Cantrell, *The History of Texas*, 4th edn, Wheeling, IL: Harlan Davidson, Inc., 2007, pp. 118–119.

12 Randolph B. Campbell, *An Empire for Slavery*, Baton Rouge, LA: Louisiana State University Press, 1989, p. 95.

13 Richard Morehead, *DeWitt C. Greer: King of Highway Builders*, Austin, TX: Eakin Press, 1984, p. 31. See also, Hogan, *The Texas Republic*, p. 60.

14 Calvert et al., *History of Texas*, pp. 120, 204–206.

15 Thad Sitton and Milam Roward, *Ringing the Children In*, College Station, TX, Texas A&M University Press, 1987, p. 24.

16 Morehead, *DeWitt C. Greer*, p. 39.

17 Calvert et al., *History of Texas*, p. 354.

18 Morehead, *DeWitt C. Greer*, p. 176.

19 Anthony Champagne and Edward J. Harpham, *Texas at the Crossroads: People, Politics, and Policy*, College Station, TX: Texas A&M University Press, 1987, p. 204.

20 Fehrenbach, *Lone Star*, p. 649.

21 Morehead, *DeWitt C. Greer*, p. 148.

22 Nick Swartsell, "Study: Inadequate Roads Cost Texans Billions," *Texas Tribune*, October 2, 2012.

23 Theodore Kim, "Many Highways Are About to Get Speedier, *Dallas Morning News*, August 29, 2011, pp. 1B, 2B.

24 For more detail on the system for attributing motor fuel tax revenues to states, www.fhwa.dot.gov/ohim/attrib.htm.

25 Highway Statistics 2009, Table FE 221, "Ratio of Apportionments and Allocations to Payments," www.fhwa.dot.gov/policyinformation/statistics/ 2009/fe221.cfm.

26 Champagne and Harpham, *Texas at the Crossroads*, p. 203.

27 www.api.org/statistics/fueltaxes.

28 James B. Reed and Jaime Rall, "Running Out of Gas," *State Legislatures*, March 2011, pp. 28–31.

29 Todd J. Gillman and Michael A. Lindenberger, "Hutchison Bill Would Let Taxes Keep Gas Tax Funds," *Dallas Morning News*, April 28, 2009, 9A.

30 AP, "Lawmakers Weighing Increase in Gas Tax to Help Build Roads," *Dallas Morning News*, November 12, 2009, 6B.

31 Jamie Rall, "Pain at the Pump: Are Gas Taxes in the Future of Transportation Funding? *State Legislatures*, June, 2013, pp. 26–29.

32 Michael A. Lindenberger, "NTTA Defends Permanent Tolls," *Dallas Morning News*, March 10, 2011, p. 5B.

33 www.fhwa.dot.gov/ohim/summary95/sb202i.pdf.

34 Highway Funding Primer, Legislative Budget Board, March 2011, p. 3; www. lbb. state.tx.us/Other_Pubs/Highway_Funding_Primer_0311.pdf.

35   Michael A. Lindenberger, "Long a Leader in Toll-Road Ventures, Texas Taps the Brakes," *Dallas Morning News*, July 5, 2009, A1, A4.

36   Michael A. Lindenberger, "Local Tax Proposal Cut From Transportation Bill," *Dallas Morning News*, May 31, 2009, Al, A25.

37   Peggy Fikac, "Woodlands Senator Seeks $3 Billion for Highways," *San Antonio Express News*, April 11, 2011.

38   Aman Butheja, "Road tolls proliterate as State Financing Falls Short," *Texas Tribune*, in the New York Times, November 30, 2012, pp. A25A, A26A.

39   Ben Wear, "Highway Leader Says Time to Turn Away from Debt for Roads," *Austin American-Statesman*, November 25, 2012.

40   David G. McComb, *Texas: A Modern History*, Austin, TX: University of Texas Press, 2010, p. 160.

41   Michael A. Lindenberger, "Texas Is Lagging in Contest for High-Speed Rail Money," *Dallas Morning News*, June 25, 2009, 6A.

42   Editorial, *Dallas Morning News*, July 12, 2009, 2P.

43   Michael A. Lindenberger, "Most Rail Funds Likely to Bypass State," *Dallas Morning News*, January 19, 2010, A1, A5.

44   Gerard MacCrossen, "Switching Tracks: Can Texas Ease Its Traffic Woes With Rail?" *Fiscal Notes*, February/March 2010, pp. 8–11.

45   Ben Wear, "TxDOT Looking at Passanger Rail Along I-35 Corrider," *Austin American-Statesman*, October 16, 2012. See also Vianna Davila, "Is Texas on Track to High Speed Rail?" *San Antonio Express-News*, October 16, 2012.

46   Michael E. Young and Ryan McNeill, "Texas Triangle Holding Most of State's Growth," *Dallas Morning News*, March 6, 2011, A1, A4.

47   http://mobility.tamu.edu/ums/congestion_data/national_congestion_tables.stm, see especially Table 7.

48   AP, "Top TxDOT Execs See Salary Jump," *Dallas Morning News*, July 9, 2012, 3A.

9 Energy and the Environment in Texas

> It has become customary . . . to damn the ancestral frame of mind that
> ravaged the world so fully and so soon. What I myself seem to damn
> mainly though, is just not having seen it . . . But God! To have viewed
> it entire, the soul and guts of what we had and gone forever now.
>
> (John Graves, 1991)[1]

To the frontier mind, the land and its resources were in endless supply—
but time was wasting, others were coming, so the choice was to maximize
profits today or share the bounty with others tomorrow. Individual
initiative searched for opportunity and seized on it when found. With
small government, low taxes, and light regulation, opportunity time and
again produced feeding frenzies that burned out the resource before its
time. Robert Calvert has written that, "Intruders into the frontier often
recklessly ravaged the natural resources of the region. This resulted in the
decimation of the great buffalo herds, the overgrazing of the range, the
stripping of timber lands without regard for the future, and the pollution
of rivers, streams, and the Gulf."[2]

While Texans have always enjoyed the beauties of nature, the urge to
preserve nature for its own sake has been suspect. John Graves, author of
the iconic *Goodbye to a River* (1960) and of the quotation above, explained
that his beloved Hill Country land, now mostly limestone and scrub cedar,
once was covered with three or four feet of top soil. But two generations of
intensive cotton farming scraped it down to rock and left him dreaming
about what it once must have looked like. What made Graves, just days
short of his 94th birthday when he died in 2013, a Texas treasure is that
few Texans, then or now, have taken time to protect the landscape, let
alone dream about what it looked like when it was pristine.

A Brief History of Texans and the Land

While the early Anglo settlers thought Texas a beautiful place, they saw
a far greater beauty in the potential of its rapid economic development.

T.R. Fehrenbach reports that, "Somewhere along the line, [Stephen F.] Austin . . . developed an obsession to 'redeem Texas from its wilderness state by . . . spreading over it North American population, enterprise, and intelligence.' . . . Destroying nature and creating civilization as they knew it was already a fetish in North American minds. Austin merely had more vision and far more ability than most."[3] Throughout the nineteenth century and well into the twentieth, Texans viewed their state as a starkly beautiful but harsh land that needed to be confronted and subdued if its riches were to be extracted and enjoyed. The land proved bountiful but fickle to generations of plantation owners and farmers, cattle and timber men, and oil and gas men. Until the mid-twentieth century, Texas was an extractive, colonial economy in which wealth drawn from land was processed elsewhere. Millions of bales of cotton left the Gulf Coast ports for the manufacturing centers of New York and Boston, London and Manchester. The millions of longhorns driven north to Kansas and Missouri railheads were slaughtered in Chicago for consumption in the East. Both are prime examples of the extractive Texas economy of the nineteenth century. The energy economy of the twentieth century began as a colonial enterprise, dominated by northern capital, but ultimately proved rich enough to draw the capitalists themselves south.

In the two decades following the end of the Civil War, not only were the great buffalo herds eliminated, but cattle herds were increased until overgrazing threatened the range. During the 1870s, the buffalo herds that had numbered in the many millions were slaughtered for hides, sport, and to deprive the remaining plains Indians of the principal resource around which their lives revolved. Texas Congressman James Throckmorton said, "It would be a great step forward in the civilization of the Indians . . . if there were not a buffalo in existence."[4] By 1880, the buffalo numbered only in the thousands and the last herd was sheltered in the new Yellowstone National Park. As the northern plains emptied, Texas ranchers sent six million longhorns to northern markets from the late 1860s through the 1880s. Half went to slaughter and half went to stock ranches in Colorado, Wyoming, Montana, and the Dakotas. Strong demand for Texas cattle led to overstocking and overgrazing. When U.S. Department of Agriculture representatives met with Texas ranchers to discuss the problem, the Texans, predictably, bristled. The cattlemen unanimously passed a resolution declaring, "That none of us know, or care to know, anything about grasses, native or otherwise, outside of the fact that for the present there are lots of them, the best on record, and we are after getting the most out of them while they last."[5] Environmentalism looked to these Texans like yet another form of federal meddling.

The timber men of East Texas took the same short-term, maximum utilization approach as the cattlemen of West Texas. Between the 1870s and 1930s, the old-growth pine forests of East Texas were decimated with little thought of conservation. Northern financiers and Texas entrepreneurs combined talents to bring the forests to market. Timber products led all other freight categories in tonnage carried on Texas railroads in the late nineteenth and early twentieth century. Timber production peaked at 2.2 billion board feet in 1907 and then began dropping.[6] Texas responded by establishing the state Forest Service (TFS) in 1917 as part of Texas A&M University. The TFS was to advise and assist private landowners in managing and improving forestry assets and products. The TFS's impact was modest and by the early 1930s production had fallen to 350 million board feet, the lowest since 1880 levels: "Most of the virgin pine had been cut, and many operators had moved to new locations, often to the Pacific coast, leaving vast cut-over areas behind them."[7]

The energy industry, also an extractive industry, drove the development of modern Texas. Texas oil and gas, once it was out of the ground, was refined and marketed by Eastern and even European corporations, led by Royal Dutch Shell (the largest European oil company), Gulf Oil (owned by the Mellon family of Pittsburgh), and Sun Oil (owned by the Pew family of Philadelphia).[8] From the first big discovery at Spindletop near Beaumont in the Upper Gulf Coast field in 1901, through the discoveries in the Panhandle and Permian Basin in the 1920s, to discovery of the great East Texas field in October 1930, Texas increasingly became identified with oil.

For the first three decades of the twentieth century, Texas took a laissez-faire approach to the oil industry as well. The major oil companies controlled most of the production and they understood the importance of managing an oil field for long-term productivity. But the majors had ignored Northeast Texas and so the discoveries around Kilgore in 1930 set off a wildcatter scramble of epic proportions. Within a year, thousands of wells producing at maximum capacity had driven the price of oil to all-time lows and threatened to reduce pressure in the field and render vast reserves unrecoverable. In a rare case of state intervention, Governor Ross Sterling authorized state troops to seize the field and limit production and he empowered the Texas Railroad Commission to regulate future production in the interest of maximizing the long-term productivity of the field.[9]

Oil and gas continue to bulk large in the Texas imagination even today. Though both production and reserves declined steadily from the early 1970s through 2005, the state's refinery and petrochemical industries continued to grow by supplementing Texas oil and gas stocks with imported oil. In recent years, both Texas and non-Texas U.S. production are up and rising while imports are down and falling. In 1972, Texas crude oil production peaked at 1.3 billion barrels annually. Texas Production bottomed out at 388 million barrels in 2005, rising slowly to 404 million barrels in 2009, before jumping to 732 million barrels in 2012. The daily capacity of Texas refineries was more than three times that, nearly 2 billion barrels annually. Just half of the oil refined in Texas is used in the state; the other half is exported to other states, mostly in the south and east through huge pipelines. Unfortunately, refineries and related petrochemical industries, critical to Texas's economic well-being, are heavy polluters. Texas is, by a wide margin, the heaviest U.S. producer of polluting gases, heavy metals, and fine particulates. Moreover, even as oil and gas production waned, Texas stuck doggedly with its historic energy sources. Only in the last decade, despite the abundant sun, wind, and agricultural plant wastes in Texas, have meaningful efforts been made to foster the development of renewable energy sources.[10]

In this chapter, we explore the history of the Texas energy and power industries, usually since 1950, though earlier where good data permit. As we shall see, Texas held a position of overwhelming dominance in the U.S. energy economy of 1950, producing nearly half of the oil and natural gas used in the U.S. As global oil supplies grew, particularly from the Middle East, U.S. domestic production fell and imports rose. Texas expanded its refinery capacity so that though it produces only about 13 percent of the oil used in the U.S., it refines and distributes about one-quarter of the oil used in the U.S. Texas has about one-quarter of the nation's proven oil reserves and thirty percent of its proven gas reserves. These are critically important state and national assets, but they tend to mesmerize, even blind, Texas officials. The state's ongoing commitment to the petroleum, natural gas, and petrochemical industries, whose beneficial products are distributed through much of the country and create good jobs in Texas, leave Texas heavily polluted. Worse, it leaves Texas officials in the position of denying the environmental impacts that flow from these industries and resisting national and international attempts to regulate their emissions.

Texas Oil and Gas Production and Reserves, 1935 to Present

Good data on U.S. crude oil production go back to 1859 but Texas did not become a major player until the early years of the twentieth century. On August 27, 1859, the Drake well in Titusville, Pennsylvania, marked the first commercially viable oil discovery in the U.S. U.S. production jumped from 2,000 barrels in 1859 to 500,000 barrels in 1860 and the race was on. Production increased steadily, to 5.3 million barrels in 1870, 26.3 million barrels in 1880, 45.8 million barrels in 1890, and 63.6 million barrels in 1900. Texas played a marginal role in the early development of the U.S. oil industry, though there were small strikes in Northeast Texas as early as the 1860s. During the nineteenth century, prior to the introduction of the automobile in the early decades of the twentieth century, the markets for petroleum products were limited mainly to industrial lubricants and kerosene for lighting.

On January 10, 1901, an Austrian engineer, Colonel Anthony Lucas, brought in the Spindletop well near Beaumont. Spindletop produced an unprecedented 100,000 barrels a day and brought entrepreneurs and would-be oil men from all over the country and the world to Texas to search for oil. Most failed, but a few struck it rich so that by 1929 Texas was the capital of the world oil industry, having produced 2 billion barrels since Spindletop. And then on October 3, 1930, Columbus M. ("Dad") Joiner brought in the Daisy Bradford #3 well in Northeast Texas near Kilgore. Within two weeks the soon-to-be-legendary H.L. Hunt of Dallas was drilling just south of Joiner's lease and by the end of November he owned Joiner's leases. The East Texas field, the largest field discovered in the world to that time, contained 5.5 billion barrels of oil. Over the next four decades, Texas stood astride the U.S. and world oil industries.

U.S. oil production increased from 63.6 million barrels in 1900, to 209.6 million in 1910, 442.9 million in 1920, and 898 million in 1930. The Texas share of that production probably ranged from one-third to one-half, but solid data on Texas production extend back just to 1935. In 1935, U.S. production was 994 million barrels, of which 376 million barrels, or 38 percent, came from Texas. Production in the U.S. and Texas grew slowly during the depression years and then more rapidly as the nation plunged into World War II. Texas provided more than 40 percent of U.S. oil production every year from 1944 to 1957. By 1957, U.S. production was 2.6 billion barrels a year while Texas production was about 1.1 billion barrels. For the next two decades, Texas produced from 35 to 40 percent of U.S. oil, reaching 40 percent in both 1975 and 1976. Texas, of course, exulted in its extraordinary wealth, while the nation suffered under high oil price. Bumper stickers, reading SECEDE AND JOIN OPEC, adorned bumpers in the elite enclaves of Houston, Midland, and Dallas.[11] But the highpoint of both U.S. and Texas production (they were obviously closely related) had come in 1972 and, struggle as they might, production fell steadily from there. Just in the last couple of years, new discoveries and advanced drilling techniques have increased production to levels seen in Texas for 25 years.

While production of U.S. oil began falling in 1972, U.S. oil consumption continued to rise and imports filled the gap (Figure 9.1). Oil imports did not comprise 10 percent of U.S. consumption until 1955 when we imported 285 million barrels. But imports soared from 15 percent in 1971, to 26 percent in 1973, and a stunning 44.5 percent in 1977. During the late 1970s, the U.S. imported about 2.3 billion barrels of oil each year. Oil embargoes, price shocks, and conservation measures held imports around 2.5 billion barrels until the early 1990s when they began rising again. The U.S. imported 3 billion barrels in 1997, cresting at 3.7 billion barrels in 2006. By 2012, it had fallen back to 3.1 billion and is expected to fall further.

In 2012, Texas produced 732 million barrels of oil, just one half of its 1972 peak production, while the U.S. (including Texas) produced 2.4 billion barrels, about 70 percent of its 1972 peak production. Since 1972, Alaska and the Gulf have played a large role in holding up U.S. production to some degree. In 2012, Texas provided 31 percent of U.S. oil production and 13.3 percent of the oil consumed in the U.S. In 2012, the U.S.

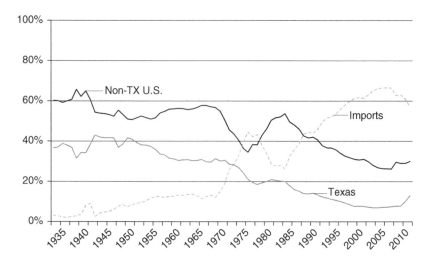

Figure 9.1   Percent of U.S. Crude Oil Supply from Texas, Non-Texas U.S., and Imports, 1935–Present.

Source: U.S. Energy Information Administration, Annual U.S. Field Production of Crude Oil, http://
tonto.eia.doe.gov/dnav/pet/hist/LeafHandler.ashx?n=PET&s=MCRFPUS1=A and Annual U.S. Imports
of Crude Oil, same except PET&s=MCRIMUS1f=A.

imported 3.1 billion barrels of oil, or 56.7 percent of the oil it consumed. The oil market is global and Texas production no longer has much effect on price, though as global prices rise Texas (though not Texas consumers) benefits while the nation in general suffers. This divergence of U.S. and Texas interests in regard to the price of oil has long fueled tension.

As with crude oil, Texas is the largest U.S. producer of natural gas, but, unlike with crude oil, domestic production is nearly sufficient to serve the U.S. market. In 2010, domestic production of natural gas fulfilled 88 percent of domestic consumption with most of the remainder being piped in from Canada. Relatively small amounts of liquefied natural gas (LNG) arrived by ship before being re-vaporized and moved into the national distribution system. In 2011, the U.S. produced and marketed 24.2 billion cubic feet (bcf) of natural gas. Texas produced 7 bcf, 29 percent of U.S. domestic production. Texas natural gas travels through an extensive system of pipelines to serve markets from California, through the Midwest, to the East Coast and New England.

During the first half of the twentieth century, natural gas was treated as a nuisance in the search for oil. Untold billions of cubic feet of natural gas were flared, or burned off, at the wellhead in the early oil fields. A few towns near the oil and gas fields used the gas for energy and some was re-injected to extend the life of depleted oil fields, but most was simply flared. After World War II, Texas passed legislation banning flaring and producers were forced to search for more productive and profitable uses for the gas. Two pipelines, the "big inch" (24 inch) and the "little big inch" (20 inch), built in 1942 and 1943 to deliver oil to the East Coast during World War II, were sold to the Texas East Transmission Corporation (TETCO) after the war. TETCO converted and extended the pipelines to move natural gas to the Midwest and East Coast. The El Paso Corporation built a new pipeline to carry natural gas from West Texas's Permian Basin to Southern California. As these markets grew, Texas production increased to serve them.[12]

In 1950, the natural gas market was just getting organized and Texas was by far its dominant player. In 1950, the U.S. produced nearly 6.3 bcf of natural gas, of which 3.1 bcf, almost exactly half, were produced in Texas. Texas's neighbors, Louisiana and Oklahoma, produced 832 and 482 million cubic feet respectively, another 13 percent and 8 percent. By 1960, U.S. production doubled to 12.8 bcf, Texas's production nearly doubled to 5.9 bcf, as did Oklahoma's to 0.8 bcf, and Louisiana's production tripled to 3 bcf. In 1960, Texas produced 46 percent of the U.S. total while Louisiana produced 23 percent and Oklahoma produced another 6 percent (Figure 9.2). Between 1960 and 1990, Texas, Louisiana, and Oklahoma provided three-quarters of the nation's natural gas. As late as 2010, Texas,

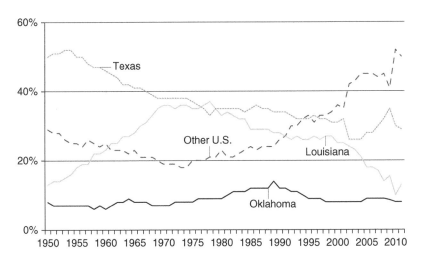

Figure 9.2 Percent of U.S. Natural Gas Supply from Texas and Other U.S. Sources, 1950–Present.

Source: Department of Commerce, Bureau of the Census, Statistical Abstract of the United States, Natural Resources, Mining and Mineral Products, various years, 1950–Present. See also U.S. Department of Energy, Energy Information Administration, Annual U.S. Natural Gas Marketed Production, http://tonto. eia.doe.gov/dnav/ng/hist/n9050us2a.htm.

Oklahoma, and Louisiana were still producing half of U.S. production, though increasingly they were supplemented by gas fields in New Mexico, Montana, the deep Gulf, and the Rocky Mountains. Recent finds, some of them huge, in Texas, Louisiana, Arkansas, and Pennsylvania have rejuvenated the natural gas market. More importantly, new drilling techniques combining fracturing shale formations (called "fracking") by pumping water, sand, and chemical gels into them at high pressure and horizontal drilling to follow the formations underground have enhanced production dramatically. The Barnett Shale near Fort Worth, where these techniques were developed, produced two billion cubic feet of gas a day in 2012, making it one of the most productive fields in the U.S. Similar finds—the Marcellus fields in Pennsylvania, the Fayetteville Shale in northern Arkansas, and the Haynesville Shale in northern Louisiana—pushed natural gas reserve estimates to a 90-year supply. They also created a natural gas glut that saw prices drop from $9 in early 2009, $2 in 2012, before recovering modestly to $4 in 2013. Many companies scaled back production at least temporarily.[13] Given the secure long-term supply and moderate prices, most experts and policymakers now see natural gas as an increasingly important energy source and as a likely transition fuel as the nation moves away from coal toward more climate-friendly energy sources.[14]

Even after more than a century of intense oil production and six or seven decades of concerted gas production, Texas has almost 25 percent of the nation's proven oil reserves and 30 percent of its proven gas reserves. Still, Texas reserves have been trending downward for decades and just a decade ago it appeared that the depletion of Texas reserves would continue apace, but new resources are being discovered all the time and new techniques are renewing the productivity of older fields. In 1950, Texas claimed 53 percent of the known U.S. reserves for both oil and natural gas. Those estimates remained above 40 percent through the 1960s before declining rapidly in the 1970s, holding at around one-quarter of both oil and gas reserves from 1980 through 2010. Even though new reserves of oil and gas are discovered regularly, Texas has been more extensively explored than other places.

In 1950, U.S. oil reserves were estimated to be 25.3 billion barrels of oil, more than half of which, 13.5 billion barrels, were in Texas (Figure 9.3). In 2010, U.S. oil reserves were estimated to be 23.3 billion barrels, just one-quarter of which, 5.7 billion barrels, were in Texas. Similarly, U.S. natural gas reserves in 1950 were estimated to be 185.6 trillion cubic feet, of which more than half, 99.2 trillion cubic feet, were in Texas. Texas gas reserves fell to just one-fifth of U.S. totals by the late 1990s, but have rebounded in the wake of recent discoveries. In 2010, U.S. gas reserves totaled 304.6 trillion cubic feet, of which about 30 percent, 89 trillion cubic feet, were in Texas.

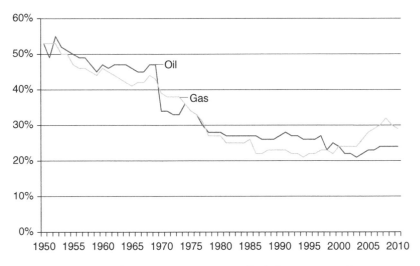

Figure 9.3 Texas Oil and Gas Reserves as a Percent of U.S. Reserves, 1950–Present.

Source: U.S. Census Bureau, *Statistical Abstract of the United States,* Petroleum and Natural Gas, multiple years, 1950–present. See also the Texas Railroad Commission, Oil Production, 1935–2008, http://www.rrc.state.tx.us/data/production/oilwellcounts/php.

The sharp drop in Texas's share of total oil reserves from 1969 to 1970 reflects the Prudhoe Bay, Alaska, discoveries of 1968.

Though the oil and natural gas industries play a smaller role in the Texas economy and job base than they once did, they continue to be disproportionately important.[15] In 2012, the oil and gas industries accounted for 8.8 percent of Texas gross state product, the value of all the goods and services produced in the state in the year, and accounted for 379,800 jobs, just 3.2 percent of the 11.7 million jobs in the state. A 2008 study by the Pew Charitable Trusts, entitled "The Clean Energy Economy," found that clean energy accounted for 55,646 jobs in Texas, 7.2 percent of the 770,385 clean energy jobs in the U.S. in 2008.[16]

Energy Consumption in the U.S. and Texas, 1980 to Present

Texas not only produces a substantial share of U.S. energy, it consumes a great deal of energy as well. In fact, Texas uses more energy than any other state, including California which is half again as populous (in 2012 California had 38.3 million residents compared to 26 million for Texas). Although Texas uses more energy than any other state, a few small states use more energy per capita. Since 1980, Texas has been the fourth most intensive energy-consuming state, behind only Alaska, Wyoming, occasionally North Dakota, and Louisiana. The cold states use a great deal of energy to heat homes and businesses in the winter, while warm states use lots of energy to cool homes and businesses in the summer. But heavy energy use by Texas is not explained by hot summers; all of the South and Southwest have hot summers and most use far less energy. As we will see, Texas uses a great deal of energy to create electricity to run industrial processes such as turning petroleum into gasoline, chemicals, and plastics.

Figure 9.4 highlights two key facts about energy usage in the United States. State energy profiles are both stable, they do not change much over time, and quite different, some states use more energy per person than other states do. In 2011, Texas used 476 million British thermal units (BTUs) of energy annually per resident, while the U.S. average was 313 million BTUs. Even more strikingly, Texas's 476 million BTUs per capita more than doubled California's 209 million BTUs and Florida's 221 million. California and Florida are garden spots with fairly temperate climates and sea breezes, but New York, no garden spot in most estimates, uses only 185 million BTUs annually per capita. Georgia and Ohio, both with substantial industrial usage, consume 306 million BTUs and 332 million BTUs per capita respectively.

Not only does Texas use more energy than almost any other state, its energy use is more carbon intensive than most other states and more of that

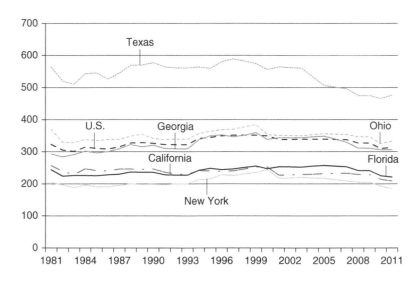

Figure 9.4 Annual Energy Consumption in the U.S., Texas, and Selected States in Million BTUs Per Capita, 1980–Present.

Source: U.S. Census Bureau, Statistical Abstract of the United States, "Energy Consumption—End Use Sector and Selected Source, by State," 1981 to Present.

energy is used for industrial purposes than in most other states. Hence, as we shall see below, Texas creates more pollution, more carbon dioxide (CO2), more toxic emissions, and more fine particulates than any other state. In fact, with just 8.2 percent of the nation's population, Texas has produced fully one-third of the nation's hazardous waste over the last two decades. As the U.S. responds to the threat of global warming by transitioning to less carbon-intensive sources of energy, Texas's traditional dependence on carbon fuels and its historically loose approach to pollution control have come under tremendous pressure.

Historically, the U.S. has been heavily dependent on carbon fuels, petroleum, natural gas, and coal. Hydroelectric power became an option for some states in the middle third of the twentieth century, nuclear power came online in the 1960s, and in the last two decades, biomass, solar, and wind have begun to contribute to our energy requirements. Each state, depending on their natural advantages, has drawn on a distinctive fuel mix and that mix has changed over time, albeit slowly, as fuel options have evolved. In 1980, the U.S. used about 45 percent petroleum, 27 percent natural gas, 20 percent coal, and 4 percent each of hydropower and nuclear power. By 2011, petroleum had declined to 36.5 percent, natural gas to 35.5 percent, coal held steady at 20.2 percent, hydropower was at 2.4 percent, while nuclear power was just over 8 percent and biomass, solar, and wind added the last 7 points. But those numbers are just averages; different states, by accident of history and by policy design, met their energy needs with different amounts and mixes of fuel.

California and Texas, the two largest states in the nation, have taken predictably different approaches. Given its own history and resources, Texas has taken a carbon-intensive approach to meeting its energy needs. In part, this was inevitable: Texas petroleum and natural gas are prepared for market in Texas plants and refineries. In 1980, Texas depended on fossil fuels (petroleum, natural gas, and coal) for 100 percent of its energy needs. The U.S. depended on fossil fuels for 92 percent of its energy needs, using hydropower and nuclear to meet the rest. California, on the other hand, used fossil fuels for 86 percent of its energy needs, using hydropower for 5 percent, and a diverse mix of nuclear, biomass, wind, and solar for the rest. In 2011, Texas used 93 percent fossil fuels to meet its energy needs; the U.S. used 82 percent fossil fuels, while California used just 72 percent fossil fuels. Figure 9.5 shows that while the U.S., Texas, and California have all reduced their dependence on fossil fuels, Texas began from a much higher base and has moved more slowly. By far the greatest difference between Texas and California is that Texas used coal, the dirtiest fossil fuel, to meet an average of 14 percent of its energy needs while California has averaged less than 1 percent since 1980.

The U.S. Energy Information Administration tracks the purposes to which energy is put throughout the U.S. Four broad categories of energy

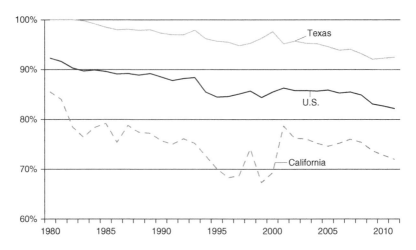

Figure 9.5 Percent of Energy Consumption from Fossil Fuels (Petroleum, Natural Gas, and Coal), 1980–Present.

Source: U.S. Census Bureau, Statistical Abstract of the United States, "Energy Consumption—End Use Sector and Selected Source, by State," 1981 to Present.

use—residential, commercial, industrial, and transportation—have been tracked since 1981. Texas's energy problem is made more complex by the fact that a larger portion of the state's energy consumption goes to more polluting industrial uses, and less to less polluting residential, commercial, and transportation uses than in most other states. For example, in 2011, U.S. energy usage was 31.8 percent industrial, 22 percent residential, 18.8 percent commercial, and 28 percent transportation. California energy usage was 23 percent industrial, 19 percent residential, 19.8 percent commercial, all three at or below the national average, and 38.2 percent transportation. California freeways burn up a lot of gas, but California battled the Bush and Obama Environmental Protection Agencies (EPAs) in the 2000s to allow it to demand better gas mileage and more robust pollution controls than demanded by national standards. Texas, on the other hand, devoted 50 percent of its energy usage to industrial purposes, 14 percent to residential, 13 percent to commercial, and 23 percent to transportation. And Texas battled the Obama EPA (the Bush administration did not bother Texas) over demands that Texas take a harder line toward industrial pollution. As with energy mix, Figure 9.6 shows that energy use has changed only slowly since 1980.

The form of energy that most people know best is the electricity that flows into their homes to insure that the lights come on when they flip the switch. Electric power came late to much of Texas. LBJ famously championed rural electrification for the Hill Country during the Depression.

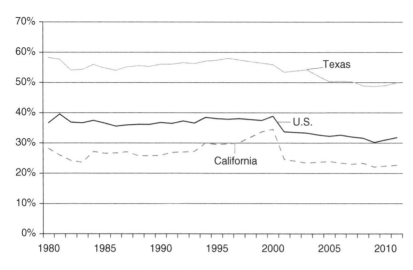

Figure 9.6 Industrial Energy Use as a Percent of Total Energy Use in the U.S., Texas, and California, 1980–Present.

Source: U.S. Census Bureau, Statistical Abstract of the United States, "Energy Consumption—End Use Sector and Selected Source, by State," 1981 to Present. Note that the bursting of the tech bubble in 2001 hit California industrial energy use particularly hard.

But the war initiated changes in Texas, especially urbanization and industrialization, which dramatically changed the state over the next several decades. In 1950, Texas was the nation's sixth most populous state, with 7.7 million residents, 5.1 percent of the total U.S. population of 152 million. But Texas produced just 3.9 percent of the electricity produced in the U.S. (Figure 9.7). Within a decade, Texas had caught up and was producing 5.2 percent of the nation's electricity for 5.3 percent of its population and by 1970 Texas was producing 7.6 percent of the nation's energy for 5.5 percent of its population. As late as 2010, Texas was producing 10 percent of the nation's electricity for 8.2 percent of its population.

The explosive build out of Texas electricity production was meant to serve industrial customers at least as much and probably more than residential and commercial consumers. Between 1950 and 1979, U.S. electricity production grew from 329 billion kilowatt hours (kWh) to 2,319 billion kWh, an increase of 605 percent. Texas, starting from further back, grew faster. In 1950, Texas produced 12.7 billion kWh and in 1979 produced 197 billion kWh, an increase of an astounding 1,454 percent. But since 1980, growth in the production of electric power in the U.S. and Texas has been much slower. U.S. electricity production has grown just 80 percent (from 2,286 kWh to 4,128 kWh) while Texas electricity production has grown just 103 percent (from 203 kWh to 412 kWh). And

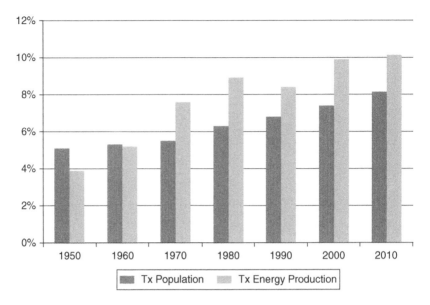

Figure 9.7 Texas Population and Energy Production as a Percent of U.S. Population and Energy Production by Decade, 1950–Present.

Source: U.S. Census Bureau, Statistical Abstract of the United States, Population section, 1950 to present; Electric Power Industry, Net Generation section, 1950 to present.

industry, because it uses power in bulk when compared to commercial and residential users, pays less. Commercial users pay about 90 percent of what residential users pay per kilowatt hour, while industrial users pay about 60 percent.

Finally, slow growth of electricity production capacity in Texas after 1980 has put increasing pressure on electricity prices for all classes of users. Throughout the 1990s, electricity prices in Texas were well below the national average. In 1990, Texas electricity prices were 29th in the nation (with 1 being the most expensive) and in 1999 they were 27th in the nation. By 2001, they were 14th in the nation and in 2006 they were 11th. As Figure 9.8 shows, Texas electricity prices were stable through the 1990s and took a sharp upward spike between 2000 and 2006. They did not fall back to the national average until 2010. What happened? Texas public policy happened.[17]

Enron was a major player in Texas politics and energy policy in the 1990s and they pushed hard for deregulation. Republican Senator David Sibley introduced Senate Bill 7 early in the 76th Texas legislative session (1999) and Governor George W. Bush signed the bill into law on June 18, 1999. Senator Sibley declared that the goal of SB7 was to bring down the cost of electric power. He said "We want this bill to bring down the cost of electricity for all Texans. If we don't get consumers lower rates, then we have been a failure—I'll be the first to say it." However, fifteen years on, rates have stayed around the national average, but supporters have not stepped forward to declare deregulation a failure.[18]

How we create electricity raises as many complex issues as whether we will have enough of it at prices that we can afford. First, electricity is generated by using fuel stocks, mostly fossil fuels, but also nuclear and renewable stocks, to heat water, creating steam that is forced past a turbine's blades to turn a shaft connected to a generator. The generator converts mechanical to electrical energy for distribution and use. In 2012, coal (37%) and natural gas (30%) were the principal fossil fuel feed stocks used in electric generation in the U.S. Of renewable fuels, nuclear power (19%), hydroelectric power (7%), and other renewables (including biomass, wind, and solar) about 5%, were the most productive. In 2011, Texas used less coal (36.3%) and more natural gas (38.2%) than the U.S. in general, but also used less nuclear power (9.1%), and about the same amount of other renewables, at about 7.4%, as the U.S.[19]

While Texas's heavy use of natural gas for electricity production is decidedly a good thing, as it is less polluting than coal, Texas has not pushed residential and commercial use of natural gas nearly as aggressively. Natural gas has long been used to heat about half of the nation's homes. But residential use of natural gas in Texas has been falling against the national average for more than half a century. In 1955, Texas accounted for 5.2 percent of the U.S. population, but Texas's 1.8 million residences served by natural gas accounted for 6.4 percent of total U.S. residences

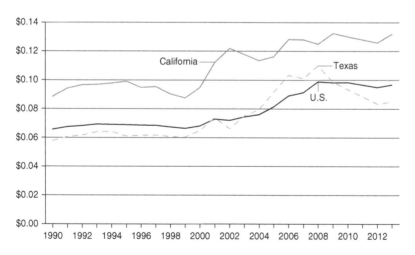

Figure 9.8 Average Price of Electricity in the U.S., Texas, and California, 1990–Present.

Source: U.S. Department of Energy, Energy Information Administration, see http://www.eia.doe.gov/cneaf/electricity/epa/average_price_state.xls, Average Price of Electricity by state.

served by natural gas. In 2011, Texas accounted for 8.2 percent of U.S. total population, while the 4.33 million Texas residences served by natural gas still accounted for just 6.5 percent of total U.S. residences served by natural gas. California, on the other hand, with a 2011 population half again as large as Texas's had more than twice as many homes (10.6 million residences) served by natural gas. With 12 percent of the U.S. population, California had 16 percent of homes served by natural gas. Interestingly, California served its 10.6 million residential customers with nineteen gas utilities, while Texas its 4.33 million residential customers with 164 gas utilities.[20] Heavier use of natural gas in Texas homes and businesses should be an obvious step in the direction of reducing the state's carbon footprint.

Coal presents U.S. policymakers with several dilemmas. First, the U.S. has about 27 percent of the world's known coal reserves, more than any other nation. The U.S. has a demonstrated reserve base of 483 billion short tons (don't ask, they call them short tons, but they are regular tons of 2,000 pounds), of which over 259 billion short tons are recoverable with current technology, a 250-year supply at current rates of usage. Over the past fifteen years, the U.S. has produced an average of 1.1 billion short tons a year.[21] Second, coal is cheaper than natural gas and much cheaper than nuclear power. Unfortunately, there is a third consideration, and that is that coal is the dirtiest form of energy, producing twice as many pollutants as natural gas.

Texas's demonstrated coal reserves account for just 2.5 percent of U.S. reserves. In 2011, Texas produced 45,904 short tons of coal from thirteen surface mines, mostly in East Texas, but brought in more than 62,262 short tons by rail from Wyoming and another 47,000 short tons from elsewhere. Texas lignite coal is low in energy content but it is also low in sulfur, which makes it less polluting than the more efficient subbituminous coal from Wyoming. As a result, Texas consumes more coal than any other state and its emissions are the highest in the nation. And as late as 2007, Texas authorities seemed on the verge of doubling down on coal. Texas then had seventeen coal-fired power plants. In early 2007, Texas power companies proposed eighteen new coal-fired plants, eleven for a single company, Dallas's TXU. Governor Rick Perry ordered the Texas Environmental Quality Commission to "fast-track" the approval process, but a coalition of local officials, led by Dallas Mayor Laura Miller, business people, and environmentalists, got in the way. Eventually, TXU was acquired in a leveraged buyout and eight of the eleven proposed coal plants were cancelled, no thanks to Texas political authorities. In fact, by 2009, another set of eight to twelve coal-powered plants were moving through the approval process.[22] However, due to the recession and the declining price of natural gas, only four new plants had been built by 2011. As natural gas prices continued to decline, a few new, more efficient, coal plant, replaced older plants, but by early 2013, when a new coal plant near Waco came online, Texas had a total of 18 coal-fired power plants. No new coal-fired plants are planned and older plants continue to slow production or shut-down entirely.

Nuclear power plants began contributing to the nation's electricity supply in the 1960s. More than 100 plants were built nationwide before the first nuclear power plant in Texas came online in 1988. When Texas brought its first plant online, California already had six units producing 25 percent of the state's electricity. Since 1993, Texas has had four units, two each at Comanche Peak southwest of Dallas and the South Texas Project southwest of Houston, producing about 9.1 percent of the state's electricity. But concerns about the safety and cost of nuclear power have hobbled the industry for decades, nowhere more so than in Texas. Today, the U.S. has 104 nuclear plants, down from 111 in 1990, producing a steady 20 percent of the nation's electricity. The 2011 nuclear catastrophe in Japan further chilled the industry in the U.S. and globally. And like coal, the prospects of new nuclear plants are undercut by the low price of natural gas.

While Texas's preference for traditional fossil fuels has made it skeptical of nuclear power, in a jaw-dropping decision in early 2011, Texas agreed to become a permanent storage site for low-level nuclear waste. The 1,340 acre Waste Control Specialists site in West Texas, near Andrews, is the only facility in the nation to accept federal and out-of-state low-level nuclear waste products, such as clothing, rags, cleaning materials, syringes and the like from nuclear power plants, chemical plants, and hospitals. The last such site, in South Carolina, closed in 2008, leaving on-site storage as the only option for those who create such waste. Waste Control Specialists won a fifteen-year license in 2009 to store 2.31 million cubic feet of waste. Opponents worry that Waste Control will move to expand its licensed storage capacity because the thirty-six states eligible to deposit waste create about 2 million cubic feet per year. Opponents also point to the $600,000 contribution that Waste Control's board chairman Harold Simmons made to Rick Perry's 2010 gubernatorial re-election campaign ($1.12 million since 2001) and $430,000 in lobbying fees as typical of Texas politics and environmental policymaking.[23]

Renewable energy generally refers to energy produced from sources that, unlike coal, petroleum, and natural gas, are not used up but occur and recur naturally. The oldest renewable energy source is wood and wood waste, which does replenish through new growth but which can be overwhelmed if harvested too quickly. Hydropower is another old source of renewable energy, used throughout history, but employed as a major source of electrical power only since the early decades of the twentieth century. Though concentrated heavily in New York and the West Coast states of Washington, Oregon, and California, hydropower still provides 62 percent of renewable electric energy supplies. Newer sources of renewable energy are biomass, including corn for ethanol, but plant wastes more generally, as well as wind and solar power.

U.S. consumption of renewable energy is about 12.5 percent of total energy consumption. Texas is still a bit below the national average. Texas has little hydropower, so its renewable energy bets have been placed elsewhere. In 2000, Texas, with 7.4 percent of the nation's population, produced just 2.2 percent of the nation's nonhydro renewable power, but by 2005, now with 7.7 percent of the nation's population, that contribution was up to 6.1 percent, mostly from a growing wind energy industry. In 2005, Texas adopted a law requiring that 5,880 megawatts of additional renewable generation capacity be built by 2015 and 10,000 mega-watts be built by 2025, of which 500 megawatts are to be nonwind renewable energy. These targets would represent an additional 5 percent of the state's total electricity demand. In 2006, Texas surpassed California to become the nation's largest producer of wind energy. In 2011, Texas produced fully one-quarter of the nation's wind energy. More than 85 percent of Texas's renewable energy production came from wind, which accounted for 7 percent of the state's total electricity usage. Texas has been quite friendly to production of wind power, investing $5 billion in new transmission lines to carry power from West Texas to the urban centers of the state, though opposition from landowners and environmentalists has been difficult to overcome.[24] Texas policymakers have not yet provided incentives to solar power energy production.

While Texas has led on wind energy, informed observers argue that a coordinated state plan to foster renewable energy has been lacking. Amy Jaffe of the Rice University's energy program has argued that "We're stuck in 30-year-old thinking, not only in the companies, but in our politicians, and we are not understanding that there is a sea change that is coming." Jeff Morris, head of the Dallas refining company Alon USA has made a similar point, saying, "They need a statewide strategy, not a little piece here, a little piece there kind of thing." Austin Mayor Will Wynn said "I'm disappointed to see the state leadership either diving under the table or, worse, pounding their chest, instead of taking part in the energy discussion." As if on cue, Governor Perry said, "If the answer is Washington, D.C., then I would suggest to you that most people in America would rather go it alone. My argument here is that we have, by our own volition, by our own innovation, led the country in a lot of the alternative energy side of things."[25]

Pollution Consequent to Energy Production and Use in Texas

Fossil fuels are of little use until they are converted into usable energy, usually in the form of electricity, transportation fuels, or chemical products. But those conversion processes, making coal into electricity, oil into gasoline, or natural gas into fertilizers and plastics, leave undesirable residuals or wastes in their wake. Because Texas produces and consumes more energy than any other state, it would have to work very hard not to produce more waste products and pollutants than any other state. Not only does Texas not work very hard to control pollution, but it also habitually resists national pressure, let alone mandates, to limit the pollution that accompanies energy production and consumption. The Obama administration and its EPA argue that cleaner air and water are important to human health and to a healthy environment more generally. The Perry administration and its Texas Commission on Environmental Quality (TCEQ) argue that tougher rules are unnecessary and unachievable, will limit economic growth, and will cost jobs.

The mission of the EPA "is to protect human health and the environment." It has a $8.5 billion budget and 17,100 employees. While its mandate is broad, its focus is defined by authorizing legislation, including the Clean Air Act of 1970, the Clean Water Act of 1972, the Resource Conservation and Recovery Act of 1976, and the Federal Hazardous and Solid Waste Amendments of 1984. The mission of the TCEQ is "to protect our state's human and natural resources consistent with sustainable economic development." TCEQ has a budget of $350 million and 2,761 employees. Both EPA and TCEQ took substantial budget cuts in 2011 and 2012.

Critics argue that the TCEQ is too business-friendly to be a credible defender of the environment. They argue that "in decision after decision, the Texas agency that is supposed to protect the public and the environment has sided with polluters." Texas leaders of course disagree. Former TCEQ Chairman Buddy Garcia, said "'From what you read and what you hear, it would almost appear we have little or no interest in taking care of the environment. . . . It's very frustrating' . . . Texas actually should be viewed as a 'model for the country.'"[26] Governor Perry describes Texas's light regulatory regime as, "the right way. We refer to it as the Texas way."[27]

The data seem to be on the side of the critics as opposed to the TCEQ. The EPA and U.S. Department of Energy's Energy Information Administration have tracked emissions from conventional, meaning non-nuclear, power plants since 1990. The principal pollutants emitted during the production of electric power, usually using natural gas and coal, are carbon dioxide (CO_2), sulfur dioxide (SO_2), and nitrogen oxides (NOx). CO_2 is by far the largest pollutant, totaling 2.2 billion metric tons in 2011. Table 9.1 shows that Texas is by far the largest producer of CO_2, producing four times as much each year over the past two decades as California. As we shall see below, Texas has been in a long-running struggle with the EPA over CO_2 emissions in the state.

The EPA also has published biennial reports on generation of hazardous wastes by states since 1991. EPA defines hazardous wastes as liquids, solids, gases, or sludges, such as cleaning fluids, pesticides, and by-products of manufacturing processes that are dangerous or potentially harmful to the environment or human health. In ten of the eleven EPA reports produced since 1991, Texas ranked number 1, producing more hazardous waste materials than any other state, usually by a wide margin (Table 9.2). For example, in 1991, the first year for which data are available, Texas produced fully 34 percent of the nation's hazardous waste materials, and in 1997, Texas produced nearly half, 46.6 percent, of the nation's hazardous wastes. In the 2007 report, Texas slipped to number 2, not because Texas had a particularly good year but because neighboring energy state Louisiana had a particularly bad year, nearly tripling 2005 hazardous waste totals. In 2007, Louisiana produced 34 percent of the nation's hazardous wastes while Texas contributed another 28.4 percent. Together the two oil producing and refining states produced nearly two-thirds of the nation's total hazardous waste output. California, more populous than Texas and Louisiana combined, produced just 1.3 percent of the nation's hazardous

Table 9.1 CO_2 Emissions from Energy Consumption at Conventional Power Plants in the U.S., Texas, and California, 1990–Present

	U.S. CO_2	TX CO_2	TX/U.S.	CA CO_2	CA/U.S.
1990	1,931,248	211,045	10.9%	52,338	2.7%
1991	1,928,035	210,362	10.9%	49,786	2.6%
1992	1,949,594	209,309	10.7%	57,646	3.0%
1993	2,033,139	244,931	12.0%	54,130	2.7%
1994	2,063,900	219,803	10.6%	61,887	3.0%
1995	2,083,509	220,223	10.6%	49,976	2.4%
1996	2,161,258	230,508	10.7%	46,847	2.2%
1997	2,232,709	237,181	10.6%	49,834	2.2%
1998	2,324,139	246,845	10.6%	52,882	2.3%
1999	2,338,660	252,540	10.8%	57,551	2.5%
2000	2,441,722	262,280	10.7%	67,411	2.8%
2001	2,389,745	253,227	10.6%	71,258	3.0%
2002	2,395,048	255,890	10.7%	59,669	2.5%
2003	2,415,680	255,073	10.6%	55,983	2.3%
2004	2,456,934	256,725	10.4%	59,820	2.4%
2005	2,513,609	258,661	10.3%	54,680	2.2%
2006	2,459,800	257,552	10.5%	59,389	2.4%
2007	2,516,580	255,092	10.1%	62,780	2.5%
2008	2,484,012	252,710	10.2%	62,548	2.5%
2009	2,269,508	242,864	10.7%	59,428	2.6%
2010	2,259,000	235,000	10.4%	45,000	2.0%
2011	2,222,000	250,000	11.3%	37,000	1.7%

Source: U.S. Department of Energy, Energy Information Administration, http://www.eia.gov/cneaf/electricity/epa/emission_state.xls.

Table 9.2 Hazardous Waste Generated by State: Comparing the U.S., Texas, and California, 1991–Present

	U.S.	*Texas*	*TX/U.S.*	*TX Rank*	*Calif.*	*CA/U.S.*	*CA Rank*
1991	305,709	104,079	34.0%	1	12,925	4.2%	8
1993	258,449	63,436	24.6%	1	14,056	5.4%	7
1995	214,093	68,513	32.0%	1	11,110	5.2%	6
1997	40,676	18,973	46.6%	1	673	1.7%	12
1999	40,026	14,924	37.3%	1	427	1.1%	16
2001	40,821	7,555	18.5%	1	807	2.0%	16
2003	30,176	6,585	21.8%	1	445	1.5%	16
2005	38,347	15,224	39.7%	1	747	1.9%	13
2007	46,693	13,272	28.4%	2	609	1.3%	11
2009	35,331	13,462	38.1%	1	700	2.0%	11
2011	34,334	15,683	45.7%	1	335	1.6%	11

Source: National Biennial RCRA Hazardous Waste Reports, http://www.epa.gov/epawaste/ inforesources/data/biennialreport/index.htm. Note that as of 1997 all wastewater treatment data contained in previous reports is excluded, which makes cursory comparison before and after that date potentially misleading.

wastes. In 2009 and 2011, Texas came roaring back to capture the number 1 spot, producing fully 45.7 percent of the nation's hazardous waste in 2011.

Texas vs. the EPA: Greenhouse Gases (CO_2)

The battle between the EPA and TCEQ is particularly intense over air pollution, especially in and around Houston. The EPA is responsible for setting national limits on ground level ozone, the principal cause of smog, while TCEQ is responsible for developing the state compliance plan, though the plan must be approved by the EPA. Smog is caused by a cocktail of transportation and industrial pollutants interacting in the atmosphere. Houston's millions of cars and trucks, together with its nine oil refineries and over 100 chemical plants, have left the city out of compliance with national rules for decades. In 2009, Houston met the 1997 EPA standard of .084 parts per million. Unfortunately for Houston, the Bush administration had lowered the standard to .075 parts per million in 2006 and the Obama administration announced plans to lower it still further, to between .06 and .07.

Texas politicians, mostly but not exclusively Republicans, have long opposed both national energy and environmental policy, especially the particular form of policy preferred by the Democrats in Washington. Led by Governor Rick Perry, Texas Republicans have questioned the science behind global warming and the economic impact that regulations or taxes on fossil fuels might have on the Texas economy. Perry said "I think the science is still out there and it's not settled yet." Barry Smitherman, former chairman of the Texas Public Utility Commission, declared he was "more concerned about climate change legislation than I am about climate change."[28] Governor Perry's spokesperson, Alison Castle, has argued that "Governor Perry has proven that stifling government mandates are not the answer to our state's energy and environmental challenges. Texas has proven it is possible to balance sound environmental policies with pro-growth economic efforts that have produced the best business climate in the country."[29]

On December 7, 2009, the U.S. Environmental Protection Agency (EPA) issued an "endangerment finding" which held that carbon dioxide emitted from automobiles, power plants, and oil refineries constitutes a public health threat subject to federal regulation. Governor Perry immediately issued a thirty-eight-page rebuttal, declaring that "It is unconscionable that unelected bureaucrats at the EPA have declared carbon dioxide a public danger despite a lack of scientific evidence to support their ruling."[30] Ten days later Governor Perry was still complaining that federal regulation of greenhouse gases would "kill jobs and raise the cost of living . . . It's time for them to take a look at the way we do things here in Texas."[31] The TCEQ called the proposed levels "arbitrary, unnecessary, and unachievable" and Debbie Hastings, a spokesperson for the Texas Oil and Gas Association, said, "I really don't think we can meet the standard." Houston Mayor Annise Parker "supported the stricter rules to protect the health of city dwellers, though she cautioned the city would need years to reach the goals."[32]

Though Texas will continue to aggressively protect its petrochemical industry from national regulation, this is a fight that Texas increasingly is bound to lose. The EPA's endangerment finding cleared the way for EPA rule-making to set limits for CO_2 from vehicles, power plants, refineries, and other large emitters. As if speaking directly to the political and business leadership of Texas, EPA administrator Lisa Jackson said, "We know that skeptics have and will continue to try to sow doubts about the science. . . . But raising doubts—even in the face of overwhelming evidence—is a tactic that has been used by defenders of the status quo for years."[33]

Nonetheless, the EPA probably underestimated Texas's tenacity. In February 2010, Attorney General Greg Abbott, with Governor Perry's support, filed suit in federal court to halt implementation of greenhouse gas rules, claiming the rules were based on bad science. Governor Perry declared that, "This legal action is being taken to protect the Texas economy . . . and protect Texas's successes against federal overreach." EPA regional administrator Al Armendariz responded, "Texas, which contributes up to 35 percent of the greenhouse gases emitted by industrial sources in the United States, should be leading the way in this effort."[34] Abbott sued twice more in 2010, once in July and again in September, still claiming the proposed rules were based on faulty climate change data and would unnecessarily slow economic activity and cost jobs. By the end of the year, Texas stood alone as the other forty-nine states, many grudgingly, prepared to implement the new rules. When a federal appeals court ruled for the EPA and against Texas in December 2010, Governor Perry responded, "Texas will do everything in its power to defeat the threat that these misguided policies impose on our state's energy industry and the thousands of jobs it sustains."[35] The new rules went into effect on January 2, 2011.

As Texas pinned its hopes on the courts to halt the imposition of stricter air pollution rules, the EPA increased the pressure on Texas by challenging its overall process and standards for issuing operating licenses to oil, gas, and chemical plants in Texas. The EPA challenged Texas's "flexible permitting" standards whereby Texas sets limits on emissions for entire facilities rather than for individual units and smokestacks within large facilities. Only Texas uses the flexible permitting system and EPA claims that it allows more pollution overall than the provisions of the Clean Air Act permit.[36] On December 23, 2010, just two weeks after the federal appeals court rejected Texas's challenge to the new greenhouse gas standards, EPA seized the industrial permitting process for 167 of the state's largest facilities, mostly oil refineries and chemical plants on the Gulf Coast, from Texas and promised not to return it until the state brought its permitting system into compliance with EPA mandates.

In 2012, the U.S. Court of Appeals for the District of Columbia again found that the EPA was "unambiguously correct" in developing regulations to limit greenhouse gases from vehicles and smokestacks. The court also held that the EPA was entitled to use climate science as a basis for its regulations despite opponents' claims that the science was flawed or in dispute. Attorney General Abbott, undaunted, declared that the court had "failed to rein-in the unelected bureaucrats at the [EPA] who are holding our country's energy independence and fragile economy hostage to a radical environmental agenda."[37] Despite this defeat, Texas won a round when the Fifth Circuit Court of Appeals held that the EPA had overstepped its bounds in taking over the state's air permitting program. Fights between Texas and the EPA will continue, but the momentum and long-term leverage favors the feds.

Texas vs. the EPA: Hazardous Waste

Two of the longest running hazardous waste pollution disputes in Texas history concern the Asarco copper smelter in El Paso and the cement plants around Midlothian. In both cases, the TCEQ tenaciously protected the polluters until the EPA forced them to change course. The American Smelting and Refining Co. (later Asarco) opened a lead smelter in El Paso in

1887. The facility was sued by the city as early as 1970 in an attempt to limit pollution and its impact on nearby neighborhoods. The smelter shut down in 1999 amid a global copper glut and law suits charging Asarco with extensive pollution throughout the Southwest. Asarco hired the prominent Houston law firm of Baker Botts in 2002 to try to get the smelter reopened to improve their leverage during a struggle with Mexican billionaire Carlos Slim for control of the company. In 2005, Asarco filed for chapter 11 bankruptcy protection from as much as $25 billion in environmental and asbestos claims. Staggering toward liquidation or takeover, Asarco stepped up its appeal to the TCEQ to get its environmental permits renewed so that it could reopen the mothballed plant. Opponents argued that the plant had pumped 7,000 tons of pollution, of which 2,000 tons were lead, into the environment when it was in good shape and would certainly do worse after eight years of deterioration and rust. Asarco made $1.6 million in contributions to Texas elected officials between 2000 and 2008, and on February 13, 2008, the TCEQ voted to approve Asarco's permit to reopen the smelter.

Texas State Senator Eliot Shapleigh (D-El Paso) and a host of Texas environmental groups were outraged and called on the EPA to intervene. Over the course of the next year the EPA did exactly that. On February 3, 2009, the EPA told the TCEQ that Asarco did not qualify under federal law for renewal of the operating permit that had been granted in 2008. EPA said that because the El Paso smelter had been shut down for eight years, it considered the shut down to be permanent and a whole new emissions permit process would be required. EPA said further that if TCEQ did not revoke their recent approval, "EPA might be forced to formally object to the permit, order any work on the smelter stopped, and initiate enforcement action."[38] The same day the EPA announced its intention to intervene Asarco withdrew its petition to reopen the plant and said that instead it would tear it down. Plant demolition took place in 2013, though cleanup will continue into 2015. Clearly, both TCEQ and EPA see the trade-off between business interests and environmental interests, but it is just as clear that they see them very differently.

A similar contest between citizens, state regulators, industry, and the EPA has been raging for decades around three huge cement plants near Midlothian. The three plants, with their ten kilns, constitute the largest complex of cement plants in the nation. Each plant has a strip mine nearby for limestone which is the principal raw material for cement. The lime-stone and other materials are heated to 2,700 degrees Fahrenheit in kilns fed by coal, natural gas, shredded shingles and old tires, and hazardous waste materials. Given the noxious inputs, it should come as no surprise that cement plants are big polluters. All three are among the top 40 pollution sites in Texas, with particularly high levels of mercury, sulfur dioxide, and fine particulates. For decades, the TCEQ has held that there is no evidence that the plants and their effluents harm public health or the environment. Governor

Perry has declared that he is proud that Texas has "a regulatory system that protects our citizens and environment without strangling prosperity."[39]

To assure they get a fair hearing from the political authorities of Texas, the cement industry and its political action committees (PACs) have spread a lot of money around. Industry PACs have contributed more than $2 million to Texas politicians since 2000, while their lobby firms have been paid another $12.6 million. Governor Perry alone received $921,714 from cement industry PACs. U.S. Representative Joe Barton (R-Arlington), whose district includes Midlothian, has received $103,500 since 2000. Barton has frequently tried to protect the cement plants from additional EPA regulation, though not always successfully. Both industry spokesmen and their political allies argued that additional regulation would cost jobs and force cement production overseas. Nonetheless, in April 2009 the EPA proposed new rules for the nation's 100 cement plants, including those at Midlothian, setting the first limits on mercury and tighter limits on particulates. Though the rules cannot take effect until 2013, they are expected to cut mercury emissions by 81 to 93 percent over time. The relationship between Texas and the EPA has shifted to one in which the agency is more likely to push past Texas objections than to be dissuaded by them.[40]

Conclusion

Edna Ferber's *Giant* is one of premier literary depictions of Texas in transition from the farming and ranching, cotton and cattle pursuits of the late nineteenth and early twentieth centuries to the oil and urban business pursuits of the mid-twentieth century. Jordan "Bick" Benedict is deeply and blindly Texan, a third generation rancher, running the Benedict family's 2.5 million acre Reata ranch. During a business trip to Washington, after a whirlwind romance, Bick marries Leslie Lynnton of the beautiful northern Virginia hunt country. Returning to Texas by train with his new bride, Bick's pride in all things Texan was wounded by his new wife's initial reaction to the state. As Texas passed by out the train window, Leslie says, "It's sort of frightening, isn't it—like something that defies you to conquer it? So huge. Why, we've been riding in it for days. And ugly, too, isn't it! I thought it would be beautiful." At Bick's pained reaction, she says, "Oh, now, don't be sulky. I'm not talking about your ancestors or something, dearest."[41]

Generations of Texans worked hard to conquer the rough land and never took time to wonder or worry that it was not beautiful in the way of more temperate latitudes. In fact, they assaulted its assets, the soil, the range, the timber, and, ultimately, the minerals that lay beneath the surface. The first major discovery of oil in Texas came at Spindletop, near Beaumont on the upper Gulf Coast, in 1901. That discovery made Texas the center of the U.S. and global oil industry for almost seventy-five years as the original discoveries were supplemented by discoveries in the Permian Basin, the Panhandle, and the huge East Texas field discovered in 1930. After World War II, extensive natural gas discoveries broadened the energy industry in Texas. New techniques have pushed the oil industry out into the Gulf and fracking has released a 90-year supply of new natural gas from rocks thousands of feet below the surface. Texas still accounts for more than 30 percent of U.S. oil production and 29 percent of natural gas production annually. Texas claims 24 percent of U.S. oil reserves and 29 percent of gas reserves.

But along with the blessings of abundant natural resources have come the environmental challenges of extracting those resources from the ground and processing them into usable energy and products. Texas leads the nation in greenhouse gas emissions, both because Texans love their cars and trucks and because coal continues to play a big role in electricity production. Texas also leads the nation, by a large margin, in the production of hazardous wastes.

Texas officials have long argued that Texas refineries and chemical plants produce not just for Texas but for the nation. Texas refineries produce one-quarter of the nation's gasoline products. The argument is that the nation should be grateful that Texas is willing to produce these beneficial, even critical, products and to be exposed to the consequent pollution. The nation, speaking, or sometimes mumbling, through the Congress, the administration, and the EPA, agrees that it needs the products but wants them to be produced with less environmental impact. Texas has resisted, arguing that Texans will lose business, jobs, and income if pollution regulations are too strict, but the Congress, President Obama, and the EPA seem less and less willing to listen.

Notes

1 John Graves, *Self-Portrait, With Birds*, Dallas, TX: Chama Press, 1991.
2 Robert Calvert, Arnoldo De León, and Gregg Cantrell, *The History of Texas*, 4th edn, Wheeling, IL: Harlan Davidson, Inc., 2007, pp. 200–201.
3 T.R. Fehrenbach, *Lone Star: A History of Texas and the Texans*, New York: Macmillan, 1968, pp. 145–146.
4 PBS, "American Buffalo: Spirit of a Nation," Introduction, 1998.
5 David G. McComb, *Texas: A Modern History*, Austin, TX: University of Texas Press, 2010, pp. 84, 86.
6 Mary Lasswell, *John Henry Kirby: Prince of the Pines*, Austin, TX: The Encino Press, 1967.
7 Robert S. Maxwell, "LUMBER INDUSTRY, Handbook of Texas Online," www.tshaonline.org/handbook/online/articles/dr102, accessed July 26, 2011. Published by the Texas State Historical Association.
8 Bryan Burrough, *The Big Rich: The Rise and Fall of the Great Texas Oil Fortunes*, New York: Penguin Press, 2009, p. 11.
9 David F. Prindle, *Petroleum Politics and the Texas Railroad Commission*, Austin, TX: University of Texas Press, 1981, pp. 21–32.

10 See the U.S. Energy Information Administration's Texas State Energy Profile at http://tonto.eia.doe.gov/state/state_energy_profiles.cfm?sid=TX.

11 Charles Homan, "The Operator," *New Rupublic*, April 20, 2012.

12 Prindle, *Petroleum Politics and the Texas Railroad Commission*, pp. 56–69.

13 Floyd Norris, "Off the Charts: Two Directions for the Prices of Natural Gas and Oil," *New York Times*, February 26, 2011, B3.

14 Ben Casselman, "U.S. Gas Fields Go From Bust to Boom," *Wall Street Journal*, April 30, 2009.

15 Erica Grieder, *Big, Hot, Cheap, and Right*, New York: Public Affairs, 2013, pp. 20–21.

16 Pew Charitable Trusts, "The Clean Energy Economy," June 2009.

17 Kate Galbraith, "Has Electric Deregulation Helped or Hurt Texans?" *Texas Tribune*, July 12, 2010, pp. 2–5.

18 A Special Report by Cities Aggregation Power Project, Inc., "The History of Electric Deregulation in Texas: The Unfulfilled Promise of Utility Restructuring," 2009, see www.capptx.com/files/HistElectricDereg_TX.pdf.

19 See http://tonto.eia.doe.gov/energyexplained/index.cfm?page=electricity_in_the_united_states, and www.eia.doe.gov/cneaf/nuclear/page/at_a_glance/states/statestx.html.

20 American Gas Association (AGA), state profiles, http://aga.org.

21 U.S. Department of Energy, U.S. Energy Information Administration, Coal Reserves, www.eia.doe.gov/cneaf/coal/reserves/reserves.html.

22 Forrest Wilder, "Coal Star State," *Texas Observer*, November 13, 2009, pp. 8–14.

23 Asher Price, "Importing Low-Level Radioactive Waste to Texas OK'd," *Austin American-Statesman*, January 4, 2011. See also Ramit Plushnick-Masti, "Commission Lets 36 States Dump Nuke Waste in Texas," *Houston Chronicle*, January 4, 2011.

24 Kate Galbraith, "Cost of Texas Wind Transmission Lines Nears $7 Billion," *Texas Tribune*, August 24, 2011.

25 Elizabeth Souder and Dave Michaels, "Texas Lags as Nation Shifts to Green Policies," *Dallas Morning News*, June 1, 2009, A1, A8.

26 Forrest Wilder, "Agency of Destruction," *The Texas Observer*, May 28, 2010, pp. 6–12.

27 Anna M. Tinsley, "Perry Touts 'the Texas Way' as He Signs Three Energy Bills," *Fort Worth Star-Telegram*, July 15, 2011.

28 Elizabeth Souder and Dave Michaels, "Texas Lags as Nation Shifts to Green Policies," *Dallas Morning News*, June 1, 2009, A1, A8.

29 Randy Lee Loftis, "EPA, Texas Activists in Sync," *Dallas Morning News*, June 24, 2009, A1, A8.

30 Dave Michaels, "EPA Plan Targets Emissions," *Dallas Morning News*, December 8, 2009, A1, A14.

31 Gromer Jeffers, "Perry Jabs Gore on Climate," *Dallas Morning News*, December 17, 2009, B4.

32 James C. McKinley Jr., "In Texas, Resistance Over Stricter Smog Limits," *New York Times*, February 3, 2010, A19. See also Ana Campoy, "Smog Fight Clouds Houston Cleanup," *Wall Street Journal*, January 20, 2010, A3.

33 John M. Broder, "Greenhouse Gases Imperil Health, E.P.A. Announces," *New York Times*, December 12, 2009, A16.

34 James Drew, "Texas Sues EPA," *Dallas Morning News*, February 17, 2010, A1, A6.

35 Dave Michaels, "State Loses in Appeal to Halt Federal Emissions Regulation," *Dallas Morning News*, December 12, 2010, 6D.

36 James C. McKinley Jr., "Texas and EPA Clash Over Air Pollution," *New York Times*, June 11, 2010, A22.

37 Randy Lee Loftis, "EPA Climate Action Upheld," *Dallas Morning News*, June 27, 2012, A1, A2.

38   Randy Lee Loftis, "Company Gives Up on Smelter," *Dallas Morning News*, February 4, 2009, p. A4.

39   Randy Lee Loftis, "Creating an Air of Uncertainty," *Dallas Morning News*, January 19, 2009, A1, A16–17.

40   Randy Lee Loftis, "Public, Industry Clash on EPA Plan," *Dallas Morning News*, June 18, 2009, A1, A11.

41   Edna Ferber, *Giant*, Garden City, NY: Doubleday & Company, 1952, p. 106.

Part III

The Coming Reality

10 The Way Forward

It's a low-tax, low-service state—so shoot us. The only depressing part is that, unlike Mississippi, we can afford to do better. We just don't.

(Molly Ivins)

One of the striking episodes in twentieth-century Texas history occurred at John Connally's Floresville ranch in January 1988. Connally was an iconic Texan, born into rural poverty, he became a protégé of Lyndon Johnson as a young man, governor of Texas in 1963, and he was seriously wounded in the Kennedy assassination later that year. After six years as governor, Connally served as Secretary of the Navy and Secretary of the Treasury in the Nixon administration, switched to the Republican Party, and made an unsuccessful run for the presidency in 1980. By 1982, Connally was in partnership with Ben Barnes as—what else—a developer. Texas was booming and Connally declared that, "We're beginning an era of prosperity like America hasn't dreamed of, and Texas will be at the forefront of it."[1] But within a very few years the price of oil collapsed and the Texas property markets and the banks that funded them went down as well. Connally declared personal bankruptcy in 1987 and he and Nellie sat through five days of public humiliation as their worldly goods passed under the auctioneer's gavel.

John Connally's biography, *In History's Shadow*, was published soon after his death in June 1993. The very last page of that biography registers his warning, born of the booms and busts in his own Texas life, that "The real question for us in Texas, as in the nation, is whether or not we have the insight and the courage to restructure our government in time to meet the changing conditions that will touch each of our individual lives."[2] As we shall see below, we have had the insight for quite some time, but not yet the courage. In fact, as Connally's goods were being auctioned off, Texas was in the process of responding to the late 1980s economic crisis in the state by lightening the tax burden on the oil and gas industry and increasing it on consumers. This was business as usual in Texas.

More than two decades later, the state's fiscal problems remain unresolved. As population grew and demographic change continued apace, state revenues tightened and unaddressed problems in education, health care, transportation, and the environment festered. Ominously, Robert Calvert, Arnoldo De León, and Gregg Cantrell close the most recent edition of their prominent book, *The History of Texas*, by warning that "almost all the challenges facing Texans in the twenty-first century will hinge upon a rethinking of how they will pay for state and local government."[3] The reason that Texas seems paralyzed in the face of growing problems is that the state's leadership has painted itself and us into a fiscal corner over the past half century. First, we ask how that happened and then we look for ways out.

A Brief History of Tax Policy in Texas

The first Anglo settlers into Texas were lured by free land and tax exemptions. Texas pioneer Noah Smithwick described this lure in the very first paragraph of his famous memoir. Smithwick, then an eighteen-year-old Kentuckian, heard the Texas empresario Sterling C. Robertson praise the new country and urge immigration. Like his competitor, Stephen F. Austin, Robertson promised new immigrants "177 acres of farming land . . . and 4,428 acres of pasture land for stock; colonists to be exempted from taxation six years from the date of settlement, with the privilege of importing, duty free, everything they might desire for themselves and their families."[4] Texans were early trained to expect low, preferably no, taxes.

From independence in 1836 through the first half of the twentieth century, Texans supported a small government with a hodgepodge of minor taxes intended to nibble a little here and there but not to bite anyone too hard. The Texan attitude in the early days was famously expressed by an anonymous land commissioner from Nacogdoches who declared, "Come what may I am convinced that Texas must prosper. We pay no taxes, . . . get our land at cost, and perform no public duties of any kind."[5] This remains the Texan view: prosperity comes from individual effort unconstrained by public imposition upon one's time, choices, or income.

Texas was born in revolution, so existing political institutions and any funds that they might possess belonged to the enemy. Hence, the framers of the Constitution of 1836 authorized the provisional government to seek loans and issue promissory notes to fund an army and navy. Following the victory at San Jacinto and the elections of 1836, the provisional government passed a $1.25 million debt to President Sam Houston and the new Congress. Houston had an instinct for frugality and a republican's fear of an idle army, so he was happy to reduce the army and most other expenses of government. Nonetheless, with scant revenues, debt continued to grow.[6]

The Land and Property Tax Regime: 1836–1900

The first Congress passed a series of taxes on imports, businesses, and property, but members knew that with little real money in the Republic revenues would arrive in a trickle. The mainstays of the Republic's tax system were tariffs on imported goods ranging from 1 to 10 percent on staples such as bread and flour, 50 percent on luxuries such as silk, and 25 to 75 percent on wine and liquor. More than half of Texas revenue during the Republic came from import fees.[7] Minor taxes on businesses, professional licenses, land fees, and voting brought some revenue, but general taxes on land, livestock, and slaves were nearly uncollectable given the tenuous state of the economy. Hence, political authorities tried to keep the tax burden low and to be neighborly about collections.[8]

Texas remained in debt throughout the life of the Republic. President Sam Houston ran an extraordinarily frugal administration, but he was still reduced to asking the Texas Congress to issue a paper currency. The first issue of "star money," so-called for the star featured on the bills, circulated at par for a time but subsequent issues quickly depreciated. By the end of Houston's term, star money was trading at eight to one American dollar. Despite the fiscal stringency faced by the new government, Texas's second president, Mirabeau B. Lamar, had visions of empire. He formed a navy to patrol the Gulf and sent military expeditions against Mexico and its territories to the west including Santa Fe. Unable to secure loans abroad, Lamar and the Congress issued "redback" dollars, named for the color of currency's reverse side, which very quickly lost their value.[9] By the time Houston returned to office in 1842, the attempt to annex New Mexico had failed—Mexican armies had twice captured San Antonio, and the republic was $7 million in debt. Houston sought to calm relations with Mexico, gain admission to the American union, and restore financial stability. To show how serious he was about controlling costs, he ordered the navy to port, withheld further appropriations, and put it up for sale. Citizens of Galveston, the navy's home port, blocked the sale but the ships remained in port.

Despite Houston's frugality, revenues came in so slowly that by the end of his second term the Republic's debt was approaching $10 million.[10] The German immigrant Wilhelm Steinert observed in 1849, by which time Texas was a U.S. state and Houston was serving in the U.S. Senate, that, "Taxation remains poorly regulated. . . . Every man makes his own estimates of the profits of his business enterprise. Real estate values are set by a board of equalization. Only a few percent tax must be paid in general, . . . I spoke with some people who owned farms and farmhouses but were not made to pay taxes." Steinert did say that trade licenses for "merchants, inn-keepers, and tavern owners" were very expensive, but, in general, one sees a regime of light taxes lackadaisically collected.[11]

Accession to the union did not change the Texan attitude toward government and taxation, though it did provide what many saw as an outside, meaning non-Texan, source of revenue. When Texas entered the union in 1845, it retained title to 150 million acres of unclaimed lands within the state. Other American states, entering the union after a period of territorial status, entered with unclaimed lands retained by the federal government. Unfortunately, too much of anything, including land, drives down its price, so the present cash value of Texas's vast landholdings was limited. Land could be given away or disposed of at "fire sale" prices to attract immigrants or rail-roads, but it could not be sold for cash to support the government. Slaves, on the other hand, had a substantial and rising value. "After statehood," the historian Randolph Campbell writes, "the value of slaves constituted more than one-third of the state's total tax assessment during the 1850s."[12] The obvious incentive of the ruling class of shareholders was to limit the cost of government and, hence, its need for tax revenues.

Fortunately, Texas had tenuous claims to parts of New Mexico and Colorado and, though that land could not be sold either, it provided a valuable bargaining chip. In 1850, Texas renounced these broader claims, assuming its current boundaries, in exchange for $10 million from the federal treasury. The U.S. kept $5 million to settle the currency debts of the Republic of Texas and Texas used some of the rest to pay off noncurrency debts incurred for goods and services prior to statehood. The remainder was dedicated to public buildings, infrastructure, and education. Texas's path to temporary fiscal stability taught lessons good and bad. Fehrenbach wrote that:

> The net result of the boundary bill was that Texas during the 1850s was financed publicly almost entirely by federal money. . . . But as Rupert Richardson [a Texas historian of the 1940s] observed, "the system may have worked injury as well as benefit. The people learned to look to outside sources rather than to taxation as the means of supporting their government and were not prepared for the day when windfalls would cease."[13]

As the Civil War loomed, Texas was back in debt to the tune of $1 million and the war itself cost mightily in blood and treasure. Once Governor Sam Houston was pushed aside in favor of Lt. Gov. Edward Clark, Texas prepared for war. Governor Clark increased the ad valorem land and property tax from 12.5 cents to 16.5 cents and then to 25 cents, raised the poll tax from 50 cents to one dollar, and reinstituted professional taxes on doctors, lawyers, and dentists. Other taxes were levied on financial transactions and liquor.[14] These revenues, as well as control over the state's future, were lost with the Civil War.

Despite the economic conditions in the war-ravaged state, the Reconstruction administration of Republican Governor Edmund J. Davis pushed education and economic recovery programs that required unprecedented revenues. White conservatives, the ashes of defeat in their mouth, thought that the little wealth they had remaining was being expropriated to educate and otherwise advantage their former slaves. They protested vigorously, holding a "Tax Payers' Convention" in Austin in September 1871. Convention leaders charged that tax rates had risen from 15 cents per $100 of assessed value before the war to $2.175 in the Davis administration. Levies to pay off railroad bonds, license taxes, and poll taxes added to the post-war tax burden.[15] These charges by Davis's opponents have passed into Texas history as proof of his administration's profligacy. True or not, as soon as Texas statehood was restored and whites in their full numbers returned to the electorate, Democrats moved quickly to restore the antebellum fiscal order. That was, of course, a fiscal order of small government and low taxes in which tariffs provided the bulk of revenues because an abundance of cheap land limited revenues from land sales and property taxes. In 1874, Texas was selling prime land for $1.50 an acre.

Governor Oran M. Roberts, citing the slow sale of land and the need to raise state revenue, encouraged the legislature to lower prices. In 1879, the legislature revised land sale policy to allow lands set aside to support public schools to be sold for $1 an acre for up to four sections (a section is 640 acres or one square mile) and to sell all other unclaimed land for 50 cents an acre with no limit on the amount to be purchased. These prices drove down all land prices in Texas, bankrupting railroads and land-holding companies and creating widespread public concern. In 1883, a state land board was empowered to reclassify,

> The remaining public domain into agricultural, timber, and pastoral acres. The first two categories sold for $3, the pastureland for $2. Payments periods lasted from ten to forty years, and interest rates ranged from five to ten percent. Moreover, until 1899 a married man could claim a 160-acre homestead with proof of three-year residence; a single man could obtain half that amount.[16]

Throughout the nineteenth century, Texas had so much land that its value stayed low and it produced little revenue from land sales or property taxes.

The Specialty Sales and Petroleum Tax Regime: 1900–1960

As the populist and progressive eras unfolded nationally and in Texas during the last two decades of the nineteenth century and the first two decades of the twentieth century, Texas elites generally resisted. The federal government and many states sought to deal with urbanization and industrialization by expanding government services and funding them with new revenues, including inheritance, income, and sales taxes. New York adopted an inheritance tax in 1885 and President Theodore Roosevelt, a former governor of New York, campaigned for a federal inheritance tax for a decade before it became law in 1916. Wisconsin adopted a personal income tax in 1911 and President Woodrow Wilson campaigned for passage and adoption of the 16th Amendment in 1913 permitting a federal income tax. Other states were slow in adopting the income tax until the Great Depression hit, reducing property values and property tax revenues, and then sixteen states adopted an income tax between 1931 and 1937. Mississippi was first to adopt a general sales tax in 1932 and by 1937 half the states had a general sales tax.[17]

Texas monitored these trends, discussed their relevance to the state, and a few people even advocated for one or another of them, but generally Texas sniffed tyranny on the winds of change. Nonetheless, Texas did begin to edge away from property taxes toward a series of modest new business and consumer taxes. As early as 1905, Governor S.W.T. Lanham successfully urged the legislature to approve a severance tax of 1 cent on each barrel of oil, a franchise tax on capital investment, and gross receipts taxes on railroads and insurance companies. In 1907, Governor Thomas M. Campbell proposed both an income tax and an inheritance tax. Campbell lost the fight for the income tax, but won a modest inheritance tax and higher licensing fees for liquor dealers. The Lanham–Campbell reforms were an important reorganization of the Texas tax structure. The arrival of the automobile in numbers in the second decade of the twentieth century brought new taxes on vehicles, drivers, and fuels. Texas governors and legislatures from the 1920s through the 1950s tinkered with but did not fundamentally reform a diffuse hodgepodge of small, narrow, targeted taxes and levies on natural resources, capital investment, professional licenses, auto license fees, gas taxes, and other specialty sales taxes.

Under the pressure of the Great Depression, some Texas leaders proposed tax reform, but their overtures were usually rejected. Governor Ross Sterling got little support when he proposed a state income tax bill in 1931. Governor Miriam "Ma" Ferguson proposed a sales tax as well as corporate and personal income taxes in 1933 but the legislature refused them all. They approved a severance tax increase to 2 cents on each barrel of oil and a small tax on pari-mutuel betting on horse races. Governor James V. Allred (1935–1939) was a supporter of FDR and the New Deal and sought to follow in its policy footsteps, but the Texas Legislature could only rarely be persuaded to go along. In a special session in 1935, Allred won an increase in taxes on natural resources and a modest new tax on chain stores. The legislature also passed the Texas Liquor Control Act and set taxes and fees on package store sales.[18] Jimmy Allred, worried that good Texans might be led astray by betting on horse races, had pari-mutuel betting repealed in a 1937 special session.

Wilbert Lee "Pappy" O'Daniel, one of the great characters in Texas political history, was elected governor in 1938 and 1940. He urged the 1939 and 1941 regular sessions of the Texas Legislature to pass a "transactions tax" of 1.6 percent on all manufacturing, wholesale, and retail transactions, except the first sale of agricultural products, to replace the ad valorem property tax. Legislators recognized the transactions tax as a sales tax and declined to go along. Instead, the 1941 regular session of the Texas Legislature passed an Omnibus Tax Bill that "placed new taxes on motor vehicle sales, stock transfers, cosmetics, and radios. It increased existing levies on oil, natural gas, utilities, insurance company premiums, and a few other items."[19] While Texas was struggling to pass narrowly targeted levies on cosmetics and radios, the rest of the nation and most of the South had adopted a new tax regime. They had supplemented the traditional property tax with state income and sales taxes. As Numan V. Bartley explained, "by 1945 all the southern states but Florida and Texas had enacted personal and corporate income taxes, and six states had adopted general sales taxes as well."[20] The southern states were poor, so they tended to keep their tax rates low even when measured as a proportion of personal income, but their systems had a balance and flexibility that they had not enjoyed before.

Population growth in the 1940s and a post-war decline in oil prices and oil revenues soon exposed the limits of Texas's revenue system. Governor Allan Shivers, a wealthy landowner, businessman, and staunch fiscal and social conservative, called a special session of the legislature in 1950 to resolve a $26 million budget deficit. Some in the legislature called for increasing taxes on business or on natural resources, but the business lobby convinced Shivers to again back increases in a number of targeted consumer taxes.[21] While this resolved the short-term budget crisis it did nothing to put Texas tax and revenue policy on a sounder footing. By 1951, all of the southern governments but Kentucky, Texas, and Virginia had adopted a general sales tax. Only Texas eschewed both the state income tax and a general sales tax. Texas was able to maintain its traditional tax system because a rise in the price of oil and the Eisenhower administration's decision to honor Texas claims to oil-rich "tidelands" in the Gulf buoyed revenues. By the mid-1950s, severance taxes and related fees accounted for one-third of state tax revenues in Texas.[22]

By the end of the decade, increased oil production in the Middle East had reduced prices and Texas oil wells were allowed to produce only nine days a month to avoid a further glut and even lower prices. With severance tax revenues down, the Texas Legislature met in January 1959 facing a $90 million dollar projected shortfall in its general revenue budget. Talk of a general sales tax was rampant but Governor Price Daniel, a moderate who had replaced the conservative Shivers in 1957, was opposed. It took three special sessions to craft a true Texas solution. Governor Daniel pushed through a "beneficiary tax" on out-of-state users of Texas natural gas, as well as increases in selective sales taxes and in fees and licenses on utilities and corporations. Unfortunately, the Supreme Court quickly struck down the beneficiary tax because it was not levied against in-state and out-of-state users—but that, after all, had been the whole point. Nonetheless, once the Supreme Court acted, the whole issue of Texas's tax structure was teed-up for the 1961 regular session of the Texas Legislature.

The General Sales Tax Regime: 1960 to Present

By 1961 the business lobby realized that tinkering with the traditional tax system was no longer an option and they were ready for change, as long as it was the right change. Teacher salaries and other government costs were rising, so a sizable tax increase seemed necessary. Governor Daniel opposed a general sales tax as unduly regressive and hard on the common people, but he did not have an attractive solution of his own. Instead, he proposed "a continuation of omnibus tax bills, including so-called sin taxes on tobacco and alcohol, and a larger share of taxes on business interests."[23] He was opposed by the Texas Manufacturing Association and the powerful oil and gas lobby, as well as by members, conservative and moderate, who saw the sales tax as the broadest path to badly needed new revenues. In his first term in the House, future Speaker Ben Barnes (1965–1969) explained that "as a conservative he preferred" the sales tax "over a corporate tax or state income tax as a way to raise much needed funds for Texas."[24] Rayford Price, another future Speaker (1972–1973), "saw the sales tax as a practical necessity. 'Oil had carried the state for many years, but the economy was changing, and we needed to draw from a new tax base. . . . The sales tax, I think, was the correct place to go at that time.'"[25] Though it took three contentious special sessions, the legislature adopted a general sales tax of 2 percent, excluding food, prescription drugs, and a few other necessities. With no viable alternative source of revenue on the horizon, Governor Daniel allowed the sales tax to go into effect without his signature. The general sales tax became the workhorse of the Texas tax system.

Revenues from the new sales tax and rising prices for oil and natural gas, as well as a brief willingness to consider additional revenues, especially for public schools and colleges and universities, made governing seem easier in the 1960s and 1970s. John Connally served three terms as governor from 1963 to 1969. In the 1963 legislative session, Connally sought almost $33 million in new revenue for a higher education coordinating board, university libraries and research, vocational education, and teacher salaries. In Connally's final term, he asked the legislature to authorize $125 million for teacher pay raises and he recommended that it be funded by a 1 percent increase in the general sales tax and that cities be allowed to impose a 1 percent addition to the state sales tax. Teachers got a pay rise and, as Table 10.1

Table 10.1 Texas General Sales Tax Rates

	State%	*Municipal%*
1961–1967	2	
1968	3	1
1969–1970	3.25	
1971–1983	4	
1984–1985	4.125	
1986	5.25	
1987–1989	6	
1990–present	6.25	
1992		2

Source: The Handbook of Texas Online, "Sales Tax," www.tshaonline.org/handbook/online/articles/mpszr.

shows, the sales tax was increased to 3 percent and the cities got the option of adding a local sales tax which most did quickly.[26]

When Connally declined to run for a fourth term in 1968, Lieutenant Governor Preston Smith moved up to governor and Ben Barnes, Speaker of the Texas House and the protégé of both LBJ and Connally, moved up to lieutenant governor. Their desire to keep the momentum of the Connally years going brought general sales tax increases to 3.25 percent in 1969 and 4 percent in 1971. Not surprisingly, Texans soon became wary that LBJ, Connally, and Barnes had led them down the path to big government, high taxes, and liberal social experimentation.

When Governor Preston Smith, Barnes, and Speaker Gus Mutcher were all caught up in an influence-peddling scandal, Texas voters went in search of honest leadership. The 1972 governor's election featured the liberal Democrat Sissy Farenthold and the conservative Democrat Dolph Briscoe. Briscoe, a wealthy cattle rancher from Uvalde and one of the largest landowners in the state, won on a platform of honesty, transparency, and no new taxes. Meanwhile, Florida's Governor Reuben Askew "pushed through Florida's legislature a corporate income tax. With that, only Texas [among the southern states] assessed no income taxes at all."[27]

In launching his 1972 campaign, Briscoe declared that "there was no need for new taxes and that the state could operate within the income generated by the existing tax structure." Briscoe's analysis of the state's fiscal situation was both correct and shortsighted. He wrote that, "it was obvious in 1972 that the state's energy-based economy would continue to increase our tax revenue for years to come. I realized that state services would have to expand to meet the challenge of a larger population, but the increase in revenue from existing taxes would be sufficient to do the job well."[28] Briscoe was right, Texas oil and gas revenues went on a steep upward climb during the 1970s, but he was shortsighted because it could not and it did not last. While the sales tax, cor-porate licenses and fees, the gas tax, and most other taxes and fees produce more revenue in a strong economy and less in a weak economy, few large revenue sources are as volatile as post-1970 oil and natural gas taxes.

Figure 10.1 shows both the real and the inflation-adjusted price of oil from 1950 through the present. The difference between the two is not dif-ficult to understand. The real price of a barrel of oil in 1950, $2.77, is its actual cost that year. The 2010 inflation-adjusted price of that 1950 barrel of oil, $26.80, is what it would cost in today's depreciated currency to buy that same barrel of oil. Adjusting for inflation isolates the real changes in the relative price of oil over time. Note four things in particular about Figure 10.1. First, note that the real price of a barrel of oil from 1950 to 1970 was so stable, barely rising from $2.77 to $3.39, that the inflation-adjusted price steadily fell. Second, note the extraordinary rise in the real price of oil from $3.39 in 1970 to $37.42 in 1980. In inflation-adjusted terms, the rise is a fivefold increase from $20.33 to $105.84. Third, in 1981 the price of oil began a slow fall that picked up speed in the mid-1980s. Finally, oil prices bounced around in the 1990s until they took off again about 2005 and they remain high today. The rollercoaster ride, up in the 1970s and down hard in the 1980s, led to broad changes resulting in a more diverse and stable Texas economy. Unfortunately, it also led to changes in the Texas tax and revenue system that left it less efficient and more brittle.

Dolph Briscoe had the good fortune to serve as governor of Texas from 1973 to 1979. Political scientists Anthony Champagne and Edward Harpham explain that,

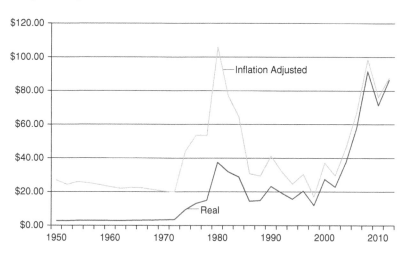

Figure 10.1 Real and Inflation Adjusted Price of Oil, 1950–Present.

Source: InflationData.com, Historical Crude Oil Prices, http://www.inflationdata.com/inflation/inflation_rate/historical_oil_prices_table.asp

As the value of oil produced in Texas rose from $4.1 billion in 1970 to $21.3 billion in 1980 and the value of natural gas rose from $3 billion in 1970 to $10.7 billion in 1980, the state budget rose from $3 billion in 1970 to $10.2 billion in 1980. In constant dollars, this translates into a real increase of 65%, an astounding number in light of Texas's history of fiscal austerity.

Energy taxes rose from 13 percent of total tax collections in 1973 to one-quarter by the end of the decade.[29] Briscoe reported that throughout his three terms as governor, "Increased revenue made it possible for us to enhance essential services, especially our highway system, and to raise the average teacher's salary more than 50 percent without increasing the state tax burden."[30] Former Lieutenant Governor William Hobby (1973–1991), the longest serving lieutenant governor in Texas history by far, offered a different take on the state of the state as Governor Briscoe gave way to Governor William Clements, the first Republican governor in Texas in more than a century. Hobby wrote that at the start of Clements's first term in 1979, "Texas ranked forty-fifth among the states in state and local tax collections and lowest among the top industrial states. . . . There were critical unmet needs in mental health, education, prisons, and the state police. The state of Texas is as big a tax break as there is."[31] But just as federal monies had lulled Texans of the 1850s into thinking they could fund state government without local taxes, the steady increase of oil and gas revenues convinced Texans in the 1970s, including the governor, that existing taxes were sufficient.

Energy prices and the revenues they generated dipped modestly in the early 1980s. Comptroller Bob Bullock began warning in 1982 that future severance tax revenues were uncertain. Nonetheless, Governor Mark White pushed a $5.5 billion tax bill through a special session of the legislature in 1984 to fulfill campaign promises of continued rises in teacher pay, more equitable school funding, and transportation improvements. This was the first tax increase in Texas in thirteen years and Governor White and scores of legislators declared that they saw no further need for tax increases. Throughout 1985, as the price of oil continued a slow downward slide, Bullock talked about the looming prospect of wholesale tax reform in Texas. Late in the year, he said, "We need new revenue. Yes, I'm talking about an income tax. It is political death to everyone who mentions it, but you have to think about it."[32] As oil price declines steepened and Texas property and financial markets began to totter, Governor White called a special session of the legislature in August 1986. White was in a tough re-election battle, but he had no choice but to call the legislature to Austin because Bullock was projecting a deficit of $2.3 billion in the current fiscal year. State leaders discussed every way imaginable to increase state revenues, including a lottery, horse racing, sin taxes, program cuts and wage and hiring freezes for state workers, and increases to the sales tax and the franchise tax. Talk of an income tax rose above a whisper. In the end, leaders settled on budget cuts totaling nearly $600 million and an increase in the general sales tax from 4.125 percent to 5.25 percent. Not surprisingly, Mark White was beaten for re-election by Bill Clements, the man he had defeated for re-election four years earlier.

Governor Clements took office just as the 1987 regular session of the legislature convened facing more deficits. Clements proposed a budget totaling $36.9 billion and toured the state calling for fiscal stringency. The Texas House called for $39.4 billion in spending and the Senate called for $40 billion. In the middle of the legislative session, state district judge Harley Clark declared the Texas school funding system unconstitutional because it was too stingy toward poor districts. When Clements agreed to consider broadening the sales tax and other revenue increases, Republican Party state chair George Strake was livid. In a meeting with the governor, Strake declared:

> We have the legislature about to break, and you're giving in, right here at the end. I know they're threatening to open the prisons and close the schools and quit building roads, but this is when you get something done. You have all the Republicans in the legislature hanging on at the end of the limb and you're sawing it off for them.[33]

Despite the partisan pressure to hold the line for more budget cuts, Clements compromised with the Democratic majorities in the legislature, though a special session was required to seal the deal. In late July, Clements signed a $38.3 billion budget and a bundle of related tax increases totaling $5.7 billion. The sales tax was increased to 6 percent and broadened to include a range of services not previously covered and increases were made to the gas taxes, tobacco taxes, and corporate franchise fees.[34] Gib Lewis, Democrat of Fort Worth and speaker during the 1987 regular and special sessions, lauded Clements for his willingness to compromise, saying, "It takes a lot of courage to make a hard decision. . . . But there comes a time and place to keep government services functioning, that you have to bite the bullet."[35]

The compromise struck by Clements and Democrats to help weather the fiscal storms of the late 1980s was courageous, but not courageous enough. Bullock continued to believe that only an income tax would allow state revenues to grow with the economy. Shortly after being elected lieutenant governor in 1990, Bullock again declared for an income tax and tried, unsuccessfully, to push it through the 1991 regular session of the legislature. The blow-back was sufficiently intense that he had to reverse field completely to insure his own political survival. Bullock proposed a constitutional amendment to prohibit an income tax unless votes approved it by referendum. As a result, the Texas Constitution now prohibits an income tax unless supported by a majority of each house of the legislature and approved by statewide vote. Moreover, two-thirds of the revenues from an income tax would have to go to property tax relief and the remaining one-third to education.

Governor George W. Bush unsuccessfully sought broad reform of the Texas tax system. Bush was first elected in 1994 and then overwhelmingly re-elected in 1998. In Bush's first term, he proposed reductions in property taxes and elimination of the franchise tax, to be funded by a 0.5 cent increase in the sales tax and a European style value-added tax. The 1997 legislature scrapped Bush's plan and produced one of their own which contained little tax relief and no new revenue. In 1999, with a presidential campaign in immediate prospect, Governor Bush pushed a smaller property tax cut and a somewhat larger cut in corporate franchise fees through the legislature. The result, of course, was that when the economy again turned down, in 2003 and more devastatingly in 2011, revenue shortfalls required ever deeper budget cuts. As we shall see, in the absence of an income tax, the revenue gap left by the decline in severance tax receipts has been closed by relentless budget cutting.

The Changing Sources of Texas Revenues

The main sources of Texas state government revenues have changed in substantial and worrisome ways. First, by the early 1950s, specialized sales taxes were already the main source of state revenues, providing 35 percent of total revenues, followed by severance taxes at 25 percent, federal transfers at 24 percent, and licenses and fees at 10 to 15 percent. Second, sales tax revenues (the top line) jumped sharply from 35 to 45 percent of total revenues with passage of the general sales tax in 1961 and rose steadily over the next three decades reflecting increases to the sales tax rate. Third, federal transfer payments accounted for a fairly steady 25 to 30 percent of total revenues until the early 1990s, 35 to 40 percent for the next decade, and 45 to 50 percent since 2004. Fourth, licenses and fees declined to a steady 8 to 12 percent of total revenues. Finally, severance tax revenues fell from 25 percent to single digits by the early 1970s, rebounded to 20 percent of total revenues by the early 1980s, before going into a steady decline broken only recently.

Figure 10.2 shows that the mid-1980s, with the collapse in the price of oil and the subsequent declines in the state's property values and banking sector, changed the sources of Texas revenues. Between 1981 and 1990, sales tax income jumped from 45 percent to 56 while revenues from the severance tax fell from 20 percent to 5 percent. Over the space of a decade, the 1980s, 15 percent of total tax revenues were shifted from the oil and gas industry to consumers. This was done in two ways, one far more visible

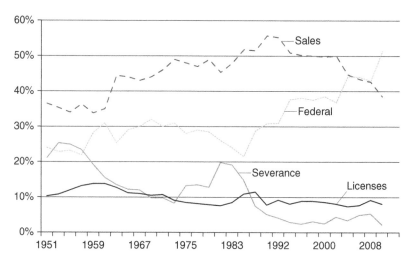

Figure 10.2 Total Texas Revenues by Source, 1950–Present

Source: *The Book of the States*, The Council of State Governments, Lexington, KY, vol. 45, 2013, "State Government Tax Revenue, By Selected Types of Tax," pp. 390–391, 397–398. See similar tables in previous editions back to 1942.

than the other. First, a quick series of increases in the general sales tax were enacted, from 4.125 percent in 1984 to 6.25 percent by 1990, with an additional 2 percent permitted to local governments. From 1990 through the early 2000s, general and selective sales taxes provided more than half of Texas state government revenues. Federal revenues rose steadily from a third toward 40 percent. Second, and much less remarked upon, is the precipitous fall in the share of Texas revenues provided by severance taxes on oil, natural gas, and other natural resources. To the extent that this decline is remarked upon, it is attributed to the late 1980s collapse in oil prices, but that is only half the story.

To get a better picture of the Texas tax system, it will be helpful to set aside federal transfer payments. This will allow us to focus directly on how Texas has chosen to raise tax revenues and how those revenue streams have changed over time. Figure 10.3 presents Texas tax revenues from 1950 to the present. In the early 1950s, Texas's selective sales taxes on automobiles, fuels, alcohol, tobacco, and other designated products produced almost half the state's tax revenues. Once the general sales tax was passed in 1961, the proportion of Texas revenues from the general and specialized sales taxes rose to 60 percent, increases in the Connally years pushed it to 70 percent, and further increases in the late 1980s and early 1990s pushed it to 80 percent of state tax revenues. Licenses and fees provided as much as 20 percent of state tax revenues around 1960, declining to 10 percent by the

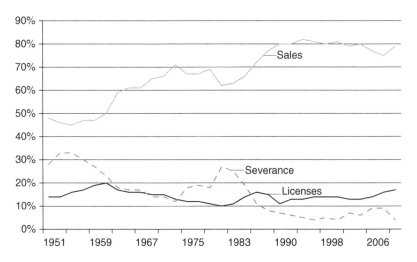

Figure 10.3 Texas Tax Revenues by Source, 1950–Present

Source: *The Book of the States*, The Council of State Governments, Lexington, KY, vol. 45, 2013, "State Government Tax Revenue, By Selected Types of Tax," pp. 390–391. See similar tables in previous editions back to 1942.

1980s and remaining in a tight 10 to 15 percent band thereafter. Severance tax revenues provided a third of state tax revenues in the 1950s and a quarter as late as the early 1980s.

But by the early 1990s severance tax revenues accounted for less than 10 percent of tax revenues and averaging around 5 percent for the last two decades. Figure 10.3, highlighting just Texas raised revenues, shows how dependent the state is on the sales tax and, glancing back at Figure 10.2, federal transfer payments. Licenses, fees, and severance taxes are important, but they don't float the boat.

Texas was the first state to levy a severance tax on oil in 1905, just four years after the Spindletop discovery. The initial tax was 1 percent of market value (the adjusted commodity price paid at the wellhead) and has been increased eight times, most recently in 1951 when it was set at 4.6 percent. The severance tax on natural gas was established in 1931 at 2 percent of market value and after several changes it has been at 7.5 percent since 1969. No other major taxes in Texas have remained unchanged for so long. Three-quarters of severance tax revenues from oil go into the state general fund and the remaining one-quarter goes to support public education. Most of the severance tax revenues from natural gas go into the state's "rainy day" fund.

What accounts for the volatility and, more importantly, the sharp decline in severance tax revenues since 1950? Texas severance tax revenues were just about $100 million in 1951. They grew steadily, but not spectacularly, reaching $200 million in 1965, before tripling to $667 million in 1975. In Figure 10.4 we show total severance tax revenues from 1951 through 1975 and then we break out oil and natural gas severance taxes. In the late 1970s, both oil and gas severance taxes rose from $500 million to more than a billion before falling back to $500 million by the mid-1980s. Oil revenues slightly outpaced gas revenues until 1985, from 1986 to 2010 gas jumped ahead, and since 2010 oil has been back in the lead. Gas revenues held up when oil revenues began to slide in the mid-1980s, jumping dramatically after 2001 as the impact of the Barnett Shale discoveries began to be felt. Unlike oil, which is an international market, on which Texas supplies have little impact, natural gas is a North American market where large increases in supply can drive down prices. The recovery of severance tax revenues from oil in the mid-2000s is a function both of sharp increases in the international price of oil and of the application of fracking techniques to oil shale formations, especially in South Texas. Increases in natural gas supplies and the deep recession of 2008 and 2009 drove down gas prices but eroded oil prices relatively little. However, and this is critical, what looks in Figure 10.4 like big increases in severance revenues in the mid-2000s hardly moves the needle in Figure 10.2's description of total revenues. Changes in Texas public policy will help explain why.

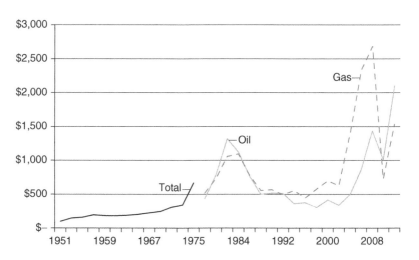

Figure 10.4 Texas Severance Tax Revenues, 1950–Present (millions)

Source: Data for 1951 through 1975 is from *The Book of the States*, The Council of State Governments, Lexington, KY, vol. 42, 2010, "State Government Tax Revenue, By Selected Types of Tax," pp. 426–427. See similar tables in previous editions back to 1942. The data from 1978 to the present, which breaks out severance taxes for oil and natural gas are from the Texas Comptroller at http://www.window.state.tx.us/taxbud/revenue_hist.html

Naturally, as the price of oil collapsed, slowly in the early 1980s and then much more rapidly in 1986 and 1987, severance tax revenues declined. The severance tax is a wellhead tax on the value of oil and gas being extracted from the ground and as the value of the product goes down so do tax revenues. But the dramatic drop in severance tax revenues had political as well as economic causes. In the late 1980s, Texas political authorities decided that the recovery of the oil and gas industry would be aided by lifting or reducing taxes on some producers. The Texas Railroad Commission, which oversees oil and gas production in the state, reports on its website that, "The reduction or elimination of state severance taxes provides an economic incentive to operators to undertake activities that produce oil and gas resources that might otherwise remain unrecovered. Texas recognized back in the late 1980s that incentives to increase the state's oil and gas production were extremely valuable."[36] Tax relief undoubtedly helped the oil and gas industry recover in the 1990s, but in the last decade the price of oil has been strong, sometimes over $100 a barrel, and the natural gas industry has been so productive, discovering new fields such as the Barnett Shale, that prices have been driven down; still the reductions and exemptions remain in place.

Critically, the reduction in severance tax revenues was partly a reflection of production and price declines, but also a reflection of changes in Texas tax policy. Just as Texas was rapidly increasing its general sales tax, it was simultaneously, but much more quietly, reducing its severance taxes. In 1989, the legislature passed the Enhanced Oil Recovery (EOR) Act which cut the severance tax rate of 4.6 percent in half for eligible wells for up to ten years. EOR wells use the injection of water or chemicals to enhance production or extend the life of the well. The program was extended in 1997 and remains in effect today. In 1993, the legislature passed the Inactive Well Program declaring that any oil or gas well not active for more than one month in the past three years would get a ten-year exemption from severance taxes if brought back online. In 1997, the period of inactivity was reduced to two years and the program has been extended and remains in effect. Most importantly, in 1989, the legislature passed the High-Cost Gas Well program. Gas production was languishing and it was thought that deeper (more than 15,000 feet) and more difficult (horizontal) drilling would be required to increase production. High-cost wells were made exempt from the severance tax until 2001, but subsequent revisions have produced a sliding scale of taxation and extended the exemptions indefinitely. Everyone realizes that techniques like deep and horizontal drilling that were thought exotic in the late 1980s and early 1990s are common today, but the exemptions remain in place and at a high cost to taxpayers. Exemptions have also been extended to oil and gas wells defined as marginal or low producing.

A study by the Texas Legislature's Legislative Budget Board (LBB), author unknown and, in fact, actively suppressed, tells a fascinating story.

In preparation for the 2011 legislative session, a study entitled "Overview of Natural Gas Tax Structures" was conducted by the LBB for the information of members. The study was not intended for public release, but was, in fact, posted to the internet by an apparently disgruntled member. Its unchallenged findings are incendiary. While this study applies just to natural gas severance taxes, one can reasonably assume that the oil lobby has been at work too. The take-away line from the study is striking: "Natural gas production in the state is taxed at 7.5 percent of market value; however, deductions, exemptions, and rate reductions have reduced many producers' tax liabilities to zero and reduced the overall effective rate to between 1.1 and 1.9 percent in recent years." The LBB study also reports that the value of high-cost gas reductions averaged $1.23 billion from 2004 through 2009, for a total of $7.4 billion. Over the same period, natural gas severance tax payments have averaged $1.9 billion, for a total of $11.4 billion. In 2009 alone, the last year covered by the study, 55 percent of all gas produced in Texas was designated high-cost gas and the effective tax rate on that gas was 1.5 percent. In 2009, natural gas severance taxes totaled $1.4 billion and exemptions and deductions cost the state $1.2 billion.[37] Every dollar that does not come in through severance taxes has to came in through sales taxes or be accounted for by deeper budget cuts.

Clearly, Texas has been moving for two decades toward reducing and perhaps eliminating the severance tax without the kind of public discussion that one would expect. Several reasons for the silence readily occur. First, the oil and gas industry is very well represented in Austin and it has always been effective in protecting its interests. Second, the public would be aroused if it were obvious that the tax burden was further being shifted from this wealthy industry to consumers. But third, the public demise of the severance tax might open a broad discussion of the efficiency of the state's tax structure. Let's have that discussion now.

Reform of the Texas Tax Regime

Texas political authorities have painted themselves into a fiscal corner. Over the course of the twentieth century, most states, even most southern states, supplemented their traditional dependence on property taxes, first with sales taxes, and then eventually with corporate and individual income taxes. Even with these new revenue sources, southern states kept their tax revenues below the national average of all fifty states, but they enjoyed the flexibility and the stability provided by the "three-legged stool" of property, sales, and income taxes. Drawing on all three sources of revenue means that each can be low and still produce a moderate but flexible and sufficient amount of revenue.

Figure 10.5 presents Texas tax collections compared to average tax collections in fourteen southern states and the U.S. In Figure 10.5, U.S.

average tax collection for the fifty states is fixed at 100 percent, meaning half the states pay higher taxes and half pay lower, and the southern and Texas tax collections are presented as percentages of the U.S. average. For example, in 1951 the U.S. per capita state tax collection was $59.59, while the southern average was $55.69 (93 percent of the U.S. average) and the Texas per capita tax collection was $45.68 (77 percent of the U.S. average). The comparisons for 1961 and 1971 are very similar; the southern rate of state tax collection is about 90 percent of the national average while the Texas rate is 75 to 80 percent. In 1981, at the height of the oil boom, Texas edged ahead of the rest of the South, collecting $574.48 (87 percent of the U.S. average) compared to the southern average of $571.50 (86 percent of the national average). The late 1980s collapse of the international price of oil, followed by Texas property and financial markets, forced changes to taxes and revenues. Figure 10.5 shows clearly that Texas per capita tax

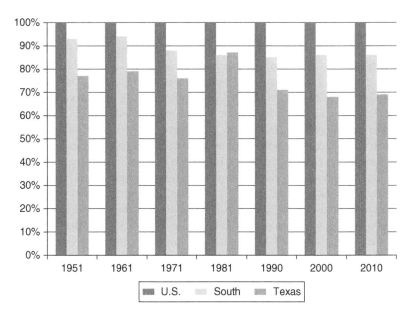

Figure 10.5 Texas Tax Collections Per Capita Compared to the U.S. and the South*

Source: *The Book of the States*, The Council of State Governments, Lexington, KY, 1951 from "State Tax Collections, by State," column labeled "1951 amount Per Capita," vol. 9, p. 212; similar table and column for 1961, at vol. 14, p. 237; 1971 from "Summary of State Tax Revenue," column labeled "Per Capita 1971, vol. 19, p. 238, 1981 from similar table and column, vol. 24, p. 409; 1990 from similar table and column, vol. 29, p. 411, 2000 from vol. 34, p. 300; 2010, "State Government Tax Revenue, vol. 44, pp. 432–433.

*Southern states are the ten confederate states other than Texas and Kentucky, Missouri, West Virginia, and Oklahoma Territory. Hence, alphabetically, Alabama, Arkansas, Florida, Georgia, Kentucky, Louisiana, Mississippi, Missouri, North Carolina, Oklahoma, South Carolina, Tennessee, Virginia, and West Virginia.

collections fell in relation to both the national and the southern averages in 1990 and thereafter. Prior to 1980, Texas tax collections averaged 77 percent of average U.S. state tax collections, while after 1990 it has averaged just 70 percent. Prior to 1980, the southern tax collection average was 92 percent of the U.S. average, while after 1990 it was 88 percent. Texas's fiscal options lie between steady as she goes, taxing and spending about 70 percent what other states do, and moving toward the average spent by the southern states.

Before we begin talking about new sources of revenue, let's really nail down the fact that Texas is a low tax state. This will require no great effort. In 1977, the Tax Foundation, a well-respected but clearly anti-tax think tank, began publishing state rankings on what they and others call "tax effort." Tax effort is generally defined as the percent of per capita personal income taken in state and local taxes. The Tax Foundation reports that from 1977 through 2010, Texas had a state and local tax burden averaging 7.9 percent, 45th among the fifty states. Only five states had a lower state and local tax burden. The Tax Foundation also presents data on per capita personal income and on the dollar amount of taxes paid per capita. While Texas has among the lowest state and local tax rates in the nation, Texas per capita income has averaged 25th in the nation since 1977, so Texans pay more in state and local taxes than the low rate might initially suggest. From 1977 through 2010, Texans ranked 25th in per capita income, 38th in amount of taxes paid, and 45th in state and local tax rate. As we shall see below, the space between 25th and 45th provides room to think about how additional revenues might be used to improve education, health care, transportation, and much else in Texas. Increasing taxing and spending to the southern average would still mean that half the southern states and nearly four-fifths of the states in the nation had higher taxes.

Texas entered the 2011 legislative session with one of the lowest tax burdens in the nation and a budget deficit of $15 billion from current spending levels and $27 billion accounting for population growth and inflation. Governor Perry led the large Republican majorities in both chambers of the legislature in cutting billions from public schools, higher education, health care, transportation, and much more. Legislators faced a less challenging environment in 2013, but even then they were unable to restore all the cuts made in 2011. Given the ongoing budget difficulties, Texans must eventually ask what additional revenues might be available. As that discussion begins, it is important to note that Texas has a regressive tax system, meaning that it bears more heavily on the poor than on the wealthy. The Austin-based Center for Public Policy Priorities (CPPP), drawing on data from the Comptroller's Office, reported that the bottom fifth of income earners in 2011 paid 14.6 percent of their income in state and local taxes while the top fifth paid just 3.6 percent.[38]

Texas has relatively high property taxes and sales taxes, but no corporate or personal income tax. The Tax Foundation reports that in 2010 Texas had the fourth highest property taxes as a percent of home value in the nation. Texans paid a rate of 1.90 percent of home value as opposed to a national average of 1.14 percent. Not much room for increase there. Texas has the 13th highest state sales tax in the nation at 6.25 percent. Eleven states have sales taxes of 6.3 to 7 percent and California has the highest sales tax in the nation at 7.5 percent. There is some room for a modest increase here, perhaps 0.5 percent, but certainly no more than 1 percent. In fact, as the 2011 regular session of the Texas Legislature faced big deficits, the CPPP suggested that a temporary 0.5 cent increase in the sales tax would raise $1.5 billion a year. They also proposed sin taxes on alcohol, tobacco, and high-sugar beverages. CPPP estimated that this "Healthy Texas Revenue Package" would raise more than $2.5 billion a year.[39]

Alternatively, Lori L. Taylor, a public finance specialist in the Bush School of Government and Public Service at Texas A&M, argued that the sales tax is honeycombed with exemptions and exclusions. Food and medicine, as well as gas, electricity, and internet access, are big exemptions. And there are dozens of smaller exemptions, "Massages are taxable, but manicures, facials, and other spa services are not. . . . Dishwasher repair is a taxable service, but auto repairs are not. . . . Laundry services . . . are taxable, but the car washing industry is tax exempt. . . . The list goes on and on." Taylor cites estimates from the Comptroller's office to the effect that eliminating most sales tax exemptions on food and medicine, even while exempting the poor, could raise as much as $4 billion and more broadly cancelling exemptions could raise another $2 to 3 billion annually.[40]

Political leaders could also review dozens of other tax rebates, exemptions, and deductions that reduce state government revenues each year. In fact, the Comptroller provides the governor and legislature at the beginning of each regular session with a book-length analysis entitled "Tax Exemptions and Tax Incidence." The March 2013 report declared that "the value of each exemption, exclusion, discount, deduction, special accounting method, credit, refund, and special appraisal" totaled $37.7 billion.[41] The $37.7 billion total for exemptions, exclusions, and discounts includes $10.9 billion in items excluded from the sales tax because they are taxed under other laws, such as motor vehicles, motor fuels, and insurance premiums. Many of the remaining exemptions are, of course, worthwhile. For example, governments and nonprofits are exempt from the sales tax. But there are dozens more, totaling $10 to 15 billion, some of which undoubtedly merit scrutiny.[42]

One exemption that has drawn some scrutiny, but not enough to bring change, is the exemption for "high-cost gas" from the gas severance tax. The exemption for high-cost gas was passed in 1989 with the support of Tom Craddick, a future speaker, as temporary assistance to gas producers during hard times. But temporary benefits have a way of becoming permanent. The exemption for high-cost gas was extended in 1995 and again in

1999 and then, after Craddick became speaker in 2003, the provision was made permanent in a "technical corrections" bill that few legislators read. Former Senator Ken Armbrister, the bill's sponsor on the senate side, later said, "I can guarantee you that nobody in the Legislature knew that was in the bill."[43] Of course, Armbrister is not speaking literally—someone knew, several people knew, and they were acting quite deliberately. The exemption remains law today and costs the Texas treasury $1 billion a year.

The biggest items on any list of potential new sources of revenue to Texas state government are corporate and personal income taxes. Texas is one of only five states (Nevada, South Dakota, Texas, Washington, and Wyoming) that have neither a corporate nor a personal income tax. Two others (Alaska and Florida) have a corporate income tax but no personal income tax. Let's look first at the corporate income tax. Forty-five states tax business capital, capital gains, gross receipts, or profits in one way or another. Some have a flat tax rate, some have tax brackets, some allow federal taxes as a deduction, and most tax financial institutions at higher rates than retail businesses. Though Texas has no corporate income tax per se, it does levy some taxes on business activity. For example, Texas has for a century taxed insurance companies and utilities. The oil and gas industry certainly consider the severance tax to be a tax on their businesses. More importantly, Texas has long had a corporate franchise tax, which it describes as a privilege tax on corporations operating in the state. The tax was 0.25 percent of taxable capital (value of the corporation) or 4.5 percent of earned income (federal taxable profits). Limited partnerships and professional services, including most legal, accounting, and financial management firms, were not subject to the franchise tax.

The spring 2006 special session of the Texas Legislature revised the way business is taxed in the state. It replaced the franchise fee with a broad new "margins tax" (many continue to refer to the margins tax as the franchise fee, so be alert). The margins tax is 1 percent on gross receipts, minus either the cost of employee compensation or the cost of goods sold, whichever is greater. Retailers and wholesalers pay 0.5 percent. Sole proprietors, general partnerships, and businesses grossing less than $600,000 annually are exempt. About 117,000 Texas businesses pay the margins tax. The margins tax provided $10 billion in 2012–2013, about 5 percent of total revenues. It had been expected to generate nearly twice that.

The best way to think about the revenue potential of corporate and personal income taxes in Texas without getting down in the weeds of hypothesized tax rates, tax brackets, standard deductions, and personal exemptions is to look at the Tax Foundation figures for per capita tax revenues for the U.S. and the fourteen southern states that levy such taxes. All fourteen of the southern states that we have been using as a comparison group (see Figure 10.5 for the list of states) for Texas have a corporate income tax averaging 6.1 percent. Kentucky, Mississippi, and South

Carolina at 5 percent are the lowest, nine states are between 5.5 and 6.5 percent, while North Carolina at 6.9 percent and West Virginia at 8.5 are the highest. Ten states have a flat tax while four vary their tax rate across three to six tax brackets. For example, Kentucky taxes corporate income at 4 percent on the first dollar, 5 percent over $50,000, and 6 percent over $100,000. Moreover, eleven of the fourteen also have a corporate franchise fee, usually ranging from $1.20 to $2.50 per $1,000 of taxable capital, a tax on deployed capital, or a gross receipts tax in addition to the corporate income tax. Given the business tax regimes of comparable states, Texas might consider a corporate income tax at the regional average of 6 percent in addition to the margins tax. In 2011, the fourteen southern states took in $99 per capita in corporate income taxes. If Texas had a corporate income tax at the southern average, the $99 per person times Texas's population of 24.8 million, it would produce $2.53 billion. A corporate income tax at the national per capita average of $129 would produce $3.31 billion.

All but one (Florida) of the fourteen southern states we have been comparing to Texas have a personal income tax. Tennessee does not tax wage income but does have a flat tax of 6 percent from the first dollar after a personal exemption of $1,250 on interest and dividend income. The other twelve states have three to six tax brackets and most offer both standard deductions and personal exemptions. Most states start with a tax of 1 or 2 percent on low incomes rising to 6 or 7 percent on higher incomes. Most states take the brackets for single filers and simply double them for married couples filing jointly. Standard deductions are usually doubled for married couples and personal exemptions are multiplied by the number of dependents. Standard deductions range from $2,000 ($4,000 for couples) to $5,400 ($10,800 for couples) and personal exemptions range from $1,000 to $3,000 per dependent. Obviously, the higher the standard deductions and personal exemptions are set, the higher one's income has to be to be subject to taxation.

Virginia provides a reasonably simple example of a state income tax system. The standard deduction is $3,000 for single filers and $6,000 for couples and the personal exemption is $930 per dependent. Virginia charges 2 percent on the first $3,000 of taxable income, 3 percent on taxable income from $3,000 to $5,000, 5 percent on income between $5,000 and $17,000, and 5.75 percent above $17,000. South Carolina shields the very poor by providing standard deductions of $6,100 for singles and $12,200 for couples and $3,000 for each dependent. On the other hand, South Carolina levies higher taxes on income above the deductions and exemptions. While Virginia's top bracket is 5.75 percent on taxable income above $17,000, South Carolina has a 6 percent bracket that kicks in at $11,400 and a 7 percent bracket beginning at $14,250.

Virginia's personal income tax took in $1,182 per capita in 2011 while Mississippi's took in just $487 per capita. The average per capita income tax revenue for the twelve southern states (excluding Florida and Tennessee) in 2011 was $755. If Texas adopted a personal income tax at the southern average (multiply per capita income tax revenue by Texas population), the 2011 revenue would have been $19.4 billion annually. An income tax set at the average of the fifty states would generate $21.4 billion. Texas is and has always been a low tax state, so it is likely any income tax would have generous deductions and exemptions and modest rates. Moreover, a constitutional amendment adopted by voters in 1993 requires that the revenue from any future income tax go two-thirds to reduce existing property taxes with the remaining one-third going to support public education. Clearly, an income tax that lowered the existing property tax would result in a more balanced revenue system and public education could certainly use an infusion of funds.[44] Although one might tinker elsewhere to some good effect, the Texas tax system cannot be thoroughly revised without adopting a state income tax.

Conclusion

Texas taxed property, business and professional licenses, and luxury goods throughout the nineteenth century. Texas adopted its first severance taxes and automobile sales and fuels taxes soon after the turn of the twentieth century. Taxes on tobacco products, alcohol, insurance companies, and public utilities also were enacted. After 1950, Texas public officials regularly nudged up selective sales taxes, licenses and fees, but the potential revenue gains in most instances were modest. The introduction of the general sales tax in 1961 created the potential for great change because it applied to a wide range of economic transactions and, as everyone understood, additional transactions could be made taxable and the rate itself, initially 2 percent, could be raised as economic circumstances seemed to demand. In fact, into the early 1980s, the Texas tax system did seem to provide sufficient revenue to meet the state's small government needs.

The second half of the 1980s was a traumatic period for Texas, its citizens, and its political authorities. After nearly two decades of strong economic growth and expanding tax revenues, the extended downturn of the late 1980s elicited dramatic policy reforms that have not been well understood. Even before the general sales tax was adopted in 1961, selective sales taxes provided nearly half of state tax revenues. As late as the early 1980s, sales taxes provided about two-thirds of state tax revenues, licenses and fees provided 10 percent, and severance taxes provided a quarter. As the economic problems in Texas gathered in the 1980s, political leaders increased the sales tax and other sources of income several times, and they provided a range of rebates, exemptions, and deductions to the energy industry to help them weather the downturn. What few Texans realize is that those incentives to the oil and gas industry were not temporary as advertised, but became permanent and increasingly expensive to the state.

Over the past two decades, Texas state government revenues have declined as a proportion of both average southern state revenues and average U.S. state revenues. Over that same period of time, the Texas Republican Party, the majority party in Texas now and for some years to come, has adopted an increasingly rigid no new taxes ideology. Hence, while there are sources from which new revenues might be drawn, in both large and small amounts, the prospects for doing so seem slim. Perhaps the most likely possibility, because it has been done so many times before, is an increase in the general sales tax of perhaps 0.5 cent. Also possible is a thorough review of the sales tax with an eye to broadening its base to cover more of the modern service economy and closing loopholes. The problem with this tack, of course, is that it would increase the regressivity of a tax regime that already bears down hard on the poor.

Bigger changes, such as the institution of corporate or personal income taxes, are less likely but, if adopted, could be mitigated by reductions in other taxes. For example, if Texas were to adopt a broad corporate income tax, it might well reduce or eliminate the franchise fee or margins tax. The result would still be a broader, more equitable tax on Texas businesses. Similarly, adoption of a personal income tax would, by constitutional requirement, require that two-thirds of the revenues be dedicated to property tax reductions and the remaining one-third to public education. Even in the face of structural budget deficits, the search for new revenues is unlikely to lead to major tax reform unless the state and federal courts force the issue. They have in the past and they may well again.

Notes

1 John Connally, with Mickey Herskowitz, *In History's Shadow: An American Odyssey*, New York: Hyperion, 1993, p. 304.

2 Ibid., p. 361.

3 Robert A. Calvert, Arnoldo De León, and Gregg Cantrell, *The History of Texas*, 4th edn, Wheeling, IL: Harlan Davidson, Inc., 2007, p. 465.

4 Noah Smithwick, *The Evolution of a State*, Austin, TX: University of Texas Press, 1985, p. 1.

5 D.W. Meinig, *Imperial Texas: An Interpretive Essay in Cultural Geography*, Austin, TX: University of Texas Press, 1969, p. 34.

6 James P. Bevill, *The Paper Republic: The Struggle for Money, Credit, and Independence in the Republic of Texas*, Houston, TX, Bright Sky Press, 2009.

7 John G. Johnson, "Tariff Policies of the Republic of Texas," Handbook of Texas Online (www.tshaonline.org/handbook/online/articles/mpt01), accessed June 06, 2011. Published by the Texas State Historical Association.

8 T.R. Fehrenbach, *Lone Star: A History of Texas and the Texans*, New York: Macmillan, 1968, p. 253. See also Wilhelm Steinert, *North America, Particularly Texas in the Year 1849*, Dallas, TX: DeGolyer Library, 2003, p. 61.

9 David G. McComb, *Texas: A Modern History*, Austin, TX: University of Texas Press, 2010, p. 53. See also Smithwick, *The Evolution of a State*, pp. 157, 171, and 201.

10 Calvert et al., *History of Texas*, pp. 87–92.

11 Steinert, *North America, Particularly Texas*, p. 124.

12 Randolph B. Campbell, *An Empire for Slavery*, Baton Rouge, LA: Louisiana State University Press, 1989, pp. 94–95.
13 Fehrenbach, *Lone Star*, p. 278.
14 Kenneth E. Hendrickson Jr., "The Confederate Governors of Texas, "pp. 228–245, in Kenneth W. Howell, *The Seventh Star of the Confederacy*, Denton, TX: The University of North Texas Press, 2009.
15 C.E. Evans, *The Story of Texas Schools*, Austin, TX: The Steck Company, 1955, p. 87; see also Fehrenbach, *Lone Star*, p. 422.
16 McComb, *Texas: A Modern History*, p. 79.
17 Dennis L. Dresang and James J. Gosling, *Politics and Policy in American States*, 6th edn, New York: Longman, 2008, p. 546.
18 Richard Morehead, *50 Years in Texas Politics*, Burnet, TX: Eakin Press, 1982, pp. 15, 23.
19 Ibid., pp. 35, 42.
20 Numan V. Bartley, *The New South, 1945–1980*, Baton Rouge, LA: Louisiana State University Press, 1995, p. 147.
21 Ricky F. Dobbs, *Yellow Dogs and Republicans: Allan Shivers and Texas Two-Party Politics*, College Station, TX: Texas A&M University Press, 2005, pp. 54–55.
22 Bartley, *The New South, 1945–1980*, p. 150.
23 Calvert et al., *The History of Texas*, p. 395.
24 Ben Barnes, *Barn Burning, Barn Building*, Albany, TX: Bright Sky Press, 2006, p. 45.
25 Patrick L. Cox and Michael Phillips, *The House Will Come to Order*, Austin, TX: University of Texas Press, 2010, p. 83.
26 Connally and Herskowitz, *In History's Shadow*, pp. 224–225. See also Morehead, *50 Years in Texas Politics*, p. 201.
27 Bartley, *The New South, 1945–1980*, p. 402.
28 Dolph Briscoe, *Dolph Briscoe: My Life in Texas Ranching and Politics*, Austin, TX: University of Texas Press, 2008, pp. 171, 256.
29 Anthony Champagne and Edward J. Harpham, *Texas at the Crossroads: Politics, People, and Policy*, College Station, TX: Texas A&M University Press, 1987, p. 7.
30 Briscoe, *Dolph Briscoe*, p. 249.
31 Bill Hobby, *How Things Really Work: Lessons From a Life in Politics*, Austin, TX: University of Texas Press, 2010, p. 82.
32 Dave McNeely and Jim Henderson, *Bob Bullock: God Bless Texas*, Austin, TX: University of Texas Press, 2008, pp. 175, 179.
33 Carolyn Barta, *Bill Clements: Texian to His Toenails*, Austin, TX: Eakin Press, 1996, pp. 352–354.
34 Barta, *Bill Clements*, pp. 360–361; see also Hobby, *How Things Really Work*, p. 132.
35 Barta, *Bill Clements*, p. 362.
36 www.rrc.state.tx.us/programs/og/severancetax.php.
37 LBB, "Overview of Natural Gas Tax Structures," www.lbb.state.tx.us/Other_ Pubs/ Natural%20Gas%20Tax%20Overview.pdf.
38 Center for Public Policy Priorities, "Who Pays Taxes in Texas," September 25, 2012.
39 Center for Public Policy Priorities, letter from William P. Hobby and F. Scott McCown to "Dear Business Leader," dated February 1, 2011, p. 3.
40 Lori L. Taylor, "Digging in the Wrong Places," *Dallas Morning News*, February 6, 2011, p. 6P.
41 www.window.state.tx.us/taxinfo/incidence/.
42 Louise Story, "Lines Blur as Texas Gives Industries a Bonanza," *New York Times*, December 2, 2012.
43 Patricia Kilday Hart, "Commentary: Tax Cut Comes at High Cost," *Houston Chronicle*, March 27, 2011.
44 For a similar analysis in more detail, see Dick Lavine, Center for Public Policy Priorities, "The Best Choice for a Prosperous Texas: A Texas-Style Personal Income Tax," June 3, 2008.

Index

Lightning Source UK Ltd.
Milton Keynes UK
UKOW06f0028271115

9 781138 783